101 CRIMES

of the century

First published in Australia in 2008 by
New Holland Publishers (Australia) Pty Ltd
Sydney • Auckland • London • Cape Town

1/66 Gibbes Street Chatswood NSW 2067 Australia
218 Lake Road Northcote Auckland New Zealand
86 Edgware Road London W2 2EA United Kingdom
80 McKenzie Street Cape Town 8001 South Africa

A record of this book is held at the National Library of Australia
ISBN 9781741106398

Publisher: Fiona Schultz
Managing Editor: Lliane Clarke
Production Manager: Linda Bottari
Designer: Simon Rattray
Cover Design: Nastasha Hayles and Hayley Norman
Printer: Ligare Pty Ltd, Australia

10 9 8 7 6 5 4 3 2 1

Front cover from left: Chaos erupts after the assassination attempt on President Ronald Reagan outside the Hilton Hotel in Washington DC, 1981. Jeffrey Dahmer in court, 1992. Bodyguards hold Pope John Paul II after he had been shot in Saint Peter's Square, 1981. Ted Kaczynski, the 'Unabomber', 1996.

101 CRIMES

of the century

Alan J. Whiticker

NEW HOLLAND

Contents

Introduction

'Crime of the century' was a catch-cry often used throughout the twentieth century. Crimes that fascinated, haunted and reviled us—crimes that transcended national boundaries and became iconic signposts in time-often earned the epitaph 'crime of the century'. Although this new century is only several years old, the world has already experienced horrific events that will be remembered as 'crimes of the century'.

The 101 crimes listed in this book is not meant to be a definitive list—there have been many other crimes committed over the past one hundred years that could have been included in this book. Crimes committed under the guise of civil or even World War could have filled another book. However, this book attempts to give the reader an overview of a wide variety of crimes since 1901 that are remembered for their historical, social and cultural impact.

In deconstructing 101 crimes committed over the past 100 years, themes reappear decade after decade—political assassination, acts of espionage and terrorism, crimes of passion, kidnapping, theft, underworld murders, sex crimes and society scandals. It has also been interesting to see the development of 'murder' terminology—the 'spree' murderer, the 'mass' murderer and lastly, the 'serial' murderer, over the past one hundred years. The different chapters also reflect the advancement in DNA technology, crime scene and accident investigation, data collection and computerisation that are now commonplace.

To appreciate the impact some crimes can have on society, we need to go no further back than the late nineteenth century. The murder of at least five prostitutes by 'Jack the Ripper' in the Whitechapel area of London in 1888 shocked the world and created something of a 'Ripper' industry.

In the early hours of 31 August 1888 the body of 43-year-old Mary Ann 'Polly' Walker was found in a dimly lit street. Walker's body had been mutilated, but the severity of the victim's injuries increased with each subsequent crime. Annie Chapman's uterus was missing when her body was found on 8 September; Elizabeth 'Long Liz' Stride, whose murder may have been interrupted on 30 September, had her throat cut but she did not have any organs missing; Catherine Eddowes (aka Mary Ann Kelly), who was killed on the same morning as Stride, had her uterus and kidney taken and was left with facial mutilation. Five weeks later, on 9 November, the body of 25-year-old Mary Jane Kelly was found inside lodgings in Dorset Street. Her throat had been slashed, her face mutilated beyond recognition, her chest and abdomen cut open and her internal organs, as well as flesh from her limbs, were left on the bed where she lay. Kelly's heart was missing and it was believed to have been thrown in the fireplace, taken away by her killer as a trophy, or even eaten.

The technological limitations of the times and the lack of knowledge of the psychological motivation for the murders hampered the investigation by London Metropolitan Police Service. Photography, for example, was used in the investigation but some people thought that by photographing the victims' retinas the murderer—the last person the victims saw before they died—would be revealed. Detectives originally thought that the murderer may have been a doctor because of the removal of vital organs but a butcher would have had just as much knowledge. London Police received a series of letters from a man calling himself 'Jack the Ripper' (one of the letters foretold of 'a double event' before the Stride and Eddowes murders, while another included part of a human kidney) and the name stuck a chord with the media and public. Vital evidence was destroyed (such as graffiti written in Goulston Street, near the 'double event' murder on 30 September, that read 'The Juwes are not The men That Will be Blamed for nothing') and at least another dozen crimes committed between December 1887 and February 1891 could have been connected to the 'Ripper' case but for a variety of reasons—professional jealousy, ignorance or incompetence—they weren't.

The failure to identify 'Jack' led to the propagation of urban legends, countless theories and a variety of suspects. Of the many people named by 'Ripper' authors as possibly being 'Jack', Montague John Druitt (1857-1888), Aaron Kosminski (1865-1919), John Pizer (1850-1897) and Frances Tumblety (1833-1903) were the main contemporary suspects. Since then, many suspects including author Lewis Carroll (1932-1898), artist Walter Sickert (1860-1942), physician Sir William Gull (1816-1890), 'Ripper' diarist James Maybrick (1838-1889) and even Queen Victoria's grandson Prince Albert Victor, Duke of Clarence (1864-1892), have been named as 'Jack the Ripper'.

The crimes of 'Jack the Ripper' were the start of a new era of iconic, violent crime breathlessly reported in all their gory detail by a developing mass media and readily consumed by the general public. 'One day men will look back and say I gave birth to the twentieth century', Jack the Ripper allegedly wrote to London Police ... and that is where we start *101 Crimes of the Century*.

Alan J. Whiticker
February 2008

1901
William McKinley Assassinated

FACT FILE

CRIME: Political assassination
VICTIM: William McKinley, 25th president of the United States, aged 58
DATE: 6 September 1901
PLACE: Pan-American Exposition, Buffalo, New York (USA)
PERPETRATOR: Leon Czolgosz
SENTENCE: Executed by electric shock at New York's Auburn State Prison on 29 October 1901

The presidency of William McKinley (1843–1901) straddled the transition from the 'gilded age' of the late 1800s to the most progressive, tumultuous and catastrophic century humankind has known. The Republican president of the United States was in the first year of his second term when, as part of his triumphant re-election tour, he opened the Pan-American Exposition in Buffalo, New York, on 5 September 1901. The following day, as McKinley shook the hands of a long line of well-wishers, he became the victim of an old world solution to new century problems—political assassination.

Detroit-born Leon Czolgosz (pronounced *chol-gosh*) was an unemployed mill worker in his late twenties who had become obsessed with the anarchist movement as he struggled between menial factory jobs in Ohio. Transposing class struggle for class hatred, he adopted the pseudonym 'Fred Nieman'—'Fred Nobody'. On 6 May 1901, Czolgosz travelled to Cleveland to hear well-known anarchist Emma Goldman speak at the Federal Liberal Club and later met with her. So extreme were his views, however, that the editor of the radical *Free Society* newspaper warned others within the anarchist movement that he might be a government agent.

The previous year, a professed anarchist named Gaetano Bresci had assassinated King Umberto of Italy as he travelled by carriage to a villa in Monza. American anarchists were shocked, but Czolgosz was deeply impressed—an ordinary labourer, like himself, taking matters into his own hands for the good of the common man. Hiss thoughts turned to killing President McKinley, who in his fanatic's mind was the embodiment of all that was wrong with the industrialised urban world—a world in which the masses were exploited for the benefit of the privileged few.

On Friday 6 September 1901, President McKinley and his travelling party (which included his wife, Ida) arrived at the Pan-American Exposition on the New York side of Niagara Falls at Buffalo. Czolgosz arrived at the exposition just as McKinley's carriage entered the grounds on its way to the railway terminal. The assassin planned to shoot the president when he stopped at the falls, but a demonstration by so-called preservationists, who were concerned that the official visit might sully the natural beauty of the area, disrupted his plans. Instead he caught a train to the Temple of Music—the president's next stop—and joined a line of people waiting to greet McKinley later that afternoon.

Czolgosz was carrying a tiny revolver concealed in his right hand by a handkerchief wrapped like a bandage. When President McKinley arrived, the unemployed factory worker was propelled towards his intended victim as the crowed surged forward, eager to get close to the president. He shot McKinley twice at point-blank range, and yelled, 'I've done my duty!' As Czolgosz was felled by a punch from one of McKinley's bodyguards, the stricken president pleaded, 'Go easy on him, boys!'

McKinley lingered for another eight days but died on 14 September 1901. It was originally thought that the president died from gangrene of the pancreas after sustaining a 'serious but unrecognised blast injury' to the area. Modern research later established that the undiagnosed injury had led to internal inflammation of his organs and the dangerous accumulation of several litres of blood plasma within the abdominal cavity. Though outwardly the president appeared to be making a good recovery after the operation to repair his wounds, his condition slowly deteriorated. Without the necessary plasma in his blood, his heart had to work twice as hard as normal, his pulse weakened and his body went into shock.

Authorities wasted no time in setting Leon Czolgosz for trial and—having determined that he had acted alone—executing him. Czolgosz was resigned to his fate and refused to speak to the two retired State Supreme Court justices appointed by New York's Eire County Bar Association to defend him. He signed a confession, which included the statement: 'I am an anarchist, a disciple of Emma Goldman. Her words set me on fire.'

On 29 October 1901, seven weeks after McKinley's death—and just 43 days after he had been indicted by a grand jury—Czolgosz was executed by electric shock.

REFERENCES:

- Fisher, Jack (2002), *Stolen Glory: The McKinley Assassination*, Alamar, New York
- McPherson, James M. (2000), *To the Best of My Ability: The American Presidents*, DK Press, New York
- *The McKinley Assassination Historical Site, www.geocities.com/CollegePark/Quad/1430*

1908

Butch Cassidy and the Sundance Kid: The Last of the Outlaws

FACT FILE

CRIMES: Robbery, murder
DATES: 1887–1908
PLACES: Argentina, Chile and Bolivia (South America) and Wyoming, Colorado (USA)
PERPETRATORS: Robert Leroy Parker ('Butch Cassidy'), 1866–?1908 and Harry Longabaugh ('The Sundance Kid'), 1867–?1908

Robert Leroy Parker was born in Beaver, Utah, in 1866, the son of English Mormon immigrants. The oldest of thirteen children, the young Parker left his family's homestead in Circleville, Utah, and worked for other ranchers, including one by the name of Mike Cassidy. In 1884 he started using the name Butch Cassidy (Cassidy was said to have been a butcher at one time, but a 'butch' was also a borrowed gun) and got involved in cattle-rustling. In 1889 he robbed his first bank, in Telluride, Colorado, escaping with a major haul. Some years later, in 1894–96, he was jailed for horse-stealing, and on his release he formed his own gang of outlaws variously known as the 'Train Robbers Syndicate', the 'Hole-in-the-Wall Gang' and the 'Wild Bunch'. One of the group's later recruits was a young man known as the Sundance Kid.

Harry Alonzo Longabaugh was born the youngest of five children to a Baptist family in Pennsylvania in 1867. Moving west with his cousin George in 1887, Longabaugh stole a horse, a saddle and a gun in Sundance, Wyoming. He was captured and jailed for eighteen months, and was thereafter known as the 'Sundance Kid'. After working as a ranch-hand for a time, he was implicated in a train robbery in 1892 and a bank robbery in 1897. Not long after, he joined the Wild Bunch. This gang of outlaws was responsible for over a dozen robberies between 1896 and 1901, which netted them, at the time, more than US$200 000.

The Wild Bunch had come under the notice of the Pinkerton Detective Agency who, acting on behalf of several government agencies, put a bounty of US$1000 on the head of each member. A wanted poster of the period mentioned that Sundance was travelling with a woman of unknown origin called 'Etta'—thought to be Ethel Place, a teacher or prostitute, depending on which story you read. With the Pinkertons bearing down on the group, the Wild Bunch decided to split up, but not before getting their photograph taken in formal attire at Fort Worth, Texas. The Pinkertons got hold of the photograph, used it to identify the outlaws and began to round them up.

In March 1901, Butch, Sundance and Etta went to New York City, from where they immigrated to Argentina on the British ship *Herminius* with the proceeds of their robberies. Taking a train from Buenos Aires to Patagonia, they bought farms in the Chubut Territory of southern Argentina and settled down. Butch called himself James ('Santiago') Ryan, and Sundance and Etta were Mr and Mrs Harry ('Enrique') Place. For two years, Butch and Sundance lived a quiet life among their neighbours—mainly Welsh, Chilean and North American immigrants—and were not troubled by their old life. Then, acting on a tip-off that the outlaws were living in Argentina, Pinkerton agent Frank Dimaio arrived in Buenos Aires with translated wanted posters of the two men. Although the wet season prevented him from travelling inland to where the outlaws lived, Dimaio alerted the local authorities to keep a watch on them.

In February 1905, two English-speaking bandits held up a bank at Cholila, 700 miles (1100 kilometres) to the south of Buenos Aires, near the Straits of Magellan. Although Butch and Sundance could not be positively identified at the men responsible, the Buenos Aires police chief ordered their arrest. Locals tipped off the pair that they were now wanted, and together with Etta Place they caught the steamer *Condor* across Lake Nahuel Huapi to neighbouring Chile. On 19 December that year, Butch and Sundance returned to Argentina and robbed the bank in Villa Mercedes, 400 miles (650 kilometres) west of Buenos Aires. The pair returned to Chile on horseback with a posse chasing them over the Andes.

When in 1906 Butch and Sundance decided to move to Bolivia, life on the run proved too much for Etta Place and she returned to California to live in San Francisco. Butch and Sundance were hired as payroll guards—of all things—at the Concordia Tin Mine, 16 000 feet (4880 metres) up in the Santa Vela Cruz range of the Bolivian Andes. Butch was keen to settle down to a law-abiding life and left the Andes for Santa Cruz, in Bolivia's eastern savannah. Here he found the place he wanted to retire to. In 1908, the outlaws quit their post when the owners of the mine learnt of their past, and the authorities then started to investigate them in regard to several hold-ups in the area. Although there is no proof that Butch and Sundance were involved in these crimes, they were later attributed to them.

In August 1908, possibly to finance their retirement in Santa Cruz, Butch and

Sundance planned to rob a bank in Tupiza, a mining centre in southern Bolivia. However, a visiting cavalry unit from the Bolivian army was staying quite close to the bank, and Butch called off the robbery. In November, he decided instead to rob an 80 000-peso (about $8000) mining payroll that was to be transported from Tupiza to Quechisla.

When the payroll turned out to be only 15,000 pesos (about $1500), Butch stole a mining company mule as 'compensation'. The payroll officers alerted the local army to the bandits' presence in the territory. Butch and Sundance fled to Oruro, a city with several thousand foreign residents.

On 6 November, the pair lodged overnight in the home of Bonifacio Casasola in San Vicente, in the Sud Chichas Province of Bolivia. A posse in the nearby town of Uyeni had warned locals to be on the lookout for 'two Yankees' and a stolen mule, and while the *corregidor* (chief administrative officer) of the Casasola household wasn't sure about the two 'Yankees', he recognised the mule as belonging to the mining company and turned them in. The four-man posse, led by Captain Justo P. Concha, surrounded the house where Butch and Sundance were staying. When a soldier entered the room, Butch shot him, and the posse then opened fire. A return volley of shots rang out, and the soldiers retreated to a safe distance and guarded the house throughout the night.

The following morning, when there was no sign of life from within the room, the soldiers entered to find Butch and Sundance dead from self-inflicted wounds. The outlaws were buried in the local cemetery that afternoon, but their bodies were exhumed ten days later so that they could be positively identified and death certificates issued. But the bodies could not be identified and, to add to the confusion, Captain Concha absconded with the payroll money and could not be questioned.

HISTORICAL AND SOCIAL SIGNIFICANCE:

- Because their bodies were never officially identified by the Bolivian government, many believe that Butch and Sundance escaped and returned to the United States. Butch, it is said, died in 1936, and Sundance is said to have linked up again with Etta Place and to have died in 1957. What is known is that the Pinkertons continued looking for Butch and Sundance until 1921.
- Writer William Goldman was paid a record US$400 000 in 1968 for his screenplay *Butch Cassidy and the Sundance Kid.* The film, starring Paul Newman and Robert Redford, made Butch and Sundance internationally famous some 60 years after their 'unofficial' death.

REFERENCES:

- Meadows, Anne and Buck, Daniel (1997), 'The Last Days of Butch & Sundance', *Wild West Magazine, USA www.historynet.com*
- *History of Butch Cassidy, www.utah.com*
- *Butch & Sundance, americanhistory.about.com*

1911
The *Mona Lisa* Stolen

FACT FILE

CRIME: Art theft
TARGET: Leonardo da Vinci's Mona Lisa (also known as La Gioconda)
DATE: 21 August 1911
PLACE: The Louvre, Paris (France)
PERPETRATOR: Vincenzo Peruggia (1881–1947)
SENTENCE: Imprisonment for one year and 15 days

The *Mona Lisa* is the world's best-known painting—and according to the *Guinness Book of Records*, the most valuable painting ever insured. Also known as *La Gioconda*, it is thought to be a portrait of Lisa del Giocondo, the wife of Florentine silk merchant Francesco del Giocondo. Leonardo da Vinci (1452–1519) began the work in 1503, and it took him four years to complete. Painted on poplar wood board and measuring just 77 centimetres by 53 centimetres (30 inches by 21 inches), this portrait of a woman—dressed in Florentine clothing, her hair hanging loose—has come to capture the imagination of future generations like no other painting before or since.

The enigmatic expression of the woman known as *Mona Lisa*—her intriguing half-smile and the way she seems to be looking slightly past the viewer—has long been the focus of speculation. Was La Gioconda pregnant? (She is certainly holding her hand across her midriff in the manner of a woman expecting a child.) She is seated against the backdrop of a visionary, mountainous landscape. The more you look at it, the more the *Mona Lisa* takes on a dreamlike quality.

Whoever the subject was, the image has achieved universal fame in the 500 years since it was painted. Leonardo sold the painting to King François I of France in 1519 for 4000 écus (approximately US$100,000 in today's terms), and in 1804, after the French revolution, it was moved to the Louvre, where millions of people have since seen it on display. Around the turn of the twentieth century, the *Mona Lisa* was moved to the wing known as the Salon Carré, where it was hung between two other masterpieces, by Correggio and Titian. Like many other works of art at the time, Leonardo's masterpiece was controversially shielded by glass to protect it. Then, on 21 August 1911, the *Mona Lisa* was stolen.

Incredibly, the theft was not discovered until the following day. On Tuesday 22

August, an artist named Louis Béroud went to the Louvre to paint a copy of the *Mona Lisa*. When he entered the Salon Carré, Béroud found only four iron pegs on the wall where the *Mona Lisa* should have been. He immediately alerted the guard, and was assured that the painting was probably away being photographed. A few hours later, the truth was known—the *Mona Lisa* was missing. The Louvre was promptly closed for a week and 60 French police scoured the building, but all they found was the frame and the protective glass panel, dumped in a nearby stairwell.

The police believed that the art thief must have hidden in the Louvre on the Sunday night and stolen the painting on Monday, when the museum was closed for cleaning. One worker later stated that he saw the painting in its place at 7 o'clock that morning, and when he noticed it missing an hour later, he assumed that it had merely been removed for cleaning. As between 600 and 800 cleaners, workmen and security guards went about their business that day (the usual guard in the Salon Carré was absent, and his replacement went out for a cigarette at about 8 am), the thief simply walked out of the Louvre with the world's most famous painting (concealed in some manner). The thief also had a 24-hour head start on police.

The police suspected that the thief had inside knowledge of the day-to-day workings of the Louvre. A thumbprint was found on the painting's ornate frame but it could not be matched to any known person. Was someone playing a joke, perhaps to focus attention on the shortcomings of the Louvre's security, or was someone going to demand a ransom for the priceless painting's safe return? As time passed, the great fear was that the artwork had been stolen on behalf of a wealthy collector and would now hang in a private room in some hidden corner of the globe—or worse, that it had been destroyed. When the Louvre reopened, people came to gaze at the empty space on the wall where the *Mona Lisa* used to hang. Some even left bouquets of flowers.

One early suspect was Gery Pieret, a former Louvre employee, who had been stealing artefacts from the museum during the past two years. When the newspaper *Paris Journal* offered a reward for the return of the *Mona Lisa*, Pieret offered to send the newspaper a Phoenician artefact stolen the previous year—and which no-one had even noticed had gone missing. After Pieret was interrogated, two Iberian heads that had been stolen four years before, in 1907, were returned. Guillaume Apollinaire, a friend of both Pieret and a struggling Spanish artist living in Paris named Pablo Picasso, was arrested and charged with harbouring an 'unknown person' involved in the theft of the *Mona Lisa*. Picasso came under suspicion in the stolen artefacts scandal simply because of his association with Apollinaire and was questioned about the *Mona Lisa*'s disappearance. But none of the three men had anything to do with the disappearance of the painting.

Two years after the *Mona Lisa* was stolen, a well-known Italian antique dealer named Alfredo Geri placed an advertisement in several Italian newspapers seeking artworks for sale. He was contacted by letter by a man named 'Leonardo' who said that he was in possession of the *Mona Lisa*. Although he assumed that the painting would be a copy, Geri contacted the director of the Uffizi museum in Florence. Together they wrote to 'Leonardo' in Paris saying they wanted to see the painting before offering a price for it. They arranged to meet the man in Milan on 22 December 1913.

'Leonardo' turned out to be Vincenzo Peruggia, a former worker in the Louvre. After protracted negotiations, ransom demands and counter offers, the *Mona Lisa* was finally recovered in the false bottom of a suitcase belonging to him. Perruggia told Alfredo Geri that he had stolen the painting in order to 'restore to Italy what had been stolen from it by Napoleon' and that he wanted the *Mona Lisa* to hang in the Uffizi. Peruggia didn't know its true history—Da Vinci took the painting with him when he went to France in 1516 at François I's invitation—and the fact that he also asked for a half a million lire ransom calls his professed motives into question. Some, however, saw him as a patriot, and he was jailed for just one year and 15 days for what was described at the time as 'the art theft of the century'.

The *Mona Lisa* was returned to the Louvre on 30 December 1913 and has hung there ever since.

HISTORICAL AND SOCIAL SIGNIFICANCE:

- The *Mona Lisa* is one of the finest examples of the *sfumato* technique, in which translucent layers of colour are applied to create the illusion of depth and form. In particular, it refers to blending tones so subtly that the transition from one to the other is almost imperceptible.
- Adelaide art historian Maike Vogt-Luerssen has argued that the *Mona Lisa* is a portrait of Isabella of Aragon, a member of the house of Visconti–Sforza.
- In a book published in 1992, US computer graphics expert Dr Lillian Schwartz of Bell Laboratories suggested, on the basis on her digital analysis, that the *Mona Lisa* is actually a self-portrait of Da Vinci as a woman.

REFERENCES:

- Ross, John (1998), *The Chronicle of the Twentieth Century* (Penguin, Melbourne)
- *The Voice of Women, www.bellaonline.com*
- *The Mona Lisa, www.about.com*

1913
The Murder of Mary Phagan

FACT FILE

CRIME: Murder
VICTIM: Mary Phagan (1900–1913)
DATE: 26 April 1913
PLACE: Atlanta, Georgia (USA)
PERPETRATOR: Leo Frank (1884–1915) was found guilty of the murder, but on 16 August 1915, while in prison awaiting appeal, he was abducted and lynched by a mob

---

In 1913, a bespectacled Jewish factory manager named Leo Frank was forcibly abducted from his prison cell and hanged by an angry mob seeking to avenge the vicious murder of 12-year-old factory worker Mary Phagan. Frank had served only a few months of his controversial life sentence and was awaiting appeal at the time. In answering one murder with another, the men responsible for the lynching provided the perfect cover for the person who really did kill little Mary Phagan.

Mary Phagan was born on 1 June 1900 in Marietta, Georgia. Although only 12 years old, she was employed by the National Pencil Factory in Atlanta to operate a machine that placed metal tips on the ends of pencils. She was temporarily laid off in April 1913 when a shipment of pencils was late in arriving, but was owed US$1.20 in back pay. On 26 April 1913 (Confederate Memorial Day in the South), Mary Phagan went to the factory to collect her wages. That night her body was found in the basement of the factory—she had been raped and murdered. Beside the body were two roughly scrawled notes.

The body was found lying in a pool of blood by an African–American nightwatchman named Newt Lee. Lee was promptly arrested, and a lynch mob had to be dispersed from outside the courthouse. Arthur Mullinax, a streetcar driver, and John Gantt, a bookkeeper at the factory, also came under suspicion and were arrested, but they were later released. Leo Frank, the 29-year-old factory manager, was unhappy with the initial police investigation and called in a private Pinkerton's detective to investigate the crime. Frank, too, was questioned about his movements on the day the girl was murdered.

At the time, Atlanta was home to the largest Jewish community in the South. Frank had moved there from New York and married a local girl named Lucille Selig in 1910. Although he was a prominent member of the local Jewish community, there were many in Atlanta and in the factory who bore grudges against him. Several women later testified that Frank had made 'sexual advances' to them at the factory and that he was 'mean' to them, but clearly this did not make him a murderer. Frank was also a Northerner—a 'Yankee' living and working in the South—and while the Civil War had ended a generation before, there were many who resented him merely because of this.

In May, Mary Phagan's body was exhumed twice, once to allow the police to check for fingerprints and the second time to check her stomach contents for drugs. On 8 May, a coroner's jury ordered that Newt Lee and Leo Frank be charged with the murder of Mary Phagan. Although this was not revealed at the time, police had also questioned Jim Conley, an African–American sweeper at the factory, about the murder.

On the day of the murder, Conley was seen trying to wash out bloodstains on his shirt, but he claimed that he had injured himself and that it was his own blood. Instead of being seen as a prime suspect, the sweeper became the prosecution's lead witness against Leo Frank.

Conley maintained that he had acted as lookout for Frank while the factory manager raped and murdered the girl and that together they had carried Mary's body into the basement. He also claimed that, on Leo Frank's orders, he had written the two notes found near the girl's body. (Their contents were not revealed to the public as the police hoped to incriminate the author in court.) On 23 May 1913, a grand jury took just ten minutes to indict Leo Frank. No action was taken or requested against Newt Lee after the nightwatchman assisted the prosecution case by testifying that Frank appeared 'nervous' on the day of the murder.

On 26 August 1913, after a 25-day trial that saw public anti-Semitism whipped to a frenzy by the prosecution case, the jury believed Jim Conley's testimony and found Leo Frank guilty. Judge L. S. Road sentenced Frank to hang and initially denied a motion for a new trial. Jim Conley was sentenced to one year on a chain gang for his role in disposing of the girl's body. Despite the United States Supreme Court finally rejecting Leo Frank's appeal in April 1915, as an act of clemency on his final day in office, Georgia governor John Slaton commuted Frank's sentence to life imprisonment. Georgia publisher (and future governor) Tom Watson called on his readership to 'take justice into their own hands and inflict the death sentence upon Leo Frank'.

On 18 July 1915, Frank had his throat slashed by a fellow prisoner at Georgia State Prison Farm in Milledgeville. He barely survived the assault. A month later, on 16 August, 25 armed men arrived at the prison farm, cut the telephone lines, captured the guards, then seized Leo Frank and drove off into the night. In the early hours of the following morning, Leo Frank was hanged in a grove in Marietta near Mary Phagan's home. Declaring his innocence to the end, Frank's only request was that his wedding ring be returned to his wife (which it was). Crowds gathered throughout the day to see the body, and photographs were taken and turned into souvenir postcards. Later that day, Frank's body was taken down to avoid it being disfigured, and was later buried in Brooklyn, New York.

No-one was ever prosecuted over the lynching of Leo Frank.

In 1982, Alonzo Mann, who was a 13-year-old employee at the pencil factory when Mary Phagan was murdered, signed an affidavit stating that, almost 70 years before, he saw Jim Conley carrying the limp body of Mary Phagan on his shoulder near the trapdoor leading to the factory basement. Conley had threatened to kill the boy if he told anyone.

When Mann later did tell his mother, he was advised to keep quiet about it because Leo Frank was dead and nothing could be done about it. In January 1983, the Anti-Defamation League submitted an application to the Georgia Board of Pardons and Paroles for a posthumous pardon for Leo Frank. In December that year, Georgia denied the motion on the grounds that although Alonzo Mann's testimony implicated Jim Conley in the murder, it did not prove Leo Frank's innocence.

It would be another three years before the Georgia Board of Pardons and Paroles issued a posthumous pardon to Leo Frank, and even then it did not officially clear his name. The pardon was based on the state's failure to protect Frank's constitutional rights while he was in custody.

HISTORICAL AND SOCIAL SIGNIFICANCE:

- The Ku Klux Klan initiated a new so-called 'invisible order' in honour of the murdered girl—the Knights of Mary Phagan. The girl's family did not condone the group and forbade the Klan from holding a service at Mary's gravesite.
- In 1987, Mary Phagan's great-niece—also named Mary Phagan—wrote a detailed account of the case, *The Murder of Little Mary Phagan*. Mary Phagan Kean believes that Frank did murder the girl.

REFERENCES:

- Phagan, Mary (1987), *The Murder of Little Mary Phagan,* Horizon Press, New Jersey
- Pou, Charles, *The Leo Frank Case, www.cviog.uga.edu*
- The Crime Library, *The Murder of Mary Phagan, www.crimelibrary.com*

1914

The Shot Heard around the World

FACT FILE

CRIME: Political assassination

VICTIMS: Archduke Franz Ferdinand, heir apparent to the Austrian throne (1863–1914) and Sophie, Duchess von Hohenberg (1868–1914)

DATE: 28 June 1914

PLACE: Sarajevo, Bosnia

PERPETRATORS: Nedjelko Cabrinovic, aged 20; Vaso Cubrilovic, aged 17; Trifko Grabez, aged 17; Danilo Ilic, aged 24; Muhammed Mehmedbasic, 27; Gavrilo Princip, aged 20

SENTENCES: Danilo Ilic was hanged, and the other six were sentenced to between 16 and 20 years' imprisonment

---

On 6 October 1908, after having occupied and administered the provinces of Bosnia and Herzegovina for 30 years under the terms of the 1878 Treaty of Berlin, Austria formally annexed them, making them part of the Austro–Hungarian empire. Prior to the treaty they had been governed by the Turks, and the annexation put paid to any hopes the Turks had of reclaiming these provinces. It also gave Bosnians full rights and privileges as members of the Austro–Hungarian empire. For a variety of complex reasons, the move provoked some disquiet among European nations, and Austria eventually defused the situation by paying a cash settlement to Turkey (which had also lost provinces in its war against Russia). But one group was not to be placated. Serb nationalists remained bitterly opposed to the annexation, having long nurtured the hope of uniting with their Bosnian brothers to form their own Serb empire. In 1914, members of an anti-Austrian secret society called the Black Hand took the bold step of planning the assassination of Archduke Franz Ferdinand—the heir apparent to the Austrian throne—on learning that he had accepted an invitation from the Bosnian mayor to inspect army manoeuvres outside Sarajevo.

The Black Hand was formed in Belgrade in 1911 and numbered many government officials, army officers and espionage professionals among its members. It had grown out of an older Serb nationalist group, and was not opposed to using violence to achieve its goal of a 'greater Serbia'. Under the direction of its leader, Colonel Dragutin Dimitrijevic (who went by the code name of 'Apis'), three young

Bosnians—Gavrilo Princip, Nedjelko Cabrinovic and Trifko Grabez—were recruited, trained and equipped with four pistols and six bombs supplied by the Serbian army. The three arrived in Sarajevo a month before the archduke and were joined by a fourth man, Danilo Ilic. Ilic then recruited further help in the form of two 17-year-old students and (to give the group a broader political base) a young Bosnian Muslim named Muhammed Mehmedbasic. Though the Serbian government learned of the plot, it made only veiled diplomatic attempts to warn the Austrians—to betray the Black Hand assassins would be to betray their own countrymen. Predictably, the Austrians failed to recognise the warnings.

Shortly after 10 am on 28 June 1914, Franz Ferdinand and his wife, Archduchess Sophie (who was accompanying her husband as part of a fourteenth wedding anniversary gift), rode into Sarajevo on their way to City Hall in a motorcade of six automobiles. The royal couple rode in the second car, behind the mayor and the city's commissioner of police. Hundreds of Bosnians lined the motorcade along Appel Quay that summer's morning and cheered the visitors on their way.

There was no hint of the assassins' intent as they mingled among the crowd of flag-waving Bosnians. Mehmedbasic missed his chance when he froze as the motorcade sped past him. Cabrinovic, the second of the assassins positioned to attack, pulled a bomb from his coat, struck its percussion cap against a lamppost and threw it directly at Franz Ferdinand's automobile. Incredibly, the archduke's driver saw the black object in flight and accelerated. Ferdinand was able to stand in his seat, deflect the bomb with his arm as he protected his wife, and watch it bounce off the folded car top and detonate behind him. Some twelve people were injured, including several members of the official party in the preceding car.

Cabrinovic swallowed cyanide and jumped into the Miljacka River, but the poison was old and only made him vomit. The would-be assassin was quickly captured. A furious Franz Ferdinand arrived at City Hall and berated the mayor, who was oblivious of the assassination attempt. Official speeches were hastily conducted, after which the archduke seemed to regain his composure. Franz Ferdinand agreed to continue on to the governor's residence for lunch, but decided at the last moment to go first to the local hospital and visit the injured. When the archduke's car took the wrong road, the driver braked and began to turn around. As the car backed up, it came to a stop two metres (a little more than two yards) from Gavrilo Princip, who was standing in front of a food store called Schiller's. Fate had presented the young Serb with his opportunity to change the course of history.

Pulling a pistol from his pocket, Princip took a step towards the car and fired twice at the royal couple as they sat upright in their seat. The car sped off, and the young assassin tried to turn the pistol on himself but was set upon by the mob. As the car headed towards the governor's residence, blood poured from Franz Ferdinand's mouth—he had been shot in the neck. His wife gasped, 'For heaven's sake! What has happened to you?' and then sank in her seat. Officials at first thought she had just fainted, but she too was fatally shot, struck in the abdomen. The Archduke implored her, 'Sopherl, Sopherl, don't die. Stay alive for the children.' (Sopherl, loosely translated, means 'Sophie dear!') When asked if he was hurt, the Archduke's final words before he slipped into unconsciousness were: 'It is nothing ... it is nothing'. The couple was pronounced dead at the governor's residence.

The 'July crisis' that followed saw Austria take a hard line against Serbia as the great European nations aligned themselves with rival sides. Germany offered Austria a 'blank cheque' for whatever action it decided to take against Serbia. Turkey, too, fell into line behind Austria. Russia, France and England came to Serbia's defence. Thirty days after the assassination, the world was at war.

All seven assassins were eventually captured. Princip and Cabrinovic remained silent during their trial, but the plot was betrayed by Danilo Ilic, who confessed to his part in the assassination. Princip was found guilty but was spared the death penalty because he was just days short of his 20th birthday. He was sentenced to 20 years' imprisonment but died of tuberculosis in Austria's Theresienstadt prison in April 1918. Cabrinovic and Grabez suffered a similar fate—both were sentenced to 20 years' jail but succumbed to tuberculosis in 1916. Cubrilovic and Mehmedbasic received lesser sentences. Danilo Ilic was the only one to be executed for the crime. Aged just 24, he was hanged in February 1915.

HISTORICAL AND SOCIAL SIGNIFICANCE:

- Disliked by many, Franz Ferdinand was buried in a crypt beneath the chapel of his castle, Artstetten, in Austria rather than in the Hapsburg crypt in Vienna. Neither his uncle, Emperor Franz Josef, nor the German Kaiser attended the funeral.
- On 1 August 1914, Germany declared war on France. Three days later, on 4 August, England declared war on Germany.
- Colonel 'Apis', the leader of the assassination plot, was convicted of treason by a military tribunal and shot at dawn on 24 June 1917. Once the full extent of the Black Hand's involvement in the assassination became known, the group was outlawed.
- World War I—the 'Great War', the 'war to end all wars'—ended on 11 November 1918. More than 10 million people lost their lives in the war.

REFERENCES:

- Lenethal, Albert V. (1973), *War: A Visual History,* Ridge Press, New York
- *Primary Documents: Germany's 'Blank Cheque', www.firstworldwar.com*
- *Assassination of an Archduke, 1914, www.eyewitnesstohistory.com*
- *Sarajevo: June 28, 1914, www.gwpda.org*

1916
The Murder of Rasputin

FACT FILE

CRIME: Murder
VICTIM: Grigori Rasputin (?1869-1916)
DATE: 30 December 1916
PLACE: Palace, St Petersburg (Russia)
PERPETRATORS: Grand Duke Dmitri Pavlovich Romanov; Prince Felix Yusopov and Dr Lazarevsky
SENTENCE: The murder was not investigated and the three perpetrators were not charged

---

Grigori Yefimovich Rasputin (?1869–1916) was a mystic and self-proclaimed faith healer who had incredible influence over the Russian royal family in the final years of the Romanov dynasty. With his searing eyes, stringy beard and long black robe, he was also known as the 'mad monk'—though he was not a monk. When during World War I Russia's military and economic fortunes took a turn for the worse, Rasputin was denounced in parliament as 'the evil genius of Russia' and a plot was hatched to rid the palace of him once and for all.

Born in Provskoye, a Siberian village along the Tura River, Rasputin was a married man with a young family (including one child born out of wedlock) when he left his home in 1901 to become a religious pilgrim. Travelling to Greece and Jerusalem, Rasputin declared himself to be a *staretz*—a holy man—who had prophetic and healing powers.

Reports of Tsarevich Alexei's haemophilia, a condition the boy inherited from his maternal great-grandmother, Queen Victoria, drew Rasputin to St Petersburg. The illness was incurable, but Tsar Nicholas II and the Tsarina Alexandra were desperate when they turned to the charismatic Rasputin, who in his native Siberia was widely reputed to possess the ability to heal the sick through prayer. Rasputin provided some momentary relief for the young boy when he came to St Petersburg in 1905—some say through a form of hypnosis rather than faith-healing—but when he was able to abate the Tsarevich's bleeding even when he returned to faraway Siberia, even the sceptics in the royal entourage were impressed. The tsar referred to Rasputin as 'our friend', and the holy man was brought to St Petersburg to attend to Alexei's needs and advise the royal family almost as a prophet in residence.

Rasputin's alleged behaviour in St Petersburg caused a scandal. His real 'power' lay in his ability to use his exotic looks—dark, brooding eyes and personal charisma—to seduce women. It was said that he took part in wild sexual orgies with his many female admirers, saying that 'one must sin' in order to be forgiven. This supposed 'man of God' shocked Russian high society with his drinking and womanising. More worrying to palace officials was Rasputin's influence over the tsar and particularly the tsarina. Concern intensified when World War I erupted and anti-German sentiment gathered strength, Alexandra being of German heritage.

Rasputin told the tsar that the Russian army would only succeed once the tsar himself took command—which Nicholas did, with disastrous results. While Tsar Nicholas was away at the front, Rasputin became the tsarina's confidant and personal adviser. Rasputin encouraged the tsar to take over control of the Russian Army and advised the unpopular, German-born tsarina on international matters. As the Russian army suffered defeat after defeat and the economy began to falter, Rasputin was denounced in the *duma* (the lower house of the Russian parliament) as 'the evil genius of Russia' and a plot began to take shape to rid Russia of him once and for all.

Duma member Vladimir Purishkevich formed a plan with the tsar's cousin, Grand Duke Dmitri Pavlovich, and the husband of the tsar's niece, Prince Felix Yusopov, to murder Rasputin. On the night of 29–30 December 1916 (15–16 December in Russia, which still used the Julian calendar), Yusopov invited Rasputin to his palace on the pretext that his wife, Irena, needed healing. Pavlovich was joined by Yusopov and a Dr Lazarevsky, but what happened that night is unclear, because there was no police investigation. What is known (largely based on Yusopov's account—he later wrote a book about the murder) is that Rasputin was fed wine and cake poisoned with potassium cyanide in a dining room in the palace basement. The poison had no effect, however, and Rasputin became increasingly inebriated. Finally, the assassins shot him in the chest, back and head and beat him with chains and a dumbbell—but still he lived. They then wrapped the semi-conscious 'holy man' in a sheet, bundled him into a car and dropped him through a hole in the ice into the Neva River.

Even then Rasputin allegedly struggled before taking his final breath. His body was found three days later.

REFERENCES:

- Oakley, Jane (1990), *Rasputin: Rascal Master,* St Martin's Press, New York
- *Rasputin, www.alexanderpalace.org*
- *The Death of Rasputin, www.timesonline.co.uk*

1917

Mata Hari: 'Spy of the Century'

FACT FILE

CRIME: Spying
DATE: 1916-1917
PLACE: Paris (France)
PERPETRATOR: Margaretha Geertruida Zelle, known as 'Mata Hari' (1876-1917)
SENTENCE: Executed by firing squad on 15 October 1917

Mata Hari, often called the 'spy of the century', was not what she seemed. Portraying herself as an exotic dancer born in India, she was in fact the daughter of a well-to-do Dutch hatter. When her marriage to a Scottish soldier soured, she became something of a 'loose' woman. Though she was found guilty of being a 'double agent' who sold secrets to the German army while spying for the French during World War I, there was never any conclusive evidence that she spied for either country. Despite this, Mata Hari was executed by firing squad on 15 October 1917 and remains one of the most talked about femme fatales of the twentieth century.

'Mata Hari' was born Margaretha Geertruida Zelle in Leeuwarden, Holland, on 7 August 1876. At the age of 18 she attended a teachers' college, but was allegedly asked to leave for having an affair with the headmaster. In 1895 she married Scotsman John Rudolf MacLeod, 20 years her senior and serving in the Dutch navy, and subsequently bore him two children. From 1897 to 1902 the MacLeods lived in Java and Sumatra (at that time parts of the Dutch East Indies), and in 1899 their children were mysteriously poisoned. Their three-year-old son, Norman, died, but their daughter, Jeanne-Louise, survived. (The lover of the children's nanny was later implicated in the crime.) In 1905 Margaretha moved to Paris, where she became something of a hit as an exotic belly dancer at the Oriental Studies Museum. Soon after she took to the Paris stage—first as 'Lady MacLeod' but later as 'Mata Hari', which is supposedly Malay for 'eye of dawn'. The McLeods divorced in 1906.

As she grew older, Mata Hari lived off 'immoral earnings'. During World War I, she had an affair with a 25-year-old Russian pilot, Vadim Maslov, who was flying with the French air force. When he was wounded, Mata Hari pleaded with officials to allow her to visit him in hospital in Germany. The intelligence section of the French army's General Staff, the Deuxième Bureau, gave her permission to do so on condition that she agree to spy on the Germans. (Her fame had brought her into contact with the crown prince of Germany, who was a fan of hers.) The plan was for her to travel to Spain, England and then to neutral Holland, where she would be free to cross over into Germany or German-occupied Belgium. When her ship docked at Falmouth, however, Mata Hari was detained by British officials, who warned her not to go to Germany and sent her back to Spain.

There she had an affair with the German military attaché, Major Kalle. He later sent a coded message to Berlin, which he knew the British were able to decode. Kalle referred to spy 'H-21'—who the British knew to be Mata Hari—providing 'valuable' information. Mata Hari returned to Holland, and when she visited The Hague at the end of 1916, the German consul offered her cash in return for bringing back information from France. The British and French had enough evidence that Mata Hari was in the pay of the German Army and when she returned to Paris in February 1917 she was promptly arrested at the Elysées Palace Hotel.

Mata Hari admitted that she had passed on information to the Germans, but it was inconsequential to the course of the war (when invisible ink was found in her luggage she originally said that it was part of her make-up). She had taken money from the Germans for 'love', she said, not for spying. One of her more fabulous claims was that she was 'working' to bring over to the Allied cause the German Duke of Brunswick–Lunenburg, who was also the heir to the British dukedom of Cumberland. This she would do by sleeping with him. But the war was going disastrously for the French, and officials decided to make an example of Mata Hari. Many also suspect that she was executed before she could further embarrass the French military officials with whom she had slept.

Tried by a military court on 24–25 July 1917, Mata Hari was found guilty and sentenced to death by firing squad. The sentence was carried out on 15 October 1917 in a field in Vincennes, outside Paris. She was not informed of the date of her execution (this was French policy and thought to be more humane) and went to her death with stoic resignation.

REFERENCES:

- Noe, Denise, *Mata Hari, www.crimelibrary.com*
- *Mata Hari timeline, www.twoop.com*
- *The Execution of Mata Hari, 1917, www.eyewitnesstohistory.com/matahari.htm*

1918
The Execution of the Romanovs

FACT FILE

CRIME: Murder
VICTIMS: Tsar Nicholas II (1868–1918); Queen Alexandra (grand-daughter of Queen Victoria; 1872–1918); Olga, aged 23; Tatiana, aged 21; Maria, aged 19; Anastasia, aged 17; Alexei, aged 14; Dr Eugene Botkin and three servants
DATE: 16 July 1918
PLACE: Yekaterinberg (later Sverdlovsk), in the Ural Mountains (Russia)
PERPETRATORS: Bolshevik troops under the supervision of Jakob Yurovski

---

The House of Romanov had ruled Russia for more than 300 years when the Bolshevik revolution swept it from power in 1917. At the height of several disastrous Russian defeats during World War I, Tsar Nicholas II was forced to abdicate in favour of an elected provisional government headed by Premier Alexander Kerensky. The tsar, his family and some of their personal staff (including Dr Eugene Botkin) were driven into exile in Tobolsk (Siberia) for their own protection. When the Bolsheviks overthrew the provisional government in October 1917, their leader, Vladimir Lenin, had the Romanovs sent to Yekaterinberg, on the eastern slopes of the Ural Mountains, and kept under house arrest. It would be decades before the world learnt the grisly nature of the fate they met there.

By July 1918, counter-revolutionary troops from the pro-royalist White Army had rallied against the Bolsheviks and were advancing on Yekaterinberg, where the royal family had been confined for several weeks in Ipatiev House. On the morning of 16 July, Tsar Nicholas, his wife, Alexandra, his four daughters, Olga, Tatiana, Maria and Anastasia, his son, Alexei, and four family retainers were ordered into the basement and shot to death. Bolshevik troops then attacked the bodies with bayonets to ensure that they were dead and smashed their skulls with rifle butts to conceal their identity. (One story tells that the girls took the longest to die, because the jewels they had sewn into their dresses deflected some of the bullets.) White Army troops regained the area soon after, but the interim Bolshevik government announced that the Romanovs had already been executed for 'innumerable foul crimes'.

The murder of the Romanov family shocked Britain and all of Europe (the

Russian royal family was related through marriage to the British royal family and many of Europe's royal houses), although stories circulated that one or two of the tsar's children might possibly have escaped—the youngest daughter, Anastasia, and Alexei, the heir to the Russian throne. Alexei suffered from haemophilia, making it highly unlikely that he could have survived on his own, but in 1922 a woman claiming to be Princess Anastasia appeared in Berlin and convinced many of the remaining members of the exiled Russian royal family that she was indeed Anastasia. In 1928, the woman, who now called herself 'Anna Chaikovsky', immigrated to the United States.

The truth of what happened at Yekaterinberg was kept secret for decades, but, as often happens, fragments of information started to circulate and were then pieced together. The bodies of the victims had been taken 22 kilometres (14 miles) into the forest, soaked with gasoline and burnt. The remains were then thrown into a swamp at the Four Brothers Mine. During communist times, the place where the Romanovs died was officially referred to as the 'scene of national revenge'. In the 1970s, on the orders of Leonid Brezhnev, Ipatiev House was burnt to the ground lest it become a shrine for royalist sympathisers. The man who reluctantly carried out that order was the then secretary of the Sverdlovsk Communist Party—Boris Yeltsen.

A young ethnographer named Alexander Avdonin became obsessed with the fate of the Romanovs and started an illegal dig of a forest area outside Yekaterinberg in the late 1970s. Avdonin found bones at the bottom of a mineshaft but was so alarmed at the repercussions of his discovery that he put them back. It was not until the collapse of the Soviet Union in 1991 that a government-sanctioned team of archaeologists completely unearthed the remains. During the next five years, the bones were stored in the police morgue at Yekaterinberg and the DNA was matched with that of the Romanovs' surviving relatives, including the Duke of Edinburgh.

In February 1998, a special state commission in Moscow announced that the more than 700 bones and bone fragments unearthed in Yekaterinberg in 1991 did indeed belong to Tsar Nicholas, his wife, Alexandra, and their staff—but to only three of their children.

REFERENCES:

- Brown, Hilary (1998), *The Romanov Dynasty* (ABC News), *www.west.net*
- *The Missing Romanovs, www.anomalyinfo.com*
- *Reflections on Russia, www.racu.org*

1919
Eight Men Out

FACT FILE

CRIME: Conspiracy to defraud
DATE: October 1919
PLACE: Chicago, Illinois (USA)
PERPETRATORS:
EIGHT WHITE SOX PLAYERS
Eddie Cicotte (1884–1969); Oscar 'Happy' Felsch (1891–1964); Arnold 'Chick' Gandil; 'Shoeless' Joe Jackson (1889–1951); Fred McMullen (1891–1952); Charles 'Swede' Risberg (1894–75); George 'Buck' Weaver (1890–1956); Claude 'Lefty' Williams (1893–1959)
FIVE GAMBLERS
'Sleepy' Bill Burns; Joseph 'Sport' Sullivan; Nat Evans; Abe 'The Little Champ' Attell; Billy Maharg
VERDICT: Not guilty, but all eight players were banned from major league baseball and their records expunged from the game

Charles Comiskey's Chicago White Sox was a divided baseball club in 1919, but it still qualified for the World Series. 'Shoeless' Joe Jackson later said that the team was split into two groups—one led by first baseman Eddie Collins and the other by second baseman Arnold ('Chick') Gandil—but the team was united in its dispute with the club's wealthy owner. Comiskey grossly underpaid his star players, and in 1917 he benched pitcher Eddie Cicotte when he got too close to 30 wins in a season—which would have entitled him to a US$10,000 bonus. This so embittered eight of the team members that they conspired to throw the 1919 World Series against the Cincinnati Reds.

Three weeks before the end of the regular season, pitcher 'Chick' Gandil allegedly approached an associate of a professional gambler named Joseph ('Sport') Sullivan and said that he could put the World Series 'in the bag' (all amounts in this story refer to US dollars) for $80,000. (In 1950, Gandil said that Sullivan approached him, but whatever the case, the 'fix' had begun.) Eddie Cicotte told Gandil that he would join in for $10,000—paid before the series began—and Gandil then recruited shortstop Charles ('Swede') Risberg, infielder Fred McMullen and pitcher Claude ('Lefty') Williams. Hitters Oscar ('Happy') Felsch, George ('Buck') Weaver and 'Shoeless' Joe Jackson said they would meet with the five players on

21 September 1921 in New York and hear what they had to say.

Gandil's plan was to test the mettle of the other players and then find out how much money they could get from the gamblers for throwing the nine-match series. Buck Weaver suggested that they ask for $80,000 in advance, and then if things got 'too hot' they would keep the money and take the cash from winning the series. Either way, they couldn't lose.

Before long another gambler named 'Sleepy' Bill Burns caught wind of the bribe. Burns and Billy Maharg allegedly approached America's biggest gambler, Arnold ('Big Bankroll') Rothstein, to finance the fix. After first declining the offer, saying that 'throwing' a World Series couldn't be done, Rothstein promised $100,000 for 'Sport' Sullivan to organise the fix through his associates Abe ('The Little Champ') Attell and Nat Evans.

The gamblers offered their bribe in two parts—$40,000 in advance and $40,000 after the series was lost (they would keep the other $20,000 for themselves)—but Sullivan passed on only $10,000 of the advance to the players and bet the other $30,000 on the Reds. When seven of the players complained to the gamblers ('Shoeless' Joe Jackson was not involved), Abe Attell offered them $20,000 every time they lost a match of the series. Still unconvinced, they decided to throw the first two matches, with Cicotte and Williams as starting pitchers.

Cincinnati won the first game 9–1, and the second 4–2. When 'Sleepy' Bill Burns asked Gandil what the players had decided for game three, the second baseman told the gambler that the fix was on. However, still upset at not having had the full amount of the advance paid, the White Sox won 3–0, with Gandil hitting a double. Burns and Maharg lost their money and Gandil told them that he needed $20,000 before the next match. The Reds won 2–0, but when the gamblers failed to produce another $20,000 after a loss in match five, the White Sox returned to their best form and won games six and seven. Chicago only needed one more win to tie the series, but Rothstein ordered Sullivan to pay the players so the series would not go to a deciding ninth game. The Reds won the game 10–5, and the series.

Rumours that the White Sox had thrown the 1919 World Series circulated throughout the winter, but it was not until a questionable 'Cubs–Phillies' game on 31 August 1920 that an inquiry was held to look into players' gambling habits. An interview with Billy Maharg blew the lid on the 1919 scandal, and Eddie Cicotte revealed everything to a grand jury formed to investigate the claims. On 22 October 1920, eight White Sox players were named as having conspired with five gamblers (Arnold Rothstein was not indicted) to throw the 1919 World Series and were suspended from playing. Without its star players, Chicago, which was in line for a shot at the 1920 pennant, quickly faded.

The trial began on 27 June 1921. The state of Illinios charged that the eight players had conspired to perpetrate a confidence game and defraud the public and White Sox pitcher Ray Schalk (who was not part of the fix), and thus injure the American Baseball League and Charles Comiskey's business interests. Despite damning evidence from 'Sleepy' Bill Burns, the jury deliberated for only two hours before finding the players 'not guilty of conspiracy to defraud the public and others'. Paradoxically, because of the judge's directions to the jury, this did not mean that the players hadn't thrown the ball games. When the verdicts were read out, the courtroom cheered and several players were carried out on jurors' shoulders.

The euphoria was short-lived. The day after the verdict, Judge Kenesaw Mountain Landis, the new commissioner of baseball, banned the players for life. 'Regardless of the verdict of juries, no player who throws a ballgame ... [or] sits in conference with a bunch of crooked players and gamblers where the ways and means of throwing a game are discussed and does not promptly tell his club about it, will ever play professional baseball.' The eight players—including 'Shoeless' Joe Jackson, who scored the highest hitting rate during the series, and 'Buck' Weaver, who never received a cent of money—never played major league baseball again. The whole affair is today referred to as the 'Black' Sox scandal.

HISTORICAL AND SOCIAL SIGNIFICANCE:

- The *Chicago Daily* reported that on the day he was arrested, 'Shoeless' Joe Jackson was approached by a young fan, who said, 'Say it ain't so, Joe.' Jackson allegedly confirmed that the fix was on—but the exchange never happened. It was just paper talk.
- The records of the 'eight men out' are still not included in baseball history. As such, 'Shoeless' Joe Jackson is not eligible for entry into the Baseball Hall of Fame.
- *Eight Men Out* is the title of a book by Eliot Asinof, which was filmed in 1988 starring John Cusack as 'Shoeless' Joe Jackson.

REFERENCES:

- Linder, Daniel (2001), *The Black Sox Trial: An Account, www.law.umke.edu*
- Bisher, Furman (1949), 'This is the Truth: By Shoeless Joe Jackson' (*Sport Magazine,* Chicago)
- *www.blackbetsy.com*
- *History Files: Chicago Black Sox, www.chicagohistory.org*

1920
Sacco and Vanzetti

FACT FILE

CRIME: Robbery and murder
VICTIMS: A paymaster and a guard
DATE: 15 April 1920
PLACE: South Baintree, Massachusetts (USA)
PERPETRATORS: Nicola Sacco (1891-1927) and Bartolomeo Vanzetti (1888-1927)
SENTENCE: Executed by electric shock, 23 August 1927

The Bolshevik revolution in Russia in 1918 produced a 'Red scare' throughout the United States of America as worker unions rallied against the continued importation of cheap labour from overseas. Following a series of strikes, riots and finally bombings, which were attributed to the anarchist movement, a nationwide fear of communists, anarchists and immigrants gripped the country and its media. By the spring of 1920, the scare seemed to have dissipated—until a robbery south of Boston, Massachusetts, ignited international headlines.

On 15 April 1920, a paymaster and guard were shot and killed during a payroll robbery in the main street of the industrial town of South Baintree. Two men opened fire on the paymaster and the guard, and a group of four or five men escaped with US$15 776 in a waiting automobile. Three weeks later, two Italian-born anarchists, Nicola Sacco and Bartolomeo Vanzetti, were arrested by police in a trap set up to capture radical elements active in the Boston area. It was thought that radicals were responsible for the South Baintree crime. Both men were carrying guns and anarchist pamphlets. When they lied about their whereabouts on the day of the robbery (both were scared of being deported), authorities felt that the pair had formed a 'consciousness of guilt' and charged them with murder and robbery. Vanzetti was also charged in relation to an attempted robbery in the nearby town of Bridgewater the previous year.

Public sentiment turned against the pair, and when Vanzetti was found guilty of the 'Bridgewater' crime, he was sentenced to a harsh 15 years' jail. The 'Baintree' trial, which was held in Dedham, became 'a *cause célèbre*' with 'worldwide reverberations'. Sacco and Vanzetti's defence lawyer, the socialist F. H. Moore, erred when he tried to prove that the pair were being tried for their radical views rather than the crime itself. After a highly politicised trial in which only circumstantial evidence was tabled and the relative guilt or innocence of either man could not be established, Sacco and Vanzetti were found guilty of murder on 14 July 1921. The entire trial was considered to be 'a gross perversion of justice'.

The Left throughout America and Europe rallied behind Sacco and Vanzetti, and for seven years they fought the death penalty. William Thompson replaced Moore as their lawyer in 1924, and for the next three years Thompson tried to prove the pair's innocence. The appeal process attracted the attention of many liberals in the United States law community, who felt that the US justice system was really on trial. On 9 April 1927, after all avenues of appeal had been exhausted, Sacco and Vanzetti were sentenced to death.

The pair's sentence sparked demonstrations and riots in London, Paris, Mexico City, Buenos Aires and Germany. There was such immense public pressure behind the case that Alvan T. Fuller, the state governor, appointed an advisory committee—the 'Lowell Committee', headed by A. Lawrence Lowell, the president of Harvard University—to investigate grounds for clemency. The committee found that the judicial process had been fair and recommended that the sentences not be commuted to life. When questions about the true nature of the 'American dream' were raised in later years, an alumni of Harvard University commented that 'not every wop has the switch to the electric chair thrown by the president of Harvard'.

Sacco and Vanzetti were executed by electric shock on 23 August 1927. As he was seated in the electric chair shortly after midnight, Sacco called out: 'Long live anarchy.' The case against Vanzetti was considerably weaker than that against Sacco. Vanzetti continued to proclaim his innocence right up to his execution. 'I wish to forgive some people for what they are doing to me,' Vanzetti declared before he followed Sacco to the chair.

Although earlier historians almost unanimously felt that both Sacco and Vanzetti were innocent and unjustly executed, some revisionist writers take the view that they were indeed guilty. The truth still lies hidden somewhere in between.

HISTORICAL AND SOCIAL SIGNIFICANCE:

- The Sacco and Vanzetti case reinforced the view among some that there are two United States of Americas—one for the rich and one for the poor.
- In 1982, author Francis Russell was informed by the son of one of the men in the getaway car that Sacco was indeed guilty but Vanzetti was innocent of 'actual participation in the killing of the two men'.

REFERENCES:

- D'Attilio, Robert (2005), *The Sacco–Vanzetti Case, www.writing.upenn.edu*
- Burnett, Paul (2005), *The Red Scare, www.law.umkc.edu*
- *Summary of Evidence in the Sacco & Vanzetti Case (2005), www.law.umke.edu*

1924
Leopold and Loeb

FACT FILE

CRIME: Murder
VICTIM: Bobby Franks, aged 14
DATE: 21 May 1924
PLACE: Chicago, Illinois (USA)
PERPETRATORS: Nathan Leopold (1904–1971) and Richard Loeb (1905–1936)
SENTENCE: Life and 99 years

On Wednesday 21 May 1924, 14-year-old Bobby Franks did not come home from the Harvard School for Boys in Chicago. Bobby's wealthy businessman father frantically searched for his son—but a phone call that night confirmed his worst fears. 'Your son has been kidnapped,' a man identifying himself as 'Johnson' said. 'He is all right. There will be further news in the morning.' Mr Franks notified the police later that night but pleaded with them to do nothing until the morning.

At 9 am the next day, the distraught father was sent a typed ransom note asking for US$10,000 in 'old bills'. Bobby Franks, it was said, would be returned safely within six hours of the ransom being paid. In reality, the boy was already dead.

The body of young Bobby Franks was discovered later that day in a drainpipe at Wolf Lake, near the Indiana border. He had been bludgeoned, tied up and disfigured with acid. Having amateurishly left a trail of clues, the killers were quickly identified as two local teenagers, Nathan Leopold and Richard Loeb. Both were sons of wealthy local Jewish families and highly intelligent. State's attorney Robert Crowe described the crime at the time as 'the most terrible criminal offence that has been perpetrated in this generation'. The killers' motive was chillingly impersonal—each was a deadly combination of sociopath and intellectual, and they wanted to show each other how easily they, with their superior intellect, could outwit the police and commit the 'perfect crime'. The pair had cold-bloodedly selected Bobby Franks as their victim.

It was Loeb who hatched the plan to commit 'the perfect crime', and he found a willing partner in Leopold, who had studied nineteenth century German philosopher Friedrich Nietzsche. Leopold was obsessed with Nietzsche's 'superman' concept and believed that a person of his intellect could operate outside the ordinary boundaries of morality. Their plan progressed to the murder of a stranger, but despite some careful preparation (opening bank accounts under false names and establishing a line of credit with a hire car company) they made major mistakes from the outset.

Leopold and Loeb left clues at almost every step of their crime. Crucially, a pair of spectacles was found at the crime scene. The lenses were a common enough type, but the hinges, which were patented by a local company, had only just come on to the market. Only three pairs had been sold—one of them to Nathan Leopold.

Local shop staff also identified the pair as the men who had bought the chisel used to bludgeon the victim, the rope used to tie him up and the hydrochloric acid used to disfigure him—even the paper on which they had typed the ransom note.

A second ransom note, instructing Mr Franks as to how he was to deliver the money, was planted in a train bound for Michigan to throw police off their trail (Leopold and Loeb had never planned to collect the ransom). A rail employee at the local station identified Loeb as having bought a rail ticket to Michigan.

Once captured, the killers turned on each other, each accusing the other of bludgeoning Bobby Franks with the chisel. Loeb took the police to where they had dumped the Underwood typewriter in a local lagoon, further sealing the case against them.

Having pleaded guilty to their heinous crime, the pair would certainly have been hanged for kidnapping and murder were it not for the brilliant defence of renowned lawyer Clarence S. Darrow. The sensational trial lasted for months—not on the basis of guilt or innocence, because the young men made a full confession in court, but on the sole question of whether the youths should be executed or imprisoned.

On 10 September 1924, Judge Caverly, visibly moved by Darrow's speech, sentenced the two killers to life imprisonment for the murder of Bobby Franks and to 99 years for his kidnapping, to be served in Chicago's Joliet State Prison.

The young killers were reunited in 1931 when they were asked to develop educational courses for other prisoners. (They wrote a maths textbook that became a standard text throughout the US prison system.) Loeb died in 1936 after a savage prison attack, but Leopold lived to write his autobiography in 1957 (*Life + 99 Years*) and was paroled the following year, after having served 33 years in prison. He moved to Puerto Rico, married a local woman and worked in the department of health until his death from a heart attack in 1971.

REFERENCES:

- Bienen, Leigh and Geis, Gilbert (1998), *Crimes of the Century,* Northeastern University Press, Boston
- *Murder Casebook* (1990), Marshall Cavendish, London
- Rackcliffe, Marianne, *Leopold and Loeb, www.leopoldandloeb.com*
- *Homicide in Chicago—1924: Leopold and Loeb, www.homicide.northwestern.edu*

1929

St Valentine's Day Massacre

FACT FILE

CRIME: Murder
VICTIMS: James Clark (aka Albert Kachelleck), aged 40; Frank Gusenberg, aged 35; Pete Gusenberg, aged 39; Adam 'Frank' Heyer, aged 39; Johnny May, aged 34; Dr Reinhardt Schwimmer, aged 28; Al Weinshenker, aged 40
DATE: 14 December 1929
PLACE: 2122 North Clark Street, Chicago (USA)
PERPETRATORS: Albert Anselmi, John Scalise, Fred Burke and another unknown associate, on the orders of Jack 'Machine Gun' McGurn and Al Capone
SENTENCE: The men were never brought to justice for this crime

On 14 February 1929, St Valentine's Day, four men disguised as police walked into a garage on North Clark Street, Chicago, lined up the seven people inside against the wall and shot them dead. At the height of the 1920s—the era of Prohibition, which was dominated by gangsters—the murder of the seven men stunned the nation. It was later revealed that Chicago mobster Al Capone ordered the 'hit' but that the real target, rival mob leader George 'Bugs' Moran, escaped the carnage. Ultimately, the St Valentine's Day massacre turned the American public against urban folk heroes like Al Capone and ushered in a new era—the Depression.

Alphonse Capone was born in New York City in 1899. He started his criminal career in his native Brooklyn when he joined Johnny Torrio's gang. Capone earned the name 'Scarface', which he hated, while still a teenager after he received three long cuts on his jaw from rival Frank Galluccio in a quarrel over a girl. Torrio moved to Chicago in 1916 and sent for Capone three years later to work in 'Diamond Jim' Colisimo's gambling and prostitution rackets. However, the *Prohibition Act*, which banned the production and selling of alcohol, opened up a new avenue of money-making for bootleggers.

Torrio and Capone maintained their powerbase and avoided incriminating themselves by hiring out-of-town hit men from New York. This strategy worked so well they conscripted a Brooklyn associate named Frank Yale to murder 'Diamond Jim' Colosimo, so that the pair could take over his rackets. Torrio, Capone's mentor and sponsor, then negotiated a 'peace plan' with his rivals to ensure that the territories and business interests of each gang were protected. Torrio may have been a gangster ahead of his time, but his peace plan did not last. By the mid-1920s, the 'beer wars' that erupted between the Torrio–Capone mob and the Irish gang run by Dion O'Bannion on the North Side of the city had turned Chicago into a violent gangland.

In 1924 Dion O'Bannion suddenly announced his retirement from the bootlegging industry and sold his illegal brewery to Torrio and Capone. On the night they took possession of the brewery it was raided by police, thanks to a tip-off from O'Bannion. In November O'Bannion was murdered by Capone's men—Frank Yale, Albert Anselmi and John Scalise—in the backroom of his florist shop. Johnny Torrio was shot in retaliation but survived, and retired to Sicily. Al Capone was now the leader of the biggest gang in Chicago.

As hard as it is to believe, Al Capone was a popular figure in Chicago. Most people hated the Prohibition laws and Capone maintained a high profile as a benefactor to hospitals and charities and as a big tipper to bus boys and beggars. Immaculately dressed—his friends called him 'Snorkey', which was street slang for 'well-dressed'—and personally charming, Capone and his entourage attended sporting fixtures and the funerals of his enemies whom he had murdered. Capone also had connections with City Hall, and his interests were well protected. But primarily, he was a thug and a murderer.

The Irish North Side mob, now headed by Hymie Weis, used George 'Bugs' Moran to intimidate Capone's gang with a series of drive-by shootings. Capone's chauffeur was shot in one incident while the mob boss sat unharmed in the back of his car, and in 1926 eleven cars drove past Capone's headquarters and machine-gunned the premises. One man and a woman (an innocent passer-by) were killed but Capone was again unscathed. Capone's response was predictable—he had Hymie Weis murdered. 'Bugs' Moran took control of the Irish mob and the war raged on for another two years. In 1928, the city elections saw voters revolt against corrupt officials who were in partnership with Capone, and it was apparent that the mobster was losing his powerbase.

On 19 January 1929, Capone gangster Patsy Lolordo and his wife, Aleina, were murdered in their Chicago home by three men—James Clark, Pete Gusenberg and Frank Gusenberg, all working for Capone's rival, 'Bugs' Moran. The murder broke a six-month truce between the warring factions and Capone and his lieutenant, Jack ('Machine Gun') McGurn (aka Vincenzo De Mora), decided to get rid of Moran and his gang once and for all.

The SMC Cartage Company on North Clark Street was a known haunt of 'Bugs' Moran. Capone led Moran to believe that a huge truckload of illegal alcohol would arrive from Detroit on 14 February knowing that Moran and his men would be there to oversee its dispersal. Also present at the garage that day were James Clark (Moran's brother-in-law), Johnny May, Adam Heyer, Al Weinshenker, Frank and Pete Gusenberg, and an optometrist named Reinhardt Schwimmer, who used his business as a cover for his criminal activities. When Capone's men arrived for the 'hit' dressed as policemen, Moran was outside the garage and hid from view, thinking that it was merely a police 'shakedown'.

On that cold Chicago morning, Capone's men—Anselmi, Scalise, Fred Burke and another unknown associate—lined up the seven men against a brick wall and fired on them with machine-guns. McGurn and Capone were in Florida at the time and had alibis.

Two months later, on 16 May 1929, Al Capone was arrested for carrying a concealed weapon as he left a three-day conference attended by many of the warring crime families in Atlantic City. Many believe that Capone was deliberately arrested on this trivial charge to allow him to escape the vengeance of 'Bugs' Moran—others believe the arrest was designed to appease the public's outrage at the gangland killings in Chicago. Whatever the reason, Capone's career as a crime boss was coming to an end. In 1930 he became the target of federal tax agents investigating the anomaly that one of Chicago's richest men had not paid tax for several years. Capone was sentenced to eleven years' jail in San Francisco's Alcatraz Prison and was fined US$80 000. By the time he was released, the gangster era was over.

Al Capone died in 1947 from the effects of syphilis.

HISTORICAL AND SOCIAL SIGNIFICANCE:

- Two of the men responsible for the massacre, Albert Anselmi and John Scalise, were murdered by Capone or his henchmen with baseball bats at a mob banquet (as dramatised in the movie *The Untouchables*) later that year. Jack McGurn was murdered in 1936, and 'Bugs' Moran spent the final years of his life in jail.
- The garage that was the scene of the crime was demolished in 1967. The wall against which the men were shot was dismantled brick by brick and sold to a Canadian businessman, who reused the bricks in the men's restroom of a bar with a gangster theme. When the bar closed, the owner tried to sell 417 'authenticated, bullet-ridden' bricks for US$1000 each because of their notoriety.
- The site of the St Valentine's Day massacre is now a landscaped lot. A tree marks the spot where 'Bugs' Moran's men were killed.

REFERENCES:

- *Haunted Chicago* (2005), *www.prairieghosts.com*
- *St Valentine's Day Massacre, www.findagrave.com*

1931
The Scottsboro Boys

FACT FILE

CRIME: Rape
VICTIMS:
Victoria Price (1910–1982) and Ruby Bates (1913–1976)
DATE: 25 March 1931
PLACE: Scottsboro, Alabama (USA)
ALLEGED PERPETRATORS: Olen Montgomery, aged 17; Clarence Norris, aged 18; Haywood Patterson, aged 18; Ozie Powell, aged 16; Willie Roberson, aged 17; Charley Weems, aged 19; Eugene Williams, aged 13; Andrew ('Andy') Wright, aged 19; Leroy ('Roy') Wright, aged 12 or 13
SENTENCE: Eight of the men were sentenced to death and 13-year-old Eugene Williams was sentenced to life imprisonment. Williams and Roy Wright were later paroled because they were juveniles. After retrials, Patterson and Norris were again sentenced to death but this was commuted to life imprisonment. Andy Wright was sentenced to 99 years and was the last of the Scottsboro Boys to be officially paroled

---

In 1931, nine black youths were arrested for the alleged rape of two white women near Scottsboro, Alabama. Despite medical reports that showed that neither woman had been raped, the nine youths—Olen Montgomery, Clarence Norris, Haywood Patterson, Ozie Powell, Willie Roberson, Charley Weems, Eugene Williams, and brothers Andrew ('Andy') and Leroy ('Roy') Wright—were charged and convicted. The trial of the 'Scottsboro Boys' and their subsequent fight for justice exposed the shortcomings of the American justice system in the racially segregated South.

On 25 March 1931, a posse of men waited at Paint Rock, Alabama, for a Southern Railway freight train to arrive. A fight had erupted en route and several white men had been thrown off one of the cars by a group of blacks. Nine blacks, whose ages ranged from 13 to 19, were charged with assault after the incident. However, two women dressed as boys who had also been riding the train—21-year-old Victoria Price and 17-year-old Ruby Bates—told police that they had been raped by the black men. After a lynch mob gathered to hang the nine youths outside Scottsboro jail, Alabama governor Benjamin Meeks Mille called in the National Guard to protect the accused.

From there, matters came to a head very quickly. Within the week a grand jury indicted the nine 'Scottsboro Boys' for rape. On 6 April, the trial began in Scottsboro before Judge A. E. Hawkins. Most of the Scottsboro Boys did not know each other, and several accused others in the group of being involved in the rapes. By the end of the following day, eight of the nine men had been tried, convicted and sentenced to death. Roy Wright's trial ended in a mistrial when some members of the all-white jury held out for the death penalty despite having been instructed to recommend life imprisonment because Wright was only 13 years old.

Although Ruby Bates wrote a letter in June 1931 denying that she was raped, the Alabama Supreme Court upheld the convictions of seven of the eight men. (Eugene Williams's conviction was overturned when it was discovered that he too was a juvenile under Alabama state law.) When the US Supreme Court reviewed the case in November 1932, it reversed the convictions on the grounds that Alabama had failed to provide counsel as required by the 'due process' clause of the 14th amendment to the United States constitution.

With no evidence that the rapes had even occurred—both 'victims' were later described as notorious prostitutes of the lowest type—this should have been the end of the matter. But Victoria Price would not be silenced. For six years, and in trial after trial, she maintained that she had been gang-raped by 'six pistol- and knife-waving' black men.

In April 1933, Hayward Patterson, the oldest of the Scottsboro Boys, was found guilty for a second time and sentenced to death. Not even Ruby Bates's surprise turn as a defence witness could sway the jury. Bates recanted the rape allegation, saying that Price had forced her to go along with the ruse in order to avoid charges of vagrancy or, worse, violation of the *Mann Act* (crossing state lines for immoral purposes). Such was the tension in Scottsboro over the case that Judge Horton postponed the retrials of the other Scottsboro Boys. When thousands of people marched on Washington in protest against the Alabama trials, Judge Horton set aside Patterson's conviction and granted him a new trial. As a result, the case was transferred to the court of another Alabama judge and Horton was voted out of judicial office at the next opportunity.

In November 1933, Patterson and Norris were again found guilty and sentenced to death. When the cases again came under US Supreme Court review in 1935, the convictions were again overturned on the basis that Negroes (the term in use at the time) had been excluded from sitting on the jury for both trials. After retrials, Olen Montgomery, Willie Roberson, Eugene Williams and Roy Wright were released in 1937—Roberson was not even in the same car as the two women but still served six years in prison, while Roy Wright and Eugene Williams were juveniles and should never have been tried as adults. (Roy Wright committed suicide in 1959.) But still the state of Alabama would not be denied.

In January 1936, Hayward Patterson was convicted for a fourth time and sentenced to 75 years in prison. The following year, Clarence Norris was convicted of rape and sentenced to death (the sentence was commuted to life imprisonment in 1938), and Andy Wright was sentenced to 99 years. Ozie Powell, who was intellectually handicapped, was sentenced to 20 years for attacking a sheriff. Despite the widespread view that the Scottsboro Boys were innocent, Alabama governor Bibb Graves declined to pardon them—the first of the accused was not paroled until 1943. After Charley Weems was paroled, Clarence Norris and Andy Wright were released in 1944 and immediately violated parole by fleeing Montgomery. Ozie Powell was paroled in 1946.

Andy Wright was returned to prison in 1946 and did not see freedom again until 1950. Hayward Patterson escaped from prison in 1948, and although he was arrested by the FBI in Michigan two years later, the state governor declined to extradite him to Alabama. In September 1951, however, Patterson was convicted of manslaughter after a bar room brawl and was returned to prison. Within a year he was dead from cancer, aged 39. Clarence Norris, who was paroled in 1946 but became a fugitive from the law for the next 30 years, was granted a full pardon in 1976 by Alabama governor George Wallace—45 years after the case first went to trial. Norris, the last of the Scottsboro Boys, died in 1989, aged 76.

REFERENCES:

- Bienen, Leigh and Geis, Gilbert (1998), *Crimes of the Century*, Northeastern University Press, Boston
- *The Scottsboro Boys* (2005), *www.law.umke.edu*

1932
The Lindbergh Kidnapping

FACT FILE

CRIME: Kidnapping and murder
VICTIM: Charles Lindbergh Jnr, aged 2
DATE: 1 March 1932
PLACE: New Jersey, New York (USA)
PERPETRATOR: Bruno Richard Hauptmann (1900–1936)
SENTENCE: Executed by electric shock, 3 April 1936

In 1927, Charles A. Lindbergh gained international fame when he made the first non-stop, solo transatlantic flight from New York to Paris in his single-engine plane *Spirit of St Louis*. Five years later, his name again made international headlines when his infant son was kidnapped from the family's New Jersey home. The elaborate ransom plot, the subsequent discovery of the child's body and the trial of German immigrant Bruno Hauptmann proved to be one of the most sensational and controversial crimes of the twentieth century.

On the night of 1 March 1932, Charles Lindbergh was working in his study, having completely forgotten that he was due at New York University for a speaking engagement. Soon after 9 pm, Lindbergh was talking to his pregnant wife, Anne, when he heard the sound of wood cracking outside. His wife heard nothing. Shortly after 10 pm, nursery maid Betty Gow went in to check on the Lindbergh's infant son, Charles Jnr, who was asleep in the nursery adjoining his parent's bedroom. At first Gow did not notice anything wrong in the darkened room, but when she turned on a heater to warm her hands before touching the baby, she realised that she could not hear the boy breathing. Charles Lindbergh Jnr was missing.

Despite his distress, Lindbergh had the forethought not to disturb anything in the room, though he noticed an envelope on the heating grille near the window and reddish clay marks on a furniture chest and on the bedroom floor. While the family's butler phoned the local police, Lindbergh contacted New Jersey State Police and his New York attorney. Before the police arrived, the women in the house checked the other rooms while the men searched the grounds using car headlights. When police arrived, Lindbergh wouldn't let them touch anything in the room. An external search found two indentations in the clay outside the window of the baby's room and the bottom section of a ladder some distance away.

State detectives arrived, and when fingerprints could not be found on the envelope, the contents were read. It was a ransom note for US$50,000. The kidnappers included the usual warnings about contacting authorities but then assured Lindbergh that the child was in 'gute care' and that he would be contacted again within two to four days. The famous aviator had every intention of paying the ransom and warned authorities not to interfere with the handing over of the money. On 4 March, Lindbergh publicly stated that the kidnappers' safety would be 'guaranteed' if the ransom exchange was successful, but the state attorney general announced that Lindbergh had no authority to make such an offer.

The following day, Lindbergh received two more letters postmarked New York and signed in the same manner as the ransom note. The first letter stated that the ransom was raised to US$70,000 because Lindbergh had involved the police and the press. The second stated that the baby was well and that they would not deal with any 'go-betweens'—Lindbergh would have to deliver the money. However, a Dr John Condon, an elderly lecturer, placed an advertisement in a Bronx newspaper declaring that he would offer his life savings if he could be used as a mediator. Soon after, Condon was contacted by letter, and after Lindbergh was convinced that this note was also sent by the child's kidnappers, Condon was allowed to deliver the ransom money.

After a convoluted series of communications between Dr Condon and the kidnappers—including a phone call with a man whose voice was described as Scandinavian or German—a package arrived on Condon's doorstep. It contained the baby's sleeping-suit and details of the ransom instructions. In another call, the man called himself 'John'. After saying that the baby was six hours away on a boat, the 'kidnapper' asked if he would 'burn'—meaning electrocution—if the baby was dead.

When the ransom money was assembled, the US treasury insisted that the bulk of the money should be gold certificate bills, which would be easier to trace. The drop-off was to be made at the Bronx cemetery on Saturday 2 April. Condon met 'John' and the exchange was made—the ransom money in return for a note detailing the child's whereabouts. Charles Jnr was said to be on a boat called the *Nelly* but no sign of the boat was found. On 12 May, two truck drivers found the child's body in woods about 7 kilometres (four and a half miles) from the Lindbergh mansion. A post-mortem revealed that the child had suffered a head injury and died on the day he was kidnapped. (It was thought that the kidnapper had accidentally dropped the baby while descending the ladder.)

By the end of 1932, 27 of the bills had been deposited throughout New York. Then, in September 1934, a customer at a petrol station used one of the US$10 gold bills and an alert manager noted the car's registration number. When German immigrant Bruno Richard Hauptmann was later arrested in his car, the 34-year-old carpenter had one of the gold bills in his pocket. Because he also matched the general description of the 'John' who had taken the ransom money in the cemetery, Hauptmann was charged with kidnapping, murder and extortion. A sum of US$13,760 was found in Hauptmann's garage. The police had their man. Or had they?

Hauptmann maintained that he was merely minding the money for a German national named Isidor Fisch who had returned to Germany. He did not even know that the package Fisch asked him to mind was full of money until his curiosity got the better of him and he opened it. Hauptmann had only recently started spending the money because Fisch owed him US$7500. The quietly spoken German immigrant was extradited to New Jersey and charged after he was found to have lied to police about his criminal past. Hauptmann's trial, which was filmed and shown in movie theatres, began on 2 February 1935.

A fair trial was always going to be difficult, given the media coverage of the kidnapping and murder of a national hero's infant son, but the circumstantial evidence began to stack up against Hauptmann. Lindbergh identified Hauptmann's voice from the original phone call, Condon identified Hauptmann as the 'John' he met in the cemetery, and Condon's phone number was found written inside a closet door in Hauptmann's home. (It was later found that it had been written by a journalist after Hauptmann's arrest.) Compounding matters, Fisch had died in Germany and could not be cross-examined, and anti-German sentiment was still running high after World War I. After a two-week trial, the German carpenter was found guilty and sentenced to death.

Bruno Richard Hauptmann went to the electric chair at Trenton State Prison on 3 April 1936. But many questions still remain about the case and the German carpenter's guilt.

HISTORICAL AND SOCIAL SIGNIFICANCE:

- The crime inspired the 'Lindbergh Law', which made kidnapping a federal crime, and also inspired the Agatha Christie novel *Murder On The Orient Express.*

REFERENCES:

- *Murder Casebook* (1990), Marshall Cavendish, London
- *The Bruno Hauptman Trial* (2005), *www.law.umkc.com*
- *Charles Lindbergh biography, www.charleslindbergh.com*

1934

The 'Pyjama Girl' Case

FACT FILE

CRIME: Murder
VICTIM: Linda Agostini (nee Platt), aged 29
DATE: 28 August 1934
PLACE: Carlton, Melbourne (Australia)
PERPETRATOR: Antonio ('Tony') Agostini (1903-1969)
SENTENCE: Tony Agostini was sentenced to six years' hard labour for manslaughter, but after serving three years and nine months was deported to Italy in 1947.

On 1 September 1934, the badly burnt body of a young woman, viciously battered about the head and wearing only pyjamas, was found in a road culvert in the township of Albury on the New South Wales–Victoria border in rural Australia. Although Sydney police reconstructed the dead woman's features and made composite drawings of what she may have looked like in life, they also took the extraordinary step of preserving the body in a formalin bath. During the next decade tens of thousands of people viewed the ghastly remains at the University of Sydney, and later Sydney police headquarters, before it was positively identified in 1944.

When the body was examined, the victim, dressed in canary yellow and white pyjamas, was determined to be between 25 and 30 years old. Her head had been protected from fire damage because it was wrapped in a towel, and she had a large laceration on the forehead and a puncture mark—most likely made by a small-calibre bullet—under her right eye. Her skull was fractured on the left side, but it was not until two days later that a local GP located the bullet with the use of an X-ray. The fact that the woman had been shot was not revealed to the public until the inquest in 1938.

An Albury dentist extracted six teeth from the dead woman's mouth for identification purposes. The lower right second molar and the upper second molar were filled with gold inlay, which was unusual for the times, and obviously offered the best prospect of identifying her. Police made a plaster cast of the woman's face (smoothing over and so concealing the gash in her forehead) and applied make-up to it to make it more 'lifelike', but still she could not be identified. In October, the body of the woman dubbed the 'Pyjama Girl' by the press was transported to the University of Sydney, where it was put on display. Images of the woman's body submerged in a formalin bath were sent to 87 police organisations in 80 countries, including England's famous Scotland Yard.

Within six months of the start of the investigation, police had reportedly conducted 5000 separate inquiries. A number of people, including a Kings Cross police sergeant and his wife, informed the police that the woman looked like the English-born wife of Italian immigrant Tony Agostini. The Agostinis had moved to Melbourne from Sydney in 1934, and inquiries revealed that Linda had left her husband and gone back to her job as a hairdresser on a Union Steamship Company ship after some 'domestic differences'.

Antonio Agostini had made many friends in his adopted country; the genial, polite Italian had secured the lease on the cloakroom at one of Sydney's best-known nightclubs, Romano's in Kings Cross. One of the many single girls living nearby in Darlinghurst Road, Kings Cross, was English girl Florence Linda Platt. After what was described as a conventional courtship for that time, Agostini married her in April 1930. The couple lived in Kellett Street, Darlinghurst, but soon Linda's social drinking developed into acute alcoholism.

In order to save his marriage, Tony Agostini took on the position of Melbourne editor of the English–Italian newspaper *Il Giornale Italiano (The Italian Newspaper)* in 1933. He hoped that the move to Melbourne would curb his wife's drinking problem, but soon Linda slipped into her old habits. After a brief separation, the Agostinis were reconciled and lived in Swanston Street, Carlton, where Tony edited his newspaper in a room below their upstairs apartment. When Linda disappeared one last time in late August 1934, Tony Agostini told his associates that his wife had finally left him for good.

In January 1938, district coroner Mr C. W. Swiney conducted an inquest at Albury courthouse into the death and identity of the Pyjama Girl. After an open finding was returned, an Italian grocer named Luigi Castellano went to the Victorian police and informed them that he knew the identity of the Pyjama Girl because her husband had confessed her murder to him. The man's name was Tony Agostini. However, the victim's dental records did not match those of Linda Agostini. The following year, rambling accusations by a Sydney physician and amateur criminologist named Dr Thomas Alexander Palmer Benbow took the focus of the murder investigation away from Agostini. When World War II was declared, Tony Agostini was interned as an enemy alien. When Italian internees were released in 1944, he was re-employed at Romano's, where he had first worked when he came to Australia.

In reviewing all the available evidence related to the long, unsolved case, Sydney detectives decided to have another look at the comparison of the dental records of Linda Agostini and the Pyjama Girl. They arranged for Agostini's dentist and two independent dentists to inspect the Pyjama Girl's body in its formalin bath. It was found that two porcelain fillings had fallen out—incredibly, the fillings were still in the mouth—and had not been noticed by the original Albury dentist who examined the body nor detected by X-ray. The porcelain work was recognised as belonging to Linda Agostini—finally, the Pyjama Girl's identity had been revealed.

When police superintendent 'Big' Bill McKay was informed of the Pyjama Girl's identity, he was shocked to find that the chief suspect was his regular waiter at his favourite lunchtime restaurant. On Saturday 4 March 1944, he sent for Tony Agostini to come to the Sydney headquarters of the CIB, and the Italian immigrant quickly confessed. At his trial in Melbourne on 19 June 1944, Agostini was able to convince the jury that the crime was not premeditated and that he had panicked after accidentally shooting his wife when she pulled a gun on him. (The fractured skull was conveniently explained as her body having being dropped down the stairs, but it's more than likely she had been subdued by a tyre lever before her body was bundled into a car and driven out of the city.)

Linda Agostini—the subject of a worldwide search to reveal her identity—was buried in relative anonymity in Melbourne's Preston General Cemetery on 13 July 1944. Found guilty of manslaughter, Agostini served three years and nine months and was then deported to Italy in 1947 because he had never become an Australian citizen. The man who committed one of the most bizarre murders in Australian criminal history remarried and lived a quiet life in Sardinia until his death in 1969.

REFERENCES:

- Coleman, Robert (1978), *The Pyjama Girl*, Hawthorn Press, Melbourne
- *The Sun*, 2 September 1934
- *The Border Morning Mail*, 3 September 1934

1934

Bonnie and Clyde

FACT FILE

CRIMES: Murder and robbery
VICTIMS: John Bucher; Deputy Gene Moore; Howard Hall; Doyle Johnson; Deputy Malcolm Davis; Constable Wes Harryman; Detective Harry McGinnis; Marshall Henry Humphrey; Major Joseph Crowson; Patrolman Wheeler; Patrolman Murphy and Constable Cal Campbell
DATES: 5 August 1932 to 23 May 1934
PLACES: Oklahoma, Texas, Minnesota, Iowa and Missouri (USA)
PERPETRATORS: Clyde Barrow (1909-34); Bonnie Parker (1910-1934); Buck Barrow (1903-1933); Raymond Hamilton (1913-1935); WD Jones (1916-1974); Henry Methvin (1912-1948)

By the early 1930s, the joint effects of the Great Depression and Prohibition—the complete ban on the production and sale of alcohol—had had a startling effect on American society. The ensuing crime spree gained momentum in the 1920s and produced any number of bootleggers, racketeers and gangsters. There was a dramatic increase in bank robberies, kidnappings and murders during this period, which produced such urban criminals as Al Capone, Meyer Lansky and 'Bugs' Siegel, and country folk heroes such as 'Machine Gun' Kelly, 'Baby Face' Nelson and 'Pretty Boy' Floyd.

Lovers Bonnie Parker and Clyde Barrow were the product of poor farming families in Texas forced to move into shanty towns outside Dallas when the Depression hit the cotton industry. Bonnie Parker already had a broken marriage behind her when she brought 21-year-old Clyde Barrow home in January 1930—and he was already on the run from police. When Clyde was captured and sentenced to two years' jail for car theft (another charge of burglary brought him a suspended 12-year sentence), Bonnie smuggled a gun into Waco Prison for him. Clyde botched his escape attempt, bringing down on his head the full wrath of his 14-year sentence. Moved to Huntsville State Penitentiary, he had a fellow inmate chop off two of his toes in order to gain an early release—and the ploy worked. He was paroled in February 1932.

Returning to Dallas and linking up with Bonnie Parker, Clyde formed his own gang and began robbing convenience stores and small banks. When Bonnie was captured in Kaufman, Texas, Clyde joined forces with teenager Raymond Hamilton.

In April 1932, the pair murdered petrol station operator John Bucher and then fled to Oklahoma. Bonnie was released for lack of evidence, but when Clyde and Hamilton were confronted by law enforcement officers at a dance in Stringtown and shot Deputy Gene Moore dead, Bonnie quickly joined her former lover. The murderous rampage of Bonnie and Clyde was about to begin.

Their first victim was a former cowboy named Howard Hall, who confronted the gun-toting pair with a meat cleaver when they tried to rob a store in Sherman, Texas. One of the gang's newest members was teenage car thief William Daniel ('WD') Jones. When a man named Doyle Johnson caught Jones and Barrow stealing his car in Temple, Texas, and jumped up on the running board, Clyde shot him in the head at point-blank range. In January 1933, Jones was again present when Clyde killed Dallas deputy sheriff Malcolm Davis, who had stumbled upon their current hideaway. Despite being wanted throughout the state for four killings, the Barrow gang were able to return to Dallas with impunity because they were shielded by a close network of family and friends.

Clyde's brother, 'Buck' Barrow, was released from prison in March 1933, and with his new wife, Blanche, in tow linked up with Clyde in Fort Smith, Arkansas. The gang set up house in Joplin, Missouri, but when money ran low in April, they started to look for a bank to rob. The police raided the house just as Clyde and 'WD' Jones returned, and in the ensuing shoot-out two policemen—Joplin Detective Harry McGinnis and Newton County Constable Wes Harryman—were killed. The Barrow gang drove throughout the night to return to Texas. After the gang's biggest robbery—US$2500 from the First State Bank in Okabena, Minnesota—the Barrow brothers split up. Buck and his wife returned to Missouri, and Bonnie, Clyde and Jones went to Oklahoma.

When Bonnie was badly burned in a car accident in Wellington, Texas, police officers raided the house the gang was staying in, but the trio managed to take hostages and escape into neighbouring Oklahoma. They were joined by Buck and Blanche Barrow on the Oklahoma–Arkansas border, and Clyde sent for Bonnie's sister, Billie, from Dallas to tend to her burn injuries. By June 1933, the Barrow gang was back in business.

Buck Barrow and 'WD' Jones gunned down town marshall Henry Humphrey while robbing a Piggly Wiggly convenience store in Fayetteville. But when they robbed the National Guard Armoury in Enid, Oklahoma, they committed a federal crime and came under the notice of the FBI. When Bonnie's injuries forced the gang to buy medical supplies in Kansas City, Clyde and Buck once again had to shoot their way out of trouble. All the male members of the gang were wounded in the shoot-out, and Blanche was badly cut by shattered glass. Buck was the most seriously injured, sustaining a head wound, and when the gang was again confronted in Dexter, Iowa, he was shot in the back. While Bonnie, Clyde and Jones escaped, Blanche stayed to protect her dying husband as the police surrounded them. She was later sentenced to ten years' jail.

When 'WD' Jones was captured in Houston, Texas, he told police that he had been kidnapped by Bonnie and Clyde and had been an unwilling accomplice to their crime spree. Sentenced to 15 years for his part in the murder of deputy Malcolm Davis, Jones turned informer. On 23 November 1933, the FBI set up an ambush for Bonnie and Clyde in Sowers, Texas, but the pair was able to escape. In January of the following year, they broke Raymond Hamilton out of a chain gang and killed Major Joseph Crowson, but the robbers later had a falling out over the distribution of stolen bank money. Having recruited new gang members, Bonnie and Clyde killed two patrolmen in Grapeville, Texas, but the net of law enforcement agencies was finally closing in.

The pair of killers became folk heroes—Bonnie wrote poetry and she and Clyde posed for photos—but the age of gangsters was coming to an end.

It was a gang member, Henry Methvin, who inadvertently provided the clue to the pair's whereabouts. Methvin's father owned a cotton farm in Shreveport, Louisiana, and Texas Rangers tracked the gang there. On the third day of their stake-out, Methvin's father Irvin was stopped and his truck disabled on the side of the road as a lure for Bonnie and Clyde. At 9.15 am on 29 May 1934 Bonnie and Clyde drove down the road in their tan Ford and slowed down as they approached the stationary truck. One hundred and fifty rounds were fired into the car before Bonnie and Clyde could reach for their guns and fire a single shot.

After the deaths of the so-called folk heroes, souvenir hunters swarmed over the death scene and stole clothing, hair and personal items from the bodies of Bonnie and Clyde.

HISTORICAL AND SOCIAL SIGNIFICANCE:

- Bonnie's wish to be buried alongside Clyde was denied. Bonnie Parker and Clyde Barrow were buried in separate cemeteries in Dallas.
- Bonnie and Clyde were immortalised both in film (*Gun Crazy* in 1950, *The Bonnie Parker Story* in 1958 and, most famously, *Bonnie and Clyde*, starring Warren Beatty and Faye Dunaway in 1967) and in song (Georgie Fame's 1967 hit 'The Ballad of Bonnie and Clyde').

REFERENCES:

- Geringer, Joseph (2005), *Bonnie and Clyde: Depression Era Duet, www.crimelibrary.com*
- *Murder Casebook* (1990), Marshall Cavendish, London

1940
Leon Trotsky Assassinated

FACT FILE

CRIME: Murder
VICTIM: Leon Trotsky, aged 62
DATE: 20 August 1940
PLACE: Coyoacán, Mexico City (Mexico)
PERPETRATOR: Jaime Ramón Mercader del Rio Hernandez (1914–1978)
SENTENCE: After serving 20 years in jail without parole, Mercader was released from Mexico City's Lecumberri Prison on 6 May 1960

Together with Vladimir Lenin and Josef Stalin, Leon Trotsky was one of the architects of the Russian Revolution in 1917. Born Lev Davidovich Bronstein in Yanovka, Ukraine, in 1879, to Jewish parents, Trotsky studied in Odessa and was arrested as a Marxist in 1898. He was exiled to Siberia in 1902 but escaped to London three years later and worked as a revolutionary journalist. Joining the Bolshevik revolution back in his homeland,Trotsky created the Red Army and was commissioner for war. When Stalin was elected general secretary of the Communist Party in April 1922, Lenin warned the party of Stalin's ambition but soon after suffered the first of a series of strokes that eventually claimed his life in 1924. Stalin later denounced Trotsky and his theory of 'permanent revolution' and ousted him from the Communist Party. Forced into exile in Alma-Ata in Central Asia, Trotsky fled overseas in 1929 but continued to attack Stalin in print and write open letters to the Soviet politburo.

Stalin tried to silence the exiled Trotsky by eliminating 'Trotskyites' within the Soviet Union and even members of Trotsky's family. Trotsky's first wife, Alexandra, was detained, their son Sergei died in prison, a daughter, Zinaida, was driven to suicide, and the KGB was allegedly behind the suspicious death of another son, Leon Sedov, in a Paris clinic in 1937. As a former communist revolutionary now in his third period of international exile, Trotsky had trouble finding a country that would allow him to write and live out the rest of his life with his second wife, Natalia. He stayed temporarily in several countries (while he lived in France, his files were stolen by Soviet agents) and was finally granted permission to live in Mexico in 1937, thanks to renowned artist Diego Rivera sponsoring him. Stalin regretted allowing Trotsky to go into exile and was determined to have his old ally assassinated. After a series of 'show trials' in Moscow in 1937, Trotsky was sentenced to death *in absentia*.

Now the Soviet secret police had to find someone to carry out the sentence.

By this time, having quarrelled with Rivera, Trotsky had moved out of Mexico City into a compound in the small village of Coyoacán. The first assassination attempt was led by Soviet agent Isoef Grigulevich and members of Mexico's Communist Party, including leading Stalinist painter David Alfaro Siqueiros. Armed gunmen raided Trotsky's house on 24 May 1940, and Trotsky, his wife Natalia and grandson Seva narrowly escaped the gunfire by taking refuge under a bed. A large bomb left by the raiders, designed to destroy Trotsky's archives, failed to go off.

Spaniard Ramón Mercader, however, had formed a relationship with Trotsky's secretary, and through her he met Trotsky only a few days after the failed attempt. The Soviet agent passed himself off as a French–Canadian supporter of Trotsky's ideals in order to gain closer access to his victim.

On 20 August 1940, Mercader visited Trotsky and, after being granted a few minutes alone with him to discuss an article the assassin had supposedly written, fatally stabbed the 62-year-old Bolshevik in the head with an icepick. Mercader had hidden the weapon in his raincoat and saw his chance as Trotsky sat in a chair reading the article. The assassin had shortened the blade of the weapon in order to hide it and to maximise its impact. Mercader later recalled: 'I laid my raincoat on the table in such a way as to be able to remove the ice axe which was in the pocket … I took out the ice axe from the raincoat, gripped it in my hand and, with my eyes closed, dealt him a terrible blow on the head.'

Mercader was handed over to the Mexican authorities, while Trotsky, his head swathed in bandages, was taken to Mexico City to be operated on. He died the following day. Mercader refused to reveal his identity or who had ordered the assassination, but was convicted of murder and sentenced to 20 years' jail. Mercader's true identity was not discovered until April 1953, and his links to the NKVD were not confirmed until after the dissolution of the Soviet Union in 1991.

Stalin buried Trotsky's reputation under so many lies and historical distortions that not even the era of 'glasnost' in the late 1980s could rehabilitate Trotsky in the hearts and minds of the Russian people. In many ways, Stalin had succeeded in assassinating his old ally all over again.

REFERENCES:

- Crystal, David (1994), *The Cambridge Biographical Encyclopedia*, Cambridge University Press, CUP, Cambridge
- Trotsky, Leon (1930), *My Life, www.marxists.org*
- Walsh, Lynn (1980), *Forty Years Since Leon Trotsky's Assassination, The Militant Tendency, www.marxist.net*

1942
The Brown-out Murders

FACT FILE

CRIME: Serial murder
VICTIMS:
Ivy McLeod, aged 40
Pauline Thompson, aged 31
Gladys Hocking, aged 40
DATE: 2–18 May 1942
PLACE: Melbourne (Australia)
PERPETRATOR: Edward Leonski (1918–1942)
SENTENCE: Hanged at Pentridge Prison, Melbourne, on 9 November 1942

In May 1942, the murder of three Melbourne women by an American GI tested the bonds that existed between the two countries. The 'Brown-out Murder Case', committed at night while Melbourne was in the grip of wartime regulations requiring all lights to be covered, was taken over by the US military. For the first and only time in Australian criminal history, a military tribunal was conducted by a foreign power on Australian soil—and the perpetrator was hanged at Melbourne's Pentridge Prison in November 1942.

Eddie Leonski was born in 1918 in New Jersey and moved to New York with his mother and stepfather. Leonski's mother had fought depression and had numerous nervous breakdowns during her son's childhood, while both his father and stepfather were alcoholics. The 24-year-old serviceman was something of a 'gentle giant', but his personality changed under the influence of alcohol.

In the early hours of Sunday 3 May 1942, part-time barman Henry Billings found the partially naked body of 40-year-old Ivy Violet McLeod in Victoria Avenue, Albert Park. She had been strangled and badly beaten. The fleshy parts of the victim's body had been torn at by hand, her arm had been broken and parts of raw scalp were showing where clumps of hair had been pulled out. There was also a shocking injury to her throat, as if the killer had tried to rip out the woman's larynx. Billings recalled seeing an American soldier stooping in the doorway of a shop next to his hotel at about 3 am that morning.

On 9 May, a 31-year-old Bendigo woman named Pauline Thompson told her husband, a local policeman, that she was going to a dance at the Music Lover's Club in

Melbourne with some girlfriends, but secretly she planned to meet a young American. When her date was 30 minutes late, Thompson gave up waiting for him. The Bendigo woman was later seen leaving the Astoria Hotel in Spencer Street with another American soldier at 11.15 pm. Thompson's strangled body was found at about 4 am on the bluestone steps of Morningside House, a boarding house in Spring Street, by the nightwatchman.

Investigating detectives entertained the theory that the killer may have been a local dressed as an American GI to distract attention, but several other women came forward and said that they too had been attacked by an American soldier but had managed to escape. In one attack, the soldier entered a woman's flat and attempted to assault her, but noise from outside in the hallway distracted the attacker and the woman was able to scream for help. The stranger ran from the scene but left behind an American GI singlet bearing the initials 'EJL'.

Four days later, on 18 May, Leonski spent the afternoon at the Parkville Hotel and reportedly consumed 25 beers up until 5.30 pm and then drank six whiskies. At about 9 pm that night, an Australian guard positioned just outside Camp Pell saw an American soldier covered in yellow mud stumbling through Royal Albert Park. Private Seymour asked the man what had happened, and the soldier told him that he had fallen in some mud while coming through the park. The man appeared to be drunk. A few hours later, the body of 40-year-old Gladys Hosking was found in the park lying face down in yellow slush; her stockings and shoes were still on but her garments were torn and disarranged and her overcoat was lying near her body. She had been strangled. At Camp Pell, Eddie Leonski was seen covered in yellowish mud in the early hours of 19 May and arrested for the murder of Gladys Hosking. The serviceman's 'reign of terror' had finally ended—after 16 days.

On 13 August 1942, Leonski's trial commenced in an impromptu court in the heart of Melbourne. The court martial was convened without the presence of civilian lawyers. When he stood to face the bench, Leonski pleaded 'not guilty'. His chance to plead guilty on the grounds of insanity was gone. The injuries to the women's throats were a symptom of Leonski's undiagnosed mental condition—he later explained the strangulations as part of his wanting 'to capture the woman's voices'.

On Monday 9 November Leonski was hung by the neck. As he was escorted to the gallows, he was singing, 'It's a lovely day tomorrow; tomorrow is a lovely day.'

REFERENCES:

- Mallon, Andrew (1979), *Leonski: The Brown-out Murderer,* Outback Press, Melbourne
- *Truth*, Melbourne, 18 August 1942
- *Herald*, Melbourne, 10 November 1942

1945
The Holocaust

FACT FILE

CRIME: Genocide
VICTIMS: Almost 6 million European Jews
DATE: 1933 to 1945
PLACE: Jews and other 'undesirables' were deported from many occupied European countries to camps in Germany, France, Poland and East Prussia for extermination.
PERPETRATORS: The Nazis

When Allied forces liberated territories previously occupied by Nazi Germany at the end of World War II, they were shocked and appalled by the scenes that confronted them. They saw with their own eyes the horror of the concentration camps established to provide slave labour for the Nazi war machine, and of the 'death camps' set up to exterminate whole groups of 'undesirable' people—Jews and priests, Slavs and gypsies, intelligentsia and the mentally retarded. But it was Hitler's 'final solution' to the 'Jewish problem' in eastern Europe that accounted for the majority of the estimated six million people systematically murdered under the Nazis' racist policies—his plan to eventually exterminate European Jewry altogether.

While historians can now plot the specific events that led to the institutionalisation of Hitler's anti-Semitic views and led a country to condone genocide, the rise of Fascism in Germany during the 1920s and early 1930s gave only a brief glimpse of the horror that was to unfold. It is now clear that Germany needed a scapegoat for the humiliation it felt it suffered at the hands of Britain, France and the United States when the Treaty of Versailles was signed in 1919. For whatever Hitler's personal reasons, the Jewry of Eastern Europe and the powerbrokers in the West (routinely characterised as Jewish industrialists and financiers) were held accountable. Hitler grabbed power in 1933 and by the end of the decade, non-Jewish Germans were forbidden from having any contact with Jewish families, and continued economic and emigration constrictions forced Jews living in large cities to move into ghettoes.

The declaration of war in September 1939 gave Hitler the cover to spread his anti-Semitic policies to neighbouring countries. After the invasion of Poland, Jewish ghettoes were set up in Lodz and Warsaw. At this stage no directive was given to the fate of these communities and they were left to their own devices, but with the surprise invasion of the USSR in 1941 Hitler demanded a 'final solution' to the presence of Jewish communities. Up to this point, the mass slaughter of captured peoples by gunfire was seen as 'uneconomical', and it didn't solve the problem of the disposal of thousands of bodies. The deportation of Jews to camps in neighbouring countries only transported the problem, and the plan hatched by Reinhard Heydrich at the Wannsee Conference (20 January 1942) to 'cleanse' Europe of Jews called for the disposal of a staggering 11 million people.

The Nazis had already trialled a forerunner of the 'final solution' among their own people with the establishment of 'Aktion T4'. The Nazi program to eliminate 'life unworthy of life' first began in October 1939 and initially focused on newborn and very young children who showed signs of mental retardation or physical deformity. However, the euthanasia program was soon expanded to include older disabled children and adults, and was eventually taken over by the SS. Six 'killing centres' were established, including a former prison at Brandenburg, where the first experimental gassings took place. The gas chambers were disguised as shower rooms, but were in fact sealed chambers connected by pipes to cylinders of carbon monoxide. (Later, hydrocyanic acid fixed on silicon tablets was used to asphyxiate victims.) Each killing centre also included a crematorium.

Between 1941 and 1942, extermination camps were set up in Sobibór, Treblenka, Chelmno, Majdanek, Belzec and Auschwitz—all in Poland. (Polish Jews made up over half of the deaths in these camps.) Dachau, Buchenweld and Bergen-Belsen were the larger German camps, while Struthof (East Prussia) and Natzweiler-Struthof (France) were in German-occupied territories. Auschwitz was the biggest of the Nazi death camps, occupying some 2000 square kilometres (770 square miles). The Auschwitz operation was conducted on such a massive scale that larger gas chambers had to be built in nearby Birkenau extermination camp. It is estimated that two million people were murdered at Auschwitz alone.

The scale of human depravity that faced American and Russian troops as they liberated Poland and finally Germany in 1945 was indescribable. The Nazis had attempted to hasten the genocide and then dismantle the killing factories they had built as the Allies advanced. American troops found mounds of bodies, as yet unburnt, and wagonloads of corpses abandoned on railway tracks.

REFERENCES:

- Minerbi, Alessandra (2005), *A New Illustrated History of the Nazis,* D&C Books, London
- *The Holocaust, www.holocaust-history.org, www.holocaustchronicle.org*

1947
'Bugsy' Siegel: Behind Blue Eyes

FACT FILE

CRIME: Murder
VICTIM: Benjamin 'Bugsy' Siegel (1906-1947)
DATE: 20 June 1947
PLACE: Beverly Hills, California (USA)
PERPETRATOR: Eddie Cannizzaro (1911-1987) on the orders of Meyer Lansky and 'Lucky' Luciano.
SENTENCE: Cannizzaro was never charged over this murder

Benjamin 'Bugsy' Siegel was a madman, mobster and dreamer. Not content with being one of New York's most feared underworld figures during the 1920s, he moved to California in 1937 to 'muscle in' on California's gambling and union rackets. After first entertaining the idea of a Hollywood career alongside his childhood friend George Raft, Siegel borrowed money from his mob friends to open a casino in the then nondescript desert town of Las Vegas in neighbouring Nevada. That mistake was to cost him his life.

Benjamin Hymen Siegelbaum was born in the Jewish neighbourhood of Brooklyn in 1906 and graduated from theft and small-time protection rackets to murder at the height of Prohibition in the 1920s. Along the way he was given the nickname 'Bugsy' by his cohorts Luciano and Lanksy because he was 'crazy as a bed bug'. (Siegel hated the name so much that he regularly lived up to the 'crazy' part by beating up anyone who made the mistake of calling him 'Bugsy' to his face.) Married to his childhood sweetheart, Esta Krakow, and the father of two young girls, Siegel was also a callous 'murderer for hire' who killed, amongst others, mobsters Joe Masseria and Bo Weinberg in order to take over their rackets. But his dark good looks, especially his piercing blue eyes, his smooth manner and his dangerous reputation made him attractive to the opposite sex and, after he moved to California, a popular party guest of the rich and famous.

As early as 1933, the mob sent Siegel to California to develop gambling opportunities under Los Angeles mobster Jack Dragna and to provide the extra muscle required to take over rival rackets. Moving to California in 1937 to escape the heat after another mob-sanctioned murder, Siegel recruited fellow Jewish gang boss Mickey Cohen as his lieutenant and targeted gambling and union organisations. Siegel originally moved his family west, but sent them back home so that he could continue a string of affairs with Hollywood starlets and mistresses. He had already previously met mobsters' courier and small-time actress Virginia Hill (some say she was sent to the West Coast by her Chicago mob bosses to spy on Siegel), and the pair started a live-in relationship and business partnership in California that would last the remainder of his life.

In Hollywood, Siegel took over the Screen Extras Guild (and attempted to extort money from Warner Brothers by refusing to supply extras) and the Los Angeles Teamsters and started the Trans-America racing 'wire' (radio) service in competition with James Ragen's Continental Wire Service. When Chicago gangsters murdered Ragen and took over his racing interests, they ordered Siegel to close down his business. His asking price was a cool US$2 million, and he refused to sell when his mob bosses baulked at paying the price. Siegel was also good at getting money out of his Hollywood contacts (one report states that he scammed $400,000 from the star community without repaying a cent), but murder was still his number one business interest. In 1939, Siegel murdered colleague Harry Greenberg on the orders of 'Lepke' Buchalter after Greenberg turned police informer, and he also murdered his brother-in-law 'Whitey' Krakow because the small-time hoodlum knew about the Greenberg hit. Siegel was arrested, but murder charges were dropped. No wonder people were scared of him.

There is a lot of mythology concerning how Siegel started the Las Vegas venture that ultimately cost him his life. The popular myth is that Siegel was a visionary who dreamed of building a large gambling palace in the Nevada desert that would attract gamblers from all over the country. (Another part of the myth says that Siegel discovered the spot where he would build his casino when 'nature called' on a cross-country car trip.) The reality is that the state of Nevada had legalised gambling in 1931 and the mob had been involved in Las Vegas since 1941. (Los Angeles hood Tony Cornero had moved his entire gambling enterprise to the Las Vegas strip and was running a very profitable casino.) When Los Angeles businessman Billy Wilkerson came to Siegel with a Las Vegas casino plan that needed funding, Siegel bought in and Wilkerson retained a one-third share in the organisation. Whatever the story, Siegel named the venture 'The Flamingo', his pet name for Virginia Hill.

Siegel borrowed money from his former partners in Murder Inc., but construction costs blew out the budget from $1 million to $6 million under his inept supervision. When his mob bosses learned that Virginia Hill was also skimming money off the top and banking it in a Swiss bank account, Siegel's bosses considered a hit on him but decided to wait until after the casino opened to see if they had a chance of recouping their money. The Flamingo opened on 26 December 1946 and despite a poor opening night the casino actually turned a profit for several months. But operating costs and a lack of customers and entertainers during the spring of 1947—and the fear that he was setting up his own organisation outside their control—sealed Siegel's fate.

On 20 June 1947, a gunman named Eddie Cannizzaro allegedly hid in the rose garden outside the home Siegel and Hill shared at 810 Linden Drive, Beverly Hills. Having been warned by her mob bosses to return the stolen money, Virginia Hill had gone to France and left Siegel behind to face the music. Cannizzaro fired nine bullets at Siegel as he sat on a sofa chair. Two of the bullets caught Siegel in the face; one of them shot out his left eye, which was later found 4.5 metres (15 feet) away in Hill's dining room. 'Bugsy' Siegel died instantly. Only two people attended Siegel's funeral at Beth Olam Cemetery—a rabbi and one of Siegel's brothers.

Virginia Hill repaid the money she owed the mob and lived overseas until her death. She died in Austria in 1966 from an apparently self-administered dose of poison. The night Siegel died, the mob took over the running of The Flamingo, which went on to become one of the most successful casinos in Las Vegas.

HISTORICAL AND SOCIAL SIGNIFICANCE:

- A famous story about 'Bugsy' Siegel concerns his hatred of Nazis because of their persecution of the Jews. In 1939, he allegedly visited Italy and was at a party hosted by Countess Dorothy Taylor de Frasso, which was also attended by Hermann Goering and Joseph Goebbels. Only good manners stopped Siegel killing the high-ranking Nazis, and he investigated organising a 'hit' on the pair when he returned to America.
- In 1991, Warren Beatty wrote and directed a film about Siegel's life called *Bugsy*. He met his future wife, Annette Bening (who played Virginia Hill), while working on the movie.

REFERENCES:

- Anger, Kenneth (1975), *Hollywood Babylon*, Bell Publishing, Los Angeles
- Tuohy, John William (1999), 'Mob Stories: Bugsy', *Gambling Magazine*, Las Vegas
- *www.bugsysiegel.net*

1947
The Black Dahlia

FACT FILE

CRIME: Murder
VICTIM: Elizabeth Short, aged 22
DATE: 15 January 1947
PLACE: Leimert Park, Los Angeles (USA)
PERPETRATOR: Unknown

Shortly after 10 am on 15 January 1947, Betty Bersinger was pushing her three-year-old daughter along Norton Avenue in the Leimert Park section of Los Angeles, not far from Hollywood. There were many vacant blocks there because World War II had put a stop to a lot of housing development, although the driveways leading from the roadway had been completed. As the pretty young housewife made her way to a shoe repair shop, she saw what appeared to be a mannequin dumped in the tall grass. The store dummy was bleached white, but the bottom half of the torso appeared disconnected from the rest of her body. Both parts were facing upwards, and there were flies buzzing around. On closer inspection it wasn't a mannequin at all—it was the body of a young woman, cut in half and completely drained of blood.

When police arrived, they found the body of a pretty young woman—her hair wet from the morning dew—lying face up. Her arms were lying above her head and her face was slashed. The lower part of her body had a number of knife marks and was missing some of the pubic hair.

One of the woman's feet was just a few centimetres from the footpath in clear view of the roadway. Detectives learned that earlier that morning a young boy taking a short cut along his usual paper route saw a black sedan pull into the lot's driveway, but he didn't see anything dumped. In the early morning light, the boy couldn't tell the make of the car or get a good look at the driver.

The sensational nature of the murder—'a pale white body severed in two, and left for the world to view', wrote author John Gilmore—resulted in the victim being referred to as 'The Black Dahlia' by a hungry Los Angeles press. (The body had a rose-coloured birthmark on one thigh, not a tattoo of a dahlia as some reports have stated, while associates of the victim stated that she was referred to as 'The Black Dahlia' before her death.)

However, it did not take long for several people on the fringe of Hollywood's film community to come forward and identify the attractive young victim.

Elizabeth 'Betty' Short was born on 29 July 1924 in Hyde Park, Massachusetts. In 1929, her father disappeared from the family home (it was thought that he had committed suicide when his empty car was found near a bridge), but he later sent a letter to the family stating that he had settled in California.

As she grew older, 'Betty' Short preferred the name 'Beth' and matured into a striking teenager who looked much older than she was. At age 19 she decided to move to Vallejo, California, and live with her father to pursue a film career.

Beth Short fell out with her father because of her constant nightclubbing. After moving to Santa Barbara she was charged with underage drinking, fingerprinted and advised to return home to Massachusetts, but she desperately wanted a film career—and stardom. She was also desperately looking for love and formed several relationships with older men, servicemen and bit-part actors.

However, Short had a genital problem that made sexual intercourse impossible—a malformed vagina delayed the onset of menstruation and did not allow penetration. (Doctors had told her mother that she would outgrow the problem as she matured.) Short liked to dress in black and dyed her hair jet black to appear sophisticated—psychologists later hypothesised that this was to hide her lack of confidence in her sexual prowess.

How Elizabeth Short met her grisly death is still open to some conjecture. What is known is that she was strangled and rendered unconscious but died of massive blood loss when the killer cut her body in half with nothing more than 'an old-fashioned kitchen knife and a strong arm'. In early newspaper reports, the press played up the fact that Short was a 'wannabe' actress and very popular with men. She was portrayed as a man-chaser, promiscuous, and even as a prostitute. Los Angeles police did not contradict this derogatory description of Short's morals—even though they knew of her sexual 'handicap'—because they knew that the fact that she couldn't be sexually penetrated would also be known by her killer.

About 50 people claimed responsibility for the death of Elizabeth Short, but police did not receive any conclusive evidence to allow them to charge anyone with her murder. The case took on urban myth status, with many scurrilous bits and pieces of information added to the facts of the case along the way—Short was a lesbian, she had had an affair with a budding actress named Marilyn Monroe, and her murder was actually an early 'snuff' film. None of this was true.

In the late 1960s, author John Gilmore, the son of a Los Angeles police officer who had met Elizabeth Short (a distant relative) when he was a boy, was contacted by a tall, thin man with a limp. Arnold Smith, alias Anderson Wilson, Grover Loving

Jnr and lastly Jack Arnold, was a would-be actor and a recovering alcoholic who had known Beth Short during the 1940s.

It was not until 1981 that Gilmore was again contacted by Arnold, who said that he had some information to sell him about the 'Black Dahlia' murder case. Arnold told Gilmore that he knew who Beth Short's killer was, but when Arnold revealed details that only the killer would have known, Gilmore formed the opinion that Arnold himself was the murderer.

Arnold was a boyfriend of Short's, but her promiscuity (it was alleged that the out-of-work actress sometimes sold oral sexual favours in order to live) and her lack of sexual contact with him drove him to murder. Arnold strangled her by shoving her panties down her throat, rendering her unconscious, and then severed her body in a bathtub and waited for the blood to drain away before dumping it in clear view of the Hollywood hills.

Arnold's signature act was cutting the woman's pubic hair and slashing at the vagina with a knife. Arnold was also the chief suspect in the murder of oil heiress Georgette Bauerdorf, whose body was found strangled in a bathtub in the 1950s.

Gilmore went to the police with his evidence, but before the facts could be drawn together to build a case against Arnold Smith, Beth Short's former 'lover' perished in a hotel room fire in 1982. Gilmore published a compelling account in his 1988 book *Severed*, but almost 60 years after the body of the Black Dahlia was found on that vacant block, the case remains officially unsolved.

REFERENCES:

- Gilmore, John (1988), *Severed: The True Story of the Black Dahlia Murder,* Granta Publications, London
- *Who Was Elizabeth Short?, www.bethshort.com*
- Anger, Kenneth (1975), *Hollywood Babylon*, Bell Publishing, Los Angeles

1948
Gandhi Assassinated

FACT FILE

CRIME: Murder
VICTIM: Mohandas K. Gandhi, aged 78
DATE: 30 January 1948
PLACE: Birla House, New Delhi (India)
PERPETRATOR: Nathuram Godse (1910-1949)
SENTENCE: Godse was hanged, alongside Narayan Apte, on 15 November 1949

Mohandas Karamchand Gandhi was born in 1869 in Poorbandar, West India. The son of the chief minister of the province and his fourth wife, a deeply religious Hindu, Gandhi married at the age of 13 and was sent to London to study law when he was 19. On his return to India in 1891, unable to find suitable work as a barrister, Gandhi accepted a contract to work in Natal, South Africa. There he came face to face with institutionalised racial discrimination, and for the next 20 years he opposed legislation that sought to deprive Indians and other minorities of their rights. Gandhi's non-violent defiance of unfair laws focused attention on his civil activities in South Africa. His establishment of a volunteer Ambulance Corps during the Boer War (1899–1902) won him the English War Medal and brought him national acclaim. Soon the world would know his name and the principles for which he stood.

Returning to India in 1914, Gandhi was a vocal advocate of 'home rule'—the complete withdrawal of English imperial interests. He became the dominant figure of the National Congress movement but never wavered from his policies of non-violent non-cooperation in achieving Indian independence. However, India's stance did not always draw a peaceful response. At the height of India's civil disobedience campaign, nearly 400 people were massacred by British soldiers at Amritsar. Gandhi was consequently jailed for two years for conspiracy related to a series of articles published in the newspaper *Young India*.

On Gandhi's release from jail, the Hindu and Muslim members of the National Congress refused to find common ground, and warring factions aligned to the two religious groups turned to bloodshed. Unable to reason with either side, Gandhi undertook a three-week fast that not only restored the non-violent aims of the 'home rule' campaign but also promoted this personal act of spiritual cleansing. By 1928, 'Mahatma' Gandhi—'the great soul'—was again elected head of India's

National Congress. After leading a non-violent, 200-kilometre (124-mile) march to the sea in defiance of the British government's monopoly on the production and taxing of salt, more than 60 000 people were arrested. Gandhi was among them and was again jailed, for three years.

Two years after his release from prison, in May 1944, Mohandas Gandhi negotiated with the British Cabinet Mission in India, which ultimately recommended a new constitutional structure for home rule in India. However, divisions between Muslim and Hindu factions within the National Congress ultimately led to the formation of separate nations, India and Pakistan, and the dream of a country united in its freedom was lost. Britain effectively relinquished 163 years of imperial rule in India on 15 August 1947—an act Gandhi described as 'the noblest act of the British nation'.

The final days of Gandhi's life were spent shaming the instigators of community and religious violence by fasting. Just as his fasting looked set to avert the country from plummeting into complete anarchy, Gandhi was assassinated in Delhi on 30 January 1948 by Hindu fanatic Nathuram Godse. At 5.17 pm, on the Prayer Ground at Birla House, the 78-year-old was shot three times as he walked with his great-nieces to make evening devotions with about a thousand supporters. Wearing his homespun *dhoti* and leaning on a simple wooden staff, Gandhi was only a metre or two (a couple of yards) from the pagoda when he was shot in the thigh, abdomen and chest. Almost instinctively he raised his hand to his forehead to signify the Hindu gesture of forgiveness of his assassin. He died half an hour later with his head cradled in the lap of his teenage great-niece Manu.

Nathuram Godse (or, in Hindu, Ram Naturam) had been plotting Gandhi's assassination with a group of Hindu nationalists for some time. A *savarna* (high-caste) Brahmin, Godse was incensed at Gandhi's 'even-handed' attitude towards Muslims and his supposed willingness to partition India into separate Hindu and Muslim (Pakistan) nations after becoming independent from Britain. (Hindu extremists wished for the return of 'Rashtah', the Hindu nation that ruled India 1400 years before.) Godse waited for Gandhi on his usual morning path, concealing his small-calibre pistol by folding his hands together in prayer, and shot the *bapu* (father) of the nation at close range.

REFERENCES:

- Crystal, David (1994), *The Cambridge Biographical Encyclopedia,* CUP, Cambridge
- Burns, John F., 'Hindu Nationalist Still Proud of Role in Killing Father of India', *New York Times*, 2 March 1998
- *M. K. Gandhi, www.mkgandhi.org*

1953

10 Rillington Place: The Evans–Christie Case

FACT FILE

CRIME: Serial murder

VICTIMS: Ruth Margarete Fuerst, aged 21; Hectorina McLennan, aged 26; Kathleen Maloney, aged 26; Rita Nelson, aged 25; Beryl Evans, aged 21; Geraldine Evans, aged 2; Muriel Amelia Eady, aged 32; Ethel Christie, aged 50

DATES: 1943–1950

PLACE: Notting Hill, London (UK)

PERPETRATOR: John Christie (1898–1953)

SENTENCE: Christie was hanged on 15 July 1953. (Timothy Evans was wrongly hanged for the murder of his infant child in 1950)

On 18 November 1949, 26-year-old lorry driver Timothy Evans walked into the police station at Merthyr Vale, South Wales, and told two detectives that he needed to get something off his mind. Evans, a small man of moderate intelligence, had disposed of his wife's body in a drain at the house in which they were lodging at 10 Rillington Place, in the London suburb of Notting Hill. Beryl Evans had died, her husband told police, when his neighbour—John Reginald Christie—had attempted to abort Mrs Evans's unwanted pregnancy. What Evans did not know was that Christie had murdered the young man's wife and infant child and then framed him for the crime when confronted by investigating police. When told by police that he would be charged with the murder of his wife and baby, Evans finally realised what had transpired. 'Christie done it!' the poor man pleaded.

Timothy Evans married 18-year-old Beryl Thorley in September 1947. The following year, the Evanses moved into Rillington Place—a nondescript, inner-city dwelling made up of six cramped rooms—and had their first child, a daughter named Geraldine. The Christies, a middle-aged couple, lived on the ground floor and had access to the small backyard area and washhouse (laundry area). When Mrs Evans became pregnant with her second child, Timothy Evans confided to his neighbour downstairs that they could ill afford another child. John Christie convinced Evans that he had enough medical knowledge to perform a backyard abortion and offered to help the young couple with their dilemma. Evans did not like the idea, but Beryl insisted and arranged for Christie to abort the pregnancy on 8 November 1949.

But Christie gassed Mrs Evans, raped her and then strangled her infant daughter while Evans was at work. When Evans returned home, Christie informed the intellectually impaired man that his wife had died from 'septic poisoning'. More than that, Evans now had to help him get rid of the body or he too would be implicated in his wife's death. According to Evans, Christie also arranged for the toddler Geraldine to be minded by a childless couple while Evans returned to Wales and told his family that his wife had left him. Although the police could not originally find the body of Mrs Evans in the drain, detectives returned to Rillington Place on 2 December and conducted a thorough search of the dwellings. The bodies of Beryl Evans and her baby daughter were found buried under the washhouse.

In his confused state, Timothy Evans admitted to the crimes when taken into custody and questioned in London. On 11 January 1950, he was indicted on the sole charge of murdering his baby daughter but reverted to his original statement and blamed everything on Christie. A former World War I veteran who served as a special constable during World War II, Christie was the star prosecution witness against Evans during the controversial trial. Despite a conviction for assaulting a woman, the quietly spoken but sincere war veteran made a huge impact on the jury.

The police felt from the outset that Evans was guilty and the crime scene was never properly investigated. Builders stated that the washhouse was being renovated on the weekend of the murders and that the bodies could not have been placed there until some days after they had finished their work. Police also missed one important clue—it would have been impossible for Evans to hide two bodies in the washhouse without Christie knowing about it, because the only access was through his flat.

Despite these inconsistencies, Timothy Evans was found guilty and, after losing his appeal, was hanged on 9 March 1950—barely three-and-a-half months after giving himself up.

Most people forgot about the murders at 10 Rillington Place—that was, until 24 March 1953. The Christies had moved, but when a new tenant rented the flat and tried to renovate an alcove at the back of the kitchen, the mummified bodies of three young women were found. A police search under the apartment's floorboards revealed the body of an older woman, later identified as Ethel Christie. A nationwide hunt found John Christie living on an embankment near Putney Bridge, by which time three more bodies had been discovered. Once captured, Christie confessed to the murders of the six women as well as that of Beryl Evans.

Police found a man's suit under the floor of the common hall area and a man's tie, tied in a reef knot, in the kitchen cupboard. They also found potassium cyanide in another area of the apartment and a tobacco tin containing clumps of pubic hair—none of which came from the bodies found in the kitchen. When police searched the garden, they noticed a human femur, in plain view, supporting the wooden fence. More bones were found in flowerbeds and under an orange blossom while blackened skull bones with teeth and pieces of a dress turned up in a dustbin. The bones were identified as belonging to two victims—Austrian immigrant Ruth Margarete Fuerst, who went missing in 1943, and Muriel Amelia Eady, who had worked at a factory with Christie. The other victims were prostitutes Christie had brought home to his flat—Hectorina McLennan, aged 26; Kathleen Maloney, aged 26; and Rita Nelson, aged 25—and his wife, whom he had murdered last of all, in 1950.

John Christie admitted to killing all six women as well as Beryl Evans, but not to killing the Evans's daughter. Christie was an hysteric, a hypochondriac and a necrophiliac. Found guilty of murder and sentenced to death, he tried to retract his confession and lie his way out of the noose.

John Reginald Christie was hanged on 15 July 1953, but justice would be too late for Timothy Evans.

HISTORICAL AND SOCIAL SIGNIFICANCE:

- Momentum for a posthumous pardon for Timothy increased during the 1950s, but it was not until 1966 that a High Court judge ruled on the case. The court ruled that Evans did not murder his daughter—the crime for which he was tried and hanged in 1950. The posthumous pardon applied only to this matter. It did not clear his name in regard to the murder of his wife.
- In November 2004, Timothy Evans's sisters failed in their attempt to have their brother's name cleared in regard to the murders of both his wife and daughter. The Evans case would not be referred to the Court of Appeal for reassessment—the 1966 pardon was said to be enough to correct the miscarriage of justice.
- The Evans–Christie case was directly responsible for Great Britain's decision to abolish capital punishment in 1964.

REFERENCES:

- *Murder Casebook* (1990), Marshall Cavendish, London
- *Timothy Evans: Miscarriage of Justice* (2003), *www.innocent.org.uk*
- BBC Online (2005), *Case Closed: 10 Rillington Place, www.bbc.co.uk*

1953

The Rosenberg Spy Scandal

FACT FILE

CRIME: Espionage
VICTIM: The United States of America
DATES: 1943–50
PLACE: New York, USA
PERPETRATORS: Julius Rosenberg (1918–1953); Ethel Rosenberg (1915–1953); Morton Sobell (b. 1917)
SENTENCE: Julius and Ethel Rosenberg were executed by electric chair on 19 June 1953. Morton Sobell was sentenced to 30 years' imprisonment but was released in 1969

The execution of US citizens Ethel and Julius Rosenberg in June 1953 escalated Cold War tensions between the United States and the Soviet Union. Found guilty of conspiring to commit espionage, the Rosenbergs were tried, convicted and executed in the atmosphere of 1950s anti-communist hysteria.

Julius Rosenberg, the son of Polish immigrants, was born in New York in 1918. An electrical engineer, Rosenberg became the leader of the Young Communist League in 1936. There he met Ethel Greenglass, who was three years his senior. The pair married in 1939 and had two sons, Robert and Michael. Julius did freelance work until 1940, when he became a civilian employee of the US Army Signal Corps. At the height of World War II, Julius and Ethel became fully fledged members of the Communist Party, but both ceased open political activity in 1943 in order to engage in espionage against their own government.

Julius Rosenberg first met with Soviet spy Feklisov in 1943 and agreed to pass on confidential information to the Soviet government—an ally of America at the time. In June 1944, Sergeant David Greenglass, Ethel Rosenberg's brother, was chosen to work on the Manhattan Project—the development of the atomic bomb. Greenglass provided sketches of a high-explosive lens developed by the Manhattan Project and passed this on to the Rosenbergs and their associates Morton Sobell and Harry Gold.

Julius Rosenberg, for his part, passed on secrets relating to the development of the radio proximity fuse, which automatically detonated a missile upon approach to a target and at such a position as to inflict maximum damage to the target. In 1945,

Rosenberg was dismissed from the Signal Corps, but it was not until the breaking of the 'Venona' code in 1950 that the full extent of the espionage ring was revealed.

By this time the Soviet Union had detonated its own atomic weapon. Ethel Rosenberg was arrested in August 1950 and stood trial with her husband, her brother and Morton Sobell—kidnapped by armed men in Mexico City and handed over to US agents at the border—in March 1951. David Greenglass agreed to cooperate with the government and implicated his sister and her husband in espionage activity. Ruth Greenglass, Ethel's sister-in-law, stated that it was she who typed the information passed on by her brother, David. Although the contents of the notes were hardly anything new to the Soviets, Ruth's testimony ultimately condemned Ethel Rosenberg to the electric chair. The Rosenbergs used their Fifth Amendment right during the trial, and although they declined to give evidence on their own behalf, maintained that they were both innocent. On 29 March 1951, Julius and Ethel Rosenberg were found guilty of conspiracy to commit espionage.

On 5 April 1951, Judge Kaufman imposed death sentences on Ethel and Julius Rosenberg for conspiracy to commit espionage and sentenced Mort Sobell to 30-years' imprisonment. Technically, the Rosenbergs should not have been given the death penalty under the *Espionage Act* of 1917. This law prohibited the transmission to a foreign government of any information relating to national defence during wartime, but the courts ruled that America was involved in a Cold War with the Soviets and the Rosenbergs were convicted under this section of the Act. By October 1952 all avenues of appeal had been exhausted, and the executions were set for June 1952. Supreme Court Justice William O. Douglas granted a stay of execution on 17 June, but this ruling delayed the executions for only two more days.

On 19 June 1953, Julius and Ethel Rosenberg were executed by electric chair in New York's Sing Sing prison. Julius was the first to die. David Greenglass was sentenced to ten years' jail in return for his testimony and was released in 1960. He later lived with his family under an assumed name. It is alleged that Greenglass may have perjured himself in testifying against his sister to save his wife from going to jail. Morton Sobell was released in 1969 and later lectured in San Francisco.

Julius and Ethel Rosenberg are the only American citizens to have been executed for being involved in espionage activities during peacetime.

REFERENCES:

- *The Rosenbergs: A Case of Love, Espionage, Deceit and Betrayal, www.crimelibrary.com*
- *Julius and Ethel Rosenberg, www.fbi.gov*
- *Timeline of Events Relating to the Rosenberg Trial, www.law.umkc.edu*

1954

Parker and Hulme: Heavenly Creatures

FACT FILE

CRIME: Murder
VICTIM: Honora Parker (nee Reiper), aged 45
DATE: 22 June 1954
PLACE: Christchurch (New Zealand)
PERPETRATORS: Pauline Parker (b. 1938); Juliet Hulme (b. 1938)
SENTENCE: Pauline Parker was sent to Arohata Borstal, near Wellington and Juliet Hulme was sent to Auckland's Mount Eden Prison. Both girls served five years at 'Her Majesty's Pleasure'

In June 1954, the murder of Mrs Honora Parker in the conservative New Zealand city of Christchurch shocked the 'shaky isles'. But the revelation that the woman had been bludgeoned to death by her fifteen-year-old daughter, Pauline, and the girl's best friend, 16-year-old Juliet Hulme, shocked the world. The reasons behind the murder—a poisonous friendship between two intelligent girls and allegations of a lesbian love affair—made the Parker–Hulme case not only one of the most infamous crimes in New Zealand's history but also one of the most startling crimes in modern times.

Pauline Parker was born in Christchurch, New Zealand, in October 1938. In August 1953 she met English-born Juliet Hulme, the daughter of physicist Dr Henry Hulme, at Christchurch Girls High School. As a child growing up in London during World War II, Juliet had suffered from 'bomb shock' as well as tuberculosis, and was sent to the Caribbean and South Africa for her health before joining her family in New Zealand, where her father had been appointed rector of the University of Canterbury. Parker and Hulme struck up an immediate friendship which quickly developed beyond the boundaries of a conventional teenage relationship. They invented a fantasy world in which they were 'heavenly creatures' with their own moral code, and composed 'novels' inhabited by famous characters from history and popular actors of the day. The catalyst for their murder plan was the decision by Hulme's parents to separate and leave New Zealand, and the refusal by Parker's mother to let her daughter go with them.

Mrs Parker, who had lived with Pauline's father, Herbert Parker, for 20 years without legally marrying him, had become concerned about her daughter's unhealthy devotion to her new friend. Pauline spent days at Juliet Hulme's home in the university grounds and the two girls dreamed of raising money to go to the United States to have their 'novels' published. Mrs Parker shared her misgivings about the friendship with Juliet's father. Dr Hulme decided to resign his position owing to a combination of marital problems and the intensity of his daughter's friendship. Because of her health, Juliet would return to South Africa with her father to finish her schooling while her mother returned to England. Pauline Parker was determined to go with Juliet.

The girls knew that Mrs Parker would not entertain the idea of Pauline immigrating to South Africa and so formulated a plan to murder her. According to the girls' own moral code, they were helping Mrs Parker get to heaven, which would make her a happier person, but most people saw the murder as a callous, misguided attempt to remove her so that Pauline Parker would get her own way. A highly intelligent girl whom Juliet considered to be 'a genius', Pauline later told detectives, 'I knew it was wrong to murder and I knew at the time that I was murdering somebody. You would have to be an absolute moron not to know murder was against the law.'

On 22 June 1954—11 days before Juliet was to leave for South Africa—the two girls lured Pauline's mother into Victoria Park on the slope of Port Hills, near Cashmere, on the pretext of going for an afternoon walk. On a deserted track, Pauline and her mother argued about her joining Juliet in South Africa. On a secluded part of the track, Juliet Hulme deliberately dropped a pretty pink stone that she was carrying in her hand, and as Mrs Parker bent over to examine the stone, Pauline hit her mother on the back of the head with half a brick inside a stocking which she had carried hidden inside her shoulder bag.

The blow did not kill Mrs Parker, and so the girls took turns bludgeoning her to death. At about 3.30 pm the girls ran into the tearooms situated in the grounds in an 'hysterical state'. 'Please help us,' they gasped. 'Mummy has been hurt. She's hurt—covered in blood.' When the groundkeeper arrived at the scene, he found that Mrs Parker had suffered terrible head injuries far beyond what could have been expected from a fall on the track.

Police were called and Pauline Parker was questioned. The following day Juliet Hulme was arrested and the pair was charged with murder.

The girls tried to explain Mrs Parker's injuries by saying that her head had bounced on the path and had kept 'bumping and banging'. Doctors later determined that the victim had been struck more than 40 times and had suffered 24 separate lacerations to the face and head. Diary entries written by Pauline Parker suggested that the girls may have enjoyed a 'pseudo-sexual' relationship, but this did not involve a physical affair. Entries in Pauline's diaries confirmed that they had carefully planned the attack ('Why could not mother die?' she wrote. 'We discussed our plans for moidering (sic) mother … I have no qualms or conscience'), but Pauline tried at first to protect her friend and said that Juliet had played no part in the attack. Juliet later said that she had hoped that the brick would be enough to scare Mrs Parker into changing her mind, but 'After the first blow, I knew it would be necessary for us to kill her'. Despite psychiatric evidence that the girls were certifiably insane when they carried out the murder—the threat of separation had heightened their paranoia, thus making them even more dangerous—they were judged to be legally sane and to have known what they were doing was wrong. On 29 August 1954, Pauline Parker and Juliet Hulme were found guilty of murder and sentenced to five years 'at Her Majesty's pleasure', because they were too young to be sent to jail. On her release, Juliet Hulme went to England to live with her mother (who had divorced and remarried) before moving to the United States, converting to the Church of Latter Day Saints (Mormons) and becoming a flight attendant. Pauline Parker changed her name and migrated to England in 1965, where she became a school teacher. In the 50 years following the crime, the formerly inseparable friends have had no contact with each other.

HISTORICAL AND SOCIAL SIGNIFICANCE:

- The Parker–Hulme Case has been turned into a book, a play and a film. The 1995 film *Heavenly Creatures* starred teenagers Kate Winslet and Melanie Lynsky as the young murderers and was directed by New Zealander Peter Jackson (who would later film the *Lord of the Rings* trilogy).
- In 1997, largely because of the success of the film, journalists tracked down Parker and Hulme. Pauline Parker was found living under the name 'Hilary Nathan' and running a children's riding school at Hoo, near Rochester, in Kent. Juliet Hulme had found international success as author 'Anne Perry'. Amongst her published works are a number of murder mysteries, including *Sudden Fearful Death*, *Face of a Stranger* and *Dangerous Mourning*.

REFERENCES:

- Furneaux, Rupert (1995), *Famous Criminal Cases Vol II*, Wingate, London
- *Parker–Hulme Murder Case (1994), www.library.christchurch.org.nz*

1954
The Murder of Marilyn Sheppard

FACT FILE

CRIME: Murder
VICTIM: Marilyn Sheppard (b.1923) and her unborn child.
DATE: 4 July 1954
PLACE: Bay Village, Cleveland (Ohio)
PERPETRATOR: Unknown

In the early hours of 4 July 1954—American Independence Day—the wife of a wealthy, good-looking doctor was bludgeoned to death in the bedroom of her Bay Village home in Cleveland Ohio. Her husband, Dr Sam Sheppard, was asleep on a sofa downstairs when he said that he was woken by his wife's screams and ran upstairs to find a large 'bushy-haired' man standing over the bloodied body of his wife. Within weeks, after public sentiment driven by sensational newspaper headlines turned against him, Dr Sheppard was charged with his wife's murder and spent ten years in jail before his eventual acquittal.

Samuel Holmes Sheppard was born in Cleveland on 29 December 1923. A star athlete at school, he was encouraged by his father to follow his two elder brothers into the family medical business as an osteopathic healer (osteopathy is the science of curing illness by manipulating bones and nerves). Sheppard married his childhood sweetheart, Marilyn Reese, and fathered a son (Samuel 'Chip' Reese Sheppard) in 1947 before graduating from the Osteopathic School of Physicians in Los Angeles the following year. The strapping 24-year-old doctor then followed his 'duty to return to Cleveland' and work in the family practice his father had founded at Bay View Hospital.

At the time of his wife's death, Sam and Marilyn Sheppard had hit a rocky patch in their marriage; Marilyn had suffered a difficult pregnancy which had affected their sex life and her husband had sought comfort with a series of affairs. But on the night of the murder, the Sheppards had hosted an informal dinner party with friends and the pair was excited by the news that Marilyn was expecting her second child. Sam Sheppard fell asleep on the downstairs sofa (he had been involved in two difficult medical cases that day) before his guests left. At 5.45 am Sheppard telephoned his friends, the Houks who lived only 100 metres away, to come quickly … someone had murdered Marilyn.

Sheppard told police that when he was awoken he had raced upstairs to find the bloodied body of his wife lying on her bed (the Sheppards slept in single beds in the same bedroom, a not uncommon practice for the time). He was immediately confronted by the dark form of a man and wrestled with his wife's attacker before being knocked unconscious. When he awoke, Sheppard checked his wife's body for a pulse and saw that she had been repeatedly beaten about the head with a blunt object. While checking on their seven-year-old son who was asleep in another bedroom he then heard the stranger fumbling around downstairs. Sheppard chased the man out of the house and wrestled with him again on the edge of the lake but the man overpowered him in a headlock and Sheppard again lost consciousness. When he came to Sheppard stumbled back to the house and raised the alarm.

The lack of physical evidence indicating an intruder had entered the house led police to suspect Sheppard had murdered his wife. At the official inquest into the murder on 21 July, Sheppard perjured himself when he stated that he had not had an affair with a hospital colleague. Whipped up by a series of articles written in the *Cleveland Press* that labelled Sheppard 'a liar' and suggested that he was being protected because of his family's wealth and social position, an angry mob surrounded the family home when Dr Sam Sheppard was arrested for the murder of his wife. Despite the lack of blood on Sheppard's clothing, the failure to identify the murder weapon (the prosecution incorrectly portrayed the weapon as a 'surgical' implement) and the injuries he suffered in wrestling with his assailant, Sheppard was already guilty in the minds of the public because he had lied about his affair. On 21 December Dr Sam Sheppard was found guilty of the murder of his wife and sentenced to life imprisonment.

The 'Sheppard' trial was a national and international sensation but it had a devastating effect on the close-knit medical family. On 17 January 1955 Sheppard's mother Ethel committed suicide and eleven days later his father, Dr Richard Sheppard, died from the effects of a bleeding gastric ulcer (Marilyn Sheppard's father also committed suicide some years later). During the next decade Sheppard was denied a retrial and the US Supreme Court twice refused to review the case. It was not until a brash young attorney named F. Lee Bailey came on board that a US Federal judge overturned the conviction in 1964 and Sheppard was released on $100,000 bail and granted a retrial. The Federal Appeal Court originally upheld the original conviction but on 6 July 1966—almost a decade to the day after the death of his wife—the US Supreme Court overturned Sheppard's conviction on the basis that the original trial was conducted in a 'carnival atmosphere' amid 'massive, pervasive and prejudicial publicity'.

Dr Sam Sheppard attempted to reclaim his life after ten years in prison, even marrying a German divorcee named Ariane Tebbenjohanns with whom he had corresponded while he was in jail, but although his medical licence was reinstated the publicity surrounding his release led to a series of malpractice suits. Sheppard's marriage disintegrated (his wife claimed 'mental cruelty') and the former athlete turned to professional wrestling in order to pay his mounting legal debts ... the professional name he used was 'Killer' Sheppard. Six months after marrying the 20-year-old daughter of his wrestling partner Sheppard drank himself to death, aged 46, in April 1970.

Three decades after his father's death Sam Reese Sheppard sought to clear his family's name once and for all by suing the State of Ohio for his father's 'wrongful imprisonment'. The bodies of his father, mother and unborn brother were exhumed for DNA testing but despite overwhelming evidence that an occasional handyman named Richard Eberling had murdered Marilyn Sheppard in an attempted rape attack, the jury ruled that 'Chip' Sheppard had failed to prove that his father had been wrongfully imprisoned. At a subsequent appeal it was stated that the law allowed only the person actually wrongfully imprisoned could sue the State and not a family member. Fifty years after the murder of Marilyn Sheppard the 'Sheppard Case' still haunts the City of Cleveland and remains a stain on the American judicial system.

HISTORICAL AND SOCIAL SIGNIFICANCE:

• The case against Dr Sam Sheppard became the inspiration of the highly successful 1960s TV series *The Fugitive* in which a doctor, who is wrongly accused of the murder of his wife, goes on the run in order to track down the man responsible. The series was made into an Oscar-winning film starring Harrison Ford in 1993.

• Sheppard's high-profile lawyer F. Lee Bailey later defended Boston Strangler Albert de Salvo, kidnap-turned-terrorist Patti Hearst and O.J. Simpson.

• Richard Eberling was found guilty of the 1984 murder of an elderly Ohio woman named Ethel May Durkin. Advances in 'blood splatter' technology placed a third person at the crime scene and Eberling's blood group could not be excluded from the sample. Eberling, who died in 1998, admitted to working in the Sheppard home prior to the murder and to accidentally 'cutting his hand' inside the house.

REFERENCES:

- Murder Casebook (1990), Marshall Cavendish, London
- McGunagle, Fred, *www.crimelibrary.com*
- *www.samreessheppard.org*

1955

Emmett Till: 'The Hate Crime that Changed America'

FACT FILE

CRIME: Kidnapping and murder
VICTIM: Emmett 'Bobo' Till, aged 14
DATE: 28 August 1955
PLACE: Money, Mississippi (USA)
PERPETRATORS: Alleged perpetrators Roy Bryant and J. W. Milam were found not guilty of Till's murder

---

In 1941, the year Emmett 'Bobo' Till was born to poor African-American parents Mamie and Louis Till in Chicago, sociologist Gunnar Myrdal published a landmark study on white America's fear of miscegenation—the interbreeding of other races into white society. Myrdal's study proved that the South's fear that black Americans wanted to intermarry and have sexual intercourse with whites was based on a myth. (It was the least popular response amongst blacks on a list of reasons to integrate.) However, so entrenched was this fear, it fuelled institutionalised hatred and resulted in segregation, democratic inequality and even murder.

Mamie Carthan was an 18-year-old high school graduate from Argo, Illinois, when she married fellow teenager Louis Till in 1940. Despite the birth of a son in 1941, the couple separated in 1942. Louis Till was drafted by the US army the following year and was killed fighting in Europe in 1945. Never fully informed of the circumstances of his death, Mamie and her son received Louis's signet ring inscribed with the initials 'L. T.'. Emmett grew up to be a confident, handsome young man who knew little of the social conditions his cousins in the South lived under. In August 1955, during summer school break, Emmett Till went to Money, Mississippi, to spend a short holiday with his mother's uncle, sharecropper Moses Wright.

At the time Emmett Till visited Mississippi, there was a lot of social unrest because of the push for black voter registration in the South, and the stakes were high. In May 1955, the Reverend George Lee was shot dead in Belzoni while driving in his car after trying to vote. A few weeks later, Lamar Smith was shot and killed in front of the county courthouse after casting his ballot. But Emmett Till lost his life because of something much simpler—a perceived slight against the wife of a white store owner.

On 24 August, Till and a number of other black teenagers went to Bryant's Grocery and Meat Market for drinks after a hot day's work picking cotton. The store was owned by a white couple, Roy and Carolyn Bryant, but sold supplies to a predominantly black community of sharecroppers and their children. When Emmett visited the store, Carolyn Bryant was serving while her husband was in town. The boys who were with Emmett at the time stated that he either whistled at the attractive young store owner or made a comment about her appearance. In doing so, he signed his own death warrant.

In the early hours of 28 August, Roy Bryant, Carolyn's husband, and his half-brother. J.W. Milam, went to Moses Wright's home. There the two men grabbed the young boy and took him to the Tallahatchie River, where they, and several unidentified men, beat Till to a pulp when the boy stood up to them. The 14-year-old was then shot in the back of the head, his body was bound with barbed wire and a large industrial fan used for ginning cotton was tied to his neck. Finally, the men pushed his body into the river.

The following day, Milam and Bryant were arrested on kidnapping charges after the missing boy's great-uncle reported the incident to police. Jailed without bond in Greenwood, Mississippi, the two men were still incarcerated when Emmett Till's body was pulled from the river. His body was so badly beaten and decomposed that he could only be identified by the fact that he was wearing his father's signet ring.

The trial of J. W. Milam and Roy Bryant opened in Sumner, Mississippi, on 19 September 1955. After a five-day trial in which Moses Wright and another black Mississippian named Willie Reed did the unthinkable and stood up in court and identified two white men as murderers, an all-white, all-male jury took just 67 minutes to find the defendants not guilty of murder. Newspapers carried photographs of the two men smoking cigars in celebration of the verdict, although kidnapping charges were still pending. The following November, a grand jury refused to indict Bryant and Milam because of a lack of evidence.

REFERENCES:

- *Emmett Till timeline (2005), www.pbs.org*
- *Emmett Till, www.emmetttillmurder.com*

1957

Ed Gein Will Get You!

FACT FILE

CRIME: Murder
VICTIMS: Mary Hogan, aged 49; Bernice Worden, aged 58
DATES: 1955–57
PLACE: Plainfield, Wisconsin (USA)
PERPETRATOR: Edward Theodore Gein (1906–1984)
SENTENCE: Found guilty, Gein was not sentenced because he was medically insane

On 17 November 1957, 32-year-old sheriff Arthur Schley went to an isolated farmhouse in rural Wisconsin with a warrant to search its premises in regard to a missing person case. When the owner, 51-year-old Ed Gein, was not home, Sheriff Schley entered the premises and found a scene of unspeakable horror. This was no ordinary crime scene.

Ed Gein was quickly arrested and at first denied any knowledge of the missing woman. A thorough search of his house the next day revealed a belt studded with nipples and parts of a face, a soup bowl made out of a hacksawed human skull, a lampshade and chairs upholstered with human skin, a patchwork shirt made of human skin with a pair of breasts, a shoebox full of human noses and female genitalia, and the faces of nine women carefully preserved and mounted on a wall. The quietly spoken handyman finally confessed under the pressure of police questioning. In a matter-of-fact manner, he told police that he liked to wear the shirt of skin around the house and often put the mummified remains of female genitalia over his crotch.

Edward Theodore Gein was born on 27 August 1906 in La Crosse, Wisconsin, the second son of George and Augusta Gein. The key to why he would later commit his gruesome crimes lay in his relationship with his mother. Augusta was a fundamentalist Christian whose puritanical views—especially her warnings to her sons about the dangers of the opposite sex—angered her eldest son, Henry, and sexually confused young Ed.

Augusta Gein ran a general store in La Crosse, but disgusted by the 'moral depravity' of the people in the town, she moved the family to an 80-hectare (195-acre) farm in 1914, where the family lived in isolation for the next 25 years.

George Gein died suddenly of a heart attack in 1940, and Henry and Ed worked as handymen in La Crosse to keep the farm going. Henry and his mother continued to clash over his drinking, while Ed, now approaching his 40s, remained devoted to his mother. In May 1944, Henry was killed in a brush fire on the family farm—it was Ed who took authorities to where his brother's body lay. Police recorded that Henry Gein had died of asphyxiation and took almost no note of a wound on the back of his head. It was never proved (but widely speculated after his arrest) that Ed Gein killed his brother because of his constant bickering with their mother.

Ed Gein and his mother lived alone for only another year. Augusta died on 29 December 1945. Timid, shy and sexually naïve (it was presumed he was still a virgin), Gein often shared a bed with his mother while listening to her rant and rage as she battled cancer. Doctors speculated that his mother's death triggered Gein's mental illness—he started by closing off areas of the house and left most of the rooms as 'shrines' to his mother.

As early as 1947, people in the area started to disappear. Eight-year-old Georgia Weckler went missing on her way home from school; Evelyn Hartley, aged 15, was abducted while babysitting; and two deer hunters, Victor Travis and Ray Burgess, vanished in 1952. However, none of the body parts found in Gein's home matched any of these victims, and it is unknown whether the Wisconsin handyman had anything to do with their disappearances. In December 1954, Plainfield innkeeper Mary Hogan disappeared from her tavern. All that was found was a bloodstain, a shell from a .32 calibre bullet and the fresh tyre tracks of a pick-up truck. It was clear that she had been murdered and her body taken away.

It was the November 1957 disappearance of shopkeeper Bernice Worden that led police to the Gein farmhouse. Gein had unnerved Mrs Worden during several recent visits to her store—enough for her to relay her concerns to her son Frank, a Plainville deputy sheriff. When she disappeared from the store, Frank Worden immediately feared that Gein had done something to his mother and informed the county sheriff. Gein later admitted to going to her store, shooting Mrs Worden in the head with a .22 calibre rifle and then taking the body back to his farmhouse in her delivery truck. He also confessed to the murder of Mary Hogan three years before.

For many people growing up in the United States in the late 1950s, Ed Gein came to symbolise the 'bogyman'. For generations to come, parents warned their children not to be out too late lest Ed Gein 'get them'.

REFERENCES:

- *Murder Casebook* (1990), Marshall Cavendish, London
- BBC Online (2005), *Case Closed: Ed Gein, www.bbc.co.uk.*
- *Ed Gein (2005), www.crimelibrary.com*

1958

The Starkweather–Fugate Murder Spree

FACT FILE

CRIMES: Robbery and murder
VICTIMS: Robert Colvert, aged 21; Marion Bartlett, aged 57; Velda Bartlett, aged 36; Betty Jean Bartlett, aged 2; August Meyer, aged 70; Robert Jensen, aged 17; Carol King, aged 16; Clara Ward, aged 46; C. Lauer Ward, aged 48; Lillian Fencil, aged 51; Merle Collison, aged 37
DATES: December 1957 to January 1958
PLACES: Lincoln, Bennet and Douglas, Nebraska (USA)
PERPETRATORS: Charles Starkweather (1939–1959) and Caril Fugate (b.1943)
SENTENCE: Charlie Starkweather was found guilty and executed by electric chair. Caril Fugate was found guilty of being an accomplice to murder and served 18 years of a life sentence.

Charles Raymond Starkweather dreamed of being a cowboy and an outlaw. The Nebraskan teenager had a fascination with guns and had already earned a reputation as a local hood in the town of Lincoln by the time he met 13-year-old Caril Ann Fugate in 1956. When he wanted to buy his girlfriend jewellery for Christmas the following year, he felt that petty theft was beneath his standing as a teenage rebel. Charlie Starkweather had grander plans.

On 1 December 1957, Starkweather held up the Crest Service Station north of Lincoln. Armed with a shotgun and wearing a baseball cap over his red hair and a bandana over his face, Starkweather took just over US$100 from the till because the new attendant, 21-year-old Robert Colvert, did not know the combination of the safe. Starkweather forced Colvert at gunpoint to drive outside the city limits and then killed him with a single gunshot to the head. Starkweather told his adoring girlfriend that his accomplice had shot the attendant, but changed his story after he was caught to say that Colvert was shot accidentally when he grappled for the gun. Charlie Starkweather was no master criminal, but he had got away with murder.

On Sunday 19 January 1958, Starkweather went to Caril Fugate's home, which she shared with her mother, stepfather and two-year-old stepsister, Betty Jean. He had been invited to go hunting with his girlfriend's stepfather, Marion Bartlett, and had borrowed a shotgun from his brother, Rodney, for the occasion. He had bought some rugs salvaged from his garbage run as a present for Caril's mother, Velda. While Caril was at work, an argument developed after Velda accused Starkweather of sleeping with Caril and slapped him. Starkweather left without his rifle, but returned later that afternoon to find Caril arguing with her mother. When Velda slapped him a second time, Starkweather fought back and was set upon by Marion Bartlett. The cowboy killer went to Caril's bedroom and retrieved his rifle, and shot Marion Bartlett in the head. He killed Velda Bartlett when she came at him with a kitchen knife and then stabbed the baby, Betty Jean, to death.

Starkweather later said that Caril was a willing participant in the murders, but she told authorities that she arrived home to find her family gone and her boyfriend telling her that they were being held hostage by the men he had been planning robberies with. Whoever was telling the truth, Starkweather either alone or with Caril's help wrapped the bodies of the adult members of the family in the rugs he had brought to the house and then stuffed the baby's body inside a cardboard box. Marion Bartlett's body was buried in a chicken coop, and Velda and the baby hidden in the outside toilet. For the next six days, Charlie and Caril told visitors and family members—and even the police, who were called by concerned friends—that the family had influenza and had moved away to quarantine themselves.

When family members visited on 27 January, they found the house deserted. A police search later that day located the three bodies, and a manhunt began. Starkweather and Fugate drove south towards a farm of a family friend, August Meyer, in the town of Bennet. Starkweather's car got bogged in a ditch about 1.6 kilometres (1 mile) away from the farm, and Fugate later told police that her boyfriend shot Meyer in a barn as the old man went to get his horses to pull the car out of the mud. (Starkweather said he shot him in self-defence when Meyer brandished a gun at him.) The pair of young killers ransacked Meyer's house and stole money, clothes, food and weapons, then headed back to their car.

Seventeen-year-old Robert Jensen and his girlfriend, Carol King, offered to take the pair to a service station to organise a tow truck, but Starkweather later pulled a gun on them and told Jensen to drive back to Lincoln. Starkweather robbed them and then shot them, but stab wounds in Carol King's abdomen did not match his knife. (He later told police that Caril Fugate stabbed her because she was jealous of her.)

The young killers decided to hide out in a wealthy area of Lincoln and chose the home of C. Lauer Ward at random. Starkweather wounded Clara Ward while her husband was at work and then shot Ward when he returned home. The bodies of Clara Ward and her housemaid, Lillian Fencil, were later found upstairs—

Starkweather said both were bound and gagged but alive when he asked Caril to watch over them.

Starkweather and Fugate left the Ward home on the evening of 28 January 1958 for the 'Badlands' area of Wyoming. Outside the city of Douglas, shoe salesman Merle Collison was shot dead when Starkweather ordered him to exchange cars. Starkweather didn't know how to release the handbrake of the car, and when a passer-by stopped to help, he saw Collison's body and fought Starkweather for control of his gun. When Sheriff William Roper pulled over to see what the commotion was about, Caril Fugate ran to him and cried, 'Take me to the police. He just killed a man.' Although Starkweather drove off without his weapon, he was apprehended soon after when police shot out his windscreen and the bleeding cowboy stopped the car, thinking that he had been shot.

The Starkweather–Fugate murder spree in America's heartland had come to an end.

Caril Fugate was so hysterical that she had to be sedated, but when she calmed down she told a story of how Starkweather had kidnapped her and held her at gunpoint while he murdered ten people. Starkweather was found guilty of the murder of Robert Jensen and executed by electric chair on 25 June 1959.

Caril Fugate was held in a mental institution but later found guilty of being an accomplice to murder and sentenced to life imprisonment. Fugate's initial life sentence was commuted to 30 to 50 years in 1973. In 1976, after serving 18 years' jail, Fugate was paroled and she eventually resettled in Michigan.

HISTORICAL AND SOCIAL SIGNIFICANCE:

- Director Terrence Malick filmed a stylised version of the Starkweather–Fugate murder spree in 1973, starring Martin Sheen and Sissy Spacek. Called *Badlands*, the television movie has become a cult classic.
- A similar movie but with a different treatment, Oliver Stone's *Natural Born Killers*, caused a furore in 1994 because of its mindless violence.

REFERENCES:

- Bardsley, Marilyn (2005), *Starkweather and Fugate*, *www.crimelibrary.com*
- *Murder Casebook* (1990), Marshall Cavendish, London
- 'Starkweather Executed', *Lincoln Evening Journal*, 25 June 1959

1959

In Cold Blood

FACT FILE

CRIME: Multiple murder, robbery
VICTIMS: Herb Clutter, aged 48; Bonnie Clutter, aged 44; Nancy Clutter, aged 16; Kenyon Clutter, aged 15
DATE: 15 November 1959
PLACE: Holcomb, Kansas, USA
PERPETRATORS: Richard Hickock (1931-1965); Perry Smith (1928-1965)
SENTENCE: Hickock and Smith were hanged on 14 April 1965 at Lansing Correctional Facility (Kansas)

On 15 November 1959, four members of a farming family in rural Kansas were bound, gagged and murdered by two small-time criminals searching for a fortune that didn't exist. Five decades later the crime continues to resonate with the family of the victims and the small-town Kansas community. The book of the case by the writer Truman Capote has left an international audience searching for an understanding of why the tragedy happened.

The son of rodeo performers, Perry Smith dreamed of finding buried treasure in Mexico, opening a hunting resort in Alaska or becoming a famous country singer. The Korean War veteran was committed to improving himself and was both well-read and a talented artist. But his dreams were dashed by his uncontrollable anger, his low self-esteem and a motorcycle accident that badly damaged his legs and left him addicted to painkillers. While serving time in Kansas State Penitentiary for robbery, Smith met 'con' artist Richard Eugene Hickock. The confident Hickock was the complete opposite of the shy and introverted Smith, but the pair formed a close, and ultimately, fatal friendship. Twice-married with children, Hickock suffered head injuries in a car accident in 1950 and according to his family, was never the same man. Hickock's specialty was bouncing cheques, but he was also a rapist and paedophile, and there is evidence that he and Smith had a sexual relationship.

Hickock's cellmate, Floyd Wells, told him of the time he spent on the Clutter ranch in Holcomb, Kansas. A chance remark by Clutter that it cost about $10,000 a week to run his ranch was translated by Wells as meaning that there were large cash resources inside the house. Hickock saw robbery of the Clutter home as 'the perfect score' because he thought no-one would connect him to the crime.

Hickock was a deluded psychopath—Smith had never killed anyone (although he had bragged about the murder of a fictitious black man in the Nevada desert) and there was no safe inside the Clutter home. Herb Clutter did not carry cash and was well known for writing cheques in his native Halcomb and Garden City; he even wrote a $1 cheque for a haircut.

After their release from prison Hickock and Smith quickly hooked up and drove to Holcomb on Saturday, 14 November 1959. Although he wanted to turn around and leave, Smith was goaded by Hickock that he didn't have the courage to commit the robbery, let alone kill anyone. Shortly before midnight, Smith and Hickock entered the unlocked house and roused Herb Clutter from his bed in the downstairs study (Bonnie Clutter, his wife, was not well and Mr Clutter tried to give her as much peace as he could).

When the robbers demanded that he open the safe, Herb Clutter told them that there was no cash in the house. Smith and Hickock followed Mr Clutter throughout the house as he reassured his family that the men were only looking for money and would soon leave. Smith bound the victims, separating the men downstairs from the two women in their bedrooms, as Hickock conducted a fruitless search for the safe. With little over $40 in cash found in the house, Smith and Hickock realised the meaninglessness of their plan. Smith later told investigators the subsequent murder of the four occupants was not so much about leaving 'no witnesses' as a battle of wills between the two perpetrators.

Smith slit Mr Clutter's throat and then shot the entire family with Hickock's shotgun. The pair wore gloves and the only evidence they left were the knots that Smith tied the victims with and two separate shoe prints in the male victims' blood. Smith souvenired Kenyon Clutter's transistor radio which became vital evidence of the crime. Psychologists later said that the pair combined to form one pathological, murderous personality but they were far from being criminal masterminds.

Floyd Wells informed authorities that he had told his cellmate Richard Hickock about the Clutter ranch. Fleeing to Mexico where their cash soon ran out, the murderers returned to Kansas where they passed more dud cheques. Kansas Bureau of Investigation officers followed the paper trail to Las Vegas and arrested them there in a stolen car on 30 December. The pair had just picked up the belongings they had posted from Mexico—including the shoes they wore on the night of the murder and Kenyon Clutter's transistor radio—when they were captured.

With indisputable physical evidence tying them to the crime scene, Hickock confessed that Smith had murdered the Clutter family. Smith was an enigma; he stopped Hickock from raping Nancy Clutter, placed a pillow under Kenyon Clutter's head and laid a bound Herb Clutter on a mattress before killing everyone in the house. He later recanted his testimony that his partner had also killed, saying that he did not want Hickock's parents to think that their son was a murderer.

A jury found the two men guilty of four counts of murder on 28 March 1960 after deliberating for just 40 minutes. Shortly after midnight on 15 April 1965, Richard Hickock and Perry Smith were hanged at Lansing Correctional Facility and then buried in unmarked graves in Leavenworth, Kansas.

HISTORICAL AND SOCIAL SIGNIFICANCE:

- *In Cold Blood* broke new ground in literature because it used the conventions of a novel in the true crime genre and quickly became a best-seller. However, the eventual execution of the murderers, six years after the actual crime, affected the author Truman Capote for the rest of his life.
- *In Cold Blood* was the subject of a 1967 film and a 1989 mini-series. Actor Phillip Seymour Hoffman won the 2005 Best Actor Oscar for his portrayal of the famed writer in the film *Capote*, which deals with the writing of *In Cold Blood*. Similarly, the 2007 film *Infamous* covers pretty much the same territory, but with a focus on the alleged sexual/emotional relationship between Capote and Perry Smith.

REFERENCES:

- Capote, Truman (1965), *In Cold Blood,* Penguin, New York
- Davis, Donna (2006), *The Party of the Century*
- *In Cold Blood: A Legacy*, *www.ljworld.com*

1960

Adolf Eichmann Captured

FACT FILE

CRIME: Genocide
VICTIMS: Unknown numbers of Jewish men, women and children
DATES: 1938 to 1945
PLACES: Austria, Germany and Hungary
PERPETRATOR: Adolf Eichmann (1906-1962)
SENTENCE: Hanged in Ramleh Prison on 31 May 1962

The kidnapping of former Nazi Adolf Eichmann, found hiding in Argentina under a false name by Israeli secret agents in 1960, captured the imagination of the entire world. The daring plan to bring to justice one of World War II's most notorious war criminals showed the world that the Jewish state of Israel would neither forgive not forget the Holocaust—the extermination of 6 million Jews by Germany between 1933 and 1945. Eichmann's trial was shown live on television before a world audience, and his execution in 1962 brought an end to the life of one of the architects of Adolf Hitler's 'final solution'.

Karl Adolf Eichmann was born in Solingen, Germany, in 1906. His family moved to Austria following the death of Eichmann's mother, and he spent the majority of his childhood in Linz—the home town of Adolf Hitler. After studying to be an engineer, Eichmann had a modest career in sales before joining the Austrian Nazi Party. In 1932 he joined the SS, and after investigating Freemasons served as an SS corporal at the Dachau concentration camp in southern Germany. Promoting himself as a 'Jewish specialist', Eichmann studied all aspects of Jewish and Zionist culture, including Hebrew, in order to promote himself inside the Nazi 'machine' that would systematically murder 6 million Jews.

Eichmann came to the attention of Heinrich Himmler and Reinhardt Heydrich and joined the SD—the powerful security service arm of the SS. In 1937, he was asked to go to Berlin and work on the solution to the 'Jewish question', and later travelled through eastern Europe scouting for opportunities to deport German Jews—he even went to Palestine to canvass support but was asked to leave by British authorities. In 1940, he put forward the so-called Madagascar Plan, which proposed that all of Europe's Jews be deported to the large island off the coast of Africa, but the plan was never implemented.

After the Anchluss, the annexation of Austria by Germany in 1938, Eichmann went to Vienna and established the Centre for Jewish Emigration. In October of that year, he organised similar offices of emigration in Prague and Berlin.

A year later, he was responsible for the forced removal of Jews in Austria and Czechoslovakia to specially sanctioned ghettoes. By December 1939, Eichmann had risen to the head of Section IV B4 in the Central Office for National Security and was directly in charge of the deportation of Jews to concentration camps in Nazi-occupied Europe.

From 1941 to 1945, Eichmann headed the Department for Jewish Affairs in the Gestapo and it was his job to solve the logistical problems of transporting millions of Jews across Europe for execution. He had already witnessed at first hand ineffective mass executions in Minsk and Lvov in Russia, and he also realised that mobile gassing vans could not handle the volume of displaced people earmarked for extermination. It was Eichmann who helped to set up the Wannsee Conference in Berlin in January 1942, where the 'final solution' to the Jewish problem was formulated—the deportation of millions of people and their extermination in gas chambers.

Eichmann thus assumed a leading role in the deportation of European Jews, the confiscation of their property and their deaths in extermination camps. In March 1944, he travelled to Hungary and oversaw the deportation of Hungarian Jews to Auschwitz in Poland. Eichmann, who had risen to the rank of lieutenant colonel, took a keen interest in operations at Auschwitz and visited the camp on several occasions. These 'personal' appearances helped seal his fate at his trial in 1961, but his complicity in history's worst case of genocide was confirmed by his correspondence with Himmler, reporting the deaths of about 4 million Jews.

When World War II ended in 1945, Eichmann was captured by the US army and interned, but he kept his identity secret and was able to escape from prison. He hid in Germany until 1950, when he was able to immigrate to Buenos Aires in Argentina with the help of remnants of the Nazi SS. Eichmann lived there for the next decade under the name 'Ricardo Klement'. In 1960, Eichmann was discovered living in Argentina by the Israeli Secret Service (Mossad). Once his identity was confirmed from his old war records, he was abducted by four Mossad agents as he waited at a bus stop on his way to work on 11 May 1960. Offered the choice of summary execution or trial in Jerusalem, Eichmann chose trial and was smuggled out of Argentina disguised as an El–Al airline crew attendant.

Although his capture was a major coup for the fledgling Jewish state, it sparked an international incident. Argentina was outraged that one of its 'citizens' had been captured on its own soil by foreign agents and demanded Eichmann's immediate return. Israel declined and committed Eichmann for trial.

Once in Jerusalem, Eichmann was placed on trial as a Nazi war criminal. During the trial, which lasted from April to August 1961, more than 100 Auschwitz survivors gave evidence against the former Nazi officer. Eichmann declared that he had been 'a very small wheel' in the complex machinery of extermination—he was simply following orders he had received from his superiors. 'Why me?' he asked. 'Why not the local policemen, thousands of them … everybody killed the Jews.'

Inside the Beth Hamishpath—the Israeli House of Justice—Adolf Eichmann was a picture of the 'banality of evil' – the title of writer Hannah Arendt's account of the trial. Eichmann was found guilty and was executed in Ramleh Prison on 31 May 1962. His body was cremated and his ashes spread over the Mediterranean Sea beyond the territorial waters of the state of Israel.

HISTORICAL AND SOCIAL SIGNIFICANCE:

- The death penalty exists on Israel's statute book only for crimes against humanity, and has been carried out only once in the nation's history—on Nazi war criminal Adolf Eichmann in 1961. It does not apply in civil cases.
- Mossad was not so successful in bringing to justice other war criminals such as Martin Bormann and Josef Mengele. Bormann was never found, but a skeleton discovered in Berlin in 1972 was later identified as his. Mengele was granted asylum in Argentina after the war. In 1960, West Germany asked Argentina to extradite Mengele. He escaped to Brazil and from there to Paraguay. Mengele allegedly drowned in Brazil in 1979.

REFERENCES:

- Minerbi, Alessandra (2005), *A New Illustrated History of the Nazis*, D&C Books, London
- *The Nizkor Project: Adolf Eichmann, www.nizkor.org*
- *Adolf Eichmann* (2005), *www.historyplace.com*

1963
The Cambridge Spies

FACT FILE

CRIME: Spying
DATES: 1933–1963
PLACE: England
PERPETRATORS: Anthony Blunt (1907–1983); Guy Burgess (1910–1963); Donald Maclean (1913–1983); Kim Philby (1912–1988)

In the 1930s, at a time when fascism was taking root in Europe and the Depression was increasing unemployment in Western democracies, communist ideology must have been appealing to some academics—although the peasants starving to death and the middle class of landowners being wiped out under Stalin's Soviet regime may have begged to differ. In the early 1930s, four young Englishmen studying at Cambridge University were won over by the communist cause. Kim Philby, Donald Maclean, Guy Burgess and Anthony Blunt worked as double agents—Soviet spies working in the bowels of British intelligence—for much of the next two decades before the truth about their duplicity was gradually revealed.

The Soviet Intelligence Service (which was known as OGPU and was the forerunner of the KGB) was well aware that many British academics sympathised with communism and saw it as the answer to both unemployment and fascism, so it actively infiltrated England's universities. The Soviets also realised that the British Secret Intelligence Agency operated on an 'old boy' system and recruited agents from leading universities such as Oxford and Cambridge. The British 'establishment' would never suspect that people it had recruited from its sacred university system could be double agents. The recruitment of four young academics in the 1930s meant that the country's future intelligence leaders were also in the Soviet's employ.

Harold Adrian Russell Philby was born in Ambala, India, in 1912, the son of a British diplomat. Nicknamed 'Kim' at school—after a Kipling character who spies for the British in India—Philby studied at Trinity College, Cambridge, in the 1930s, and together with Donald Maclean, Guy Burgess and Anthony Blunt became a communist sympathiser. During the late 1930s he was a journalist and he became a war correspondent during the Spanish Civil War. By the time he was employed by the British Secret Intelligence Agency in 1944—as head of anti-communist counter-espionage—he was already a double agent. A newspaper journalist by profession, Philby became first secretary of the British embassy in Washington after World War II and liaised with the CIA on matters affecting the Cold War.

Francis de Moncy ('Guy') Burgess studied at Eton, Dartmouth and Cambridge. Burgess later worked with the BBC (1936–44), wrote war propaganda and joined MI5. A member of the foreign office, and second secretary under Kim Philby in Washington, he was also a homosexual. One of Burgess's early relationships was with Frederick Anthony Blunt, an art historian. Some believe that the Soviets recruited Blunt to act as a 'talent scout' for young recruits to the Communist Party after he made a trip to Russia in 1933. During the war, Blunt worked in British intelligence and passed on information to the Soviet government. After the war he held the position of surveyor of the Queen's pictures (1945-72) and was director of the Courtauld Institute of Art from 1947 to 1974.

Duart ('Donald') Maclean joined the diplomatic service in 1934 and was recruited as a Soviet agent during the war. One of Stalin's chief informants, Maclean was head of the American Department of the British Foreign Office at a time when Britain had access to a lot of classified information about America's atomic weapons program. An alcoholic—nervous and tense—the others in the espionage ring thought Maclean was most likely to crack under pressure if caught and interrogated.

In 1949, FBI agent Robert Lamphere learned that a member of the British embassy in Washington was sending messages to the Soviets as early as 1944–45. The FBI intercepted a message sent from an agent codenamed 'Homer'—second secretary Douglas Maclean—but Maclean was not identified for another two years. Kim Philby, who was living with Guy Burgess at the time, tipped off Donald Maclean that his cover had been blown in April 1951. When Burgess was recalled to London because of 'serious misconduct' the following month, he and Maclean secretly defected to the Soviet Union. Anthony Blunt helped Maclean escape to the Soviet Union, but the leading art historian's identity as a double agent remained a secret. (Blunt was even knighted in 1956.)

British intelligence was convinced that Maclean and Burgess had been assisted by a 'third man' within the diplomatic service, but Philby remained composed under increased scrutiny. He resigned his position in 1956 but was denied his pension until cleared by an internal investigation. In 1956, when Maclean and Burgess reappeared in Moscow, Philby was a journalist in Beirut but was publicly cleared of any involvement in the 'Maclean–Burgess' affair. Once again in the employ of the British SIS, he was confronted by his friend Nicholas Elliot about his double agent status in Beirut in December 1962 and confessed.

Kim Philby disappeared from Beirut on 23 January 1963 before he could be interrogated by the British. He later married the former wife of fellow Cambridge spy Donald Maclean, but she later returned to England and Philby married a Russian woman. In 1964, Anthony Blunt confessed to being part of the espionage ring in return for immunity from prosecution. Blunt was allowed to keep his official posts, and the full extent of his involvement in spying was not revealed until 1979 following the annulment of his knighthood.

Why did the Cambridge spies betray their country? Not for financial gain, nor for the notoriety. (All but Blunt died in obscurity in the Soviet Union.) There are some who believe Philby was a triple agent—infiltrating the Soviets so he could feed information back to the British—but given his later life in exile in Moscow, this seems unlikely. Philby and the others obviously believed in what they were doing, but today their motives still remain unclear.

In the world of espionage, there is no monopoly on the truth.

HISTORICAL AND SOCIAL SIGNIFICANCE:

- Guy Burgess and Donald Maclean defected to the Soviet Union in 1951. Kim Philby was revealed as the 'third man' in 1963. Anthony Blunt confessed to his part in the espionage ring in 1964 but was given immunity from prosecution.
- Historians now refer to the Cambridge spies as the 'Cambridge Five'—Philby, Maclean, Burgess, Blunt and an unnamed associate. Who was he?
- Kim Philby was a close friend of former MI6 agent turned novelist Graham Greene. Some believe Greene left the British SIS rather than expose his friend as a spy, but this is just speculation.
- Philby published his autobiography, *My Silent War*, in 1968. Graham Greene wrote the introduction.

REFERENCES:

- Creig, Charlotte (2005), *Criminal Masterminds*, Arcturus Publishing, London
- BBC Online (2005), *Case Closed: Kim Philby, www.bbc.co.uk.*

1963

The Profumo Affair

FACT FILE

CRIMES: Misleading parliament (Profumo), perjury (Keeler) and living off immoral earnings (Ward)

DATE: March–June 1963

PLACE: London (England)

PERPETRATORS: John Profumo (1915–2006); Christine Keeler (b. 1942); Dr Stephen Ward (1914–1963)

SENTENCE: Christine Keeler was sentenced to nine months' jail for perjury on an unrelated matter; John Profumo resigned from the House of Commons for misleading parliament; Dr Stephen Ward committed suicide on the last day of his trial on the charge of living off immoral earnings

---

The Profumo Affair, which erupted in March 1963, became the biggest political sex scandal of its day. The revelation that an English Conservative Party politician—no less than the secretary of state for war—had had an affair with a showgirl shocked British society. The further revelation that the woman, Christine Keeler, had also slept with Yevgeny Ivanov, a naval attaché to the Soviet embassy in London, compromised national security at the height of the Cold War. The scandal ushered in the 'swinging sixties', with Christine Keeler becoming an icon of a new era in sexual permissiveness.

John Profumo was a respected member of London society and a high-ranking member of the Tory government. Married to the actress Valerie Hobson, he was educated at Harrow and Oxford and first entered parliament in 1940. Profumo was the secretary of state for war (a position that no longer exists) when he had a brief affair with Christine Keeler in 1961. Profumo ended the affair after only a few weeks, but when rumours of the relationship became public the following year, Profumo denied the affair in the House of Commons in March 1963. Misleading the British parliament was the beginning of the end of Profumo's stellar political career.

Christine Keeler had run away from home as a teenager and became a topless dancer at Percy Murray's club in London. There she befriended Mandy Rice-Davies, a teenage model from Birmingham, who was also a dancer at Murray's. The attractive young girls were recruited by society doctor Stephen Ward to 'entertain' his rich clients. John Profumo first met Keeler at a party given by Lord Astor at

Cliveden in 1961. Keeler was living with Ward in a largely platonic relationship at the time, and the pair often stayed in a cottage on Astor's estate Ward rented on weekends. Keeler was swimming in the nude when she attracted Profumo's attention, and Ward and a group of his friends were invited to join Astor's house guests the following day. Profumo was introduced to Keeler by Ward, who provided him with her phone number.

Profumo was so smitten with Keeler that he did not realise, or chose to ignore, the potential for scandal and the potential political fallout. Another of Ward's friends, Soviet naval attaché Yevgeny Ivanov, was also vying for Keeler's attention. The society doctor later remarked to Keeler that with Profumo on one arm and Ivanov on the other, she had the potential to start a third world war. He wasn't far off the mark. After that first weekend, Profumo pursued an affair with Keeler, even bringing her to his Regents Park home late at night to make love to her. Profumo gave Keeler gifts and some money 'for her mother', but Keeler saw the relationship as an affair of 'convenience' and was not surprised when Profumo ended the affair by letter just weeks later.

What she didn't know at the time was that Profumo had been warned off the Keeler–Ward–Ivanov association by MI5. As far as he was concerned, the affair was over and the matter closed.

But Keeler's erratic love life, and her friendship with Ward and fellow showgirl Mandy Rice-Davies, conspired to expose Profumo's involvement in the affair to the British public. Snippets of the liaison filtered into the British press, and Profumo's political enemies learned of the affair and were determined to use it against him. It was Keeler, however, who proved to be the weak link in the chain of secrecy protecting Profumo. Two West Indian men, John Edgecombe and Aloysius ('Lucky') Gordon, were fighting for Keeler's affection, and Edgecombe went into hiding after slashing Gordon's face. Keeler refused to help Edgecombe find a solicitor, and although scared of Gordon, threatened to be a witness in any court action relating to the knife attack in order to get rid of Edgecombe. While visiting Mandy Rice-Davies at Ward's flat, Edgecombe shot a hole in the door and police were called. Almost immediately, the whole sordid story started to unravel in the press, which quickly latched on to the combination of sex and politics.

On 22 March 1963, John Profumo denied in the House of Commons that he had had an affair with Christine Keeler. However, the press had incriminating letters given to them by Keeler that suggested otherwise, and he was forced to resign in June. An investigation by MI5 revealed that 'Honeybear' Ivanov had asked Keeler to find out from Profumo when nuclear warheads were being delivered to West Germany. Ivanov was recalled to Moscow before he could be further implicated in the unfolding scandal. Further investigation revealed that Ward was actually running a callgirl ring and used Keeler and Rice-Davies to recruit young girls. Ward was arrested and charged with living off immoral earnings.

At Ward's trial, Christine Keeler, Mandy Rice-Davies and Vickie Barrett (alias Janet Barker) gave sensational testimony about the sexual activities of British society. Quote of the trial went to Mandy Rice-Davies, who—when told that Lord Astor had denied he had paid her for sex—stated, 'He would, wouldn't he?' Ward committed suicide on the day that his judgment was to be handed down. (Keeler later said in her autobiography that the doctor was a Soviet spy.) Christine Keeler was sentenced to nine months' jail for giving false evidence in the assault case against 'Lucky' Gordon at the Old Bailey in December 1963. Gordon had not assaulted her, she said, but by that time she had sold her story to the press and was financially self-sufficient. Keeler later married, had a son and divorced, but has not been in the news for more than 30 years.

Back in the 1960s, however, with the world in 'James Bond 007' spy frenzy, the Profumo Affair proved that sometimes the lives of the rich and powerful are just as fascinating as fiction.

REFERENCES:

- BBC Online (2005), *Case Closed: The Profumo Affair, www.bbc.co.uk*
- *The Profumo Affair, www.nzgirl.co.nz*
- Cowell, Alan, 'John Profumo, British Minister Ruined by Sex Scandal, Dies' (10 March 2006, *New York Times*)

1963

The Great London Train Robbery

FACT FILE

CRIMES: Conspiring to rob a mail train; carrying out a robbery with offensive weapons; assault; and receiving money knowing it to be stolen
VICTIM: Royal Mail train driver Jack Mills
DATE: 8 August 1963
PLACE: Ledburn, Buckinghamshire, UK on the Glasgow to London mail train
PERPETRATORS: Ronald Arthur Biggs; William Gerald Boal; Roger John Cordrey; Ronald 'Buster' Edwards; Brian Arthur Field; Leonard Dennis Field; Douglas Gordon Goody; James Hussey; Roy John James; Robert Alfred Welch; Charles Frederick Wilson; Thomas William Wisbey
SENTENCES: Thomas Wisbey, Robert Welch, James Hussey, Douglas Gordon Goody, Ronald Biggs, Roy John James and Charles Wilson were sentenced to 30 years; Roger Cordrey to 20 years and William Boal to 24 years (both reduced on appeal to 14 years); and Brian Field and Leonard Field to 25 years (both reduced on appeal to just 5 years). John Wheater was also convicted and sentenced to three years in prison.

On 8 August 1963, as the result of signal boxes having been tampered with, the Royal Mail's Glasgow to London travelling post office (PTO) train was stopped at the Bridego Railway Bridge, Ledburn, near Mentmore in Buckinghamshire. A 12-man gang, led by London criminals Bruce Reynolds and Thomas Wisbey, robbed the train of £2.6 million (worth about £40 million in today's money). No guns were used in the robbery, but the train driver, Jack Mills, was struck on the head with an iron bar by Ronald ('Buster') Edwards and never fully recovered from the attack. The gang always regretted the injury to Jack Mills, who never returned to work and died prematurely in 1970. 'Without Mr Mills being attacked,' Ronnie Biggs later reflected, 'it would've been, for me, a clean, very neat piece of what I call crookery.'

A diesel locomotive pulling four Royal Mail carriages left Glasgow at 6.50 am that day on its way to London, carrying 40 post office workers and over £2.6 million cash, which was on its way to the Royal Mint to be destroyed. Approaching Bridego Bridge over a deserted road in Buckinghamshire, north of London, the train was stopped by railway signals. The robbers, their faces hidden by balaclavas and helmets, took just 15 minutes to remove 150 mailbags from the train and take them down a steep embankment to a waiting lorry. When the train driver, Jack Mills, tried to stop the robbery, he was hit on the head with a steel pipe by 'Buster' Edwards.

Thirteen members of the gang were eventually identified after police raided Leatherslade Farm in Oxfordshire on 13 August. The farmhouse had recently been rented by a London solicitor, John Wheater, and although it had been abandoned by the time the police arrived, the robbers had left enough incriminating evidence to enable police to trace their identity. It was a friendly game of Monopoly—played with real money—that proved their undoing. Police found fingerprints on the Monopoly board and game pieces and on £1, £5 and £10 notes left behind in the robbers' rush. Roger Cordrey, who had fixed the railway signals that stopped the train, was the first to be arrested. He was caught in the middle of a giant shopping spree. Scotland Yard traced fingerprints to the other gang members, but the 'inside man' who had identified which train to stop and rob was not identified.

The robbery was investigated by teams led by Chief Superintendent of Buckinghamshire CID Ernest Fewtrell and 'Flying Squad' Detective Chief Superintendent Jack Slipper of the Metropolitan Police. It was Fewtrell who had a hunch that the gang was still hiding out in the area. The hunch proved to be correct when neighbours living near the Oxfordshire farmhouse alerted local police to the comings and goings. Fewtrell was due to retire soon after the Great Train Robbery, but postponed his retirement until after convictions were secured. Slipper continued to hunt down many of the escaped robbers even in retirement. In the 1970s, he chased Ronnie Biggs to Australia and Brazil and was on hand to greet the 'Great Train' robber when Biggs voluntarily returned to England in 2001 after 28 years on the run.

In 1964, Ronald ('Ronnie') Biggs, Gordon ('Doug') Goody, Roy James, Robert Welch, Thomas Wisbey, James Hussey and Charley Wilson stood trial and were each sentenced to 30 years' jail—far in excess of the usual life sentences for murderers. Although he was not aware of the robbers' intentions when he rented the farmhouse, John Wheater was sentenced to three years for not informing police after the robbery that he had rented the farmhouse on the gang's behalf. Ronald ('Buster') Edwards escaped to Mexico but returned to England when he became homesick, and was captured in 1966. Edwards and Jimmy White were sentenced to 15 years and 18 years respectively. Roger Cordrey was the only robber to plead guilty, and despite returning his share of the money (£80,000), he was jailed for 20 years. Bruce Reynolds spent five years on the run before being captured in 1968 and was sentenced to 10 years' jail.

On 12 August 1964, Charley Wilson coshed a prison warder and escaped from

Winson Green Prison in Birmingham along with three other men. On 8 July 1965, Ronald Biggs, the youngest of the train robbers, escaped from Wandsworth Prison and met up with his wife and family in Adelaide, South Australia, after undergoing plastic surgery and assuming a new identity—Terry Cook. Fleeing to Melbourne, Biggs was discovered working as a plumber and quickly disappeared again. After the tragic death of his young son in a road accident threatened to expose his whereabouts, Biggs escaped from Australia and settled in Rio de Janeiro, Brazil. Hastily fathering a son to a local dancer, Biggs avoided extradition and became something of a cause célèbre for the next 30 years. Wilson was recaptured in Canada in 1968.

The majority of the stolen £2.6 million was never recovered.

HISTORICAL AND SOCIAL SIGNIFICANCE:

- In February 1974, British mercenaries captured Ronnie Biggs after they lured him onto their yacht *Rio*. Biggs was released in Barbados when a court ruled that his capture was illegal.
- The 1988 film *Buster*, starring pop singer Phil Collins, was a highly romanticised account of 'Buster' Edwards's life on the run after the robbery. Later a flower seller outside London's Waterloo Station, Edwards committed suicide in 1994, age 62.
- In 2001, 71-year-old Ronald Biggs ended 35 years on the run when he voluntarily returned to England after a series of strokes. He was immediately imprisoned to serve out his original 30-year sentence in Belmarsh Prison.
- When former Flying Squad Detective Chief Superintendent Jack 'Slipper of the Yard' Slipper died in 2005, an ailing Ronnie Biggs asked to be released from prison to attend the funeral of his nemesis and pay his final respects. His request was denied.

REFERENCES:

- Creig, Charlotte (2005), *Criminal Masterminds*, Arcturus Publishing, London
- BBC Online (2001), *Flashback: The Great Train Robbery*, *www.bbc.co.uk.*
- *The Great Train Robbery, www.madfrankiefraser.co.uk*

1963

The Assassination of John F. Kennedy

FACT FILE

CRIME: Political assassination

VICTIM: John Fitzgerald Kennedy, aged 46, 33rd President of the United States

DATE: 22 November 1963

PLACE: Dallas, Texas

PERPETRATOR: Lee Harvey Oswald (1939–1963). Oswald was murdered before he could come to trial for either the Kennedy assassination or the murder of Dallas Police Officer J.D.Tippit

On Friday 22 November 1963, President John F. Kennedy was killed by an assassin's bullet as he rode in an open motorcade through Dallas, Texas. Kennedy was one of the most popular and charismatic leaders the world has known, and his death has haunted an entire nation for over 40 years. Later that afternoon, alienated loner Lee Harvey Oswald was quickly implicated in the president's death when he was arrested in a movie theatre and charged with the murder of a Dallas policeman.

Lee Harvey Oswald was born on 18 October 1939 in New Orleans. His father died two months before Oswald was born and his mother, Marguerite, was forced to put Lee Harvey and his two brothers into foster care for several years. Oswald's mother remarried and the family reunited and moved to Fort Worth, Dallas, but the marriage soon ended. The Oswalds moved to New York, but Lee Harvey's childhood was troubled, dislocated and dysfunctional. Intelligent and articulate, he suffered from a form of dyslexia, and this disability hindered his success at school. However, even at a young age, he developed an interest in communism and Marxist ideology.

In 1956, shortly after his seventeenth birthday, Oswald joined the US Marines. Trained as a radar operator, he was stationed in Japan the following year and became part of a team that monitored U2 spy aircraft. When he was told that he was being transferred to the Philippines, he responded with a self-inflicted gunshot wound. Punished by Marine authorities, Oswald decided to defect to the Soviet Union, but did not inform his unit of his intentions and returned to the United States in November 1958. In order to prepare for life in the Soviet Union, Oswald took a

Marine Corps course in Russian before securing a discharge on the grounds that his mother needed his support. Travelling to Finland, he arrived in Helsinki and applied for a traveller's permit to the Soviet Union. In Moscow, on 15 October 1959, Oswald consulted Soviet officials before visiting the United States embassy and renouncing his American citizenship.

Though in America he had been vocal in his praise of life under communism, Oswald's two-and-a-half years in Moscow were to prove a personal and ideologcal disappointment. Despite his marriage to a Russian girl, Marina Prusakova, in 1961 and the birth of a daughter the following year, he tired of the Soviet Union and managed to return to America with his family in June 1962, settling in Fort Worth, Texas. The marriage floundered as Oswald became increasingly involved in political issues, especially the 'Fair Play for Cuba' Committee. Oswald was filmed by local security agents handing out pro-Castro pamphlets in New Orleans and tried to ingratiate himself with Soviet consulate authorities on a trip to Mexico. Emotionally, Oswald was spiralling out of control.

Oswald started work at the Texas Book Depository on 16 October 1963, by which time he was living in Dallas apart from his estranged wife, who had given birth to a second daughter. On the night before the Kennedy assassination, Oswald visited his wife in Irving, Texas, and took possession of a rifle and telegraphic sight that he had purchased by mail order. Dismantling it and wrapping it in brown paper (he told colleagues it was curtain rods for his workplace), Oswald took the rifle to work on the day the president's motorcade was scheduled to pass under his window.

John F. Kennedy, his wife, Jackie, Vice President Lyndon Johnson, and his wife, Bird, arrived in Fort Worth. Texas, on 21 November 1963. At 11.22 am the next day, the presidential jet left Fort Worth for the 13-minute flight to Love Field, Dallas. After acknowledging the crowd, Kennedy and his wife took their places in the presidential limousine behind Texas Governor John Connally and his wife. The motorcade began its slow journey to the Dallas Trade Mart, where the president was to address a group of local businessmen and civic leaders in order to bolster support for his re-election in 12 months' time.

Taking his position behind a cardboard barricade he built for himself on the sixth floor, Oswald took aim as the presidential motorcade slowed down at the top of the intersection of Houston and Elm Streets and drove down past Dealey Plaza. Three shots were fired; the first missed its intended mark, but the second hit the president in the back and exited his throat. The bullet, referred as the 'magic bullet' by those who questioned its 'irregular' trajectory, then hit Governor Connally in the back near the right armpit, exited under the right nipple and shattered his right wrist. The bullet then carried on with diminishing velocity and struck the governor in the left thigh. (Incredibly, it was recovered in 'pristine' condition from the stretcher on which Connally was carried into the hospital.)

President Kennedy was wearing a back brace for a war injury that plagued him, and instead of slumping forward was kept upright, which made him an easy target. The third bullet struck the president in the head, shattering his skull. Amateur film showed First Lady Jackie Kennedy climbing onto the back of the limousine to retrieve part of her husband's skull.

It was 12.30 pm. President Kennedy was pronounced dead at Parkland Hospital at 1.00 pm.

After the shots rang out in Dealey Plaza, Oswald returned to where he was then living, in suburban Dallas, and allegedly shot dead policeman J. D. Tippit 45 minutes after the Kennedy shooting. Hiding in the Texas Theatre in Oak Cliff, Dallas, Oswald was captured by several policemen who had been alerted by a ticket seller. Although he denied all charges—'I'm just a patsy,' he famously declared after his capture—Oswald was charged with the murders of President Kennedy and the Dallas policeman.

At 2.38 pm, in the presence of his wife, Bird, and Kennedy's widow, Jackie, Vice President Lyndon Johnson took the presidential oath of office aboard Air Force One with the body of the slain president on board. The following day, Saturday 23 November, Oswald was visited by his wife, mother and brother, Robert. Soon after 11 am on Sunday, Oswald was taken from his cell at Dallas police headquarters to be transferred to the county jail. As he was led out in handcuffs by several detectives, a short, stocky man lunged forward from the crowd of reporters and stuck a .38 calibre gun at Oswald's stomach. A single shot fired by former Chicago bar owner and small-time mobster Jack Ruby killed Oswald, started a conspiracy industry and silenced the killer's true motives forever.

HISTORICAL AND SOCIAL SIGNIFICANCE:

- JFK was the fourth US president to be assassinated, after Abraham Lincoln (1865), John Garfield (1881) and William McKinley (1901).
- On 29 November 1963—just one week after the shooting—President Lyndon Johnson issued Executive Order No. 11130 and empowered a presidential commission to investigate the assassination. Kennedy's death resulted in a 'conspiracy industry' that tried to implicate the Mafia, Cuba, the CIA, the FBI and even President Johnson in the assassination.

REFERENCES:

- Groden, Robert J. (1993), *The Killing of a President*, Bloomsbury, London
- Lois E. Anderson (1986), *John F. Kennedy*, Bison Books, London
- *Murder Casebook* (1990), Marshall Cavendish, London

1963
The Murder of Lee Harvey Oswald

FACT FILE

CRIME: Murder with malice
VICTIM: Lee Harvey Oswald, aged 24
DATE: 24 November 1963
PLACE: Dallas Police Station, Texas
PERPETRATOR: Jack Ruby (1911-1967)
SENTENCE: Life

The world had not yet comprehended the death of John F. Kennedy, the 35th President of the United States of America, when his alleged assassin—24-year-old Lee Harvey Oswald—was gunned down under the very noses of the law enforcement officers assigned to protect him on 24 November 1963. Incredibly, Oswald's 'assassination' took place in front of a crowd of photographers, journalists and other media workers—shown live on television as the chief suspect of the murder of the most powerful man on the planet was paraded through Dallas Police Station after a press conference.

Whatever Dallas nightclub owner Jack Ruby's motivation, his murder of Lee Harvey Oswald raised more questions than it could have possibly have answered. Was Ruby, as he originally told detectives, a patriot who hoped to spare America's First Lady Jackie Kennedy the public spectacle of Oswald's trial? Or was Ruby, as many believed, a Mafia stooge assigned to kill Oswald before the troubled young man could reveal a conspiracy to murder the President of the United States of America?

Worse still, Oswald's death robbed authorities of the opportunity to cross-examine him under oath and reveal his real motivations for killing the president, his complicity in any conspiracy or his complete innocence of the crime. Did Oswald fire the fatal head shot that killed the president? Or the 'magic bullet' that entered the president's throat, deviated then shattered Governor's Connally's wrist? Was there a second shooter ahead of the motorcade secreted on the grassy knoll? Although improvements in ballistic technology in the last 20 years have supported the 'lone gunman' theory (a bullet can, in fact, deviate in the air and the trajectory of the fatal third shot was consistent with the angle from the Texas Book Depository and the speed of the motorcade), the conspiracy theories have continued. But did Oswald and Ruby know each other?

Jack Ruby was born Jacob Rubenstein in Chicago in 1911. One colourful report of the time was that Ruby had worked for Al Capone, Jake 'Greasy Spoon' Guzik and even Frank 'The Enforcer' Nitti, but Ruby was nothing more than a low-level criminal with aspirations of greatness. He moved to Dallas and worked at a number of nightclubs before opening the Carousel Room. Although several witnesses came forward after Oswald's death and stated that Oswald had frequented Ruby's club, there is no known connection between the pair. A tenuous link was that Ruby had visited Cuba in the final days of the Battista regime—ostensibly to talk to crime figures—and Oswald was a Cuban sympathiser. In September 1963 he travelled to Mexico and tried to gain a transit visa to Cuba as a 'friend' of the Cuban revolution.

Ruby was well known to local police enforcement officers—many drank at his Carousel Club and he casually handed out advertising cards to officers at the Dallas Police Station the day the president died. He had spent the previous two days at police headquarters taking a keen interest in proceedings. On the day Oswald was murdered, Ruby accessed police headquarters via a down ramp but inexplicably, the policeman guarding the access later stated that he did not see Ruby pass him. Although it was an hour past Oswald's scheduled transfer time, Ruby climbed under a metal rail that blocked vehicular access and arrived just as the suspect was being transported to the county jail. Doped up on antibiotics and dexedrine tablets, Ruby pushed to the front of the crowd of newsmen and journalists and shot Lee Harvey Oswald at almost point blank range. Ruby was immediately arrested.

It was determined by the Warren Commission that Ruby was acting of his own volition. The FBI declared that they could find no connection between Ruby and the crime community. Chief Justice Earl Warren and the future president, Republican Congressman Gerald Ford, travelled to Dallas to interview Ruby in 1964. Ruby stated that, 'I may not live tomorrow to give any further testimony … I can't say it here … it can't be said here.' Ruby wanted to be transferred to Washington but he was never again questioned about the Kennedy assassination. Shortly before his death from lung cancer, Jack Ruby promised to 'tell all' if only he could be moved from Dallas. He died on 3 January 1967 before a new trial could begin. He never married and had no children.

REFERENCES:

- Groden, Robert J. (1993), *The Killing of a President* (Bloomsbury, London)
- *Murder Casebook* (1990), Marshall Cavendish, London
- *Unsolved: Lee Harvey Oswald* (1984), Orbis Publishing, London

1964
The Boston Strangler

FACT FILE

CRIME: Serial murder by strangulation
VICTIMS: 13 women, aged 19 to 80
DATES: June 1962 to January 1964
PLACE: Boston, Massachusetts
PERPETRATOR: Albert DeSalvo (1931-1973)
SENTENCE: Life imprisonment for the 'Green Man' assaults, De Salvo never stood trial for any of the Boston murders. He was stabbed to death by an unknown convict at Walpole Prison (Massachusetts) in 1973.

In the late 1950s, a man posing as a representative of a modelling agency talked his way into the homes of ordinary Bostonian women with nothing more than a clipboard and the promise of a potentially lucrative modelling career. The fit, ordinary looking man with jet-black hair was even able to talk the women into taking their clothes off so he could measure their vital statistics—before raping them. Nothing more was heard of the 'Measuring Man', as police tagged him, until Boston was paralysed by a series of strangulations in the early 1960s.

In 1964, 33-year-old ex-army boxing champion Albert DeSalvo was arrested for a series of brutal assaults in Massachusetts and Connecticut. Dubbed 'the Green Man' by police because of the work clothes he wore during the assaults, DeSalvo harboured a darker secret. Sent to Bridgewater mental institution for observation, DeSalvo revealed himself to be a dangerous schizophrenic who was not only responsible for the 'Measuring Man' assaults in the late 1950s but also for the strangulation deaths of at least 11 women in Boston over the previous two years.

Albert De Salvo was born on 3 September 1931 in the working class suburb of Chelsea in Boston, the third of six children in an abused and abusive family. His father, Frank, beat his wife and children, taught his sons to steal and 'sold' three of his children—including Albert—to a farmer in Maine for US$9. Introduced to sex and pornography at an early age by his father, DeSalvo escaped his violent upbringing by joining the army in 1948 and being posted to Germany. There he met a German girl from a good Catholic family and returned to the United States with her after serving five years. Discharged from the army when charges of sexual assault of a nine-year-old girl could not be proved, DeSalvo returned to Boston and tried to settle into the routine of a respectable family man with his young wife and three children.

Although he had a steady job, DeSalvo drifted into 'breaking and entering' because of his sexual insatiability. (DeSalvo's wife later told police that he would demand sex up to 12 times a day.) In 1961, he served 11 months in prison for 'lewd and lascivious behaviour', but in June 1962, just weeks after his release, DeSalvo strangled his first victim—55-year-old seamstress Anna Slesers, who lived alone. On the last day of June, DeSalvo strangled two women on the same night, and by the end of the year his victims numbered eight. Despite a police force of 2600 men working around the clock—and the fact that over 5000 known sex offenders were questioned during the investigation—the murders continued into the New Year. Joan Graff, a Sunday school teacher, was murdered on 23 November 1963 during a national day of mourning for President John F. Kennedy, assassinated the previous day.

Choosing his victims at random, the man dubbed the 'Boston Strangler' by the media killed old and young alike. Mary Sullivan, his youngest and final victim, was a teenager. The killer's modus operandi was much the same—the women were beaten, strangled and raped—but several copycat killings gave police the false impression that there was more than one 'strangler' responsible for the unsolved murder spree. It was clear, though, that no woman was safe, and Boston was gripped by fear. Peter Hurkos, a psychic detective from Holland who seemingly had the ability to see visions of a crime or killer from physical objects associated with an event, was even brought into the case, but still there was no breakthrough.

When Albert DeSalvo was arrested for the 'Green Man' crimes in November 1964, psychiatrists little knew what they were confronted with. When DeSalvo boasted of his sexual conquests to a fellow inmate, he could not resist talking about his involvement in the deaths of 13 women—the 11 known victims, as well as 80-year-old Mary Mullen, who died in June 1962, and 69-year-old Mary Brown, murdered in June 1963. (Mullen suffered a heart attack and died in De Salvo's arms, while Brown was beaten and stabbed to death—because of the different methods, these deaths were not initially linked to the 'Boston Strangler'.) DeSalvo gave accurate, word-perfect accounts of his crimes and drew sketches of the apartments he broke into. He even described the 'strangler's knot' he used to murder his victims. However, this was not a confession, and there was not enough evidence to corroborate his version of events.

John Bottomly, the Assistant Attorney General of Massachusetts, was assigned to the 'Boston Strangler' case and formed a good relationship with the troubled

DeSalvo. Bottomly was able to convince DeSalvo to give a thorough account of the 13 deaths on the understanding that the information would not be used in court. It was more than likely that DeSalvo was insane and would never face trial in any case, but the police desperately needed a confession in order to close the case. 'I knew it was getting out of control,' the Strangler told the assistant district attorney. Once he had confessed to the crimes, Boston police were shocked to realise that Albert DeSalvo had been on their list of suspects all along—but only under the list of 'break and enter' offenders.

DeSalvo escaped prosecution—and a potential death sentence—because his attorney, Lee Bailey, allowed him to stand trial for the 'Green Man' assaults. Medical evidence confirmed DeSalvo's shattered state of mind, and he was sent to Bridgewater Hospital for treatment. Although he escaped from Bridgewater in 1967 and was later recaptured and transferred to Walpole Prison, he never did stand trial for the Boston murders. 'Society right from the very beginning started to make me an animal ... that's why I started all that killing,' DeSalvo told a journalist in 1973, shortly before his death. On 25 November that year, the Boston Strangler was found dead in his cell— having been repeatedly stabbed by an unknown hand.

HISTORICAL AND SOCIAL SIGNIFICANCE:

- New York psychiatrist Dr James Brussel was one of the first professionals to provide a profile of the 'Boston Strangler'. His description of a muscular man in his thirties, possibly Italian or Spanish—a paranoid schizophrenic in search of his sexual potency—was incredibly accurate.
- In Walpole Prison, DeSalvo made costume jewellery and specialised in 'choker' necklaces. 'I thought the chokers would be a good gimmick,' he said.
- Actor Tony Curtis, unrecognisable with a putty nose, gave the performance of his career in the 1968 film *The Boston Strangler*.

REFERENCES:

- BBC Online (2005), *Case Closed: The Boston Strangler, www.bbc.co.uk.*
- Smith, Jo Durden (2005), *100 Most Infamous Criminals*, Arcturus Publishing, London
- *Murder Casebook* (1990), Marshall Cavendish, London

1964

Mississippi Burning

FACT FILE

CRIME: Murder; conspiracy to deprive the three young men of their constitutional rights.
VICTIMS: James Chaney, aged 21; Andrew Goodman, aged 20 and Michael ('Mickey') Schwerner, aged 24
DATE: 20 June 1964
PLACE: Meridian, Mississippi (USA)
PERPETRATORS: Jimmy Arledge; Horace Doyle Barnette (deceased); Sam Bowers (b. 1924); Edgar Ray Killen (b. 1925); Billy Wayne Posey ; Cecil Price (1937–2001); Alton Wayne Roberts (1928–2005); Jimmy Snowden
SENTENCE: Roberts and Bowers were sentenced to ten years, Price and Posey to six years and the others to four years each. Arledge, Snowden and Horace Doyle Barnette, three years. None served more than 6 years jail. Mississippi never charged anyone with murder. Edgar Ray Killen was tried four more times before being found guilty in 2004. Sheriff Lawrence Rainey was found not guilty of conspiracy along with dam owner Olen Burrage and Klansman Frank Herndon.

In the summer of 1964, three civil rights volunteers who were working in Mississippi to help register black voters—Andrew Goodman, James Chaney and Michael Schwerner—were murdered and their bodies hidden near a local dam. Investigations by the FBI later revealed that local law enforcement officials had been involved in the crime and subsequent cover-up. The FBI investigation, headed by Alabama agent John Proctor, was called MIBURN—an abbreviation of 'Mississippi Burning'. The case would not finally be concluded until 40 years after the crime was committed.

In 1964, President Lyndon Johnson's administration passed the *Civil Rights Act*. The Act had attempted to stop discrimination in voter registration, but the reality was that very little had changed in the past 100 years in most southern states. Intimidated blacks were often afraid to vote, and the Justice Department just didn't have the resources to monitor voting booths in every county.

Continued resistance by certain politicians in southern states, especially Alabama governor George Wallace, actually kept the registration of black voters down. (The accepted practice was to administer literacy, knowledge or other tests to keep African–Americans from registering to vote.) In Mississippi alone, less than 6 per cent of eligible black voters were registered.

In January of that year, a 24-year-old New Yorker, Michael ('Mickey') Schwerner, and his wife, Rita, arrived in Mississippi to open up the Lauderdale County (Meridian) office of the Congress of Racial Equality (CORE). Schwerner, a Jew, earned the ire of local Klansmen when he promoted voter registration amongst the black communities and organised a boycott of a local store that sold goods to blacks but did not hire them. One of the local black volunteers, 21-year-old James Chaney, found a voice in the organisation, while 20-year-old student Andrew Goodman arrived in Meridian from New York on 20 June—the day the trio lost their lives.

On 16 June, the Klan broke up a meeting at the Mount Zion Church in nearby Longdale while looking for Schwerner and then burnt the church to the ground. On 20 June, after returning to Meridian, Schwerner, Chaney and new recruit Goodman, having recently completed a three-day course in Ohio, decided to visit Longdale, in nearby Neshoba County, to inspect the damage. Having interviewed several witnesses to the beatings and firebombing of the Mount Zion Church, they were returning to Meridian along Highway 16 when local police spotted their clearly marked CORE wagon. County deputy sheriff Cecil Price arrested the three civil rights workers on suspicion of starting the church fire and took them to Neshoba County jail.

Only some of what happened over the next six hours is known. Price met with local Klan leaders Sam Bowers and Edgar Ray Killen and discussed what to do with the three 'troublemakers'. (It was never proved in court that county sheriff Lawrence Rainey had knowledge of the plot.)

A group of men, including a 26-year-old ex-marine named Wayne Roberts, were recruited to shadow the civil rights workers out of the county following the trio's release at 10 am.

The group of locals intercepted Chaney, Goodman and Schwerner on Highway 492 and drove them to a farm owned by local businessman Olen Burrage. There Roberts executed the trio at point-blank range, and their bodies were buried in a hollow near the farm dam with the help of a front-end loader.

The focus of the subsequent FBI investigation was to gather information rather than search for the bodies. A US$30 000 reward brought forward a number of leads concerning the network of relationships shielding the murderers. On 4 August 1964, the bodies of the three young men were unearthed, with members of the local police, including Price and Rainey, as witnesses. On 4 December 1964 the FBI arrested 21 suspects in connection with the murders of the three civil rights workers. Nineteen men were eventually charged with conspiring to deprive the three young men of their constitutional rights. However, obtaining a verdict from the jury of seven white men and five white women—and federal judge William Harold Cox, a known segregationist—was going to be difficult.

On 20 October 1967, the jury returned verdicts against seven men, including Deputy Sheriff Price, Imperial Wizard Sam Bowers and the alleged 'trigger man' Wayne Roberts, but acquitted eight others. In the case of three other defendants, including Klansman and Baptist minister Edgar Ray Killen, the jury could not reach a verdict. (One of the jurors stated that he would not convict a preacher.) Killen survived two subsequent trials, but the FBI reopened the case in 1999 and justice was finally served in June 2005 when Killen was ordered to serve three 20-year terms—one each for the manslaughter of Andrew Goodman, James Chaney and Michael Schwerner—for his conspiracy in the 'Mississippi Burning' case.

HISTORICAL AND SOCIAL SIGNIFICANCE:

- In January 1965, President Lyndon Johnson asked Congress to ratify a tough voting rights bill in his State of the Union speech. When Congress stalled, civil rights leader Rev. Martin Luther King and his supporters marched from Selma to Montgomery in Alabama to register African–Americans to vote.
- It took the 'federalising' of the Alabama National Guard and the addition of another 2000 guards to allow the 3000-strong march to Montgomery to begin on 21 March 1965.
- Congress finally passed the bill (known as the *Civil Rights Act* of 1965 or the *Voting Rights Act* of 1965) on 5 August, but racial unrest in the nation continued.
- In Mississippi, the state with the worst voting registration record, enrolment of black voters subsequently grew from 6 to 44 per cent in three years.
- The 1989 film *Mississippi Burning*, staring Gene Hackman, was a fictionalised dramatisation of the FBI investigation.

REFERENCES:

- Linder, Douglas (1967), *The Mississippi Burning Trial: United States vs Cecil Price et al., www.lawumkc.edu*
- BBC Online (4 August 1964), *On This Day, news.bbc.co.uk*

1964

Nelson Mandela: The Rivonia Trial

FACT FILE

CRIMES: High treason, sabotage and conspiracy to overthrow the government
DATE: 11 June 1964
PLACE: Johannesburg (South Africa)
PERPETRATORS: Nelson Mandela (b. 1918); Walter Sisulu (1912-2003); Govan Mbeki (1910-2001); Raymond Mhlaba (1920-2005); Elias Motsoaledi (1924-1994); Andrew Mlangeni (b. 1923); Ahmed Kathrada (b. 1929); Denis Goldberg (b. 1933)
SENTENCE: Life imprisonment

The jailing of nationalist and political activist Nelson Mandela in 1962 by the discredited white South African regime started a chain of national and international events that would not see their conclusion until 27 years later. With the white government's apartheid policies crumbling around it, Mandela was released from prison in February 1990. Having galvanised so much support, Mandela was elected President of the Republic of South Africa the following year—his dignity in the face of an unjust prison sentence had changed an entire nation of people.

Rolihlahla Dalibhunga Mandela was born on 18 July 1918, the son of a Thembu tribal chieftain, in a small village in the Transkei province of South Africa. Given the English name 'Nelson' by a schoolteacher, Mandela was raised by the acting regent of the Thembu people after his father's death in 1927. Mandela attended Fort Hare University, became a lawyer in Johannesburg and in 1944 joined the African National Congress (ANC). With friends Oliver Tambo and Walter Sisulu, Mandela formed the Youth League of the ANC when he felt that the ANC leadership was too conservative. The same year he married his first wife, Evelyn Mase, the mother of his first three children.

For the next 20 years, Nelson Mandela was involved in a campaign of non-violent defiance of the South African government's apartheid policies. In 1952, he was arrested for violating the *Suppression of Communism Act* (which was intended to crush any mass movement against apartheid) and was banned from attending meetings for the next two years. In 1956, Mandela, along with 155 other political activists, was accused of attempting to overthrow the South African government by violent means. After a four-year trial, charges of high treason against Mandela were dropped. During this time, Mandela divorced his first wife and married Winnie Madikizela in 1958. The same year, Hendrik Frensch Verwoerd, the former minister of native affairs and the 'father' of apartheid legislation, became South African prime minister.

On 21 March 1960, South African police opened fire on unarmed anti-apartheid protestors in Sharpeville, killing 69 civilians—most of whom had bullet wounds in the back, having been shot as they ran away from the police. The government declared a state of emergency and banned the ANC and other minority opposition groups. Nelson Mandela responded to the banning of the ANC by forming the underground movement Umkhonto we Sizwe ('Spear of the Nation' or 'MK'), whose policy was to target and destroy government utilities and symbols of apartheid—but not to harm people. In 1961, Mandela 'illegally' escaped the country and studied guerrilla warfare in Africa and Europe.

Returning from overseas after a year on the run, Mandela was arrested by South African security police and sentenced to five years' jail on Robben Island. In November 1963, the government brought further charges against him and seven others for high treason, sabotage and conspiracy to overthrow the government. Although Nelson Mandela and the other accused escaped execution, they were sentenced to life imprisonment at the end of the so-called Rivonia Trial.

Found guilty of the crimes on 11 June 1964 and later sentenced to life imprisonment at the brutal Robben Island Prison (the South African government did not want to make martyrs out of the group by executing them) Mandela was confined to a small cell without a bed or plumbing and was forced to do hard labour in a quarry. He could write and receive a letter every six months, and was allowed to meet with a visitor for 30 minutes once every year. In the late 1960s, his mother and eldest son were killed in separate car accidents, but Mandela was not allowed to attend either funeral. While in prison, Mandela led a civil disobedience campaign among prisoners that effectively forced the South African government to improve prison conditions.

During the 1970s and 1980s, Mandela became the symbolic leader of an international movement (led by exiled colleague Oliver Tambo) to end apartheid in South Africa. For the last nine years of his prison sentence, after contracting tuberculosis, Mandela was moved to Pollsmoor Prison, where he effectively lived under house arrest while the Botha government negotiated with him. In 1989, F.W. de Klerk became South African president, and bowing to political, social and economic pressures, immediately instigated a program to end apartheid. International sanctions had cost the country US$4 billion between 1988 and 1990, but de Klerk knew that the apartheid goal of congregating blacks into separate homelands was impossible to maintain. The South African president lifted the ban on the ANC, suspended executions and released most of the prisoners from the 1964 Rivonia Trial.

Finally, in February 1990, de Klerk ordered Mandela's release.

Upon his release, Nelson Mandela led the ANC in its negotiations with the minority National Party government to bring an end to apartheid and the armed struggle in the Natal province, and to establish a multiracial government. In September 1992, Mandela and De Klerk signed the 'Record of Understanding', which promised to formally investigate the role of the police in propagating violence and established an elected constitutional assembly. The following year, Mandela and the South African president were jointly awarded the Nobel Peace Prize for their efforts. In 1994, the ANC won 252 of the 400 seats in the country's first free elections, with Nelson Mandela elected president of South Africa. On 10 May 1994, Nelson Mandela was formally inaugurated as president of South Africa, which he held until June 1999.

HISTORICAL AND SOCIAL SIGNIFICANCE:

- Mandela's achievement in leading his country to freedom did not come without personal sacrifice—even after his release. In 1992 he separated from his wife, Winnie, after she was convicted of kidnapping and being an accessory to assault by men acting as her bodyguards.
- On his 80th birthday—18 July 1998—Nelson Mandela married Graca Machel, the widow of the former president of Mozambique. Mandela stood down as South African president in 1999 after preparing the way for his successor, ANC president Thabo Mbeki. Despite being diagnosed with prostate cancer in 2001 and losing two of his adult children to AIDS, Mandela showed that he was still internationally active in his eighties when he spoke out against poverty and Third World debt in London in 2005.

REFERENCES:

- *On the Rivonia Trial, www.anc.org.za*
- *Nelson Mandela, www.nobelprize.org*
- *Mandela timeline, www.time.com*

1964

Malcolm X Assassinated

FACT FILE

CRIME: Murder
VICTIM: Malcolm X (1925–1965)
DATE: 21 February 1965
PLACE: Audubon Ballroom, Manhattan, New York (USA)
PERPETRATORS: Talmage Hayer (alias Thomas Hagan); Norman '3X' Butler; Thomas '15X' Johnson
SENTENCE: Life imprisonment

Malcolm X emerged as the Nation of Islam's most important leader in the late 1950s and early 1960s—eventually eclipsing his mentor Elijah Muhammad, whom many inside the religion considered a living prophet. In May 1964, Malcolm X established the Organisation of Afro-American Unity (OAAU), a secular political group. A pilgrimage to Mecca that year softened his political approach, however, and on his return to the United States he saw integration as the real hope for the future. Slowly, his message started to reach all races and creeds. But Malcolm X's renouncement of Elijah Muhammad created powerful enemies within the Nation of Islam. On 21 February 1965, Malcolm X was shot dead as he began an address at the Audubon Ballroom, New York.

Malcolm X was born Malcolm Little on 19 May 1925 in Omaha, Nebraska, one of eight children of outspoken Baptist Minister Earl Little. In 1929, Malcolm's family had their home in Lansing, Michigan, burnt to the ground because of Earl Little's support of black nationalist leader Marcus Garvey. Two years later, Earl Little's body was found lying on a trolley track—a victim of the white supremacist group the Black Legion—but at the time his death was ruled to be an 'accident'. Malcolm's mother suffered the first of several nervous breakdowns, and he and his siblings were placed in foster homes and orphanages.

Although he was a bright student, Malcolm drifted into petty crime. He moved to Boston in 1946, and was later sentenced to ten years' jail on burglary charges. Malcolm used this time to rekindle his interest in education but was also converted to the religious organisation Nation of Islam (NOI) by his brother Reginald. By the time he was paroled in 1952, Malcolm was a firm follower of NOI leader Elijah Muhammad, and the following year he forsook his slave name 'Little' for the letter

'X' to symbolise the loss of his tribal African name. (Malcolm's Muslim name was actually El-Hajj Malik El-Shabazz.) Malcolm X's ability to articulate Elijah Muhammad's sternest teachings—to despise the white society that had enslaved African–Americans and which was now actively working against them achieving equality—made him a stark alternative to the non-violent leadership of Martin Luther King for African–Americans.

Malcolm X at first believed that it was impossible to achieve equality with 'White' America and solution lay in the formation of a separate NOI state within America (by bloodshed, if necessary). However, when he discovered that Elijah Muhammad was conducting affairs with as many as six women (and had fathered several children), he broke away from NOI in March 1964 and founded his own religious organisation, the Muslim Mosque, Inc.

Malcolm X's renouncement of Elijah Muhammad created powerful enemies within the Nation of Islam. In February 1965, his family home in East Elmhurst, New York, was firebombed. On 21 February, Malcolm X was shot dead as he began an address at the Audubon Ballroom, New York. A man in the crowd of 400 created a disturbance, which drew Malcolm X's bodyguards away from him. At the same time, a black man rushed the stage and shot Malcolm X in the chest with a sawn-off shotgun. Two other black men quickly charged forward and fired handguns at him as he lay dying on the stage. Angry members of the crowd held and beat the assassins as they tried to escape the ballroom.

Although the assassins were identified as disgruntled members of the Nation of Islam, Elijah Muhammad expressed his 'shock and surprise' at Malcolm X's murder. Talmage Hayer, the man convicted of Malcolm X's assassination, later signed an affidavit that his co-accused, Norman 3X Butler and Thomas 15X Johnson, were not involved in the murder, and named three other New Jersey men.

Fifteen hundred people attended Malcolm X's funeral on 27 February 1965 in Harlem. After the service, friends took the shovels away from the local gravediggers at the Ferncliff Cemetery in Hartsdale, New York, and buried Malcolm X's body themselves.

REFERENCES:

- Hutchinson, Effie Ofari (2005), *Revisiting the Malcolm X Assassination, www.alternet.org*
- *Malcolm X website, www.cmgww.com*

1965

Jack the Stripper

FACT FILE

CRIME: Serial murder

VICTIMS: Gwyneth Rees, aged 22; Hannah Tailford, aged 30; Irene Lockwood, aged 26; Helen 'Teddie' Barthelemy, aged 22; Mary Fleming (alias Mary Turner), aged 30; Margaret McGowan, aged 21; Bridie Esther O'Hara, aged 28

DATES: January 1964 to February 1965

PLACE: London (England)

PERPETRATOR: Unknown

In January 1964, the body of a 30-year-old waitress and part-time prostitute named Hannah Tailford was found floating in the Thames River by rowers belonging to the London Corinthian Club at Hammersmith Reach. Naked except for a pair of stockings which had been rolled down around her ankles, the victim had been gagged with her own panties, which had been thrust down her throat. Detectives established that Tailford's body had been thrown in the water about 2.4 kilometres (one-and-a-half miles) upriver in an area called Duke's Meadow. Although the exact cause of death was never established, head injuries suggested that the victim had been knocked unconscious or drowned in a pond or bath. Tailford had disappeared from the flat she shared with her boyfriend ten days earlier.

On 8 April 1964, the naked body of a 26-year-old, red-headed prostitute named Irene Lockwood was found entangled in reeds at Duke's Meadow. Lockwood worked the Bayswater Road and Notting Hill districts, and was known to have attended vice parties and appeared in blue movies. She was also pregnant. Lockwood had last been seen outside Cheswick Pub the day before her body was found, and she too appeared to have been attacked from behind, beaten about the head and then dumped in the water.

The similarities were obvious—the bodies of prostitutes, naked and with head injuries, dumped in the Thames near the same spot. But not all of the murders that punctuated 'Swinging London' in 1964–65 fitted this pattern.

At the end of April 1964, the body of Helen ('Teddie') Barthelemy was found dumped in an alleyway in Brentford. She was naked and had been suffocated, but there were no marks on her throat. Police believed that she had been suffocated with a pillow. Barthelemy was also a prostitute and worked as a stripper in Blackpool.

The deaths of the three known prostitutes were linked to the 1963 murder of Gwyneth Rees, whose body had been found in an ash tip near Cheswick Bridge. Her body was also naked, except for a single stocking. Police referred to this case as the 'Cinderella Murder', because they had made a plaster cast of her foot to identify her. Other murders, in May and June 1964, were also linked to these crimes.

The London media referred to the man responsible for the 'Thames Nude Murders' as 'Jack the Stripper', an obvious play on London's most infamous unknown killer. As the murders continued, London detectives appeared to have as much chance of discovering the identity of the killer as their predecessors had in 1888.

On the day that Barthelemy's body was found, 54-year-old Kenneth Archibald walked into Notting Hill Police Station and confessed to the murder of Irene Lockwood. Archibald had already been questioned about the murder—one of his business cards was found in Lockwood's flat—but at the time he denied ever having met the prostitute and said he had no idea how one of his cards came to be in her flat. But now he was confessing to her murder and provided intimate details of her final moments. 'I must have lost my temper and put my hands around her throat,' he told London detectives. 'She could not scream. I then proceeded to take her clothes off and rolled her into the river.'

Archibald took police to where he and Lockwood allegedly argued about money and retraced his steps on the night of the murder, but he did not confess to the other crimes. Although police were convinced that the same person was responsible for all the murders, Archibald knew a lot about the Lockwood crime and was charged with her murder. Then, during his trial, which began on 19 June 1964, Archibald retracted his confession. He was acquitted by a jury four days later, because there was no evidence linking him to the crime other than his confession.

Because the body of Helen Barthelemy had not been dumped in the Thames, vital evidence had survived. Minute particles of paint—specks of different colours (yellow, orange, green and black)—were found on her skin. This suggested that her body had been hidden before being dumped in Brentford. The paint contained a lead acetate base, like the paint used to spray-paint cars and furniture. If the body wasn't lying in a spray shop, it had definitely been kept near one. Other forensic tests determined that Barthelemy had been murdered fully clothed (her underclothes restricted blood flow after her death) and that her body had lain on a rough sack and been stored flat on a shelf.

Police appealed for prostitutes and male customers to come forward in confidence and provide information. Twenty-three prostitutes came forward, and by the end of April 60 men and woman had provided information. Female officers worked undercover dressed as prostitutes, shadowed by their male colleagues.

On 14 July 1964, the body of a fourth woman was found naked and left in a sitting position outside the garage of a home in a Cheswick cul-de-sac. Mary Fleming (alias Mary Turner) was a prostitute and the mother of two small children, and had been attacked from behind and her body stripped. The same kind of paint flecks that were found on the previous victim were also found on Fleming's body. She had been dead for three days. Local residents recalled seeing a dark van in the cul-de-sac, which had most likely been used to dump the woman's body.

The body of a fifth victim, Margaret McGowan, was found in a car park near Kensington High Street in West London on 25 November 1964. McGowan was short, like the previous victims, and had been strangled, and her body was left naked and speckled with paint. The body, hidden between two slabs of concrete, had been in the car park for over a week. Ten weeks later, on 16 February 1965, the naked body of prostitute 'Bridie' O'Hara was found in Acton. Her body was partially mummified, suggesting that it had been kept near a heat source for some time, and investigation revealed traces of oil and fibre—as if the body had been wrapped in a tarpaulin—and spray-paint flecks.

Police issued a statement that they had narrowed the list of suspects, but suddenly the murders stopped. The murders had taken place roughly every three months—in January, April, July, November and February—but then stopped. The suicide of a London family man who left a note stating that he could 'no longer stand the strain' was not originally linked to the murders, but when the dead man's background was investigated, his duty roster at the security firm where he had worked fit the pattern of the murders. No physical evidence was found in the man's home or garage, but police were convinced he was the killer.

Out of deference to the suspect's family, the man's identity was never revealed. 'Jack the Stripper', like his famous namesake, took his secrets with him to his grave.

REFERENCES:

- BBC Online (2005), *Case Closed: Jack the Stripper, www.bbc.co.uk*
- *Murder Casebook* (1990), Marshall Cavendish, London
- *Jack the Stripper, www.murderuk.com*

1966
The Moors Murderers

FACT FILE

CRIME: Serial murder
VICTIMS: Pauline Reade, aged 16; John Kilbride, aged 12; Keith Bennet, aged 12; Lesley Ann Downey, aged 10; Edward Evans, aged 17
DATES: July 1963 to October 1965
PLACE: Saddleworth Moor, Manchester (England)
PERPETRATORS: Ian Brady (b. 1938); Myra Hindley (1942–2002)
SENTENCE: Life imprisonment

In July 1963, 16-year-old Pauline Reade disappeared from the Gorton district of Manchester, in England, while walking to a dance. John Kilbride, aged 12, went missing the following June. Six months later, Keith Bennet, also 12, disappeared on the way to his grandmother's house. On Boxing Day 1964, 10-year-old Lesley Ann Downey disappeared from Ancoats fairground without a trace. Police were baffled by these disappearances until the following October, when they charged two sadists—27-year-old Ian Brady and his 23-year-old girlfriend, Myra Hindley—with kidnapping and murder. The discovery of several bodies on Saddleworth Moor, north of Manchester, would establish a new benchmark for depravity.

In 1965, 17-year-old David Smith fell under the influence of his sister-in-law's boyfriend, Ian Brady. A sadist obsessed with Nazism, Nietzsche and the Marquis de Sade, Brady talked the impressionable young man into 'rolling a queer'. It was Smith who picked up 17-year-old Edward Evans from the local pub and brought him back to Brady's ordinary estate house in Wardle Brook Avenue, Manchester, so that they could rob the teenager. Smith was in the kitchen when Myra Hindley, the older sister of his wife, Maureen, rushed in and told him to come and help Brady. Smith entered the room just as Brady smashed a hatchet into Evans's head. As the young man fought back, Brady struck Evans again and again. 'It's done,' Brady said. 'It's the messiest yet. It normally takes only one blow.'

Incredibly, possibly because they felt that he was part of the family and wouldn't tell anyone, the pair of killers let a shaken David Smith return home. That night, Smith and his wife, Maureen, armed themselves with a screwdriver, hid in a public telephone box and worked up the courage to call the police. A detective dressed as a delivery man knocked on the door of Brady's home and found the killers home.

When police raided the house soon after, they found the body of Edward Evans wrapped in carpet. They also found much more.

A search of the house found a luggage deposit ticket hidden in the spine of Myra Hindley's first communion missal. The ticket was for two luggage cases deposited at Manchester station. The luggage was full of sadomasochistic paraphernalia, pornographic material and personal effects belonging to a missing child, Lesley Ann Downey. Worse still, there were lewd photographs of the young girl and an audiotape sickening in its inhumanity. On the tape, the child pleaded to be allowed to go home. The audio tape also had gargled sounds, Brady's threatening voice and Hindley's demands made to the frightened girl. Hindley later stated that the tape, which finished with the sounds of Christmas carols, was not 'as bad as it sounds'.

Police were also able to piece together the final moments of 12-year-old John Kilbride from Brady's handwritten notes and photographs of Myra Hindley posing innocently on Saddleworth Moor pointing to where the bodies of the missing children may be buried. Frustratingly, the pair made no confessions and steadfastly refused to reveal the fates of their victims. The bodies of Leslie Ann Downey and John Kilbride were found, but the other victims were not located. Hindley seemed more upset over the death of her pet dog when it was accidentally killed by forensic detectives testing for links to the victims. Other than that, the pair remained sullen and dispassionate throughout their trial.

These were no ordinary killers.

Myra Hindley and Ian Brady were office co-workers at Millwards Merchandisers in Manchester. Hindley, a plain-looking, aloof teenager, came under the spell of the brooding 'teddy boy', who had had a troubled childhood in Glasgow. Hindley willingly let Brady beat and whip her, and joined him in his murderous outings. The pair formed what criminologists describe as a 'foile à deux'—a depraved partnership in which neither is capable of murder without the actions and support of the other. Hindley dyed her hair blonde (to make her look 'more German') and dressed in the provocative miniskirts and high boots of the time. More than that, Brady could not drive a car, and Hindley not only befriended the children whom the pair abducted but also drove them to their deaths. (Brady would follow on his motorbike.)

Brady had long had a fascination with moorland, and the pair covered their tracks by bringing humus and soil back to their garden from their murderous 'picnics' on the moors. In this manner, they could explain their trips away.

On 6 May 1966, Ian Brady was found guilty on three counts of murder (the deaths of Pauline Reade and Keith Bennet could not be proved because their bodies were not found), while Hindley was found guilty on two counts (Downey and Kilbride).

The 'Moors Murderers' were sentenced to life imprisonment. In Britain, 'life' usually meant a 12- to 20-year period of incarceration, but relatives of the victims publicly swore that they would take matters into their own hands and kill the pair if either was released from prison.

In the 1970s and 1980s, Hindley actively campaigned for parole, believing that she would be released after 25 years. In 1986 she finally cooperated with police, and possibly anticipating her release from jail, revealed where the body of Paula Reade had lain hidden on the moor for the past 20 years.

The British home secretary then increased her minimum jail term to 30 years. For Brady's part, he did not seek release and was placed in a mental institution in 1985.

The body of Keith Bennet was never recovered, and Myra Hindley never did see freedom. A heavy smoker, this personification of evil for many Britons died from respiratory failure 11 days before the 2002 ruling that stripped the Home Secretary of his powers to overrule the parole board's recommendations on life sentences.

At the time of publication Ian Brady is still alive and is currently being kept alive at Ashworth Hospital in Liverpool. Officials denied his wish to be allowed to end his four decades in captivity by starving himself to death.

HISTORICAL AND SOCIAL SIGNIFICANCE:

- In 1972, prison governor Dorothy Wing was severely reprimanded for taking Myra Hindley for walks outside the jail—possibly in readiness for her parole.
- In 1973, prison officer Pat Cairns became Hindley's lesbian lover and was convicted of trying to plot her lover's escape from prison.
- Such was the hatred for the pair—and Hindley in particular—that Hindley's family was assaulted by protestors at the funeral of her sister, Maureen, who had turned the killers in.

REFERENCES:

- BBC Online (2005), *Case Closed: The Moors Murderers, www.bbc.co.uk*
- *Murder Casebook* (1990), Marshall Cavendish, London
- Williams, Emlyn *Beyond Belief: A Chronicle of Murder and its Detection*, (1968) Random House, London

1966

Charles Whitman: Deadly Sniper

FACT FILE

CRIME: Murder

VICTIMS: Margaret Whitman (mother), aged 44; Kathleen Whitman (wife), aged 23; Marguerite Lamport, aged 45; Mark Gabour, aged 15; Edna Townsley, aged 51; Karen Griffith, aged 17; Patrolman Bill Speed, aged 22; Paul Sonntag, aged 18; Claudia Rutt, aged 18; Roy Dell Schmidt, aged 29; Dr Robert Boyer, aged 33; Harry Walchuck, aged 38; The unborn son of Claire Wilson; Thomas Aquinas Ashton, aged 22; Thomas Karr, aged 24

Eleven died at the campus, two died later (unborn child and Karen Griffith) plus wife and mother = 15

DATES: 31 July to 1 August 1966

PLACE: Austin, Texas, USA

PERPETRATOR: Charles Whitman (1941-1966)

In the summer of 1966, ex-marine Charles Whitman was a troubled man. The 25-year-old former military sniper suffered from increasingly violent urges and had sought psychiatric help. His parents had recently separated, and he had driven to Florida to bring his mother back to Austin, Texas, to live near him and his wife, Kathleen. Whitman's father became the focus of his growing hatred as he regularly phoned his son and asked him to bring his mother back home to Florida. Finally Whitman snapped. He went out and murdered at random as many people as he could—hoping that he too would be killed—after killing his wife and mother to save them from the 'embarrassment' his actions were bound to cause them.

On 31 July 1966, Charles Whitman typed a note outlining his concerns about his health and asking that after his death an autopsy be performed to discover if he had any medical disorder that made him act so violently. He wrote a tirade of abuse about his father, whom he hated with 'a mortal passion', and gave his reasons why his mother and wife had to die. Later that day, he picked up his wife from work and dropped her off at home. He then took a pistol and drove to his mother's apartment and stabbed and shot her to death. Whitman put his mother's body in bed and covered it with a blanket as if she were sleeping. He left a note beside her body that said 'I love my mother with all my heart'.

Back at home, in the middle of the night, Whitman added to his suicide note ('12.30 am. Mother already dead') and then went to his bedroom and killed his wife as she lay sleeping. The last addition to the note read: '3 am—Wife and mother both dead'. At 9 am Whitman drove to a local hardware store and bought a second-hand .30 calibre M1 carbine. After buying hundreds of rounds of ammunition, he bought more guns, hired a foldaway three-wheeled trolley and returned home. Dressing in grey workman's overalls, he loaded up his stash of weapons—7 guns, 3 hunting knives, 1000 rounds of ammunition, 3 gallons (about 14 litres) of petrol, and sundry food and hardware supplies—and drove to the administration offices of the University of Texas, which were housed in a 307-foot (94-metre) tower with commanding views of the city of Austin.

When Whitman reached the university offices, he told the receptionist that he was a maintenance man and pushed his arsenal-laid trolley to the lift. The lift only went to the 27th floor, and Whitman had to unpack his trolley and carry two guns four short flights of stairs up to the observation deck. Edna Townsley, another receptionist working near the exit to the observation deck, was beaten by Whitman with the butt of a gun and hidden behind the desk. After the remainder of his stockpile had been placed on the deck (a young couple left the area, oblivious to the bloodstains near the receptionist's desk, before the shooting started), Whitman walked down the stairs just as a family got out of the lift. Marguerite Lamport and her 15-year-old nephew Mark Gabour were killed by a gunshot volley, while other family members in the group were injured and retreated to the lift. Whitman then shot Edna Townsley dead before returning to the observation deck of the tower and barricading the door with furniture. It was 11.45 am.

Once positioned on the deck, Whitman had the protection of an 18-inch thick (4.5-centimetre-thick) limestone parapet. With classes expected to finish at 12.20 pm, the experienced sniper took his bolt-action .35 Remington rifle with telescopic sights and spied for potential victims. Three people were dead before anyone knew what was happening. (Student Karen Griffith would die in hospital from her injuries a week later.) By 11.52 pm police had received hysterical phone calls reporting a sniper firing from the tower. Traffic cop Bill Speed, one of the first officers to respond to the calls, was killed as he took cover behind a balustrade. Teenage couple Paul Sonntag and Claudia Rutt were killed as they strolled along a mall. Roy Dell Schmidt, an electrical repairman, visiting lecturer Dr Robert Boyer and Harry Walchuck, a postgraduate student, were the next to die. Such was the speed of the volley of shots and the varying directions from which they came that police originally feared that there was a group of snipers on top of the tower.

Most victims died within the first 15 minutes, including the unborn baby of freshman Claire Wilson, who was severely injured. By 12.30 pm police marksmen were in position and firing at the tower. When marksmen firing from light aircraft failed to stop Whitman, Austin police chief Robert Miles decided not to use a helicopter and ordered his men to storm the tower. Three officers, Ramiro Martinez, Houston McCoy and Jerry Day, made their way into the tower and were met by university employee Allen Crum. Having just finished 20 years' service in the air force, Crum insisted on joining the team and was quickly deputised and given a rifle. While Officer Day took Mark Gabour's mother downstairs to be treated for her injuries, the others crawled past the victims' bodies on the stairs, dismantled the barricades and used a desk to shield them as they crawled out onto the observation deck.

Circling the sniper, Allen Crum fired a shot at Whitman that forced Whitman to run back into the vision of Officer Martinez. Although shot, Whitman still had hold of his rifle when Officer McCoy shot him with a shotgun. When Martinez saw that the sniper was still moving, he rushed him with McCoy's shotgun and shot him in the head at almost point-blank range. At 1.20 pm it was all over … 11 people had been killed, two others would later die and more than 30 people were injured.

An autopsy later revealed that Charles Whitman had a small tumour in his brain in the area that determines emotional responses. A report commissioned by Texas Governor John Connally stated that the tumour was malignant and would have killed Whitman within the year. It was believed that the illness contributed to the ex-marine's loss of control that hot summer's day in 1966.

HISTORICAL AND SOCIAL SIGNIFICANCE:

- The crimes of Charles Whitman provided the basis for director Peter Bogdanovich's 1968 cult movie *Targets*, in which the setting was transferred from a tower to a suburban drive-in.
- *The Deadly Tower*, a 1975 television movie starring former child actor Kurt Russell in an early adult role, was a faithful recreation of the events in Austin, Texas.

REFERENCES:

- *Murder Casebook* (1990), Marshall Cavendish Ltd, London
- MacLeod, Marlee (2005), *Lost Innocence*
- *www.crimelibrary.com*

1968
Martin Luther King Jr Assassinated

FACT FILE

CRIME: Murder
VICTIM: Rev. Martin Luther King Jnr (1929-1968)
DATE: 4 April 1968
PLACE: Memphis, Tennessee (USA)
PERPETRATOR: James Earl Ray (1928-1998)
SENTENCE: 99 years' imprisonment

In August 1963, the Reverend Martin Luther King Jnr led a march to Washington, DC, to demonstrate the commitment of the American people—of all creeds and religions—to seek equal rights in every facet of American society. King was named *Time* magazine's 'Person of the Year' in 1963 and, a few months later, received the 1964 Nobel Peace Prize. King then threw himself into new causes—voter registration in Selma, Alabama—which led to the famous 'freedom march' from Selma to Montgomery—domestic poverty, Chicago slums and the war in Vietnam as well as factions within the equal rights movement. He was planning another massive march on Washington—'a demonstration of such intensity and size' that Congress would have to finally take notice of the nation's poor—when he was shot and killed in Memphis, Tennessee, on 4 April 1968.

Martin Luther King Jnr was born in Atlanta, Georgia, in 1929 and graduated from Crozer Theological Seminary in Chester, Pennsylvania, in 1953. Granted his doctorate two years later upon completing his dissertation, he became pastor of the Dexter Avenue Baptist Church in Montgomery, Alabama, at a time when the local black community was boycotting local bus companies in protest at the South's strict code of social segregation. The boycott lasted 382 days and brought Dr King and the civil rights movement to the attention of the entire world. King was arrested and his home was bombed, but ultimately the Supreme Court declared bus segregation to be unconstitutional and outlawed racial segregation on public transportation. It was the first of many important victories for the articulate, quietly spoken minister.

After several high-profile victories in the South, King was stung by the criticism directed at him by militant blacks in the North, especially Malcolm X, who could not see the benefit of peaceful, prayerful protest in the face of continued discrimination, injustice and violence. When King attempted to form a new coalition of equal support for civil rights and the peace movement, he also met with criticism from within his own ranks that he was spreading resources—and himself—far too thinly. In early 1968 he was invited to Memphis, Tennessee, to address striking sanitation workers. It was a minor cause in the scheme of things, but for Marin Luther King there were no small causes, only just ones.

On 4 April 1968, Martin Luther King was shot and killed as he stood on the balcony of the black-owned Lorraine Hotel. He was talking to Ralph Abernathy and Jesse Jackson at 6.01 pm when he was struck in the neck and died at the scene soon after. Almost perversely for a man of peace, but in scenes not uncommon in the history of humankind, King died a violent death and his passing caused a wave of destruction in more than 60 major cities across the United States.

On 8 June 1968, 40-year-old escaped convict James Earl Ray was captured at London's Heathrow Airport carrying a forged Canadian passport. It was alleged that Ray was a segregationist and had killed Dr King when the opportunity presented itself because of the civil rights leader's profile in the South. Positioning himself in a window of a rooming-house bathroom, the former US army marksman had a clear view of the balcony outside King's room and fired a .30 calibre Remington Gamemaster Model 760 rifle. On 10 March 1969, on the advice of his lawyer and in order to avoid the death penalty, Ray pleaded guilty to killing Dr King and was sentenced to 99 years in prison. Three days later he sacked his lawyer and claimed that a mysterious figure named 'Raoul' (later Raul) had framed him. There was an elaborate FBI-led conspiracy, it was alleged, and James Earl Ray was merely a 'patsy'. The 'conspiracy theory' had a familiar ring to it, but few were buying. James Earl Ray maintained this stance until his death in 1998.

HISTORICAL AND SOCIAL SIGNIFICANCE:

- Shortly before his death, Ray met with King's son, Dexter, and told him that he did not shoot his father, but may have been 'partially responsible without knowing it'. The King family believed him.
- On 9 December 1999, a Memphis jury handed down a verdict that King's assassination was the result of a conspiracy rather than the act of lone gunman James Earl Ray. However, it did not exonerate Ray.
- In 2000, the US Justice Department stated that it had uncovered no reliable evidence of a conspiracy being behind the 1968 assassination of Martin Luther King Jnr.

REFERENCES:

- BBC Online (4 April 1968), *On This Day, www.bbc.co.uk*
- *House Select Committee On Assassinations: Investigation of the Assassination of Martin Luther King, Jnr*
- *www.parascope.com*
- *Ray's death won't end assassination conspiracy* (23 April 1998), *www.cnn.com*

1968
Robert F. Kennedy Assassinated

FACT FILE

CRIME: Assassination
VICTIM: Robert Francis Kennedy, aged 42
DATE: 6 June 1968
PLACE: Los Angeles, California (USA)
PERPETRATOR: Sirhan Sirhan (b. 1944)
SENTENCE: Death, commuted to life imprisonment

The assassination of Robert Kennedy in June 1968, almost five years after the death of his brother John and just two months after the murder of Martin Luther King, raised many questions about American society during the volatile 1960s. It also robbed the country—and potentially the world—of one of its greatest leaders.

Robert Francis Kennedy (1925–1968) was born in Brookline, Massachusetts, the third son of self-made millionaire and later US ambassador to Britain Joseph P. Kennedy. Bobby Kennedy studied at Harvard and at Virginia University Law School before serving in the navy during World War II. During the 1950s—before he was appointed attorney general during the presidency of his older brother, John—he was a member of the Select Committee on Improper Activities, taking on union leaders such as Teamster boss Jimmy Hoffa and busting mob rackets. In 1964, the year after John Kennedy's death, Bobby Kennedy left the White House after disagreeing with the Vietnam War policies of Lyndon Johnson's administration. In 1965, he became the Democratic senator for New York, and when in March 1968 President Johnson announced that he would not seek re-election, the younger Kennedy began his bid for the Democratic Party presidential nomination.

Despite an unapologetically unpopular platform (he spoke out against the war in Vietnam before it became fashionable to do so and advocated support for the poor despite being a multimillionaire), Kennedy pulled away from his closest rivals, Eugene McCarthy and Hubert Humphrey. In South Dakota, Kennedy won 50 per cent of the Democrat vote to Hubert Humphrey's 30 per cent and Eugene McCarthy's 20 per cent. On 4 June 1968, Robert F. Kennedy won the California Primary for the

Democratic nomination with 46 per cent of the vote against McCarthy's 42 per cent, with the remaining 12 per cent shared amongst uncommitted delegates. Just before midnight, he delivered what was to be his final speech at his campaign headquarters in the Embassy Ballroom of the Ambassador Hotel in Los Angeles:

> *I think we can end the divisions within the United States. What I think is quite clear is that we can work together in the last analysis … We are a great country, an unselfish country and a compassionate country. And I intend to make that my basis for running.*

Against the wishes of his main bodyguard, Bill Barry, Kennedy turned away from the crowd of supporters and disappeared through a gold curtain behind the rostrum, using a back exit via the hotel kitchen to get to the pressroom. As the presidential candidate walked through the kitchen passageway and mingled with his staff, newsmen, supporters and hotel workers, no-one noticed the small man standing beside an ice-making machine. There had been no attempt by security to screen anyone, as it was never certain that Kennedy would even come that way. No police were inside the building at the time of the shooting.

At 12.23 am on 5 June, as Robert Kennedy paused to shake the hand of dishwasher Jesus Perez, Jordanian immigrant Sirhan Bishara Sirhan steaded his elbow on a stainless steel bench and shot at Kennedy from just over a metre (4 feet) away. Kennedy was struck behind the ear and in the armpit, and fell to the ground while he still held Perez's outstretched hand. Eight men, including author George Plimpton, Kennedy aide Jack Gallivan, former Olympian Rafer Johnson, and actor and former LA Rams linesman Rosie Grier, wrestled the gunman to ground as he continued to fire. Johnson knocked the gun out of the man's hand and placed it in his pocket. Some supporters tried to harm the gunman, but Kennedy's bodyguards protected him on the ground as someone screamed, 'We don't want another Oswald!'

Ethel Kennedy knelt over her husband's semiconscious body as the senator strained to speak. Someone put ice on the back of Kennedy's head to stop the bleeding and made a pillow for his head with the jacket of a blue suit. Kennedy's tie and shoes were taken off as his hand clutched a rosary to his chest. Twenty-three minutes after the shooting, Kennedy was taken by ambulance to the Good Samaritan Hospital. Five other victims were also transported to hospital, but only Kennedy was mortally wounded.

Robert Kennedy was operated on later that day. Of the two hollow-nosed bullets that struck him, one had travelled through his armpit and lodged in his neck. The second had penetrated his skull and spread on impact. After an operation lasting

3 hours and 40 minutes, Kennedy was kept in intensive care on the fifth floor of the hospital. The following day, surrounded by family and friends, he died there at 1.44 am—some 25 hours after being shot.

Why? The second Kennedy assassination of the decade was almost expected—given the cold acceptance of the nature of political life in a gun-happy American society. The 24-year-old assassin was allegedly upset by Kennedy's support of Israel during the Six Day War the previous year. (He was found to be carrying a newspaper clipping outlining Kennedy's pro-Israeli views, and 5 June was the first anniversary of the Arab–Israeli war.) Sirhan was a member of a middle-class Greek Orthodox family who had immigrated to the United States from Jordan on a United Nations-sponsored program, and the murder weapon was eventually linked to his brother Munir.

But as had been the case following the deaths of John F. Kennedy and Martin Luther King, Sirhan's act of madness spawned its own conspiracy theories. Some say that Sirhan was brainwashed either by a foreign or US government agency; others said that he was a dupe and that the real killers were the Mafia. Sirhan Sirhan was found guilty on one count of murder and five counts of attempted murder and sentenced to death, but this was commuted to life imprisonment.

Robert Francis Kennedy's body was flown back to New York for full funeral rites at New York's St Patrick's Cathedral on Fifth Avenue on 9 June 1968. A special 21-car train bore the senator, his family (his pregnant wife, Ethel, would later bear him an eleventh child) and his supporters south to Washington, DC, where he was buried in Arlington War Cemetery. Thousands lined the tracks to witness RFK's final journey.

HISTORICAL AND SOCIAL SIGNIFICANCE:

- RFK's death continued the tragedy of the Kennedy family. He was the fourth child buried by his parents, Joseph and Rose—after Joe Jnr (1944), Kathleen (1948) and Jack (1963). Ethel Kennedy's parents both died in a plane crash, as did her brother George.
- Robert Kennedy was buried 14 metres (47 feet) away from the headstone of the grave of his brother John. RFK was buried at 11 pm, the first night-time burial at Arlington War Cemetery.
- Republican candidate Richard M. Nixon successfully won the presidential race the following November, setting the United States on the path of international (Vietnam) and national (Watergate) disaster. Interestingly, Nixon composed and delivered his famous 1952 'Checkers' speech from inside the same hotel where RFK was shot.

REFERENCES:

- BBC Online (6 June 1968), *On This Day, www.bbc.co.uk*
- 'For Perspective and Determination', *Time* magazine, 14 June 1968
- *RFK Assassination, www.crimelibrary.com*

1968

The Krays: Brothers in Arms

FACT FILE

CRIME: Murder
VICTIMS: George Cornell and Jack ('The Hat') McVitie
DATE: 1966–67
PLACE: London (England)
PERPETRATORS: Ronnie Kray (1933–1995); Reggie Kray (1933–2000); Charlie Kray (1926–2000)
SENTENCE: Ronnie and Reggie Kray were sentenced to life (30 years). Charlie Kray was sentenced to 10 years for being an accessory to murder

Despite their feared reputations, the Krays—twins Ronnie and Reggie and their older brother, Charlie—were as much a part of 'Swinging London' in the sixties as the British spy scandals and the Beatles. The Krays rubbed shoulders with 'establishment' figures and appeared to be just as glamorous as the pop stars and actors who frequented the twins' clubs. But just as the sixties came to a spectacular end, so too did the reign of the 'kings of the London underworld'—when the Krays were jailed for murder in 1969.

When identical twins Ronnie and Reggie Kray were born in 1933 to Charlie and Violet Kray of Hoxton, in London's East End, their brother, Charlie, was seven years old. The Krays moved from Hackney to Bethnal Green in 1939. But when their father, Charlie, was drafted into World War II he quickly deserted and spent the next decade on the run. The Krays grew up hard, bitter and with a strong anti-authoritarian streak. The influence of their grandfather, former bare-knuckle boxer Jimmy 'Cannonball' Lee, led all three boys to take up amateur boxing. Elder brother Charlie was a natural athlete and a keen boxer, but it was the twins who really took to the sport.

Ronnie Kray was the 'dominant' twin but suffered severe mood swings and engaged in bouts of violence outside of the boxing ring. He was also homosexual at a time when homosexuality was not accepted in social circles, least amongst hardened criminals. Reggie, the quieter of the two and secretly bisexual, was just as ruthless in disposing of opponents in and out of the boxing ring. In 1951, the twins were called up for national service, but were dishonourably discharged for assaulting a police officer while AWOL and attacking prison guards while awaiting court martial in a military prison in Somerset. Once discharged, they were free to pursue their

The Wild Bunch with Harry 'Sundance Kid' Langbaugh (left) and Robert LeRoy 'Butch Cassidy' Parker (right), Texas, 1855.

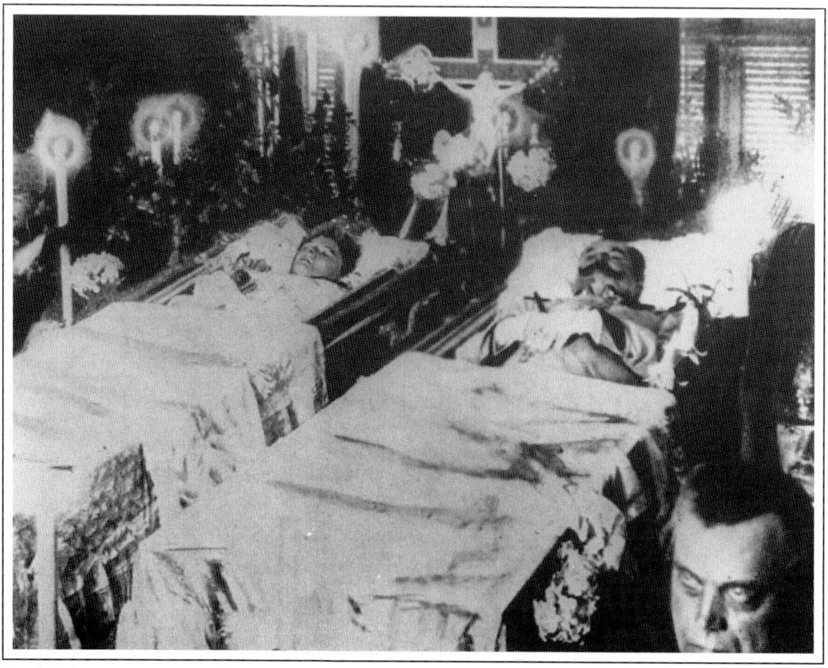

Archduke Franz Ferdinand and his wife Sophie lying in state after their assassination in Sarajevo, 1914.

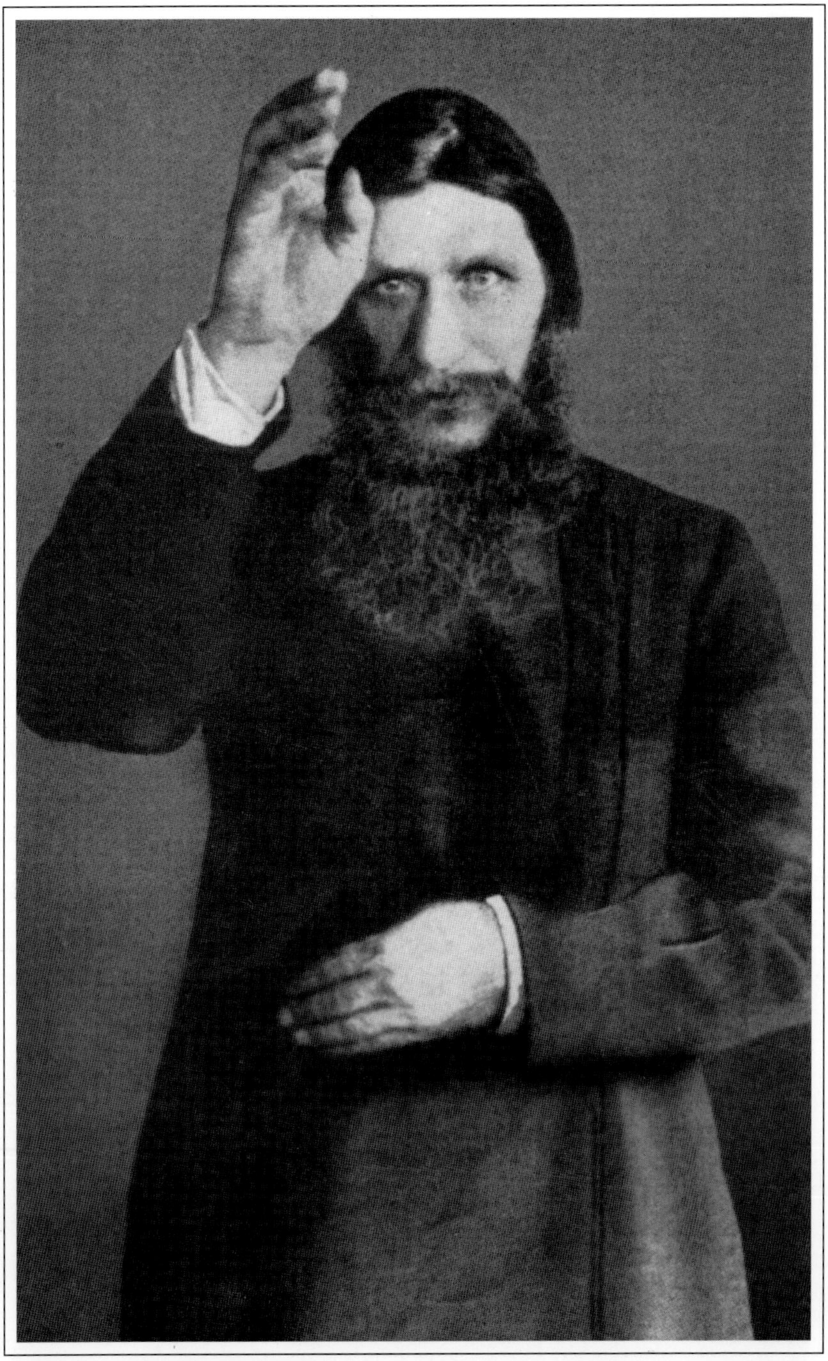

Grigori Efimovich Rasputin, mystic and spiritual advisor to the Russian court, in 1905.

Gangsters Bonnie Parker and Clyde Barrow loved the camera and frequently posed for it. They were ambushed by Texas Rangers and killed in 1934.

The remains of serial murderer John Christie's fifth victim are removed from 10 Rillington Place, London, 1953.

The kitchen of serial murderer Ed Gein where parts of his victims' bodies were found in 1957. His devotion to his dead mother was the inspiration for Hitchcock's movie *Psycho*.

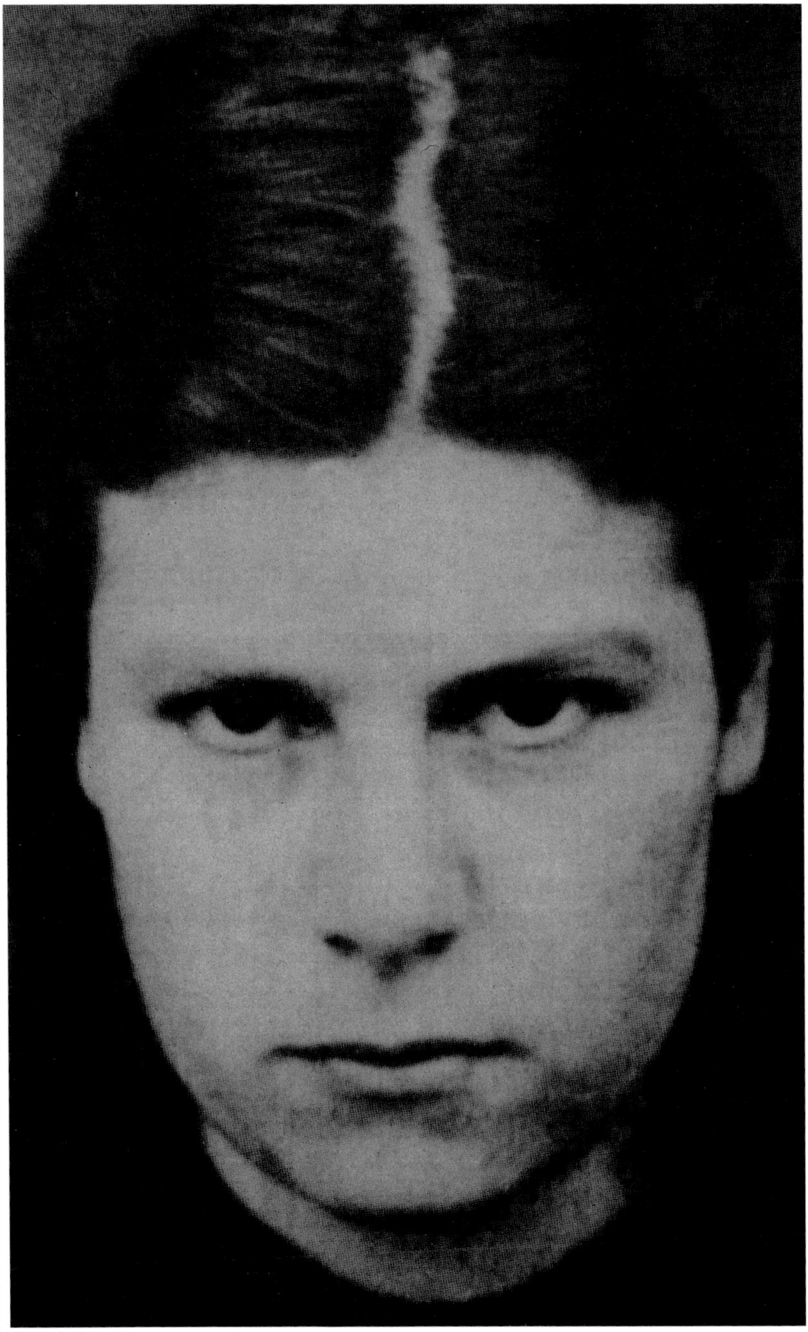

'Heavenly creature' Pauline Parker who, with her close friend Juliet Hulme, murdered her mother in Christchurch, New Zealand in 1954.

The burnt-out car of slain civil rights workers James Chaney, Andrew Goodman and Mickey Schwerner near Philadelphia, Mississippi, 1964.

Russian Andrei Chickatilo, considered the worst serial killer of modern times, was tried and executed in 1994.

Charles Manson is led from the courthouse after a hearing on chargers of possessing stolen property, Los Angeles, 1969.

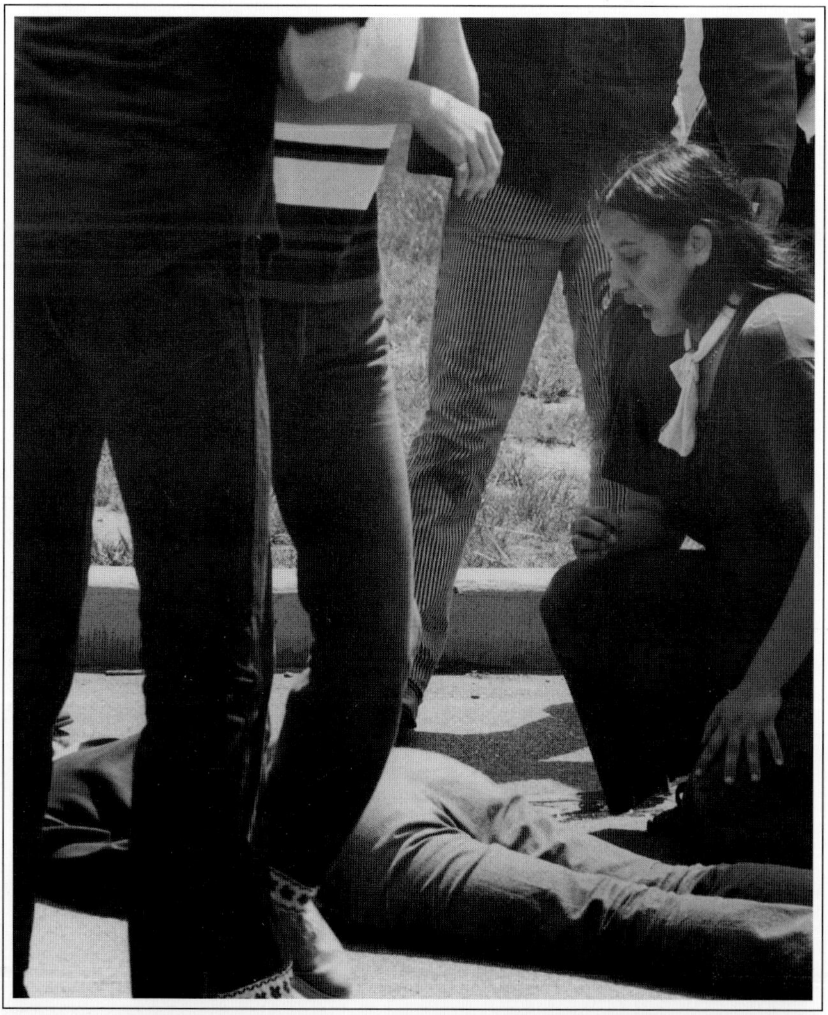

Student Mary Ann Vecchio kneels over the body of fellow student Jeffrey Miller, shot during an anti-war demonstration at Kent State University, Ohio, 1970.

dual careers of boxing and petty crime, but their reputations as fearless standover men made them a bigger success in London's underworld than in their chosen sport.

Imposing figures as they were, the Krays surrounded themselves with a group of Cockney and Scottish criminals they called 'The Firm'. Graduating from standover rackets to career criminals, the Krays opened a billiard hall on Mile End Road before establishing their own nightclub, The Double R, in Bow Road in 1957. Their elder brother, Charlie, remained in the background of the family organisation—after managing the twins' boxing careers he looked after the nightclub accounts—and was in awe of his brothers' 'intense' relationship. However, whenever they were in trouble, they would turn to their older brother for help. Charlie Kray was clever, but never violent. All he had to say was his last name and people would do what he wanted.

In the 1950s Ronnie Kray had been certified insane while serving a prison sentence but had successfully exploited a loophole in the law and applied to be transferred to another prison after the medical certificate lapsed.

In 1966, a taunt by fellow criminal George Dixon about Ronnie Kray almost cost Dixon his life. When Dixon called Ronnie 'a fat poof' at the Blind Beggar pub in Bethnal, it was not the type of personal slur Kray could forgive. Ronnie Kray pulled a gun on Dixon but the revolver jammed and Kray allowed him to live. George Cornell was not so lucky; Ronnie Kray shot him dead in front of stunned customers at the Blind Beggar for allegedly talking to a rival gang about the twins' 'business interests'. Such was the code of silence amongst the criminal community that police could not gather enough evidence to charge anyone with the crime. However, another ruthless, careless and pointless murder the following year would prove the Krays' undoing.

In 1967 Ronnie Kray talked his brother into killing an associate named Jack ('The Hat') McVitie. Ronnie and Reggie stabbed McVitie to death in the latter's flat. After McVitie tried to escape the attack by throwing himself out of the window, Reg Kray allegedly nailed McVitie to his wooden floor with one stab but the reality was much worse – according to his autobiography, Reggie drove a carving knife into McVitie's face, just below the eye. His brother Charlie and some other associates allegedly disposed of the body, but no trace of McVitie was ever found. Detective Inspector Leonard ('Nipper') Read of Scotland Yard was determined to bring the Krays to justice (they were already suspected of being involved in the 'breaking out' of Frank 'The Mad Axeman' Mitchell from Dartmoor Prison in 1966), and his team began dismantling the East End 'wall of silence' that protected the brothers. Although their case was weak, police arrested the Krays on 9 May 1968 in the hope that taking them off the streets would encourage people to speak out. The move worked.

In early 1969, the Krays and eight members of 'The Firm' stood trial for the murders of George Cornell and Jack McVitie. After a 39-day trial, the longest and most expensive trial ever at the No. 2 Court at London's Old Bailey, the jury deliberated for 6 hours and 55 minutes before finding Ronnie and Reggie Kray guilty of murder. Ronnie Kray and John Barrie were convicted of murdering George Cornell. The twins, along with Ronald Bender, and Christopher and Anthony Lambrianou were found guilty of McVitie's murder. Charlie Kray and Freddie Foreman were sentenced to ten years' jail for being accessories to McVitie's murder. Cornelius Whitehead was sentenced to seven years, and Albert Donaghue, the only member of the gang to plead guilty, got two years. Anthony Barrie was found not guilty and was released.

Ronnie and Reggie Kray were sentenced to a minimum of 30 years in jail—the longest sentence ever handed out at the Old Bailey. In 1982, the twins were allowed to attend the funeral of their mother, Violet, who had died of cancer. The brothers arrived separately and heavily guarded—Ronnie Kray was brought from Broadmor Hospital for the legally insane, while Reggie was brought from Pankhurst Prison on the Isle of Wight, where he was held as a maximum security Category 'A' prisoner. Ronnie Kray died of a heart attack in 1995, while Reggie served more than the minimum 30-year sentence before he was diagnosed with cancer and released in August 2000.

Reggie, who had converted to Christianity and now wanted to be remembered as a 'poet and philosopher', wanted to finish his life as a free man. The former East End criminal got his wish, but enjoyed only 35 days of freedom before dying on 1 October 2000, at the age of 66.

HISTORICAL AND SOCIAL SIGNIFICANCE:

- In 1990, a decade after his release, Charlie Kray brokered the film rights to the family's story. *The Krays*, starring pop group Spandau Ballet's Gary and Martin Kemp, was a success, but Charlie squandered the money and returned to a life of crime. In 1997 he was jailed for trying to import £69 million worth of illegal drugs and died in prison in 2000—five months before the death of his last surviving brother.

REFERENCES:

- BBC Online (4 March 1969), *On This Day, www.bbc.co.uk*
- Kray, Reg and Ron, with Reg Dinenage, *Our Story* (1988) Pan Book, London
- *The Krays, www.eastlondonhistory.com*

1969
Teddy Kennedy and Chappaquiddick

FACT FILE

CRIME: Leaving the scene of an accident
VICTIM: Mary Jo Kopechne, aged 29
DATE: 18 July 1969
PLACE: Chappaquiddick, Martha's Vineyard, Massachusetts (USA)
PERPETRATOR: Senator Edward ('Teddy') Kennedy (b. 1932)
SENTENCE: Two months' imprisonment (suspended)

Born in 1932, Edward ('Teddy') Moore Kennedy was the youngest of four sons and five daughters born to Joseph and Rose Kennedy. After studying at Harvard and at Virginia University Law School, he was admitted to the bar in 1959. Teddy Kennedy was elected Democratic senator for Massachusetts at the young age of 30 in 1962—the position vacated by his brother John F. Kennedy when he became president. The youngest Kennedy was an important part of the mythical Kennedy political 'dynasty', but even more pressure was placed on the last of the family line following the assassinations of his brothers John (1963) and Bobby (1968). Then, on the night of 18 July 1969, Teddy Kennedy's political destiny changed forever.

Senator Teddy Kennedy delivered the eulogy for his brother Bobby at St Patrick's Cathedral, New York, on 8 June 1968.

A year later, on the night of 18 July 1969, Kennedy, some of his slain brother's campaign staff and several of his own staff held a party on Chappaquiddick Island, Massachusetts, as part of the Edgartown Regatta off Martha's Vineyard.

Teddy planned to race the *Victura* (his brother Bobby's boat) and his boat the *Resolute* during the weekend. The six men and six women rented a small cottage on Chappaquiddick Island, which was separated from Martha's Vineyard by a 200-metre (655-foot) channel of water, ostensibly to reminisce about working for Kennedy's brother Bobby the previous year.

At about 11.15 pm that night, Kennedy decided to return to his motel in Edgartown and took with him 29-year-old secretary Mary Jo Kopechne, who had asked for a lift back to town. En route to the dock to catch a ferry back to Edgartown, Kennedy took a wrong turn and drove onto a narrow wooden bridge.

Kennedy's 1968 Oldsmobile went over the side of the bridge, and he and his female passenger were submerged in a tidal lake. Kennedy somehow struggled out of the car, but despite his attempts during the next 20 minutes, he could not reach Mary Jo Kopechne. He then walked back to the cottage where the party was being held and raised the alarm. Two of his staff, lawyers Joe Gargan and Paul Markham, went to the scene and frantically dived in the water for 45 minutes, hoping to rescue the girl from the car. Teddy Kennedy sat on the side of the bridge 'shocked and in a state of disbelief'.

Gargan and Markham drove Kennedy to the ferry so that he could return to Edgartown and report the accident, but when the ferry did not arrive, Kennedy decided to dive into the water and swim the channel. The US senator was disoriented and was rambling about the Kennedy 'curse', but he made a commitment to his staff to report the matter once he stepped ashore in Edgartown. Instead, inexplicably, he went to his room and did not report the accident for another ten hours. The girl's body was recovered the following morning at about the same time that Kennedy was making a police report in the presence of Paul Markham.

For the next week Teddy Kennedy retained his silence about the accident, but there was growing speculation that he would be charged with leaving the scene of an accident, failing to report an accident or, at worst, criminal manslaughter. Kennedy made it clear to police that he had not been drinking that night; he had been injured and was in a state of shock. (Although the nature of his injuries was never made clear, Kennedy later attended the girl's funeral, accompanied by his pregnant wife, Joan, wearing a neck brace.) Six days later Kennedy pleaded guilty to leaving the scene of an accident—meaning that he would not have to give evidence—and was given a two-month jail sentence, which was immediately suspended.

In a nationally televised speech, Kennedy accepted responsibility for the accident, but was unable to explain why he had not reported it. Most newspapers doubted Kennedy's story—was he just buying time to save his political career? Although he kept his seat in Congress, the public backlash all but meant that Teddy Kennedy would never take his place in the White House.

REFERENCES:

- *American Rhetoric: Ted Kennedy: Chappaquiddick Speech, www.americanrhetoric.com*
- BBC Online (18 June 1969), *On This Day, www.bbc.co.uk*
- *The Truth About Chappaquiddick* (2000), *www.ytedk.com*

1969
The Manson 'Family'

FACT FILE

CRIME: Serial murder
VICTIMS: Gary Hinman, aged 34; Steven Parent, aged 18; Sharon Tate, aged 26; Jay Sebring, aged 35; Abigail Folger, aged 25; 'Voytek' Frykowski, aged 35; Leno LaBianca, aged 44; Rosemary LaBianca, aged 38
DATES: 27 July to 9 August 1969
PLACE: Los Angeles, California (USA)
PERPETRATORS: Susan Atkins (b. 1948); Bobby Beausoleil (b. 1947); Clem Crogan (b. 1948); Linda Kasabian (b. 1947); Patricia Krenwinkel (b. 1948); Charles Manson (b. 1934); Leslie Van Houten (b. 1951); Charles ('Tex') Watson (b. 1946)
SENTENCE: Death sentences for Atkins, Crogan, Krenwinkel, Manson, Van Houten and Watson were commuted to life imprisonment. Kasabian turned police witness and was granted immunity from prosecution. Bobby Beausoleil was sentenced to death for his part in the Hinman murder but this was commuted to life imprisonment

---

The 1960s—the decade of peace and love—ended with a shuddering jolt with the murders of actress Sharon Tate and four other people in the Hollywood hills on the night of 8 August 1969. At first, the deaths of Leno and Rosemary LaBianca the following night in the nearby suburb of Los Feliz were not linked to the Tate murders (despite some disturbing similarities), but through a circumstantial series of events, a commune of 'hippies' living in the Los Angeles desert were implicated in the crimes. Their leader, a charismatic ex-con and failed musician, was later found to be responsible for ordering the murder spree. His name was Charles Manson.

By 1967, Charlie Manson had spent more than half his 32 years in jail. Surrounding himself with a band of gypsy-like misfits, Manson used acid (LSD) and sex to control the 'family' of disaffected young women and disparate young men. Two of the women even bore children for him. 'The Family' set up residence at the Spahn 'Movie' Ranch in the Santa Susana Mountains—a former cowboy set used for the television shows *Bonanza* and *Gunsmoke*—before moving to Barker Ranch in Death Valley. Manson talked himself into the home of Beach Boy Dennis Wilson and actually wrote the B-side of a Beach Boy single, but record producer Terry Melcher stopped short of offering the budding musician a record deal—a move that embittered Manson.

In July 1969, Manson sent three of his 'family' to convince 34-year-old music teacher Gary Hinman to part with some of the $20 000 drug money that was rumoured to be hidden in his Malibu home. One of the trio, a former porn star named Bobby Beausoleil, murdered Hinman while Susan Atkins and Mary Brunner looked for the money, cleaned the home of prints (all, except one) and wrote 'Political Piggy' on the wall above the victim's head. They also crudely drew a cat's paw—the symbol of the Black Panther movement. In Manson's deranged mind, he was 'Jesus Christ' and he was going to spark a race war that he termed 'Helter Skelter' after a song on the Beatles' *White* album.

On the hot summer's night of 8 August 1969, Manson ordered four members of his family—Charles ('Tex') Watson, Susan Atkins, Patricia Krenwinkel and Linda Kasabian—to go to 10050 Cielo Drive in the Hollywood Hills and kill everyone in the house. The home was formally rented by Terry Melcher but was now occupied by actress Sharon Tate, the American wife of famed Polish director Roman Polanski. Tate, who was eight months pregnant, had invited celebrity hairdresser Jay Sebring, coffee heiress Abigail Folger and her boyfriend 'Voytek' Frykowski, to stay with her while her husband was in London.

Manson's family arrived shortly after midnight and, after cutting the telephone wires, climbed the security fence. They hid in bushes as a car drove out the driveway, and as 18-year-old Steve Parent stopped at the gates, Watson shot him four times with a huge Buntline Special revolver. Parent was visiting a friend, Will Garretson, in the mansion's guesthouse and didn't even know the occupants of the house. Incredibly, Garretson did not hear anything that night because he was playing his stereo loudly and was oblivious to the mayhem that unfolded.

Watson, Atkins and Krenwinkel broke into the main house while Linda Kasabian sat in the group's battered car. Startled by the intruders (Abigail Folger thought they were Sharon's friends at first and smiled at them from her bed), the occupants were tied together with a long nylon rope. Sebring was shot as he lunged for Watson's weapon, and Frykowski was stabbed by the women and shot by Watson before making a dash for the door. Watson then beat him with his pistol, breaking the handle, before Folger ran outside.

While Watson stabbed Sebring to death, Krenwinkel followed Folger outside and stabbed her to death on the lawn. Frykowski was stabbed to death by Watson while Atkins turned her attention to Sharon Tate, who was tied to Sebring, stabbing her to death as she pleaded for her life and that of her unborn baby. The killers then scrawled the word 'Pig' on the front door, leaving a bloodied handprint behind.

Later that night, Charles Manson went back to the house to see his 'family's' handiwork, and wiped the place clean of prints. He also looked for a lost knife—

Atkins's murder weapon—but it had fallen down the side of the sofa. It was later recovered by crime scene detectives.

The following night, Leno LaBianca and his wife, Rosemary, were chosen at random to be 'the family's' next victims. Manson, Watson, Atkins and Kasabian were joined by two new recruits—17-year-old Leslie Van Houten and Steve ('Clem') Grogan—but Kasabian again sat in the car and refused to take part. After Manson left the house, Leno La Bianca was stabbed to death in his pyjamas while his wife was murdered in her bedroom. Leno La Bianca had the word 'WAR' scratched into his abdomen with a carving fork, while Rosemary La Bianca was stabbed a total of 57 times. 'Death to Pigs' and 'Healter Skelter' [sic] were written on the walls in blood.

Because the two crimes were investigated by rival factions of the Los Angeles police force, information was not shared between the two teams. When a local boy found the murder gun and turned it over to police, it was not passed on to investigators. However, detectives investigating the murder of Gary Hinman were struck by the use of the word 'pig' in each crime. It was not until members of 'the family' were arrested on 12 October for car theft (Manson's group stole Volkswagens and converted them into dune buggies to sell) that detectives were able to link the crimes.

When Susan Atkins bragged to her cell mates about the Tate–LaBianca killings, police offered her immunity from prosecution to testify against Manson. When she stalled, they shifted their attention to Linda Kasabian, who eventually told police the details of the two nights of murder.

During the trial, which started on 15 June 1970, Manson's followers—including Lynette ('Squeaky') Fromme, who was later jailed for life for firing a gun at President Gerald Ford in 1975—followed his every move, shaving their heads when he did and even carving swastikas into their foreheads. After the longest trial in US history, the members of the group were found guilty and sentenced to death, but in 1972 the state of California revoked the death penalty—before Charles Manson or his 'family' of murderers could be executed.

REFERENCES:

- Bugliosi, Vincent (1974), *Helter Skelter*, Arrow Books, London
- *Murder Casebook* (1990), Marshall Cavendish, London

1969
The Zodiac Killer

FACT FILE

CRIME: Serial murder
VICTIMS: David Faraday, aged 18; Betty Lou Jensen, aged 18; Darlene Ferrin, aged 22 Cecilia Ann Shepard, aged 22; Paul Stine, aged 29; Michael Mageau and Bryan Hartnell were seriously injured.
DATES: 20 December 1968 to 11 October 1969
PLACE: San Francisco, California (USA)
PERPETRATOR: Unknown

In the final years of the 1960s, five people were randomly selected and murdered by an unknown killer in San Francisco. The killer called himself 'Zodiac' and taunted the police for years with letters that mocked their failure to capture him. Although the murders ceased in 1969, the unknown killer stayed in communication with the media and the San Francisco police department—even sending them a Halloween card—for the next decade. Despite claiming responsibility for as many as 37 deaths (the official number is 5) the Zodiac killer was never captured.

On 20 December 1968, teenagers David Faraday and Betty Lou Jensen were parked in a lover's lane in the Vallejo Hills above San Francisco when shots were fired into their car. Jensen rushed from the car as the gunman leaned inside and shot her boyfriend in the head. The terrified girl got only 10 metres (32 feet) away from the car before the gunman caught up to her and fired five shots into her body. The gunman then escaped in his own car. A woman motorist noticed the bodies on the ground and drove to the next town (Benica) to alert local police. David Faraday was still alive when the police arrived at the crime scene but died later in hospital.

The crime was motiveless—neither victim had been robbed or sexually molested—and the police investigation failed to identify anyone who had a grudge against the young lovers. Then, on 4 July 1969, the gunman struck again.

Just 3 kilometres (2 miles) away from where Faraday and Jensen lost their lives, 22-year-old waitress Darlene Ferrin was sitting in a car with a boyfriend, Mike Mageau, just before midnight when a car pulled alongside them. The car moved away and then returned, stopping on the other side of the stationary car with its headlights shining on the couple. Mageau assumed it was the police, and as he instinctively reached for his licence, gunfire rang out. Mageau was hit in the neck and back, but Ferrin was fatally wounded. After firing four shots into the car, the unknown gunman drove away.

A few minutes later, a man contacted Vallejo police and left a phone message about a murder on the Columbus Parkway: 'You will find the kids in a brown car. They are shot with a .9-millimetre Luger. I also killed those kids last year. Goodbye.' When the police arrived, they found Ferrin dead but Mageau still alive. Mageau was able to give a description of his attacker—a man with a round face and brown, wavy hair.

The killer was determined to let police know what he had done. On 1 August, three letters were sent to local newspapers confessing to the three murders and including a description of the ammunition used. Each letter also contained part of a coded message. Code experts who combined the three parts of the message could not decipher the code, but Salinas schoolteacher Dale Harden and his wife were successful. In part the message was: 'I like killing because it is so much fun … it is more fun than killing wild game in the forrest [sic] because man is the most dangeroue [sic] animal of all.'

The message was deliberately misspelt to confuse the police, but it gave an eerie insight into the killer's psyche. The letters were published to try to draw information from the public, but the following month a newspaper editor received the following note: 'Dear Editor, this is the Zodiac speaking …' The San Francisco serial killer had at last been christened. There was also a symbol on one of his letters—a circle with a cross inside it, not unlike the sights of a rifle—that would become the killer's calling card.

On the afternoon of 27 September, Bryan Hartnell and Cecilia Ann Shepard, two Seventh Day Adventist students, were picnicking at Lake Berryessa, 21 kilometres (13 miles) north ofVallejа, when they were approached by a hooded man. The man ordered Shepard to tie her boyfriend with clothesline that he had brought with him, and then tied her. He then stabbed the pair in a frenzied attack after telling them both that he was going to kill them. Thinking that the pair was dead, the man drew his symbol on their car, but he was interrupted by a fisherman who heard the victims' screams. Incredibly, Hartnell and Shepard survived the attack, but the 22-year-old girl died two days later without coming out of a coma. Hartnell survived despite the repeated stab wounds to his back and told police that the man also had the same symbol sown on his hood. It was definitely the Zodiac killer.

On 11 October, 29-year-old taxi-driver Paul Stine was shot dead on a busy intersection near the former military facility, the Presidio, in San Francisco. The motive at first appeared to be robbery, but the suspect was logged in by police as being a 'negro male adult'. Police questioned a white, stocky male near the crime scene but allowed him to go because he did not match the suspect. Was this the Zodiac killer? Three days later, the *San Francisco Chronicle* received a letter from the Zodiac killer confessing to the crime. Inside the letter was part of the victim's shirt, which the killer had cut off to verify the crime. 'Zodiac' also claimed responsibility for seven other murders—two more than had been committed—and police tried to link him to earlier murders in 1963 and 1966. That Christmas, high-profile attorney Martin Belli received a card from 'Zodiac' asking for help before he killed again. Inside the card was another piece of Paul Stine's shirt.

Although 'Zodiac' remained in contact with authorities until 1974, he did not commit another crime after the failed abduction of a woman and her baby from a San Francisco freeway in March 1970. Was Zodiac in prison, did he die or was he cured of his need to kill before he was caught? Although a number of suspects were investigated, the SFPD closed the case in April 2004 after 35 years.

The Zodiac murders can almost be called the 'perfect crimes'—if it weren't for so many victims still calling for justice from their graves.

HISTORICAL AND SOCIAL SIGNIFICANCE:

- In 1990, a 'copycat' killer murdered four people in New York City. The man, who mimicked the modus operandi of the Zodiac killer, was identified as Herbiberto Seda, and was captured and jailed.
- The Zodiac killer was the basis of the character 'Scorpio' in the first *Dirty Harry* movie. The climax of the movie involves the hijacking of a school bus. A film based on Robert Graysmith's book *Zodiac* was released in 2007 and focused on the theory that convicted paedophile Arthur Lee Allen (1933–1992) was responsible for the unsolved crimes.

REFERENCES:

- *Murder Casebook* (1990), Marshall Cavendish, London
- Goodyear, Charlie, 'Files Shut on Zodiac's Deadly Trail', *San Francisco Chronicle*, 7 April 2004
- *Zodiac Killer, www.rotten.com*

1970
The Kent State Massacre

FACT FILE

CRIME: Killing of unarmed protestors
VICTIMS: Allison Beth Krause, aged 19; Jeffery Glen Miller, aged 20; Sandra 'Sandy' Lee Scheuer, aged 20; William Knox Schroeder, aged 19; 9 others were injured.
DATE: 4 May 1970
PLACE: Kent State University, Ohio (USA)
PERPETRATORS: Unknown elements of the Ohio State National Guard

During the early months of 1970, American students in colleges and universities held a nationwide student strike against the escalation of the Vietnam War. The previous December, President Nixon had introduced a lottery system of inducting draftees, and for many students the threat of being sent off to a war that they did not believe in was very real. In May, a massive demonstration was held at Kent State University in the small town of Kent, Ohio. Local students were joined by protestors from other colleges, radical 'adult' elements and even local biker groups for the inevitable confrontation. On Monday 4 May, US National Guardsmen fired on a group of unarmed protestors on open ground known at Kent State University as the 'Commons'. Four innocent people were killed in the shooting, sending shockwaves through college campuses, middle America and the world.

On Friday night, Mayday 1970, violence erupted in the streets of Kent after bars closed their doors early in order to avoid trouble. Store windows were smashed, there was some looting, and tensions ran hot throughout the town over the weekend. The following day, Kent mayor Leroy Satrom asked Ohio governor James Rhodes to send in the National Guard when rumours spread that 'revolutionaries' were going to take over the university campus. The National Guard was hastily deployed that evening, and the campus's ROTC (Reserve Officers' Training Corps) building was set alight. (The building was boarded up and already earmarked for demolition.) When the local fire service attempted to put out the blaze, radical elements among the protestors cut the hose lines while others cheered and pelted the firemen, the police and the National Guard with rocks. The following day, Governor Rhodes threatened to declare a state of emergency (he never did) and to ban demonstrations, but he failed to consult the university administration, which wanted to close the university, and further inflamed the situation by comparing the protestors to 'brownshirts … communist[s] … nightriders and … vigilantes'.

On the Sunday night before the major protest, students refused to disperse after holding another rally on the campus, and two people, including a wheelchair-bound Vietnam veteran, were bayoneted when the National Guard broke up a 'sit-in'. On Monday 4 May 1970, a protest was planned for the Commons for 12 noon, by which time the number of protestors had swelled to almost 2000. Just before noon, the National Guard tried to disperse the crowd with tear gas and was pelted by rocks by sections of the protestors.

As a group of 77 National Guardsmen marched through the Commons, they found themselves trapped by the crowd on three sides of a football field. Deciding to withdraw up a hill known as Blanket Hill, the guardsmen again came under 'fire' by rock throwers and were verbally 'attacked' by angry students. When they reached the top of the hill, 29 of the guardsmen turned around and fired 67 shots at the unarmed students.

The Adjunct General of the Ohio National Guard later stated that the firing, which lasted only 13 seconds, started when a 'sniper' shot at them. No sniper was ever identified and not one guardsman was injured, but when the tear gas cleared, four unarmed students were dead and nine others were injured.

Allison Krause was standing among the protestors with her boyfriend, Barry Levine, when the shooting started. The 20-year-old student was shot from a distance of 105 metres (114 yards)—the length of a football field—away from the guardsmen and could not have been considered a serious threat. Nineteen-year-old Jeffrey Miller, who had recently transferred from Michigan State University, was running away from the guardsmen when he was shot through the cheek and killed instantly from a distance of 80 metres (87 yards). The National Guard, who were firing M-1 semi-automatic rifles, which had a range of just over 3 kilometres (2 miles), killed two students who were merely changing classes. Sandra Scheuer, an honours student in speech therapy who played no part in the protests, was shot dead as she walked to class 120 metres (130 yards) away. William Shroeder, who was actually in the Army Reserve and had received a ROTC scholarship, was shot dead with a textbook in his hand.

The shooting of unarmed students caused further waves of protest around American colleges, but there was also the feeling amongst President Nixon's 'silent majority' that the dead students were 'subversives' and deserved what they got. (Vice President Spiro T. Agnew famously commented without a hint of irony that if the protestors had not been throwing rocks they would not have been shot. Nixon commented a few days later, 'What are we going to do to get more respect for the police from our young people?') Kent State was closed for six weeks and

100 000 people marched on Washington, DC, to protest against the war just a week after the student killings.

A President's Commission later reported that the National Guard was ill trained for riot duty, but that although the guardsmen's actions were 'unnecessary, unwarranted and inexcusable', they were not criminally liable because they had felt their own safety threatened. An FBI report debunked the 'sniper' theory and ruled that the National Guard was not surrounded and that no guardsman had been struck by a rock. The state of Ohio later settled out of court in a wrongful death and injury suit and paid $675 000 to the victims. The families of the dead received just $15 000 each.

Kent State was a turning point as far as public opinion was concerned about the war in Vietnam. The US military had turned on its own civilians.

HISTORICAL AND SOCIAL SIGNIFICANCE:

- On 14 May 1970, two black students were shot dead while protesting unarmed at the Jackson State University in Kentucky.
- Singer David Crosby was inspired to write a song about the event. Crosby, Stills, Nash and Young released their song 'Ohio' two weeks after the killings. Harvey Andrews, Dave Brubeck and even the Beach Boys also wrote song tributes.
- Documentaries based on the tragic event include *Confrontation at Kent State* (1970), *Allison* (1971) and *Kent State: The Day the War Came Home* (2000).
- In 1997 David Crosby, Stephen Stills and Graham Nash (without Neil Young) performed at the 27th anniversary concert at Kent State University.

REFERENCES:

- *Recollections of the Kent State Riot, www.okstate.edu*
- Kent State, May 4 1970: *America Kills Its Children, www.spectacle.org*
- *Kent State Shootings, www.wikipedia.org*

1972
Bloody Sunday

FACT FILE

CRIME: Unlawful killing
VICTIMS: Patrick Doherty, aged 31; Gerald Donaghy, aged 17; John Duddy, aged 17; Hugh Gilmour, aged 17; John Johnston, aged 59; Michael Kelly, aged 17; Michael McDaid, aged 20; Kevin McElhinney, aged 17; Bernard McGuigan, aged 41; Gerald McKinney, aged 35; William McKinney, aged 26; William Nash, aged 17; James Wray, aged 22; John Young, aged 17; At least 14 other people were wounded.
DATE: 30 January 1972
PLACE: Derry, Northern Ireland
PERPETRATORS: Unknown members of the British Paratrooper Brigade and the Royal Anglican Regiment

---

On 30 January 1972, a demonstration organised by the Northern Ireland Civil Rights Association gathered in the streets of Derry, Northern Ireland, to protest against the government's 'internment policy' of jailing people thought to have IRA links without charge. Since the previous August, 342 men had been imprisoned without trial. Despite the banning of civil rights marches, thousands of protestors (conservative figures put the number at between 2000 and 3000, while some writers say that the crowd was as large as 15 000) set off from the Bishops Field in Creggan at about 3 pm.

As the march reached a British army barricade at William Street, a minor confrontation occurred between local youths and British troops. The rock throwers were dispersed by water canon, rubber bullets and capsicum spray, and by 4 pm the protestors were starting to disperse. Some time later, British troops opened fire on the crowd. Within minutes, 14 men—half of them teenage youths—were dead.

In 1920, Britain passed the *Government of Ireland Act* and created Northern Ireland by dividing the 6 north-eastern counties from Ireland's 26 other counties. The counties of Fermanagh, Antrim, Tyrone, Derry, Armagh and Down were dominated by 'Unionists'—predominantly Protestants who wanted to remain part of Britain—while the 26 other counties were made up of Irish 'Nationalists' or 'Republicans'. In Northern Ireland, Nationalists found it difficult to win political representation because of gerrymandered electoral boundaries that ensured a Unionist majority. The threat of attack from militant Republicans (as occurred in every decade up until 1962) made the Unionists increasingly uneasy and ensured that power would never be shared.

The Northern Ireland Civil Rights Association was formed in 1967 to demand electoral and social reform. After demonstrators were attacked in the streets of Derry City by local police in October 1968, Northern Ireland prime minister Terrence O'Neill announced a reform package to address local government issues. This angered Unionists and failed to satisfy Nationalists. Rioting exhausted the resources of local police, and in August 1969 British soldiers were deployed. In Belfast, 6 people were killed, 150 houses burnt and 3500 people displaced. The Irish Republican Army, which had been relatively quiet during the mid-1960s, reignited its campaign against British rule in Northern Ireland.

Many of the events of 'Bloody Sunday'—30 January 1972—are still in dispute and are currently being re-investigated by the British government. However, it is known that a group of youths broke away from the main crowd in Derry and tried to break through the barricades built by the British Paratrooper Regiment. The youths attacked the British guard with stones and shouted insults, and although the confrontation was not intense, two people were shot and wounded by British soldiers. John Johnston, aged 59, was shot as he waited in nearby William Street. (He died four days later.) The order to arm with live rounds was given after a report of an IRA sniper was lodged, but when one protestor was killed, the attack on the British soldiers escalated sharply.

When the order was given to mobilise in an arrest operation, British troops turned on the unarmed crowd and chased them down to the Free Derry Corner. Despite a cease-fire order from British headquarters, more than 100 shots were fired into the fleeing crowd by members of the Paratrooper Brigade and the Royal Anglican Regiment. Fourteen civilians were killed. Most of the victims were shot in the back as they ran away or as they stopped and tried to help the injured. Some were shot as they stood beside a rubble barricade—22-year-old James Wray was wounded and then shot again at close range—while other victims were later alleged to have been carrying weapons. Gerald Donaghy was shot in the stomach and taken to a house to be treated. His pockets were turned out in order to identify him, but a later police photograph of the dead man showed nail bombs in his pocket. Not one British soldier was shot during the melee.

The British Paratrooper Brigade stated that it had reacted to the threat of gunmen and nail bombs from within the crowd. However, the official coroner for the City of Londonderry, retired British officer Major Hubert O'Neill, had a different view when he handed down his findings in August 1972. 'The army ran amok that day,' he said. 'They were shooting innocent people ... I would say without hesitation that it was sheer unadulterated murder.' Although the commission of inquiry, under Lord Chief Justice Lord Widgery, established by Edward Heath's government supported the army's account of the day, as early as 1974 the British government's official view was that the victims were 'innocent of any allegation that they were shot whilst handling firearms or explosives'.

Forensic evidence, later discredited, appeared to confirm that some of the victims had handled explosives before their deaths. The same Greiss tests helped to wrongfully convict people suspected of involvement in a spate of IRA retaliation bombings that killed scores of innocent drinkers in English pubs during the 1970s. The 'Birmingham Six' (Paddy Hill, Gerry Hunter, Dick McIlkenny, William Power, John Walker and Hugh Gallaghan), the 'Guildford Four' (Paul Hill, Gerard Conlon, Patrick Armstrong and Carole Richardson) and the 'Maguire Seven' (Annie Maguire, Paddy Maguire, Vincent Maguire, Patrick Maguire, Sean Smyth, Guiseppe Conlon and Pat O'Neill) were released from prison after their convictions were quashed in the 1980s. The soldiers responsible for the murder of 14 civilians would not be so easily found.

The 'Bloody Sunday' massacre was a turning point in the troubled history of Northern Ireland. The deaths of 14 unarmed civilians gave the IRA—and its mainstream offshoot, the Provisional IRA—tremendous support from a new generation of radical, disaffected youth who had grown up with the presence of British troops in their homeland. For the next 20 years, Republican groups waged a 'war' against Unionists and the British that led to the deaths of many more innocent people. Finally, in January 1998, British prime minister Tony Blair set up the Saville Inquiry to review all the available evidence about the 'Bloody Sunday' massacre—but eight years later, a final report is yet to be handed down.

HISTORICAL AND SOCIAL SIGNIFICANCE:

- The massacre was also known as 'Sunday, Bloody Sunday' after the 1971 Peter Finch film, which was not about politics but a failed three-way love affair.
- In 1972, former Beatles John Lennon and Paul McCartney separately recorded pro-Ireland songs. Lennon's 'Sunday, Bloody Sunday' appeared on his *Some Time in New York City* album. McCartney's 'Give Ireland Back to the Irish' was released as a single but banned by the BBC.
- U2's anthemic 'Sunday, Bloody Sunday' was released in 1982. The song is not pro-rebel or pro-British … it is pro-peace.

REFERENCES:

- 'Bloody Sunday', *The Guardian*, 30 January 1970, *www.guardian.co.uk*
- *Background to Bloody Sunday* (2005), *www.bloodysundaytrust.org*
- The Saville Inquiry (1998), www.bloody-sunday-inquiry.org
- *www.bloody-sunday-inquiry.org*

1972
The Watergate Cover-up

FACT FILE

CRIME: Burglary, conspiracy to pervert the course of justice and wiretapping
VICTIMS: The people of the United States
DATE: 17 June 1972
PLACE: Watergate Building (Democratic Party campaign headquarters), Washington, DC (USA)
PERPETRATORS: Richard M. Nixon (1918–1994); E. Howard Hunt (b. 1918); G. Gordon Liddy (b.1930)
WHITEHOUSE BURGLARS
James McCord (b. 1924); Bernard Barker (1924–2006); Eugenio Martinez (b.1924); Frank Sturgis (1924–1993); Virgilio González (b.1925)
SENTENCE: Nixon resigned to avoid impeachment but was pardoned by his presidential successor, Gerald Ford. The Watergate burglars pleaded guilty; Gordon Liddy and Howard Hunt were sentenced to 20 years. Liddy served four and a half years; Hunt served 33 months

---

On 17 June 1972, shortly after 2.30 am, five men were caught breaking into offices of the Democratic National Committee in the Watergate Building in downtown Washington, DC. What made this seemingly commonplace crime unusual was that the five men were white—burglary was a predominantly 'black' crime in a 80 per cent black district—and that the men were wearing business suits (some with US$100 bills stuffed in the pockets) and possessed surgical gloves, walkie-talkies, pen-size tear-gas guns, bugging devices and photographic equipment. When the men were bailed later that Saturday, it was discovered that one of them, James McCord, was the security co-ordinator of President Nixon's re-election committee. Two of the burglars' address books contained the phone number of White House consultant E. Howard Hunt, with the abbreviations 'W House' and 'WH' beside it. This was no usual burglary.

Two *Washington Post* reporters, Carl Bernstein and Bob Woodward, traced a US$25,000 cheque deposited into burglar Bernard Barker's bank account as one donated to President Nixon's re-election campaign fund. This was the first news report to tie the burglary to the White House. By September, the two *Post* reporters revealed that John Mitchell, Nixon's attorney general, controlled a secret Republican slush fund that was used to finance White House-sanctioned intelligence-gathering operations against the Democratic Party leading up to the November 1972 presidential elections. The FBI soon confirmed that the Committee to Re-elect the President (deridingly referred to by the acronym CREEP) had been involved in a highly illegal 'dirty tricks' campaign involving spying, sabotage and political smearing of the Democratic Party. These illegal activities had their origin in the leaking of the 'Pentagon papers' to the *New York Times* in June 1971. Highly classified papers—the defence department's history of just how badly the Vietnam War was going—were leaked by Daniel Ellsberg, a former defence analyst who worked for the US government.

The White House quickly put together a 'plumbers' unit—a group of trained counter-intelligence officers—to 'plug' the leaks and find their source. They did more than that; Howard Hunt and Gordon Liddy authorised a break-in of the office of the psychiatrist who was treating Ellsberg for depression. The information was leaked to discredit Ellsberg before his trial in 1973 for releasing classified information. (The trial was aborted because of government 'misconduct' when it became known that the White House had illegally authorised phone taps on people it suspected of leaking information.) The 'Ellsberg' burglars included the Watergate team of Barker and Martinez.

The irony was that none of the 'dirty tricks' was necessary. Richard Nixon was re-elected to a second term in a landslide victory, defeating the Democrat nominee, George McGovern, by a record 520 college electoral votes to 17. (Libertarian candidate John Hospers garnered 3673 popular votes, which translated to one college vote.) Despite the ease of Nixon's victory, the 'Watergate' story gathered momentum during 1973 and threatened to consume Nixon's second term as president.

Bernstein and Woodward were kept on track in their investigations by an 'informer' close to the White House. Codenamed 'Deep Throat' after an infamous pornography movie of the period, the mole provided 'deep background' material to Bob Woodward, who would meet the unnamed source in an underground garage in Arlington, Virginia. For more than 30 years, the informer's name remained a secret between Woodward, Bernstein and their editor, Ben Bradlee. The White House continued to deny any knowledge of the Watergate burglary and press secretary Ron Ziegler attacked the *Washington Post* for its 'shabby journalism'.

With increasing media coverage, however, White House aides H. R. Halderman and John Ehrlichman, as well as the new attorney general, Richard Kliendienst, resigned over the scandal in April 1973. White House counsel John Dean was fired when he refused to take the blame for the White House 'cover-up' of the burglary and told President Nixon that he was duty-bound to inform any investigation that a 'cover-up' had indeed been discussed. The following June, when the US senate began televised hearings on the Watergate investigation, Dean stated that he had discussed the burglary cover-up with the president on 35 occasions. But a stunning revelation was provided by a former White House appointments secretary, who innocently informed the court that since 1971 an increasingly paranoid and suspicious President Nixon had recorded almost all appointment and telephone conversations in the Oval Office. In taping himself, Nixon had potentially given prosecutors the evidence for his own impeachment for being party to a criminal act.

For the remainder of 1973, President Nixon steadfastly refused to hand over the Oval Office tape recordings to the special prosecutor assigned to the Senate Watergate Committee. When he finally relented and turned over the subpoenaed tapes in December of that year, Nixon could not explain an 18-minute gap on one of the tapes. In February 1974, the special Watergate prosecution team obtained guilty pleas from seven White House aides, while the officers of eight corporations pleaded guilty to charges of making illegal contributions to CREEP. Mitchell, Haldeman and Ehrlichman were three of the members of the White House inner circle to face charges of obstruction of justice and perjury.

Finally, in order to avoid impeachment, Richard Nixon, the 37th president of the United States became the first leader to resign the presidency. On 9 August 1974, Richard Nixon bade a tearful farewell to the White House and retired into private life.

HISTORICAL AND SOCIAL SIGNIFICANCE:

- Woodward and Bernstein's book *All the President's Men* won them the 1974 Pulitzer Prize for Literature.
- In June 2005, former FBI vice president Mark Felt 'outed' himself as 'Deep Throat', the person who informed Bob Woodward of the extent of the Watergate cover-up. The 91-year-old said that he did this because the behaviour of Nixon and his White House staff threatened the independence and the integrity of the FBI.

REFERENCES:

- Bernstein, Carl and Woodwood, Bob (1973), *All the President's Men*, Simon and Shuster, New York
- *Watergate, www.watergate.info*
- *The Watergate Story, www.washingtonpost.com*

1972

The Munich Massacre

FACT FILE

CRIME: Mass murder

VICTIMS: David Berger, aged 28; Anton Fliegerbauer, a German police officer, aged 32; Ze'ev Friedman, aged 28; Yossef Gutfreund, aged 40; Eliezer Halfin, aged 24; Yossef Romano, 31; Amitzur Shapira, aged 40; Kehat Shorr, aged 54; Mark Slavin, aged 18; Andre Spitzer, aged 27; Yacov Springer, aged 51; Moshe Weinberg, 33

DATE: 5 September 1972

PLACE: Munich, West Germany

PERPETRATORS: Luttif Afif; Adnan Al-Gashey; Jamal Al-Gashey; Afif Ahmed Hamid; Khalid Jawad; Yasuf Nazzal; Mohammed Safady; Ahmed Chic Thaa

---

On 5 September 1972, during the Munich Olympic Games, nine Israeli athletes were taken hostage by members of the Palestinian terrorist organisation Black September. Two Israeli athletes were killed in the earlier stages of the attack, but a botched rescue attempt at Fürstenfeldbruck airbase later that night resulted in the deaths of all nine hostages, all but three of the Palestinian terrorists and a German police officer. The 'Munich Massacre' threatened to bring a premature end to the 1972 Olympics, but its impact was more long-term than that. The deaths of innocent sportsmen competing under the banner of peaceful competition was seen as an attack on the civilised world and launched a new era of terrorism in the Middle East.

Israeli athletes had enjoyed a night out from the Olympic village to watch a performance of *Fiddler on the Roof* on 4 September. At 4.30 am the next day, eight Palestinian terrorists scaled a 2-metre (6-foot, 6-inch) fence protecting the compound that housed the apartments being used by Israeli, Uruguayan and Hong Kong athletes. The Palestinians were dressed in tracksuits and carried duffel bags full of weapons. Israeli wrestling referee Yossef Gutfreund was awoken by someone trying to break in to the apartment and used his 130-kilogram (286-pound) frame to block the door and warn the other athletes to escape. Weightlifter Yossef Romano was shot and killed when he grabbed one of the intruder's guns, but two Israeli athletes managed to get away and sound the alarm while eight others hid from the terrorists.

The Palestinians captured nine Israelis—weightlifters David Berger and Ze'ev Friedman, wrestlers Mark Slavin and Eliezer Halfin, and officials Yossef Gutfreund (wrestling), Yacov Springer (weightlifting), Amitzur Shapira (track), Kehat Shorr (shooting) and Andre Spitzer (fencing)—after allowing competitors from Uruguay and Hong Kong to leave unharmed. As the intruders transferred the Israelis to a different room, wrestling coach Moshe Weinberg was killed when he returned to the apartment after the initial attack. Grabbing a fruit knife and attacking three of the terrorists, Weinberg was shot in the chest and head. When authorities arrived, Weinberg's body was thrown from the balcony of one of the apartments as a warning that the terrorists meant business.

The *fedayeen* ('men of sacrifice') terrorists demanded the release of 234 Palestinians jailed in Israel, as well as two in German prisons, or the hostages would be killed. Israel refused to bow to their demands. As the drama unfolded, the image of a masked terrorist, standing on the apartment balcony dressed in black, was televised around the world. The delicate negotiations were shown live on German television, and the terrorists were able to watch as German police took up vantage points on the roof of the apartment and then demanded that they be removed.

Despite the fact that German police had no special hostage training, West German authorities refused Israel's request to allow the deployment of a Special Forces unit in the Olympic village to rescue the hostages. Instead, West Germany tried to negotiate with the Palestinians. Chancellor Willy Brandt and his minister for the interior Hans-Dietrich Genscher offered terrorist spokesman 'Tony' (Yasuf Nazzal) money and safe passage out of Munich, but the reply was unequivocal. 'Money means nothing to us; our lives mean nothing to us.'

Deadlines were pushed back three hours, and then another five hours as negotiations continued. Egyptian Olympic officials offered to act as mediators but the Egyptian government refused to assist in any police action against the terrorists. When the terrorists demanded that they be flown to Cairo with the hostages, Manfred Schreiber, the Munich police commissioner, felt that a rescue attempt before the hostages left Germany was their only hope.

At 10.10 pm two helicopters transported the eight terrorists and eleven hostages to a local airbase, where a vacant Boeing 727 aircraft was waiting. (The terrorists thought they were going to Reims airport.) However, German police were hiding inside the plane and had been ordered to overpower the terrorists once they entered. Five snipers were positioned to shoot the remaining terrorists, but the plan hit a number of immediate problems—there were eight terrorists (the authorities did not know this), the snipers had no special training in sharpshooting and were not in radio contact with each other, and the police inside the plane abandoned their post once the helicopters landed. Local police also refused to involve the Israeli Mossad chief, Zwi Zamir, in the planning of the rescue.

While the terrorists held the pilots and the hostages at gunpoint, leaders Yasuf Nazzal and Luttif Afif inspected the plane. Finding it empty, they ran back to the helicopters and were immediately fired upon by the snipers. A gun battle ensued, but German authorities had not arranged for armoured personnel carriers and the battle raged for almost an hour. At four minutes past midnight one of the terrorists jumped out of the easternmost helicopter, sprayed it with gunfire and threw a hand grenade into the cockpit. Springer, Halfin, Friedman and Berger died—the last victim from smoke inhalation. The terrorists shot at fire trucks to stop them from putting out the blaze, and a German police officer was killed in the crossfire.

Two kidnappers were killed trying to ignite the second helicopter, but Adnan Al-Gashey riddled it with gunfire, killing all five hostages—Gutfreund, Slavin, Shorr, Spitzer and Shapira. Two more kidnappers were killed, but three others were located by police pretending to be dead (Sadafy and cousins Adnan and Jamal Al-Gashey). Yasuf Nazzal ('Tony') escaped from the airport on foot but was tracked down by police dogs and shot dead. By 12.30 am, the carnage was over.

Later that same day, Olympic competition was suspended for one day out of respect for the murdered athletes. At a memorial service in front of 3000 athletes, 80,000 spectators and a huge world audience, IOC president Avery Brundage made no mention of the dead athletes. (The Olympic flag flew at half-mast, along with the flags of most of the competing nations, but the Arab countries participating in the Games demanded that their flags remain untouched.)

The Israeli team left Munich the following day. (The Egyptian team departed on 7 September because it feared reprisals.) Israel, outraged by the murders and the official snubs, would not forget so easily.

On 29 October, a German Lufthansa jet was hijacked and demands were made to release the three surviving Black September terrorists who had been responsible for the Munich massacre. The men—Mohammed Safady, Adnan Al-Gashey and Jamal Al-Gashey—were released, but they and many of the terrorists responsible for planning the Munich massacre were tracked down and executed by Israeli secret service agents during the late 1970s. Today, only Jamal Al-Gashey remains alive, and is in hiding somewhere in Africa.

REFERENCES:

- Calahan, Alexander B. (1995), *Countering Terrorism: The Israeli Response to the 1972 Munich Olympic Massacre and the Development of Independent Covert Action Teams, www.fas.org*
- Jonas, George (2005), *Vengeance: The True Story of an Israeli Counter-Terrorist Team* (Simon & Schuster, New York)
- ABC Online, *Munich Massacre Remembered, www.abc.net.au*

1974
The Disappearance of Lord Lucan

FACT FILE

CRIME: Murder, assault
VICTIM: Sandra Rivett, aged 29
Lady Lucan, the former Veronica Duncan, was seriously injured.
DATE: 7 November 1974
PLACE: 46 Lower Belgrade Street, London (England)
PERPETRATOR: Richard John Bingham (b. 1934), 7th Earl of Lucan
SENTENCE: Lord Lucan escaped and was never bought to justice but a 1975 inquest named him as the murderer

On 7 November 1974, the nanny hired by the estranged wife of Lord Lucan was murdered at the Lucan family home in London. Lady Lucan was also seriously injured in the attack, and dropped a bombshell on British society and the subsequent murder investigation when she identified her husband—Richard Bingham, the 7th Earl of Lucan—as her attacker. Lord Lucan's disappearance before he could stand trial seemed to support his involvement in the murder and assault that night. Or did it?

Richard John Bingham, later Lord Lucan, was born on 18 December 1934. Bingham attended Eton College and joined the Coldstream Guards in 1953, but the great passion in his life was gambling. He married Veronica Duncan in March 1963, and assumed the prestigious title in the Irish peerage in January 1964, upon the death of his father, Charles. Lord and Lady Lucan had three children—Frances (b. 1964), Charles (b. 1967) and Camilla (b. 1970)—and lived in a four-storey mansion in Lower Belgrade Street, London. In the early 1970s, Lady Lucan was prescribed medication for postnatal depression while Lord Lucan was addicted to gambling and suffering heavy financial losses. The marriage faltered, and during Christmas 1972 Lord Lucan moved out of the family home into a nearby apartment in Elizabeth Street.

In March 1973, Lord Lucan obtained a court order granting him custody of the children while Lady Lucan voluntarily checked into a psychiatric clinic. Lord Lucan was confident he would be awarded full-time custody of his children, but in June

1974 the court ordered the children return to their mother. Lord Lucan was incensed by the decision and obsessed with the idea of winning the children back. He hired a private detective to monitor his wife's behaviour, but when he could no longer afford to do that, he took on the task himself and secretly taped his access visits in the hope of gathering incriminating evidence against her.

On the evening of Tuesday 7 November 1974, Lord Lucan dropped a friend off in the London suburb of Chelsea before heading off the Clermont Club for a late meal with friends. Tuesday was the night that his children's nanny, petite, 29-year-old Sandra Rivett, did not normally work, and Lucan thought that his wife would be home alone with the children. However, Rivett was working that night, and at about 8.40 pm she ventured downstairs into the family's basement kitchen to make evening tea. When she was missing for some time, Lady Lucan left the children upstairs and went down to see why she was taking so long. She told an inquest held in June 1975 that the time was about 9 pm when she peered from the ground floor into the basement and heard a noise in the downstairs cloakroom.

A figure then rushed out of the cloakroom and began hitting Lady Lucan around the head with a length of pipe. When she screamed, someone told her to 'shut up' and she recognised the voice as belonging to her husband. Her attacker tried to gouge her eye out and shoved three gloved fingers down her throat, but she grabbed the man's testicles and the man collapsed on the kitchen floor. It most definitely was her husband who had attacked her, she told the inquest, but after she went upstairs to grab a wet cloth from the bathroom, she ran from the house and struggled into the nearby pub, The Plumber's Arms, covered in blood. 'Help me, help me, help me,' she cried. 'He's in the house. He's murdered the nanny!'

When police arrived at the home of Lady Lucan, they found the body of Sandra Rivett in the basement hidden inside a blood-soaked sack near the door between the breakfast room and the kitchen. She had been beaten to death with a lead pipe covered with surgical tape—the same weapon that had struck Lady Lucan—which was found at the top of the stairs. She told police that her husband had mistaken the nanny for her and bludgeoned her to death in the dark. Lord Lucan, via letters to friends that were presented at the inquest, told a completely different story.

On the night of the murder, Lord Lucan allegedly telephoned a family friend named Madeleine Floorman at about 10 pm. The caller, whom Floorman identified as Lucan, was incoherent and upset. At 10.30 pm, Lucan telephoned his mother and told her to go to his former home and to collect the children because there had been a 'catastrophe'. At 11.30 pm, he arrived at the home of friends in Sussex, 68 kilometres (42 miles) away, in a borrowed car. A family friend, Susan Maxwell-Scott, informed police that Lucan told her a story of 'incredible co-incidence'. While walking to his dinner reservation, he had passed his family home and—through the basement window, which was at road level—seen his wife struggling with a man. Letting himself in through the front door, he slipped in the blood and the man had escaped. He then took his wife upstairs to wash her wounds and calm her down when she started to scream 'Murder!' and ran out of the house. Realising how bad things looked for him, Lucan left the children in their bedrooms and drove to Sussex to talk to friends.

Lord Lucan wrote three letters to his brother-in-law, Bill Shand Kydd, that night and left Sussex the following day in the borrowed car, which was found three days later at the port of Newhaven. Lord Lucan has not been sighted since. The letters, revealed at the inquest, intimated that despite his innocence Lucan now considered suicide because he wanted to spare his children financial ruin and the sight of their father standing in the dock on the charge of murder. However, the inquest jury retired for only 31 minutes before handing down a verdict of 'murder by Lord Lucan'. It was the last time an inquest exercised its right to name a murderer—that right under British law was abolished by the *Criminal Law Act* of 1977.

Friends of Lord Lucan believed he caught a commercial boat or ferry out into the English Channel and simply jumped overboard and drowned. His body was never found—launching 30 years of urban mythology and enough worldwide sightings to rival Elvis.

HISTORICAL AND SOCIAL SIGNIFICANCE:

- Lord Lucan's son and heir, George Charles Bingham (b. 1967), could not inherit the earldom until his father was declared legally dead. Finally, in 1992, the High Court ruled that Lucan was legally dead, but probate was not granted until 1999—25 years after his disappearance. His son, known by the courtesy title 'Lord Bingham', assumed control of his father's estate.

REFERENCES:

- *Lord Lucan Mystery, www.lordlucan.com*
- BBC Online (7 November 1974), On This Day, *www.bbc.co.uk.*

1976

The Raid on Entebbe

FACT FILE

CRIME: Attempted hijacking, murder

VICTIMS:

Israeli soldier Colonel Yonatan ('Yonni') Netanyahu

4 unnamed hostages

civilian Dora Bloch, aged 75

DATE: 4 July 1976

PLACE: Entebbe International Airport, Uganda (Africa)

PERPETRATORS: Seven Baader-Meinhof and PFLP hijackers led by Wilfred Bose and supported by the Ugandan regime of Idi Amin

---

Four years after the Munich Massacre, Israel was again confronted with the deadly situation of its citizens being held hostage by pro-Palestinian terrorists. While the stance of Israeli Prime Minister Yitzak Rabin's government was the same—it would not negotiate with terrorists—Israel was determined this time to rescue the hostages rather than leave their fate in the hands of a foreign country.

On 27 June 1976, Air France Flight 139 left Ben Gurian Airport for Paris via Athens. Shortly after it took off from Athens, the Airbus A300 carrying 244 passengers and a crew of 12 was hijacked by four men. Two hijackers from the Popular Front for the Liberation of Palestine (PFLP, an offshoot of the Palestinian Liberation Organisation) masqueraded as South American tourists, and two from a German Red Army group known as the Baader-Meinhof Gang diverted the plane to Benghazi in Libya. The terrorists demanded the release of 40 Palestinians imprisoned in Israel and 13 others detained in foreign countries such as Kenya and Germany within 48 hours or they would blow the plane up and kill the hostages. Although the hijackers said that they would not negotiate, they released one female passenger before refuelling and flying to Entebbe the following morning.

Uganda was ruled by the pro-Palestinian dictator Idi Amin. In 1972, Idi Amin severed ties with Israel and allowed Yasser Arafat's Palestinian Liberation Organisation to train in Uganda. The hijackers were later joined by three other men, including leader Wilfred Bose. Bose was working under the orders of Palestinian terrorist Wasim Haddid, an associate of Carlos ('The Jackal') Ramirez.

The hostages were held in the transit hall of Entebbe's Old Terminal, and non-Jewish passengers were separated from the Israeli and Jewish group. The non-Jewish passengers were told that they would be released and flown to France while the group of 105 Israeli and Jewish passengers would be held hostage. Incredibly, the flight crew of Air France Flight 139, headed by Captain Michael Bacos, refused to leave their passengers and stayed behind in Entebbe. (Bacos was severely reprimanded for this decision by Air France on his return and was suspended.) The other passengers were forced onto the departing plane by Ugandan soldiers, who were clearly on the side of the terrorists.

More than 200 Special Forces troops in five Israeli Air Force 3-130 Hercules transport aircraft were deployed to Uganda. Supported by the Kenyan government, which was opposed to Amin's regime, the Israeli elite force planned to land at Entebbe International Airport at night without the knowledge of the hijackers, Ugandan troops or airport ground control.

After refuelling at Ophir, on the Sinai Peninsula, Israeli troops landed just before midnight on 3 July and headed for the terminal building in a convoy of Land Rovers accompanied by a black Mercedes designed to fool guards in the control tower that it was an official Ugandan convoy. The convoy drove right up to the front door of the terminal without being challenged. Storming the building, Israeli troops called for the hostages to get down and shot one man as he leapt up and ran towards them. They killed three terrorists who were sitting at a table before taking the hostages to the waiting convoy. In the ensuing gun battle, three other hijackers, including Wilfred Bose, 45 Ugandan troops and 3 hostages were killed.

As the hostages were being loaded onto the transport planes, Colonel Yonatan ('Yonni') Netanyahu was shot and killed as he ran up the ramp of the Hercules after guarding the rear of the convoy. Netanyahu was the elder brother of Benjamin Netanyahu, who went on to become prime minister of Israel from 1996 to 1999. It was later revealed that American hostage Dora Bloch had been transferred to Kampala Hospital when she suffered a choking attack. When Amin learned that the Israelis had rescued the hostages, he ordered two of his guards to take the 75-year-old grandmother from her hospital bed and murder her.

But 'Operation Thunderbolt', later known as 'Operation Entebbe', had been a success.

REFERENCES:

- Jewish Virtual Library (2005), *The Entebbe Rescue Mission*, *www.jewishvirtuallibrary.org*
- Onyango-Obbo, Charles (1997), 'Entebbe Raid of 1976 Recalled', *The East African*, *www.africannews.com*
- *Palestine Facts*, *www.palestinefacts.org*

1976

Gary Gilmore's 'Death Wish'

FACT FILE

CRIME: Murder
VICTIMS: Max Jensen and Benny Bushnell, aged 25
DATES: 19–20 July 1976
PLACE: Provo, Utah (USA)
PERPETRATOR: Gary Mark Gilmore (1940–1977)
SENTENCE: Executed by firing squad on 17 January 1977

Gary Gilmore was a career criminal who committed his first crime at the age of ten while on his newspaper round. Despite his high IQ, he fantasised about being a mobster. At the age of 14 he was sent to a correctional institute for wayward boys. Four months after his release, Gilmore was arrested again and sentenced to 15 years for robbery. When he murdered two men in 1976, however, Gilmore entered the big-time. With the death penalty controversially reinstated in the United States, Gilmore's decision to fight the justice system in order to be executed made him an international cause célèbre.

In April 1976, Gary Gilmore was released from prison after serving four years of a nine-year stretch for a second armed robbery. The 36-year-old moved to Utah under the sponsorship of his cousin Brenda Nicol and her husband, Johnny. Gilmore moved in with Brenda's parents, Vern and Ida, in Provo, south of Salt Lake City, and was given a job in Vern's shoe repair shop. The ex-convict so impressed his employer that he was given another job in an insulation factory. Gilmore met Nicole Baker, a 19-year-old divorcee and mother of two, through a co-worker at the shoe store, and within a week they were living together. There was an instant attraction between the pair, who believed that they had met in a previous life.

A compulsive shoplifter, Gilmore could not escape his own recklessness, and in June 1976 he stole nine guns from Swan's Market in the suburb of Spanish Forte. He attempted to sell the guns—with Nicole and her children in his car so that the police would not suspect him—but the buyer did not show and Gilmore argued with Nicole and beat her and her children. When another store robbery was foiled, Gilmore dumped Nicole's car, threw the keys away and hid his guns. The next day

Nicole and Gilmore's probation officer convinced him to plead guilty to a minor charge so that she could get her car back. Gilmore was set to appear in court on 24 July 1976.

Gary and Nicole's relationship quickly deteriorated. Gilmore's drug-taking and drinking made him difficult to live with, and Nicole started seeing other men. After another fight, Gilmore hit her and threw her out of their home. On 19 July, he drove to Nicole's parents' home looking for her in his new pick-up truck, but she was not home. Instead, he took Nicole's mentally disturbed older sister for a drive—looking for a convenience store to rob. At the Sinclair Service Station in Orem, Gilmore threatened attendant Max Jensen with a .22 Browning automatic pistol and stole US$125. Gilmore then ordered Jensen into the restroom and shot him dead at point-blank range as he lay on the floor.

Gilmore drove around aimlessly that night searching for Nicole until the pick-up truck ran out of petrol. Increasingly desperate, he walked to a 7–11 store and got a lift back to his pick-up with some local youths. When they dropped Gilmore at the car, they saw him place a gun under the seat. By the time he got the pick-up back to a service station, it was overheating.

The owner of the garage, Norman Fulmer, offered to fix it. On the evening of 20 July, Gilmore went into the office of the City Center Motel, which was next-door to the shoe repair shop where he first gained employment after moving to Utah, and mortally wounded motel manager Benny Bushnell. After stealing a cashbox with approximately US$125 in it, Gilmore accidentally shot himself in the hand while trying to dispose of the murder weapon.

Walking back to Fulmer's garage to pick up his truck, Gilmore went into the restroom to clean his wound and left bloodstains. Fulmer, who had heard of the motel shooting over the radio, noticed Gilmore's wound but waited until he had left in his truck before contacting police. The local police already had a description of the man they wanted—before he died Benny Bushnell had described the man to a customer who found him lying in a pool of blood. From the description posted by police, Vern and Ida knew that it was Gary Gilmore the police were looking for and rang his cousin Brenda Nicol to warn her that he may turn up. Gilmore did contact her, telling his cousin that he had been injured while preventing a robbery, and told her to bring bandages and painkillers to where he was hiding. Brenda informed the police, but they did not want a potential shoot-out and kept him under surveillance.

When Gilmore got tired of waiting, he drove off followed by the police. Stopped and ordered out of his truck, he was arrested at gunpoint while lying on the ground. After being treated for his wound, Gilmore admitted to killing the two men but did not sign a confession.

Gary Gilmore's trial began on 5 October 1976 in Provo, Utah. Just two days later, he was found guilty of first-degree murder and sentenced to death. Given the option of appealing, Gilmore chose instead to be executed by firing squad. Despite his objections, Gilmore's lawyers filed appeals and stays of executions. The American Civil Liberties Union and the National Association for the Advancement of Colored People opposed the use of the death penalty, and over the next two months Gilmore's execution was delayed three times. On 16 November, both Gilmore and Nicole Baker attempted suicide (Gilmore would try again a month later), but both were unsuccessful.

Gary Gilmore was executed by firing squad at 8.06 am on 17 January 1977 after a restraining order on the execution was overturned. A hood was placed over his head, a target was attached to his shirt, and the five-man firing squad took aim and shot him from behind a screen. So that none of the executioners could be sure that they fired the bullet that killed Gilmore, one of the five rounds was blank. The paradox of Gary Gilmore's case was that he had to lose his appeal in order to gain what he wanted—execution.

HISTORICAL AND SOCIAL SIGNIFICANCE:

- Gilmore's final words, 'Let's do it', became a T-shirt catchphrase after his death. His death was the first of more than 100 executions to take place in the United States since the death penalty was reinstated in some states in 1976.
- Two people received Gilmore's corneas within hours of his death, and his organs were donated to medical research.
- British punk band The Advert had a minor hit with the song 'Gary Gilmore's Eyes'.
- In 1979, writer Norman Mailer won the Pulitzer Prize for Literature with his account of Gilmore's crimes, trial and execution, entitled *The Executioner's Song*. Tommy Lee Jones won an Emmy Award for his portrayal of Gary Gilmore in the television movie based on the book.

REFERENCES:

- *Murder Casebook* (1990), Marshall Cavendish, London
- Petch, Simon (1997), 'Norman Mailer, Gary Gilmore and the Untold Story of the Law', *Australian Humanities Review, www.lib.latrobe.edu.au*
- BBC Online (17 January 1977), *On This Day, www.bbc.co.uk*

1977
David Berkowitz: Son of Sam

FACT FILE

CRIME: Serial murder
VICTIMS: Donna Lauria, aged 18; Christina Freund, aged 19; Virginia Voskerichian, aged 19; Alexander Esau, aged 20; Valentina Suriani, aged 20; Stacey Moscowitz, 20;
Five other people were shot and wounded.
DATES: December 1975 to July 1977
PLACES: Suburbs of New York (USA)
PERPETRATOR: David Berkowitz (b. 1953)
SENTENCE: Imprisonment for 365 years

In the summer of 1976, a series of random murders paralysed New York City. The 'city that never sleeps' lived up to its name until 24-year-old David Berkowitz was finally captured, in June 1977. By then six young people had lost their lives—shot with a .44 calibre handgun as they sat in their cars or walked home from bars in the early hours of the morning—and another five people had been seriously wounded. For 13 months the unknown killer taunted police by leaving letters at the scene of his crimes, signing them 'Mr Monster', 'Sam's Creation.44' and finally 'Son of Sam'.

David Berkowitz was born 'illegitimate' and given up for adoption. Deeply upset by the death of his adopted mother from cancer when he was just 14, Berkowtiz developed into a spoilt bully who found it difficult to form relationships with the opposite sex. (He described himself as a 'girl-hater'.) When his father remarried, the podgy, shy loner joined the army and renounced his Jewish faith and became a Baptist. Berkowitz was reunited with his birth mother, and although he was a welcome guest in her home and formed a good relationship with his half-sister, his adoptive father became increasingly concerned about his son's mental state during the early part of 1976. By this time, Berkowitz was living in a one-bedroom apartment in the Bronx and had become completely isolated from the rest of society.

But Berkowitz had already begun his attacks. On Christmas Eve 1975, he stabbed a young woman as she left a supermarket in the New York suburb of Co-op City, inflicting a superficial back wound. When she began to scream, Berkowitz ran from the scene but attacked another teenage girl on his way home. These were the 'Son of Sam's' 'practice runs'. Berkowitz bought a .44 calibre Charles Arms Bulldog revolver and was driven to kill by 'demonic voices', although he later recanted this. More than likely, Berkowitz killed out of his anger against women and for the fame his crimes would bring him.

In the early hours of 29 July 1976, two teenage women, Donna Lauria and Jody Valentine, were sitting in a car outside Donna's home in the Bronx. As Jody got out of the car, Berkowitz stepped from the curb and shot Donna through the windshield with a gun concealed in a brown paper bag. The first bullet fatally struck her in the neck, while a second entered her forearm as she raised it to protect herself. Jody Valentine was hit in the thigh, and as she slumped back into the car she fell against the car horn and raised the alarm. Twelve weeks later, 18-year-old Rosemary Keenan and her friend Carl Denaro were shot as they sat in their car outside a bar in Flushing, Queens. Both survived the attack despite five shots being fired. It was later revealed that Berkowitz had mistaken Denaro for a girl because of the male victim's shoulder-length hair.

On 27 November 1976, two young women were shot as they sat on the front porch of their home. Eighteen-year-old Joanne Lomino was left paralysed from a bullet to her spine, while 16-year-old Donna DeMasi, who was visiting her friend, was shot in the neck. The stranger had suddenly crossed the road in front of them and, as he asked for directions, begun to shoot. Although police tried to link the random shootings, differences in descriptions of the suspect (Lomino and DeMasi both described the shooter as having fair hair) had them perplexed. But there was no mistaking the weapon used—a .44 Bulldog revolver.

The suspicion that New York was dealing with a solitary madman was confirmed in January 1977 when John Diel and his girlfriend, Christina Freund, were fired upon as they sat in their Pontiac Firebird outside a restaurant in Queens. As Diel started the car in freezing temperatures, Freund was shot dead with a single bullet fired through the passenger side window.

A police taskforce, known as 'Operation Omega', was set up to investigate the killings. In March 1977, not far from where Christine Freund lost her life, 19-year-old Virginia Voskerichian was shot dead at 7.30 pm walking along the footpath in Forest Hills. Unknown to the police, the killer was looking for a new opportunity to deliver them a letter.

On the night of 16 April 1977, 18-year-old Alexander Esau and his girlfriend, Valentina Suriani, were killed in their car. Berkowitz left a note addressed to Captain Joe Borelli, the deputy chief of the Omega taskforce, saying that he had been ordered to kill by his 'father Sam, a vampire'. Although the contents of the letter were not released to the public, *New York Daily News* reporter Jimmy Breslin leaked the fact that the killer was in contact with police.

When Breslin was contacted by the 'Son of Sam' on 30 May 1977, the killer's nickname was reported in the city's newspapers. Berkowitz was excited by his new-found notoriety, and on 26 June 1977 he shot teenagers Sal Lupio and Judy Placido as they sat in their car outside the Elephas disco in Queens. Miraculously, both survived.

On 31 July, Bobby Violante and Stacy Moscowitz parked in a 'lover's lane' in South Brooklyn, some distance from the crime scenes in the Bronx and Queens, at 2 am. Both were shot through their car's windscreen—Violante lost his sight in one eye and suffered a burst eardrum, Moscowitz clung to life for another 38 hours before dying of her wounds. But Berkowitz had made a mistake.

Having parked his white Ford Galaxy next to a fire hydrant in a nearby street, he received a parking fine. A witness, Cacilia Davis, saw him rip the ticket up when he returned to his car at 2.20 am. Davis was at first too afraid to tell the police, but when she did so three days later, police ignored her evidence for another week. Police unearthed a ticket for a Ford, registration number 561 XLB, licensed to a David Berkowitz.

When he was captured, Berkowitz smirked for the cameras and asked arresting detectives, 'What took you so long?' Police found satanic messages written on his apartment wall and more 'Son of Sam' letters in his room and his car. At his trial, he claimed that he took the name 'Son of Sam' from the devil, who spoke to him through his neighbour Sam Carr's black Labrador dog and had urged him to kill.

Sentenced to 365 years in prison, Berkowitz became a born-again Christian and continues to write letters. Each June, when his parole comes up, he asks the New York governor not to release him.

REFERENCES:

- *Murder Casebook* (1990), Marshall Cavendish Ltd, London
- BBC Online (2005), *Case Closed: David Berkowitz, Son of Sam, www.bbc.co.uk*

1978

The Aldo Moro Murder

FACT FILE

CRIME: Kidnapping and murder
VICTIM: Aldo Moro (1916–1978)
DATES: 16 March to 9 May 1978
PLACE: Rome (Italy)
PERPETRATORS: The Red Brigades

The call by the Red Brigades (*Brigate Rosse)* to 'strike one to educate one hundred' focused world attention on the volatile world of Italian politics in the 1970s. The Red Brigades were a left-wing Marxist group formed in northern Italy in 1969. Those recruited by the Brigades—mostly students, unionists and labourers—originally sought to create a 'revolutionary' Italian state and to break away from the country's alliance with the West. Although this would be achieved through armed struggle if required, the Red Brigades became fractured and increasingly militant in the mid-1970s and became involved in sabotage, kidnapping—and murder.

The Red Brigades broke into factory offices and trade union headquarters before graduating to more violent activities such as bombings and kidnapping. The revolutionary group expanded into Rome, Genoa and Venice with a mandate to 'strike at the heart of the state'. But soon they abandoned their responsibilities to Italy's workers and carried out lethal attacks against rival political parties; two members of an Italian neo-fascist party were murdered in 1974, and police killed a Brigades member in 1976. The Red Brigades carried out terrorist attacks against magistrates and jurists in order to influence political trials against their members.

By 1978, the Marxist group had little to do with the workers' struggle and, under the influence of an influx of students and radicals, moved inexorably to the hard left of politics.

On 16 March 1978, members of the Red Brigades kidnapped former Italian prime minister Aldo Moro on the Via Fani as he travelled to a session of parliament. Five security guards assigned to protect Moro were killed when the 61-year-old politician was abducted at gunpoint. Moro—who had been prime minister on two previous occasions (1963–68 and 1974–76) and was expected to be the country's next president—was kidnapped because he was trying to broker a *compromesso storico* ('historical compromise') between the Italian Communist Party (PCI) and his own Christian Democrats (DC).

As party president of the Christian Democrats, Moro agreed that a coalition government formed with the communists was the best chance to finally establish 'national solidarity' at a time of political, economic and social crisis in Italy. For the next 55 days, the Red Brigades negotiated with Italian authorities as the country—and the world—waited for Moro's release. The terrorists would spare Moro's life if 13 members of the Red Brigades who were on trial were released. The Brigades announced that they would try Moro as a 'political prisoner' and execute him if need be. However, Moro's capture had a negative effect on the Brigades' plan. Parliament empowered Guilio Andreotti to form a majority government with the help of the Communist Party for the first time in Italian history.

The government refused to negotiate with the terrorists and launched the largest police investigation in the country's history. The Brigades published photos of Moro in captivity and tried to use the Vatican as a go-between. A personal appeal from Pope Paul VI could not convince the terrorists to release their captive.

On 9 May 1978, the Red Brigades placed Aldo Moro in a car and told him to cover himself with a blanket, possibly on the pretext of transporting him to another destination. The terrorists shot Moro ten times and later left the car in Via Caetani—symbolically, halfway between the offices of the PCI and the DC. The following year, philosopher Antonio Negri was arrested and charged with planning the kidnap and murder of Aldo Moro, leadership of a terrorist group and plotting to overthrow the Italian government. Negri was found not guilty on most of the charges in 1980 and fled to France while on appeal. While his arrest was seen as politically motivated in order to close down the investigation, he voluntarily returned to Italy in 1997 to serve the remainder of his 17-year sentence. Negri wanted to show that the methods the Red Brigades utilised to bring about social and political change in the 1970s were now a thing of the past.

The murder of a popular political figure such as Aldo Moro was seen as an assault on Italy's politics, its law enforcement agencies and, indeed, its society as a whole. Moro's death was condemned by former leaders of the Red Brigades who had been sent to jail, other left-wing radicals and all political parties.

REFERENCES:

- Katz, Robert (1979), *The Death of a Statesman, www.theboot.it*
- Wehling, Michelle (1997), *Aldo Moro, www.uwgb.edu*

1978

Georgi Markov: The 'Umbrella Murder'

FACT FILE

CRIME: Murder
VICTIM: Georgi Markov (1929-1978)
DATE: 11 September 1978
PLACE: Waterloo Bridge, London (England)
PERPETRATOR: Unknown

On 11 September 1978, former Bulgarian dissident Georgi Markov died an agonising death in a London hospital. Four days earlier, the 49-year-old novelist and playwright—and, more recently, BBC journalist and broadcaster for the German Deutsche Welle—complained to doctors that a stranger with a foreign accent had jabbed him in the leg with the tip of an umbrella as he waited for a bus. Although the man apologised as he quickly walked away, Markov almost immediately felt a stinging sensation where the umbrella tip had struck him. When he arrived at work at the BBC, he noticed that a red pimple had formed on his leg. That evening he developed a high temperature. He was admitted to St James's Hospital in Balham, and three days later he was dead.

An autopsy conducted with the help of British government scientists located a minute, 1.5-millimetre metal sphere in the victim's calf muscle. (The pellet had not dissolved in the bloodstream, as had obviously been expected.) The pellet was 90 per cent platinum and 10 per cent iridium and had two holes bored into its hollow centre, which was big enough to hold 0.28 cubic millimetres of poison.

Taking into consideration the symptoms and the amount of toxin used, government analyst Dr David Gall believed that ricin was the only toxin that could have been used. The presence of a poisonous pellet in the victim's leg confirmed that Georgi Markov had been deliberately murdered. That Markov was a known critic of communist Bulgaria and had defected to England a decade before, cast suspicion on the Bulgarian government and the Soviet Union's KGB.

After coming to London in 1969, Markov worked for the BBC's World Service, Radio Free Europe, as a broadcaster and journalist. He was a vocal critic of the Bulgarian communist regime, and it was thought that it was his attacks against Todor

Zhivkov's government that led to plans to silence Markov once and for all.

KGB defector Oleg Gordievsky later informed Western Intelligence that Bulgarian interior minister Dimiter Stoyanov had requested KGB assistance with the assassination and that this was approved by Soviet leader Yuri Andropov.

An unknown person slipped a toxin into Markov's drink at a dinner party given by colleagues at Radio Free Europe, but Markov only became ill. Another attempt while he was on a trip to Sardinia also failed, so the Bulgarian secret police came up with the 'umbrella' plan. A poisonous pellet containing deadly ricin would be injected under Markov's skin using the tip of a modified umbrella.

Markov worked a double shift at the BBC and usually caught a bus home to rest after the morning shift. On the afternoon of 7 September 1978, he parked his car on the south side of Waterloo Bridge, which crosses the Thames, and waited to catch a bus to the BBC studios to start the evening shift.

As he stood in the queue for the bus, he felt a sharp pain in his right thigh. A heavy-set man with a thick accent apologised to Markov as he picked up his umbrella from the ground and then walked away from the bus queue.

Ricin is a naturally poisonous compound derived from castor beans (*Ricinus communis*). When the beans are boiled down during the process of making castor oil, the residue compound is ricin. Because castor bean plants are found all around the world and the process is easy and inexpensive, the toxin is available worldwide. One gram of ricin is enough to kill 36 000 people.

According to CNN, in 1992 General Vladimir Todorov, a former Bulgarian intelligence chief, was sentenced to 16 months' jail for destroying ten volumes of material relating to Markov's assassination. Another agent, General Stoyan Savov, committed suicide rather than face prosecution for his involvement in the cover-up. Another agent, alleged operations commander Vasil Kostev, was killed in a car crash. Informants told British authorities that the KGB recruited a 'low-level Italian' criminal to carry out the murder.

The man later fled to Denmark, where he was questioned, before going to Hungary and the Czech Republic. In June 2005, in his book *Kill Wanderer*, Bulgarian journalist Hristo Hristov revealed the name of Markov's assassin as Francesco Gullino.

REFERENCES:

- CNN.com/world (2003), *Ricin and the Umbrella Murder, www.cnn.com*
- *Ricin, www.chemsoc.org*
- Open Society Justice Initiative (2005), *Book Names Murderer of Georgi Markov*, *www.justiceinitiative.org*

1978
Ted Bundy: Serial Killer

FACT FILE

CRIMES: Serial rape and murder
VICTIMS: Laura Aime, aged 17; Brenda Ball, aged 22; Margaret Brown, aged 21; Caryn Campbell, aged 23; Georgann Hawkins, aged 18; Lynda Healy, aged 21; Debbie Kent, aged 17; Kimberley Leach, aged 12; Lisa Levy, aged 20; Donna Manson, aged 19; Denise Naslund, aged 19; Janice Ott, aged 23; Roberta Parks, aged 22; Susan Rancourt, aged 18; Melissa Smith, aged 17; Nancy Wilcox, aged 16
DATES: 31 January 1974 to 9 February 1978
PLACES: Seattle (Washington), Salt Lake (Utah), Aspen (Colorado) and Tallahassee (Florida) in the United States
PERPETRATOR: Theodore ('Ted') Bundy (1946–1989)
SENTENCE: Executed by electric chair at Starke Prison, Florida, on 24 January 1989

Theodore Robert ('Ted') Bundy was such a prolific murderer during the 1970s—and such a unique case study in sociopathic behaviour and sexual deviancy—that investigating detectives tracking his litany of murders across the United States coined a new term to describe his crimes. Bundy was more than a repeat murderer—he could more accurately be described as a mass murderer except that his crimes were spread over several years and several states. He was, instead, deemed to be a 'serial killer'—the term used by FBI profiler Robert Ressler and Dr Robert Keppel in the 1970s to describe the perpetrator of a series of then unsolved sex murders.

Seattle, Washington, was the scene of a series of violent attacks, sexual assaults and disappearances during 1974. In that year alone, 12 pretty young women disappeared from the north-western seaboard city. On 14 July, two women, Janice Ott and Denise Naslund, went missing at Lake Sammamish Park in separate incidents. Witnesses told detectives that they saw a good-looking young man, with his arm in a cast, talking to young girls on the day they disappeared. The following September, the bodies of the two women (and the thighbone of a third victim) were discovered by grouse hunters in Taylor Mountain, a little more than 3 kilometres (2 miles) east of where they had gone missing. A search of the area during the next six months yielded three more bodies—just a fraction of the number of women who had gone missing in the Seattle area.

Just as the murders seemed to stop, a similar series of crimes occurred in Salt Lake City, Utah, between October 1974 and August 1975. Despite some distinct similarities, detectives investigating the two cases did not initially link the crimes to one person. Once again, however, pretty young girls were disappearing in broad daylight. A murder case in the snow resort of Aspen, Colorado, in January 1975 also had investigators perplexed.

A young nurse, 23-year-old Caryn Campbell, left her boyfriend and his children at the Wildwood Inn to return to her room to get a magazine. When she did not return after 20 minutes, her boyfriend went looking for her. Campbell's body was not discovered until the snow thawed the following year; she had been bashed with a blunt object and raped.

Finally, detectives in Salt Lake got a lucky break. Carol La Ronch told them that a handsome young man posing as a policeman had tried to abduct her in the car park of a shopping mall on the pretext that her car had been broken into and that she would have go with him to file a report. Although her suspicions heightened when the man was driving a Volkswagen—hardly a police vehicle—she still got in the car. When he tried to snap handcuffs on her, she reacted quickly and he only succeeded in cuffing one wrist. He then pulled a gun on her, but she made a quick decision that was to save her life. La Ronch opened the door and tumbled out of the car onto the road. She was picked up by a passing motorist and was able to give a good description of the man—lean, good-looking, with wavy brown hair. More than that, the description and the make of the car matched the suspect in the Seattle murders.

On the night of 16 August 1975, 29-year-old Ted Bundy was arrested in his Volkswagen convertible by a suspicious police patrolman after the car had been seen travelling without headlights and ran two red lights. On inspecting the car, the patrolman discovered a 'burglary kit'—a bag containing a knitted ski balaclava, a mask made out of women's stockings, a steel bar and a pair of handcuffs. Bundy was placed under arrest.

Detectives at first found it difficult to entertain the idea that the likeable, charming university student could be responsible for the spate of disappearances in the Salt Lake area. Released, then rearrested and re-released on bail, Bundy was found guilty of aggravated kidnapping in the La Ronch case in December 1976.

During the next 12 months, as Bundy mounted his own defence against charges that he was involved in the murder and disappearance of other girls and young women, he twice escaped from custody but was recaptured. Then, on 31 December 1977, he successfully escaped from Garfield County Jail in Denver and began a six-week rampage that led him to Tallahassee, Florida.

The murder of two college girls at the Chi Omega Sorority House in January 1978 made national headlines, but few suspected that Seattle and Salt Lake suspect Ted Bundy was involved. The breakthrough came the following month when the 14-year-old victim of a botched abduction was able to give police a clear description of her attacker and the licence plate number of what proved to be a stolen van—although not soon enough to save the life of Bundy's final victim.

The abduction, rape and murder of 12-year-old Kimberley Leach plumbed new depths of depravity (Bundy secreted the body in bushland so that he could return and abuse it) and galvanised police efforts to capture him. Bundy was captured on 15 February 1978, but it took another two days to confirm his true identity. Ted Bundy was such a good liar that he almost talked his way into freedom once again.

For the next two years, Bundy battled to beat the death penalty. Although he had a high IQ, Bundy erred by committing murder in Florida—one of the few states in America that still had the death penalty in the liberal 1970s—and no amount of charm and guile could keep him from the executioner's chair.

Clinical psychologists who studied him during the next decade noted his insatiable obsession with sex and murder. Originally, Bundy was addicted to pornography and was a kleptomaniac, but his lust for violence and power over women eventually overpowered him.

Ignoring a late bid to have his death penalty commuted to a life sentence (Bundy offered to reveal the burial sites of his other victims if he was kept alive), the state of Florida sent him to the electric chair on 24 January 1989. Huge crowds kept vigil outside Starke Prison, Florida, and cheered at 7.07 am when Ted Bundy finally paid for his crimes with his life.

REFERENCES:

- *Murder Casebook* (1990), Marshall Cavendish, London
- BBC Online (2005), *Case Closed: Ted Bundy, www.bbc.co.uk*
- The Crime Library (2003), *Robert D. Keppel, Ph.D. An Interview, www.crimelibrary.com*

1978
The Jonestown Massacre

FACT FILE

CRIME: Mass-induced suicide
VICTIMS: 914 members of the 'People's Temple' congregation;
Leo Ryan, US congressman, aged 53; Greg Robinson, photographer, 27;
Robert Brown, NBC cameraman, aged 36; Don Harris, NBC reporter, aged 41
DATE: 18 November 1978
PLACE: Jonestown, Guyana (South America)
PERPETRATORS: The Reverend Jim Jones (1931–1978) and other congregation leaders

---

In November 1977, one thousand members of the Reverend Jim Jones's 'People's Temple' congregation left San Francisco to set up a religious community in Guyana, South America. By the following year, stories of sexual exploitation, forced labour in oppressive conditions, and the confiscation of passports and valuables filtered back to the American relatives of the congregation members. Californian congressman Leo Ryan investigated the sect's activities and living conditions in Guyana on behalf of many of these relatives. When Ryan and his press entourage arrived at the congregation's headquarters in November 1978—a tropical haven named Jonestown—a cataclysmic chain of events was set off that was to shock the world.

James Warren ('Jim') Jones was born in Crete, Indiana, in 1931, the son of a Klansman in the heart of America's Bible belt. Jim Jones was preaching at the age of 12 and paid his own way through religious studies at Indiana University. In the late 1950s, Jones was something of a rarity as a preacher in that he reached out to both poor urban blacks and middle-class white Americans.

In 1963, Jones had 'visions' of an impending nuclear holocaust and relocated his first People's Temple to Ukiah, California, to await Armageddon. He later moved his tax-exempt church to San Francisco, where he achieved a modicum of respectability and received several humanitarian awards.

Jones adapted the concept of 'revolutionary suicide' from the Black Panthers, and schooled his followers in mass-induced suicide as a form of protest against 'racism and fascism'. He was also bisexual, and was investigated by authorities over allegations of sexual abuse and tax evasion in 1977. This investigation prompted Jones to leave the country with many of his followers.

On 24 October 1978, at the instigation of concerned relatives, a US House Foreign Affairs Committee authorised Senator Leo Ryan to travel to Guyana and investigate the living conditions of many of his former constituents.

The Reverend Jim Jones had no choice but to comply—he was facing legal action that threatened to cut off funding from the United States—but he insisted on several conditions. Ryan was not to bring 'traitors' with him—former sect members—or the press.

The congressman disregarded these conditions and arrived in Guyana with four members of the so-called Committee of Concerned Relatives, reporters from Washington and San Francisco newspapers, and an NBC film crew. Ryan threatened that if Jones turned him away he would film the refusal and show it to the world, and then there would be a full-scale congressional investigation.

Jim Jones gave the world film footage of an event that it would never forget.

Leo Ryan's chartered plane landed at an airstrip at Port Kaituma, several kilometres (about 5 miles) from Jonestown, on 17 November 1978. The visitors were given a friendly reception by sect members, who had been instructed by Jones to smile and appear happy. For his own part, Jones withdrew from the visitors and appeared sullen and unhappy about their presence in Jonestown.

Dinner at 8 pm was followed by singing and dancing, and Ryan gave a speech saying that he had enjoyed the music, remarking that Jonestown looked like 'the best thing' that had happened to the congregation. His words were met with spontaneous applause, and the celebration continued into the night.

The following morning, 18 November, the atmosphere amongst the visitors and the congregation quickly changed. Towards the end of the festivities the previous night, a young woman named Monica Bagby handed a note to NBC journalist Don Harris asking him to help her and a friend leave Jonestown the following day.

Nine sect members attempted to escape at daybreak, and Jones's security force—heavily armed Guyanese soldiers—attempted to stop them. Journalists began asking questions of their own, and Jones was asked about the apparent unhappiness of some of his followers. Jones pleaded with Ryan and his group on camera to leave Jonestown.

About 20 people asked to go back to America with Ryan, but when a woman attempted to leave Jonestown, Jones forbade her to take their son with her. An emotional stand-off ensued, but Jones was persuaded to let the American group leave. Leo Ryan was stabbed in the arm by a sect member, while another man, Larry Layton—known as Jones's 'robot'—boarded the plane with a concealed gun.

All the while, NBC video footage captured the drama, including a tractor driving a wooden wagon onto the airstrip and blocking the plane from leaving.

Suddenly, 20 armed soldiers stood up in the wagon and opened fire.

On the runway, congressman Ryan and three of the press crew—Greg Robinson, Robert Brown and Don Harris—were hit by a volley of bullets. Brown's video camera continued filming and captured the mayhem. On the plane, Layton shot Monica Bagby dead and killed three other defectors. Surviving members of the press crew ran into the jungle and hid. Back at the Jonestown compound, the Reverend Jim Jones revealed his plan to the congregation. According to Jones, Layton had killed the pilot and the plane had crashed into the jungle (the original plan), and authorities would soon arrive. There was now only one solution, for which they had long been prepared—they would commit mass suicide.

The Jonestown medical staff prepared two 50-gallon (228-litre) drums of Flavor-Aid laced with Valium and cyanide. Members of the congregation formed an orderly line, giving drinks to their children and squirting the poisonous drink into the mouths of their babes with a syringe, and then went and lay down in the fields and waited to die in each other's arms.

Although the men, women and children were told that it would be a painless end, many suffered convulsions and died a slow, agonising death. After the armed guards shot some of the congregation and took their own lives, the Reverend Jim Jones shot himself with a pistol. A nurse, Annie Moore, used the same gun to kill herself moments later—the whole episode was tape-recorded by Jones.

Survivors of Leo Ryan's press crew and several members of the congregation who escaped the carnage sounded the alarm. When Georgetown soldiers and media representatives from the United States arrived, they met with a sight unprecedented in peacetime history: more than 900 bloated bodies—276 of them children—were lying in the Guyanese sun following the worst case of mass-induced suicide the modern world had seen.

HISTORICAL AND SOCIAL SIGNIFICANCE:

- Jim Jones had been invited to President Jimmy Carter's inauguration in January 1977.
- When the bodies were flown back to America, many could not be identified. Several cemeteries refused to take them before the Evergreen Cemetery in Oakland, California, accepted 409 bodies in 1979.
- Jonestown itself has all but vanished—stripped by villagers, consumed by a fire in the early 1980s, and overgrown by the jungle.

REFERENCES:

- *Murder Casebook* (1990), Marshall Cavendish, London
- Durden Smith, Jo (2005), *100 Most Infamous Criminals*, Arcturus, London

1978

John Wayne Gacy: Killer Clown

FACT FILE

CRIME: Serial murder
VICTIMS: 33 men and boys
DATES: 1972–79
PLACE: Chicago, Illinois (USA)
PERPETRATOR: John Wayne Gacy (1942–1994)
SENTENCE: Executed by lethal injection on 9 May 1994.

The discovery that local businessman John Wayne Gacy was a sadistic serial killer responsible for the murder of 33 men and youths shocked Chicago. Gacy, twice married but a closet homosexual, had often dressed as a clown to entertain local children at hospitals and parties. He was also active in local politics—a photograph published the year before his capture in December 1979 revealed his beaming, corpulent figure standing beside First Lady Rosalind Carter—much to the embarrassment of the Democratic Party. As the world later realised, underneath the façade of Gacy's social respectability lurked the cunning mind of a killer and the latent depravity of a truly sinister man.

John Wayne Gacy Jnr was born on St Patrick's Day in 1942 in Chicago. An overweight child who was abused by his violent, homophobic father, Gacy suffered from blackouts in his youth after being injured in a play accident. It was revealed at his murder trial that Gacy did not mature emotionally and suffered from 'cringes of doubt [and] quakes of total helplessness' as an adult. Gacy developed an alter ego named 'Jack Hanley'—a tough cop who protected him from his fears—and maintained that it was his other self who murdered the young men he lured to his Chicago home for sex.

After leaving high school without graduating, Gacy worked as a clothing salesman and then met his first wife, Marilyn Myer. Gacy and his wife moved to Waterloo, Iowa, to manage his father-in-law's KFC store. There he raised two children and lived a comfortable life, but Gacy harboured a dark secret. Privately homosexual, he was consumed by sexual fantasies of dominating young men. In 1968, one of his KFC employees filed a complaint with local police that Gacy had tied him up and sodomised him. Gacy was convicted of sexual assault and sentenced to ten years' jail. Although the scandal ended his first marriage, he was released within 18 months and began his murderous assault on Chicago society in 1972.

Had Gacy remained in prison for the entire ten-year period, 33 people would not have perished.

On his release, Gacy got a job as a chef, met his second wife, Carol Hofgren, and moved to Des Plaines, Illinois. The marriage broke up in 1975 when Gacy admitted to being gay, but by then he was already a killer. Gacy used his new business, a construction company called PDM Contractors, to attract young runaways. Five of his victims once worked for him. Gacy also frequented gay bars, and picked up hitchhikers, homeless men and male prostitutes. Because Gacy was grossly overweight and considered himself to be unattractive, he would ply his victims with alcohol and then sodomise, strangle or drown them. He also used handcuffs to subdue his victims, fooling them into handcuffing themselves as part of a 'trick'. The real trick, he would tell his panic-stricken victims, was to have the key to the handcuffs. Gacy then buried their bodies with lime under and around his house. Four of his victims, however, were dumped in the Des Plaines River ... possibly because he was running out of space.

A few days before Christmas 1978, 15-year-old Robert Priest went missing from a pharmacy in Des Plaines, Illinois. Priest told his mother that he was going to see a man about a summer job. When he failed to return, the owner of the pharmacy where Priest worked told authorities that the man most likely to have offered the boy a job was a construction builder named Gacy, whose company was renovating the pharmacy. When police went to Gacy's home in the suburb of Norwood Park, they found a trapdoor leading to a crawlspace under his home. There they found the bodies of 7 victims. Another 21 victims were buried around the outside of the house.

The testimony of two men who escaped Gacy gave prosecutors an insight into the accused's warped mind. Jeff Rignall testified that Gacy had picked him up in the New Town section of Chicago and sexually assaulted him. Inexplicably, Gacy let him go—possibly because he felt Rignall couldn't identify him. Police did not take Rignall's claim that he was sexually assaulted seriously. Rignall could give only a vague description of his attacker, so for several weeks he waited on the same highway where Gacy had picked him up trying to identify the work vehicle that his attacker drove. After recognising the car, Rignall followed the driver to a home in Summerdale Avenue, Northwood Park. Police had decided not to prosecute Gacy because of a lack of evidence.

Robert Donnelly also had a near escape from the killer. Donnelly told police that Gacy plied him with alcohol, handcuffed him, banged his head against the wall and then submerged his head in a bathtub full of water before raping him. However, Gacy convinced the police at the time that it was consensual sex, and the police told Donnelly that they would have to wait until Gacy committed another crime before they could investigate him. When the traumatised man broke down while describing the rape to the court, Gacy rolled his eyes and laughed loudly. It was clear that he despised his victims.

Despite evidence at his trial that Gacy was legally insane, he was found guilty and sentenced to death on 12 March 1980. The jury deliberated for just two hours. During the 14 years Gacy sat on Death Row, he gained some notoriety as an artist, and his paintings of garish clowns, animals, dwarfs and Jesus with the crown of thorns became the latest fad in 'celebrity art'. In one two-year period, he painted over 250 pieces and earned nearly US$10,000 (Gacy sold 6 artworks at a display of inmate art at the Illinois State Fair). Gacy was assaulted by other prison inmates and tried to blame everyone else for his plight—his lawyers, his trial, the prison system and even his victims. As he was led to his execution by lethal injection shortly after midnight on 9 May 1994, he was still complaining:

'Taking my life won't compensate for the lives of others,' Gacy said matter-of-factly. 'This is only a state murder.'

A combined lethal dose of the anaesthetic sodium pentothal, pancuronium bromide and potassium chloride ended John Wayne Gacy's complaints once and for all.

HISTORICAL AND SOCIAL SIGNIFICANCE:

- The parents of Robert Priest filed a US$85 million lawsuit against the Iowa Board of Control for releasing Gacy in June 1970 after serving only 18 months of his 10-year sentence. The matter was settled out of court.
- After his execution, Gacy's brain was removed for scientific study. While no abnormality was found, sections of it were later kept by forensic psychologist Dr Helen Morrison.

REFERENCES:

- *Murder Casebook* (1990), Marshall Cavendish, London
- Durden Smith, Jo (2005), *100 Most Infamous Criminals*, Arcturus, London
- BBC Online (2005), *Case Closed: John Wayne Gacy, www.bbc.co.uk*

1979
The Mountbatten Murders

FACT FILE

CRIME: Mass murder
VICTIMS: Lord Mountbatten of Burma, aged 79; The Dowager Lady Brabourne, aged 82; Nicholas Knatchbull, aged 14; Paul Maxwell, aged 15
On the same day, 18 British soldiers were killed in two explosions at Warrenpoint in Northern Ireland, and civilian Michael Hudson, aged 28, was caught in crossfire and killed
DATE: 27 August 1979
PLACE: Donegal Bay, Republic of Ireland
PERPETRATOR: Thomas McMahon
SENTENCE: Life imprisonment; released in 1998

Sir Louis Mountbatten, First Earl Mountbatten of Burma, First Sea Lord and the last Viceroy and first Governor-General of India, was also the uncle of Prince Philip and the cousin of Queen Elizabeth II. On 27 August 1979, Mountbatten was killed along with three other members of his party while sailing on Donegal Bay in the Republic of Ireland. The Irish Republican Army had planted a bomb on his boat. Some hours later, 18 British soldiers were killed when two bombs were exploded at Narrow Water Castle on the bank of the Newry River in County Down, Northern Ireland. It was the highest loss of lives suffered by the British army in a single day since it had arrived in Northern Ireland a decade before, and combined with the 'Mountbatten Murders', struck at the heart of the British government and the royal family.

Louis ('Dickie') Mountbatten served in two world wars and was made Chief of Combined Operations by Winston Churchill in 1941. In October 1943, Mountbatten was appointed as Supreme Allied Commander South East Asia Theatre, and it was his experience in this region during the last years of World War II that led to his appointment as Viceroy of India after the war. Mountbatten oversaw the establishment of an independent India and Pakistan, and the title 'Earl Mountbatten of Burma' was created in recognition of his great diplomacy during this period.

Mountbatten later served as First Sea Lord and from 1959 to 1965 was Chief of the Defence Staff. Immensely popular with his wartime colleagues and the British public, Mountbatten was particularly close to his great-nephew, Prince Charles, the heir to the British throne.

Approaching 80 years of age, Mountbatten refused to have bodyguards, and although local police watched his home for one month each year when he visited Ireland, his boat was moored unguarded on Donegal Bay. On 27 August 1979, Mountbatten was holidaying at his summer home, Classebawn Castle, in Mullaghmore, County Sligo, in the northwest of the Republic of Ireland.

While sailing in his boat *Shadow V* on Donegal Bay shortly before midday with his family, a bomb planted by the IRA 'blew the boat to smithereens', as one witness described it, and threw the seven occupants into the water. Those killed were Mountbatten, the Dowager Lady Brabourne (the mother-in-law of his eldest daughter, Patricia), one of Mountbatten's twin grandsons, Nicholas Knatchbull (Patricia's son), and a teenage crew member named Paul Maxwell.

Local fishermen rushed to the scene and rescued the survivors. Mountbatten was alive when help arrived, as was Lady Brabourne, but he died soon after from massive blood loss from injuries to both legs. Lady Brabourne died in hospital the next day.

Mullaghmore is just 19 kilometres (12 miles) from the Northern Ireland border, and the assassination was carried out by local IRA members. In claiming responsibility for the crime the following day, the IRA stated that, 'This operation is one of the discriminate ways we can bring to the attention of the English people the continuing occupation of our country.' No mention was made of the loss of innocent lives, including local boy Paul Maxwell and the women and children.

Meanwhile, just across the border in Northern Ireland, the IRA's South Armagh Brigade planted two booby traps at Narrow Water Castle in Warrenpoint, County Down. The target was the British Parachute Regiment; the reason was reprisal for the 'Bloody Sunday' deaths in 1972.

A 500-kilogram (1100-pound) bomb hidden under a haystack on a flatbed lorry parked close to the castle was detonated as an army convoy drove past. Six soldiers were killed. Twenty minutes later, a second bomb exploded on the opposite side of the road, closer to the castle's gate lodge. Twelve soldiers from the Queen's Own Highlanders—who had been airlifted to the area from their Bessbrook base in County Armagh after the first bombing—were killed by the second explosion as they took cover. The death toll included Commanding Officer Lieutenant-Colonel David Blair, the most senior army officer killed in Northern Ireland to that date.

A gun battle broke out between the bombers, who were positioned on the other side of a narrow canal that formed part of the border, and soldiers from the tower house of the castle. The soldiers had been ordered not to cross into the Republic of Ireland, and the men responsible for the carnage escaped. In the crossfire, innocent bystander Michael Hudson was killed. It was later discovered that the 28-year-old was the son of the Queen's coachman.

The murders of Lord Mountbatten and his family were described as 'a day full of tragedy for Donegal Bay'—and, indeed, the world. On 5 September 1979, the day on which local funerals were held for the six soldiers killed at Warrenpoint, Lord Mountbatten was given a state funeral.

The president of Ireland, Patrick Hillery, and the prime minister, Jack Lynch, later attended a memorial service for Lord Mountbatten in Dublin. A memorial service for the British soldiers was held on 26 September at the Royal Garrison Church at Aldershot. Despite its heavy losses, the British Parachute Regiment completed its 18-month tour of duty. The deaths of 18 soldiers further escalated 'the troubles' in Northern Ireland and set the stage for bitter reprisals during the 1980s. Loyalist paramilitarists killed a number of Catholic civilians in Northern Ireland in reprisal for what became known as the Mountbatten Murders and the Warrenpoint Massacre.

Local Irish police investigated the Mountbatten Murders. Two hours after the bombing, they detained 31-year-old Thomas McMahon who was driving in the area. On 23 November 1979, McMahon was sentenced to life in prison for his part in the murders of Lord Mountbatten and three others in the Donegal Bay bombing.

No-one was ever prosecuted for the Warrenpoint Massacre. In 1998, McMahon was released from prison under the 'Good Friday Agreement', which constituted a new peace agreement between Britain and Ireland.

REFERENCES:

- Crystal, David (1994), *The Cambridge Biographical Encyclopedia*, Cambridge BBC. Online (27 August 1979), *On This Day, www.bbc.co.uk.*
- University Press, Cambridge, *A Nation Mourns, www.time.com*

1979
The Iranian Hostage Crisis

FACT FILE

CRIME: Kidnapping
VICTIMS:
66 US embassy staff captured
13 released on 19-20 November 1979
1 person released on 11 July 1980
52 people released on 20 January1981
8 US servicemen were killed in the Great Salt Desert near Tabas, Iran, on 25 April 1980 while attempting to rescue the hostages
DATE: 4 November 1979
PLACE: Tehran, Iran
PERPETRATORS: Iranian militants under the leadership of the Ayatollah Khomeini

The historian Gaddis Smith wrote that the capture and detainment of 66 US hostages between November 1979 and January 1981 'absorbed more concentrated effort by American officials and had more extensive coverage on television and in the press than any other event since World War II'. The hostage crisis, which cost the lives of eight US servicemen in a botched rescue attempt, brought down the presidency of Jimmy Carter, and revealed the vulnerability of US military, diplomatic and intelligence personnel in the Middle East.

In January 1979, Islamic fundamentalists took control of Iran and forced the Shah of Iran (Muhammad Reza Shah Pahlevi) into exile. For 30 years, the United States had provided Iran with economic, political and military support in order to ensure a steady supply of oil, but when it agreed to allow the ailing Shah into the United States to be treated for cancer, the revolutionary Islamic regime turned on its former ally. President Carter knew that the decision would leave US embassy personnel at risk from reprisals, but against his better judgment he went ahead on humanitarian grounds. On 1 November 1979, the new Iranian leader, Ayatollah Khomeini, labelled the United States government the 'Great Satan' and 'Enemies of Islam'. Thousands of Iranians demonstrated outside the US embassy in Iran and attacked US-owned businesses.

On 4 November, 500 Iranian students, calling themselves 'Iman's Disciples', occupied the embassy grounds and seized the embassy building. As staff rushed to destroy confidential documents, the students overpowered the token number of Marine guards and took 63 hostages. Three more hostages were taken from the Iranian foreign ministry, while six US embassy staff escaped and were hidden by staff at the Canadian and Swiss embassies. The students demanded that the Shah be returned so that he could stand trial, and stated that they would hold the embassy staff hostage as long as they felt that the United States was contemplating a coup—perhaps one similar to the coup it had carried out in 1953 to install the Shah.

The hostage crisis lasted 444 days and spanned the entire year of 1980. President Jimmy Carter, his presidency already in trouble because of the economic crisis the United States faced in the late 1970s, stated that his priority for the remainder of his term would be the safe return of the hostages.

Iranian oil imports were suspended, Iranian diplomats were expelled from the United States and US$8 billion worth of Iranian assets were frozen. The Iranian students paraded the blindfolded hostages in public and in front of television cameras, and displayed sensitive intelligence documents—some painstakingly pieced together after having been shredded—to prove that the US embassy was a front for the CIA and was spying on the Iranian people. Several embassy staff, including 33-year-old Dr William Dougherty, had worked for the CIA in Iran.

On 19–20 November, the Ayatollah Khomeini released 13 female and African–American hostages because, he said, women and minorities also suffered from American 'oppression'. The remaining 53 hostages (who included two women, Elizabeth Ann Swift and Kathyrn Koob, and an African–American, Charles Jones) remained on display until 20 January 1980, when the Canadian embassy successfully smuggled out the six US embassy staff using Canadian passports. President Carter refused to publicly acknowledge the Iranian demands for the release of the hostages—the return of the Shah for trial, an apology for the 1953 coup that installed him in power and a commitment not to interfere in Iranian politics in the future—and tried to end the crisis by diplomacy. Something needed to be done to break the stalemate, and with Carter's popularity diving in the polls (1980 was a presidential election year), the president realised that it had to be something daring and drastic. In April 1980, he approved 'Operation Bear Claw'.

On the night of 24–25 April, the United States conducted an ill-conceived mission aimed at rescuing the Iranian hostages. As transport aircraft prepared for a Special Forces landing on an airstrip in the Great Salt Desert in eastern Iran, the mission had to be aborted because of mechanical damage suffered in a sandstorm.

During the pull-out a helicopter collided with a C-130 plane and eight soldiers were killed. When the dead bodies of the US servicemen were displayed in Tehran, Cyrus Vance, Jimmy Carter's secretary of state, who had opposed the mission, resigned. Carter was soundly beaten by Republican candidate Ronald Reagan in the election for the US presidency later that year.

But by July 1980, relations with Iran had started to thaw. On 11 July, 28-year-old New Yorker Richard Queen was released by his captors because of an illness later diagnosed as multiple sclerosis. When the Shah died in Egypt at the end of that month, the Islamic hard line softened. The invasion of Iran by neighbouring Iraq (led by the US-backed dictator Saddam Hussein) in September 1980 changed Iranian revolutionary leadership's priorities.

On 4 November 1980—exactly one year after the hostages were taken—Republican Ronald Reagan was elected the 40th president of the United States. The knowledge that a new, right-wing government was taking power hastened the resolution of the crisis. Iran was now ready to negotiate.

Using Algerian diplomats as go-betweens, Carter negotiated the 'payment' of US$8 billion in frozen assets (the Iranians wanted US$30 billion) and the lifting of economic, diplomatic and political sanctions in return for the hostages' release. Carter desperately wanted the remaining 52 hostages freed in the final days of his presidency—one final accomplishment to end a wretched year—but the Iranians held firm. Carter allegedly took a phone to Ronald Reagan's inauguration on 20 January 1981, hoping that he would secure the hostages' freedom, but it was not to be. President Reagan spoke to the hostages minutes after he took office, and they were flown to freedom and landed at Frankfurt Air Force Base in West Germany.

Waiting there to welcome them was Reagan's special emissary, former president Jimmy Carter.

HISTORICAL AND SOCIAL SIGNIFICANCE:

- After the aborted mission to rescue the hostages in April 1980, President Jimmy Carter approved a second rescue attempt codenamed 'Credible Short'. The mission was abandoned in November 1980 after Carter lost the presidential election.
- In December 1979, Penelope Laingen, the wife of one of the hostages, tied a large yellow ribbon around a tree outside her house. The American public followed suit until the hostages returned home. The idea was based on the popular 1973 song 'Tie a Yellow Ribbon Around the Old Oak Tree'.
- In 2000, the hostages and their families attempted to sue Iran under the 1996 US Anti-terrorism Act. Two years later, the US government ruled that damages could not be paid to the victims because of the terms of the agreement made when the hostages were freed.

REFERENCES:

- Jimmy Carter (2005), *The Hostage Crisis in Iran, www.pbs.org*
- Various articles, *www.jimmycarterlibrary.com*
- CBS News (2001), *Iran Hostage Anniversary, www.cbsnews.com*

1980
Death of an Ex-Beatle

FACT FILE

CRIME: Murder
VICTIM: John Lennon, aged 40, former Beatle and peace activist
DATE: 8 December 1980
PLACE: Dakota Building, New York City (USA)
PERPETRATOR: Mark David Chapman
SENTENCE: Life imprisonment

On 9 October 1980, ex-Beatle John Lennon celebrated his 40th birthday and his son Sean's fifth birthday. His new album and single were doing well, and an optimistic and rested John Lennon was again doing the rounds of publicity interviews and looking forward to the future. On 8 December 1980, he gave what was to be his final interview to San Francisco DJ Dave Sholin and sat for a photo session with famous photographer Annie Leibovitz before leaving for a quick limousine ride to the Record Plant to mix Yoko Ono's new song 'Walking on Broken Ice'. As he left the Dakota Building with Yoko and Sholin at about 5 pm, Lennon was asked to sign a copy of his new album, *Double Fantasy*, by a heavy-set, bespectacled fan. Six hours later, that unknown man shot John Lennon dead.

John Winston Ono Lennon used his celebrity status as a member of one of the most successful bands in the history of pop music to promote peace and to pursue a creative artistic partnership with his Japanese-born second wife, Yoko Ono. As the unofficial leader of the Beatles (Lennon was the founder of the group and the one who coined the name 'Beatles'—itself a clever pun and a homage to Buddy Holly's backing group, the Crickets), he was one-half of the 'Lennon–McCartney' songwriting partnership that wrote the soundtrack to the 1960s. Lennon was directly responsible for writing such classic songs as 'Help!' 'Strawberry Fields Forever', 'Lucy in the Sky with Diamonds', 'Revolution' and 'Come Together' but was also a talented author (*In My Own Write* and *A Spaniard in the Works*) and actor (*A Hard Day's Night* and *How I Won the War*).

By the end of the 1960s, the former 'mop-top'—now pressing 30 years of age—was ready to spread his artistic wings. In March 1969, Lennon married his second wife, Yoko Ono, in Gibraltar and together the pair staged a series of 'events' to promote world peace. In July the Lennons held court to local and international media in their bedroom in a Toronto hotel and spoke out against the war in Vietnam.

However, their antics did not endear them to Lennon's legion of fans, his former Beatle bandmates or the US government. After the Beatles disbanded in 1970, Lennon recorded the song 'Imagine'—arguably the greatest 'peace' song of all time (English fans rated the anthem amongst the top three songs of the twentieth century)—before moving to New York. The mid-1970s saw Lennon's solo career stagnate, and after an 18-month separation from Yoko (Lennon called this his 'lost weekend' period), he reunited with her and settled down to an ordinary domestic life following the birth of their son, Sean, in 1975.

For five years John Lennon stayed out of the celebrity limelight, living in New York's famous Dakota Building and opting for the relative obscurity of being a 'house husband' while his wife attended to their business interests. Lennon spent time building relationships—he took a hands-on role in raising Sean, established a better relationship with his eldest son from his first marriage, Julian, and was again on speaking terms with his former songwriting partner Paul McCartney. But most importantly, he strengthened his love for Yoko and rejuvenated his creative talents. By the summer of 1980, he was ready to record again. Only this time, Yoko Ono would be his recording partner. The album was called *Double Fantasy*; the first single was called '(It's Just Like) Starting Over'.

Mark David Chapman was a deluded loner. Born in Georgia in 1955, Chapman was the product of a broken marriage and a troubled adolescence who had struggled to find his place in society. A YMCA volunteer, college dropout and security guard, he originally idolised celebrities such as John Lennon but became increasingly disenchanted with what he saw as 'phoneys'. (*Catcher in the Rye*, a famous novel about teenage alienation, was Chapman's favourite book.) After a failed suicide bid in Hawaii in 1977, Chapman travelled to Tokyo at the same time as John and Yoko were visiting the country. In the first of several eerie incidents that deliberately mirrored Lennon's life, Chapman married a Japanese travel agent, Gloria Abe, but his personal life became increasingly erratic.

After his marriage broke down, Mark Chapman became increasingly agitated and quit his job. (He signed his last work card 'John Lennon'.) The ex-Beatle's re-emergence in the media coincided with Chapman's mental breakdown; in October 1980 the 25-year-old purchased a snub-nosed .38 calibre revolver and a one-way ticket to New York. In his own mind, in order for him to finally be someone, John Lennon had to die.

Mark Chapman loitered around the Dakota Building from 30 October to 9 November (he travelled to Atlanta to obtain dumdum bullets for his gun from an old friend because he did not have a gun licence) and then phoned his estranged wife to tell her that he was coming home. He told his wife that he had 'won a great victory' over his inner demons. Three weeks later, after suffering a series of hallucinations, Chapman returned to New York and carried out his plan. At 10.50 pm on 8 December, as John Lennon and Yoko Ono returned from the recording studio, Chapman was waiting for them. As the Lennons walked past, oblivious of the man whose album Lennon had signed earlier that day, Chapman took a combat stance and called Lennon's name. As the music superstar turned around, Chapman fired five shots into Lennon's body. The ex-Beatle collapsed in the doorway of the Dakota Building, fatally wounded.

Jay Hastings, the 27-year-old front desk clerk at the Dakota Building, called for a police car from the nearby 20th Precinct station, and two police officers bundled the stricken singer into the car and took him to nearby Roosevelt Hospital. John Lennon was pronounced dead on arrival—any one of the four bullet wounds would have been fatal. When other officers arrived at the crime scene, they found Mark Chapman reading a copy of *Catcher in the Rye* with the murder weapon nearby after it had been kicked away by Hastings. That winter's night thousands of fans surrounded the Dakota Building and crammed Central Park West, and held a candlelight vigil in memory of the slain ex-Beatle.

John Lennon's murder not only robbed the world of a great artist, it also took away a man who had just found himself.

HISTORICAL AND SOCIAL SIGNIFICANCE:

- Mark Chapman pleaded guilty to murder and was sentenced to life imprisonment with a minimum parole period of 24 years. He has been denied parole every year since 2002.
- After Lennon's death, his 'final' studio album, *Double Fantasy* (in collaboration with his wife, Yoko Ono), went to No.1 in most countries around the world. Lennon's death ended decade-long conjecture that the four Beatles would re-form. In 1995, Paul McCartney, George Harrison and Ringo Starr re-formed to rerecord the John Lennon songs 'Real Life' and 'Free As a Bird' with the original Lennon vocals.

REFERENCES:

- *Murder Casebook* (1990), Marshall Cavendish, London
- Kane, Larry (2005) *Lennon Revealed*, Running Press, Philadelphia
- BBC Online (8 December 1980), *On This Day, www.bbc.co.uk*

1981

The Yorkshire Ripper

FACT FILE

CRIME: Serial murder

VICTIMS: Patricia Atkinson, aged 32; Jacqueline Hill, aged 20; Emily Jackson, aged 42; Jean Jordan, aged 20; Barbara Leach, aged 20; Wilma McCann, aged 28; Jayne MacDonald, aged 16; Vera Millward, aged 40; Yvonne Pearson, aged 21; Irene Richardson, aged 28; Helen Rytka, aged 18; Marguerite Walls, aged 47; Josephine Whitaker, aged 19

Six other women were attacked by the Yorkshire Ripper but survived

DATES: 30 October 1975 to 17 November 1980

PLACE: Northern England (Leeds, Bradford, Manchester, Huddersfield and Halifax)

PERPETRATOR: Peter Sutcliffe (b. 1946)

SENTENCE: Life imprisonment

Between 1975 and1977, four prostitutes were murdered and three others savagely attacked in the north of England. Then, on 26 June 1977, a 16-year-old shop assistant named Jayne MacDonald was murdered on her way home from a night out with friends. MacDonald, who had spoken to two prostitutes earlier that night, was probably asking for the time, but it was enough to convince her attacker that she too was a prostitute. The following morning her battered and stabbed body was found in a vacant block near her home. The murderer, dubbed the 'Yorkshire Ripper', had struck fear into northern England's red-light district. It is a cruel, hollow reality, but the unsolved murders only gained national—and later international—attention after someone who wasn't a prostitute was murdered.

A 28-year-old prostitute named Wilma McCann, found stabbed and bludgeoned to death in a soccer field close to where her four young children slept in their modest Chapeltown house in Leeds, was the 'Ripper's' first victim, in October 1975. Four months later, Emily Jackson, also from Leeds, was bashed with a hammer and stabbed 52 times with a screwdriver. A year later, in February 1977, the murderer claimed his third victim, Irene Richardson. He struck again two months later in nearby Bradford, killing 32-year-old Patricia Atkinson. The only pieces of evidence the police had to go on were a footprint made by a large industrial shoe left at the scene of one of the murders and the fact that the killer used a hammer to subdue his victims and a sharp implement to mutilate them. The country was in a state of shock after the death of pretty teenager Jayne MacDonald, but the West Yorkshire Police, despite their best endeavours, seemed almost helpless to stop the attacks. The 'Yorkshire Ripper' later regretted killing MacDonald—acknowledging it as a grave mistake—but it didn't stop him from killing again. His name was Peter Sutcliffe.

Peter Sutcliffe was born in North Yorkshire in 1946, the eldest of six children. A weak child with a speech impediment, he left school at 15 and became, among other things, a grave-digger and a truck driver. Sutcliffe had a cruel streak and had experienced poor relationships with the opposite sex. However, he was calm and gentle with his girlfriend, Sonja, whom he married in 1974. She was a quiet woman who developed schizophrenia, and Sutcliffe was both loving towards her and protective of her. The Sutcliffes bought a house together—a period of relative domestic happiness for the budding killer—but Sutcliffe could not control his hatred of women for long. Women, but especially streetwalkers, had become for him hated symbols of his own sexual inadequacy. Authorities later learned that he attacked several defenceless women from behind with a brick in a sock long before the murders began.

Having got away with five murders in two years, Sutcliffe chose Manchester for the scene of his next crime. On 1 October 1977 he killed part-time prostitute and mother of two Jean Jordan, hiding her body in bushes. Sutcliffe had made the mistake of paying his victim with a brand new £5 note from his truck-driving wages, but was disturbed by a passing car before he could retrieve it from his victim. The 'Ripper' waited eight days before returning to the undiscovered crime scene to retrieve the note. When he couldn't find the note in the dark (it was found near the body), Sutcliffe tried to decapitate the body with a pane of glass to throw detectives off the 'Ripper' trail. After the body was discovered, detectives tried to trace the £5 note and actually interviewed Sutcliffe at his place of work twice before the end of the year.

When three more victims were discovered in the early part of 1978, police intensified their efforts to capture the 'Ripper', but Scotland Yard's card index system—a manual system of cross-referencing every piece of information and evidence gathered about the investigation—proved to be far too unwieldy. The 'Yorkshire Ripper' continued his attacks throughout 1978 and 1979, striking victims in the suburbs of Bradford, Halifax and Huddersfield. Nine women had been murdered and the task of finding the killer was becoming no easier. West Yorkshire Police went to the extraordinary extent of spending £1 million on a publicity campaign to catch the 'Ripper', but they focused too much attention on hoax letters and the infamous 'Ripper' audio tape in which a man with a 'Geordie' or Yorkshire accent goaded police to capture him. All this did was to hide Peter Sutcliffe's identity under a mountain of false leads.

By 1980, the 'Yorkshire Ripper' had gained international notoriety, but still the murders continued. Four more women lost their lives—two in 1979 and two in 1980—with several others surviving attacks and giving police vague descriptions of their attacker. All the time Sutcliffe kept up a facade of respectability—picking up his wife from work to 'protect' her from the 'Ripper' and not having to explain his many absences to her because of her constant illness. Over the 1980–81 Christmas–New Year break, police heightened their presence around the red-light districts in the 'Ripper's' favourite haunts, and on the night of 2 January 1981, the police finally got lucky. Peter Sutcliffe, the 'Yorkshire Ripper', was arrested by two police in Sheffield for soliciting a prostitute in a car park.

Sutcliffe originally told the police that his name was Peter Williams, but after establishing that the number plates on his car were stolen they arrested him. Sutcliffe asked if he could relieve himself and the arresting police agreed. Under cover of darkness, Sutcliffe disposed of a ballpein hammer and a sharpened knife, which were later recovered. Sutcliffe was kept in custody for 24 hours and calmly confessed to 13 murders the following day.

While the reign of the 'Yorkshire Ripper' had come to an end, the fallout from the shortcomings of the police investigation and charges of journalistic harassment of witnesses would dominate Sutcliffe's trial. Finally, on 22 May 1981, Peter Sutcliffe was found guilty on 13 counts of murder and sentenced to life imprisonment.

HISTORICAL AND SOCIAL SIGNIFICANCE:

- Sutcliffe tried to feign paranoid schizophrenia during his trial but because his wife suffered from the condition doctors believed that he was able to fake the symptoms. Sutcliffe was sane when he committed the crimes and was simply a sadist who enjoyed killing defenceless women.
- On 10 January 1983, Sutcliffe was attacked and seriously disfigured by a patient wielding a knife in the hospital wing of Parkhurst Prison on the Isle of Wight. He needed 84 stitches after the attack and was transferred to Broadmoor High Security Hospital the following year.
- On 21 March 2006, 49-year-old Sunderland man John Humble was sentenced to six years for each of three letters he sent to the police purporting to be the Yorkshire Ripper, and eight years for the infamous hoax tape.

REFERENCES:

- *Murder Casebook* (1990), Marshall Cavendish, London
- BBC Online (2005), *Case Closed: Peter Sutcliffe, www.bbc.co.uk*
- *The Yorkshire Ripper, www.execulink.com/~kbrannen/*

1981

Ronald Reagan Assassination Attempt

FACT FILE

CRIME: Attempted assassination

VICTIMS: Ronald Reagan, 40th president of the United States, aged 69;
James Brady, aged 40; Timothy J. McCarthy, aged 31; Thomas Delehanty, aged 46

DATE: 30 March 1981

PLACE: Washington, DC

PERPETRATOR: John Hinckley Jnr (b. 1955)

SENTENCE: Found not guilty by reason of insanity and confined to St Elizabeth's Hospital in Washington, DC

On 30 March 1981, just 69 days after his inauguration, President Ronald Reagan barely survived an assassin's bullet after giving a speech at a labour conference at the Hilton Hotel in Washington, DC. President Reagan, who was originally thought to be unharmed, was quickly bundled into his car and—when it was discovered that he was bleeding—taken to George Washington University Hospital. His condition became critical ...

Ronald Reagan, 40th president of the United States, was a talented sportsman in his youth and a sports announcer in Illinois before he moved to Hollywood and started his film career.

After his nationally televised endorsement of 1964 Republican presidential candidate Barry Goldwater, the Republican Party groomed Reagan as its nominee for governor of California for 1966. A decade later, Reagan emerged as the hope of the Republican Party and the American people, who were looking for change after four years under Jimmy Carter's administration. Despite being almost 70 when he ran for the presidency, Ronald Reagan swept to power in November 1980.

Outside the Hilton Hotel on that day in March 1981, 24-year-old John Hinckley fired six shots from a Rhom revolver before he was pounced upon by secret service agents, Washington police and members of the press.

Reagan was hit in the chest under his left arm when a stray bullet ricocheted off the windscreen of the presidential limousine. The bullet was of an exploding type, but it did not explode. However, Reagan's condition became critical because of blood loss and a collapsed lung. James Brady was shot in the left temple and a bullet lodged in his brain, causing him to be partially paralysed. Timothy McCarthy was shot in the stomach and Thomas Delehanty in the neck.

John Hinckley Jnr was the son of one of the major supporters of George H. Bush—Reagan's Republican vice president. Hinckley Snr was the chairman and president of Vanderbilt Energy Corporation in Texas. His youngest child, John Jnr, was a popular sportsman in elementary school but grew increasingly isolated as a teenager. An occasional student at Texas Technical University and a failed songwriter, Hinckley wrote to his family about a fictitious girlfriend while living a subsistence lifestyle in California. He became obsessed with the former child actress Jodie Foster, watching the 1976 movie *Taxi Driver* 15 times. In the film, a character played by Robert De Niro hatches a plan to assassinate a political candidate. De Niro's 'Travis Bickel', the taxi-driver in the film, later kills a pimp in order to rescue a child prostitute played by Foster, and becomes an unlikely hero.

In 1980, when Hinckley read that Jodie Foster was studying at Yale University, he moved to New Haven, Connecticut, to be nearer to her and enrolled in a writing course. Hinckley phoned the actress and left notes and poems for her, but did not form any reasonable contact with her. In his deranged mind, Hinckley decided that he would gain Foster's 'respect and love' by assassinating President Carter.

The troubled young man followed Carter across the country during the president's re-election campaign and was arrested at Nashville Airport, in Tennessee, for possession of a gun. Hinckley returned home to Colorado and was under psychiatric care for his depression. A psychiatrist diagnosed 'emotional immaturity' as the root of Hinckley's problem and recommended that his parents cut him off financially.

However, after Ronald Reagan's inauguration in January 1981, Hinckley changed his target to the newly elected president. Hinckley flew to Hollywood before boarding a bus for Washington, where he booked in at the Park Central Hotel on 29 March. The following day he wrote a letter to Jodie Foster outlining his intention to assassinate the president and impress her with his 'historical deed'. At 1.30 pm John Hinkley Jnr stepped forward out of a crowd of reporters and shot Ronald Reagan outside the Hilton Hotel.

On 21 June 1982, John Hinckley Jnr was found not guilty by reason of insanity and was confined to St Elizabeth's Hospital in Washington, DC.

REFERENCES:

- McPherson, James M. (2000), *To the Best of My Ability: The American Presidents*, DK Press, New York
- *Forgotten Coverage of the Hinckley Assassination* (2005), *www.hereinreality.com*
- *John W. Hinckley, Jnr: A Biography* (2005), *www.law.umkc.edu*

1981
Pope John Paul II Shot

FACT FILE

CRIME: Attempted murder
VICTIM: Pope John Paul II, aged 60
DATE: 13 May 1981
PLACE: St Peter's Square, Rome (Italy)
PERPETRATOR: Mehmet Ali Ağca (b. 1958)
SENTENCE: Life imprisonment. Ağca was extradited to Turkey in 2000, where he is currently serving another life sentence for an unrelated murder

During World War II, Karol Jozef Wojtyla was a seminary student in his native Poland. Ordained a Catholic priest in 1946, he became a professor of moral theology and was named Archbishop of Cracow. Created a cardinal in 1967, Karol Wojtyla became the first non-Italian Pope in 450 years when he succeeded John Paul I (and took his name) in 1978. An articulate, analytical and popular pontiff, he travelled the world during the first ten years of his papacy and renewed interest in the Holy Catholic Church, especially in communist countries. In 1981, Pope John Paul II barely survived an assassination attempt by Turkish national Mehmet Ali Ağ ca as the pontiff greeted a crowd in St Peter's Square in Rome.

Mehmet Ali Ağca was born in Turkey in 1958. A petty criminal and street gang member, he became a smuggler in Turkey and neighbouring Bulgaria. He later went to Syria, where he trained in weaponry and terrorist tactics. A self-described mercenary of no political persuasion, Ağca was willing to do anything for money. In 1979, under orders from the Grey Wolves terrorist group, he killed the left-wing newspaper editor Abdi Ipekçi in Istanbul. Caught and sentenced to life in prison, Ağca escaped and, with the help of the Grey Wolves, fled to Bulgaria.

Ağca later alleged that he was working for the Bulgarian government when he shot the Pope. The KGB had instructed the communist government, Ağca said, to assassinate the Pope because of his support of Poland's Solidarity movement. However, Ağca later renounced this story and Pope John Paul II himself rejected claims of a Bulgarian connection with his shooting. Ağca later gave a hint of the real reason behind this unprecedented crime. 'To me [the Pope] was the incarnation of all that is capitalism,' he said. The Turk entered Rome on 10 May 1981, by train from Milan. In Rome, he later claimed, he met up with three accomplices—one Turk and two Bulgarians. The plan was for Ağca, and a second gunman named Oral Celik to shoot the Pope in St Peter's Square and then detonate a bomb to create chaos and allow the assassins to escape.

On 13 May 1981, the two Turkish terrorists sat in St Peter's Square writing postcards and waited for Pope John Paul II to arrive. At 5.19 pm Mehmet Ali Ağca shot the Pope in the abdomen and hand as the pontiff entered St Peter's Square in an open car to address a waiting audience. Ağca fired only two shots before he was grabbed by members of the crowd. Celik fled the scene and did not shoot at the Pope or set off a bomb. Doctors credited the decision by Archbishop Stanislaw Dziwisz, the Pope's private secretary, to take the pontiff directly to hospital in his vehicle instead of waiting for an ambulance with saving his life. Severely wounded, Pope John Paul II was operated on for six hours at Gemelli Hospital and was hospitalised for 22 days. Four days after he was shot, John Paul II was strong enough to recite the angelus. 'Pray for the brother who shot me,' the pontiff said, 'whom I have sincerely forgiven.' On 20 June that year, the Pope was hospitalised for an infection linked to his injuries and underwent further surgery.

At Ağca's trial, his defence descended into insane ranting, including claims that he was Jesus, and he was sentenced to life imprisonment. Two days after Christmas 1983, Pope John Paul II met with his would-be assassin in his prison cell in Rome.

The two spoke privately for some time. John Paul II said, 'What we talked about will have to remain a secret between him and me. I spoke to him as a brother whom I have pardoned and who has my complete trust.'

In 2000, Italian president Carlo Azeglio Ciampi pardoned Mehmet Ali Ağca, and the Italian justice minister then authorised Ağca's extradition to Turkey to serve a prison sentence for another killing.

After his recovery, Pope John Paul II continued the hectic pace of his papacy—travelling the world and greeting crowds in a bullet-proof cart often referred to as the 'pope-mobile'—but his health slowly declined in the 1990s. Pope John Paul II died on 2 April 2005, aged 84.

HISTORICAL AND SOCIAL SIGNIFICANCE:

- On 26 June 2000, Pope John Paul II released the 'Third Secret of Fatima', in which he explained that Ağca's assassination attempt was the fulfilment of this third secret.
- In March 2005, newly released files from the Stasi, the secret police of communist East Germany, appeared to confirm that the KGB had ordered the Bulgarian and East German secret services to kill Pope John Paul II.

REFERENCES:

- BBC Online (13 May 1981), *On This Day, www.bbc.co.uk*

1981

Wayne Williams: The Atlanta Child Murders

FACT FILE

CRIME: Serial murder
VICTIMS: 29 African-American children, youths and young men
DATE: July 1979 to May 1981
PLACE: Guildford, Woolwich, Birmingham (USA)
PERPETRATOR: Wayne Williams (b. 1958)
SENTENCE: Found guilty on two counts of murder, Williams was sentenced to two life terms, to be served consecutively in Fulton County Prison, Georgia

---

In 1979, a series of child murders in the predominantly black suburbs of Atlanta, Georgia, ignited the already strained racial tensions of that state. All the victims were black and many thought that the murders were the work of the Klan, a paedophile network or even some type of payback crimes for the spate of muggings and shootings of white businessmen in the city of Atlanta. The following year, the bodies of black children continued to be found until the person or person(s) changed their attention to young black men and began dumping their bodies in the Chattahoochee River. Twenty-nine victims were attributed to the 'Atlanta Child Murderer' before 22-year-old Wayne Williams was arrested in June 1981 after a major manhunt and charged with two of the murders. Most extraordinarily, Williams broke the mould with what authorities thought they knew about serial killers. Like his victims, Wayne Williams was black.

Wayne Bertram Williams was born in Atlanta, Georgia in 1958, the only son of two Dixie Hills schoolteachers. Williams was spoilt, intelligent and fascinated with electronics but he was also a habitual liar who was content to plunge his parents into bankruptcy with his get-rich schemes. A self-employed talent scout looking for the next Michael Jackson, Williams told anyone willing to listen that he had a major recording deal in the offing, but in reality had very few friends or professional associates.

Williams was also homosexual and his attraction to young black males—some of them street hustlers who were keen to sell their sexual favours—was later seen as a prime motivation in his crimes. Williams had not been in trouble with the law before (in 1976 he was caught impersonating a police officer, but charges were not laid) but he was a 'scanner freak' obsessed with listening to police conversations on CB radio.

Often he would be the first to arrive at a car accident or crime scene, video or photograph it and then sell his images to news agencies. Outsmarting the police was another motivating factor and it is believed he used his inside knowledge of police procedures to pick up his younger victims and evade capture.

From July 1979 to July 1980 eight boys were abducted, strangled and their bodies dumped in woods, dumpsters and landfill areas around Atlanta. Tony Carter, found stabbed to death, and seven-year-old Latonya Wilson, who was kidnapped from her house, were later added to the list of child murders when their bodies were discovered. Four more murders occurred in late 1980 before the killer started dumping bodies in the Chattahoochee River.

On 5 November 1980, United States Attorney General Benjamin R. Civiletti directed the FBI to participate in the investigation of several missing and murdered children in Atlanta, Georgia. In addition to working an independent investigation, the FBI collaborated with the local law enforcement Task Force and provided additional manpower, guidance and technical assistance, but frustratingly the murders continued into 1981.

Seven more victims were found in the early part of 1981, four of them in the Chattahoochee and South Rivers, before the killer changed his focus to young adult males. This may have been a deliberate ploy to put police off the track (with the list of 'victims' now numbering 24, authorities still had difficulty determining whether the murders had been committed by the same person or if some were related to other crimes), or a reflection of the educational and news programs warning children and their parents to be aware of strangers.

Soon after a revolt in the Techwood Homes project area by disgruntled black residents demanding something be done about the murders, the body of 21-year-old Eddie Duncan was discovered in the Chattahoochee River. Although a lot of physical evidence was destroyed, there were distinct similarities to that of an earlier murder, of 16-year-old Patrick Rogers, the previous November.

When two of the next four victims were again given up by the Chattahoochee, police decided to stake out a number of bridges within the boundaries of eleven major streets connected to Memorial Drive. On 22 May 1981 an alert police officer heard a splash underneath the Jackson Parkway Bridge and saw a white 1970 Chevrolet sedan speeding from the scene. The driver, 22-year-old Wayne Williams, told authorities that he was on his way to audition a singer named Cheryl Johnson for a recording contract. Police found no trace of the woman and put Williams under round-the-clock observation. Two days later, the body of Nathaniel Cater—who lived in the same apartment complex as Latonya Wilson—was found floating in the Chattahoochee River. The police finally had a suspect.

Consummately confident in his innocence, Williams held impromptu press conferences on his front porch with news teams while authorities built their case. Although police believed that Williams and his father 'did a major clean-up' of the house in the days before the final victim's body was found, 19 different fibres associated with Williams—his bedspread, bathroom, gloves, carpet, clothing and dog—were matched to two murder victims. Eyewitnesses also placed Williams in the presence of several of the victims and their bloodstains matched samples found in Williams's car. On 21 June 1981 Wayne Williams was arrested and charged with the murder of two victims—Nathaniel Carter and Jimmy Ray Payne.

On 27 February 1982, Wayne Williams was found guilty on two counts of murder in the Fulton County Superior Court, Atlanta, Georgia. Although Williams was sentenced to only two consecutive life terms, prosecutors introduced evidence of a 'pattern' relating to ten of the other unsolved murders.

However, many questions still remain about the other 27 victims listed among the 'Atlanta Child Murders'. Chet Dettlinger, the former assistant Atlanta police chief turned author, raised doubts that Williams was responsible for any or all of the 29 murders alone when he told CNN in 2005, 'I don't know if Wayne Williams is innocent or not. I just don't think they proved him guilty of anything.'

Whatever the full story, there is one inescapable truth: the 'Atlanta Child Murders' suddenly stopped when Wayne Williams was captured.

HISTORICAL AND SOCIAL SIGNIFICANCE:

- Wayne Williams continues to proclaim his innocence. In 2005 DeKalb County Police Chief Louis Graham stated that he planned to reopen the investigation into the murder of five Atlanta victims killed between February and May in 1981. The cases were originally linked to another suspect, but the case was closed after Williams was arrested in 1981. Authorities in neighbouring Fulton County, Georgia, where the majority of the murders occurred, have declined to reopen the cases.

REFERENCES:

- *Wayne Bertram Williams* (2005), *www.crimelibrary.com*
- *Wayne Williams* (2005), *www.nndb.com*

1981

The Anwar Sadat Assassination

FACT FILE

CRIME: Assassination
VICTIMS: Anwar Sadat (1918-1981) and six others, with 28 wounded
DATE: 6 October1981
PLACE: Cairo, Egypt
PERPETRATORS: Khalid Ahmed Showky El-Islambouli and seven others.
SENTENCE: Islambouli and five other of his co-conspirators were executed on 15 April 1982.

Mohammed Anwar el-Sadat (1918–1981) was one of a family of 14 children born into a poor Egyptian-Sudanese family in the Tala District of Egypt. After playing his part in the coup that ousted King Farouk in 1952, Sadat succeeded Gamal Abdel Nasser as Egyptian president in 1970. In 1973–74 Sadat also assumed the role of prime minister—a period in which Egypt was involved in the Yom Kippur War against sworn enemies Israel. As early as 1971, Sadat raised the issue of signing a peace agreement with Israel providing that all occupied territories were returned to neighbouring Arab states. However, during 1972–73, Sadat stated that war was inevitable unless the US forced Israel to accept the United Nations resolution to withdraw from occupied territories captured during the Six-day War in 1967.

On the feast ofYom Kippur—6 October, 1973; the holiest day of the Jewish calendar—Egypt and Syria (backed by nine other Arab states) launched a surprise attack on Israel. But the Israeli army recovered brilliantly and Egypt was on the brink of a disastrous defeat when, on 22 October, the United Nations directed all parties to immediately 'terminate all military activity'. With war a diplomatic and military failure, Sadat sought a peaceful end to the conflict by continuing to negotiate with the Israeli government before announcing that he would be willing to enter into a peace agreement with Egypt's former enemy.

The peace agreement between Egypt and Israel was sponsored by newly elected US President Jimmy Carter in 1978. Carter invited the Egyptian president and Israeli Prime Minister Menachem Begin to his presidential retreat at Camp David resulting in 1978's Camp David Peace Accord. Sadat and Begin were jointly awarded the Nobel Peace Prize for their efforts, but Sadat was severely criticised for his initiative by other Arab leaders and hard-line Muslims from within his own country. In 1979 the Arab League suspended Egypt's membership because of its peace agreement with Israel (it was not readmitted until 1989). Despite Sadat's good intentions internationally, Egypt's growing economic problems in the late 1970s led to civil and social unrest.

In September 1981, Sadat outlawed protest and declared that the Shari'a would be the basis of all new Egyptian law. He was condemned internally and internationally for the severity of a crackdown on Muslim groups, Coptic organisations and university students in which 1600 people were arrested. A blind Muslim cleric, Omar Abdel-Rahman, issued a fatwa approving Sadat's assassination and members of the Egyptian Islamic Jihad organisation took up the challenge.

On 6 October 1981, during the annual holiday parade that marked the Suez crossing in the Yom Kippur War, Sadat was assassinated by radical Muslim fundamentalist army regulars led by army First Lieutenant Khalid Islambouli. Several times that afternoon, soldiers broke from their ranks and ran up to Sadat and saluted him. As Mirage jets flying overhead distracted the crowd, a military truck towing a large gun stopped in front of the official reviewing stand and a group of assassins ran from the truck, threw grenades and fired assault rifles over the heads of the crowd. Sadat was wounded when Khalid Islambouli, a member of Egypt's Bombardment Force (Air Force), ran towards the official dais and shot Sadat at almost point black range. Islamnouli allegedly shouted 'I have killed Pharaoh and I do not fear death!' Among the officials who scattered for their lives was UN Foreign Minister Boutros Boutros Ghali, James Tully, the Irish Minister for Defence, and four international military advisors. Among seven people killed were the Cuban ambassador, a Greek Orthodox priest and Sadat.

Sadat's successor, Honsi Mubarak, the Egyptian vice-president and a former air force pilot, was unharmed despite sitting beside his president when he was killed. In the subsequent trial of the assassins in December 1981, it was revealed that the conspirators were members of a militant group called Jama'at al-Jihad (Organization for Jihad).

REFERENCES:

- Anwar el-Sadat, *www.jewishvirtuallibrary.org*
- The Assasination of Anwar Sadat, *www.ibiblio.org*
- Sadat, *www.elsadat.info*

1983

The Death of Benigno Aquino

FACT FILE

CRIME: Murder
VICTIM: Benigno 'Ninoy' Aquino, aged 50
DATE: 21 August 1983
PLACE: Manila International Airport, The Philippines
PERPETRATOR: Rolando Galman
SENTENCE: Galman was shot by troops before he could be charged with the crime. Several members of the military team assigned to protect Aquino on the tarmac are serving life sentences.

Benigno 'Ninoy' Aquino (1932–1983) was a leading opposition leader in the Philippines during the Marcos regime of the 1970s. Born in Concepción, Tarlac, Aquino was elected mayor of Tarlac at the age of 22 in 1954—the same year he married American-educated Corazón Cojuangco. In 1961 he became governor of Tarlac and six years later became the youngest elected Senator in the country's history. When President Ferdinand Marcos declared martial law in 1972 Aquino was jailed on trumped up charges of 'murder and subversion' and was sentenced to death in November 1977. Bowing to international pressure, especially from the United States of America, President Marcos commuted the sentence to life in exile to allow Aquino to receive medical attention for a heart problem in 1980.

After he recuperated from surgery 'Ninoy' Aquino and his wife Corazón continued their opposition to the Marcos regime whilst living in America during the next three years. In August 1983, with President Marcos in his sickbed after a kidney transplant, Aquino decided to return to the Philippines and press the government to lift martial law and, if need be, to 'suffer with his people in this time of crisis'. On 21 August, as his plane sat on the tarmac of Manila International Airport, Benigno Aquino had a speech in his hand to deliver to the Filipino people denouncing the Marcos regime. The speech was never delivered.

Despite the protection of his own bodyguards and the presence of a large government military team on the tarmac 'Aquino was fatally shot in the head as he was escorted off the airplane. Troops immediately shot dead a 'gunman', Rolando Galman, whom they claimed was responsible for Aquino's murder. The brazen nature of the assassination—in front of the world media—shocked the Filipino people and international observers. Most suspected that Aquino's death was ordered by the ailing Ferdinand Marcos, his wife or cronies, such as Eduardo 'Danding' Cojuangco (Cory Aquino's cousin) or high-ranking military personnel such as General Fabian Ver. The Agrava Commission, formed by Marcos to investigate the murder, not surprisingly found many of the high-ranking military officials did not have a case to answer. However, some members of the military team 'protecting' Aquino on the tarmac that day were later jailed for their part in Aquino's murder. Rolando Galman's motivations for killing Aquino or the exact role that he played in the actual shooting, was never made clear.

Aquino's funeral, conducted on 31 August 1983 by the Catholic Archbishop Jaime Sin, lasted twelve hours with over two million people lining the streets during the procession of his body to Manila Memorial Park. Aquino's murder galvanised the Filipino people into action and opposition to the Marcos regime cut across class boundaries. During the next two years Aquino's widow, Cory Aquino, led the call for non-violent regime change in the absence of her husband. Further revelations of the lifestyle excesses of Imelda Marcos, continued governmental mismanagement by those acting on behalf of a gravely ill Ferdinand Marcos and only guarded support by the US Reagan administration, added fuel to the firestorm that would ultimately destroy the Filipino dictatorship.

In November 1985 the Marcos government called a snap election—the first since martial law was enforced in 1972—in the hope that opposition parties would not have time in the 57 days before the 7 February elections to mount an organised campaign. Cory Aquino, the focal point of government opposition since her husband's death, led the unified UNIDO Party into the 1986 elections. When Marcos declared himself the winner, the Filipino people conducted a 'People Power' bloodless revolution and refused to accept the decision. At the same time Marcos was declaring himself President, Cory Aquino was being inaugurated as the 'people's president' at Club Filipino in San Juan, Metro Manila.

After he lost the support of his military advisors, Ferdinand Marcos, his wife and staff fled into exile to Hawaii (the 72-year-old former dictator died there in 1989) and Cory Aquino was officially named the first woman President of the Republic of the Philippines. She proclaimed a provisional constitution in March 1986, which was adopted in a landslide popular vote the following year.

REFERENCES:

- Crystal, David (1994), *The Cambridge Biographical Encyclopedia*, Cambridge
- *Sun Star Davao* (1983), *www.sunstar.com.ph*

1984

The Milperra Bikie Massacre

FACT FILE

CRIME: Murder and affray

VICTIMS: John 'Shadow' Campbell; Mario 'Chopper' Cianter; Phillip 'Leroy' Jeske; Robert 'Foghorn' Lane; Tony 'Dog' McCoy; Ivan 'Sparrow' Romcek; Leanne Waters

DATE: 2 September 1984

PLACE: Viking Tavern, Beaconsfield Street, Milperra, Sydney (Australia)

PERPETRATORS: 43 bikies were charged with murder and affray.

SENTENCE: Nine men were found guilty of murder and sentenced to life; 21 men were found guilty of manslaughter and sentenced to between 10 and 14 years' imprisonment; 12 men were found guilty of affray and were released after spending almost three years in jail awaiting trial. Tony 'Snod' Spencer committed suicide in prison before his trial.

At 1 pm on Sunday, 2 September 1984, while the rest of Australia enjoyed barbecues and picnics on Father's Day, rival bikie gangs faced off in the crowded car park of a suburban tavern in Milperra, Sydney. What was supposed to be a 'swap meet' organised by the British Motorcycle Club—an opportunity for bike enthusiasts to show their club colours and swap bike parts—turned into a pitched battle that raged for 20 minutes. Swap meets had long been seen as 'neutral ground' for rival clubs but not on this day. Simmering hatred between the Bandido and Comanchero bikie groups was the spark that ignited the bloodshed that afternoon. At the end of the melee, 7 people lay dead with 15 others injured.

The Bandido bikie club was formed by members of the Comancheros after complaints that the self-appointed 'supreme commander' was running the club like a paramilitary organisation in order to take over rival clubs. The Comancheros were a powerful Sydney-based gang led by Scotsman William 'Jock' Ross.

Ross, for his part, said that the split occurred because he was opposed to drug trafficking, which was starting to infiltrate the club. A number of bashings and shootings during 1984 only inflamed the division. In July 1984, the Bandidos, led by Tony 'Snod' Spencer, declared war on the Comancheros. On Father's Day morning a group of Bandidos drove past the home of 24-year-old Comanchero Glen Eaves and told him that they would be out 'in force' at the Viking Tavern in Beaconsfield Street, Milperra (in western Sydney) that afternoon to confront their former brothers-in-arms. The Comancheros were already armed and waiting when the Bandidos arrived at the tavern and a stand-off ensued until Comanchero leader 'Jock' Ross waved a machete at the group. A gun was fired and the resulting melee lasted 20 minutes. Weapons including baseball bats, knives, chains, machetes, shotguns and a Rossi .357 rifle, were used with wanton disregard for life. Police later discovered that one of the Comancheros had gone to the 'meet' with three sticks of gelignite and a hand grenade—enough firepower to kill everyone there—but did not explode them. Instead, when uniformed police and the NSW Tactical response group arrived at the scene, seven people lay dead—four Comancheros, two Bandidos and a 14-year-old girl who had gone to the swap meet with a member of the Rebels bike gang—while 21 others required hospitalisation.

On the footpath near Beaconsfield Road, 'Shadow' Campbell had died after being moved there by Bandidos after taking a shotgun load to the face. Nearby in the car park, fellow Bandido Mario 'Chopper' Cianter lay on his back with his eyes starring blankly at the sky. Between two Harley Davidson motorbikes lay Robert 'Foghorn' Lane, the vice president of the Comancheros, who had been killed by a .357 magnum Rossi rifle blast to the centre of his chest. Tony 'Dog' McCoy lay nearby, his face covered with blood, and his Comanchero colours pelted with shot. Phillip 'Leroy' Jeske, the Comanchero 'sergeant at arms' had also been killed by the .357 Rossi—the blast shooting a hole through the club crest of his jacket.

The fourth Comanchero to die was Ivan 'Sparrow' Romcek who had been hit in the face and neck with a shotgun blast at close range. Beside him was a 'Louisville Slugger' baseball bat that he had been using as a weapon.

The petite body of 14-year-old Leanne Waters, dressed in blue denim and wearing a striped woollen jumper, struck a stark contrast to the other victims. The girl had been struck in the jaw by a stray .357 magnum bullet and had died near the entrance of the Viking Tavern. Waters, a ward of the state, was selling raffle tickets when shot and had allegedly moved into the line of fire to protect her boyfriend when the fighting started. Waters' guardians did not even know she was at the tavern that day.

The police investigation was hindered by the fact that the bikies would not talk because of a 'code of silence' and loyalty to their respective clubs. Many of the victims were carrying false drivers' licences, which made identification difficult. However, Bandido club secretary Bernie Podgorski turned informer and, after being granted immunity from prosecution, assisted the squad of 250 police working on the case to secure convictions. Raids on both bikie clubhouses revealed other weapons and evidence of a 'hit list' of who was to be killed. But there was also a random nature to the murders—it was as if the stand-off had got out of hand and people were killed just because they were closest. The 'Milperra Massacre' Task Force eventually laid seven murder charges against 43 people (17 Comancheros and 26 Bandidos)—a total of 301 counts of murder. It was the largest number of murder charges laid for a single event in the history of Australia.

While awaiting trial, Tony 'Snod' Spencer, who had been identified as firing the Rossi rifle that killed three people, including Leanne Waters, hanged himself in prison on 28 April 1985. The trial of the remaining 42 defendants got under away in April 1986 after they had been spilt into two groups—31 charged with murder and 11 with the lesser charge of affray. On Friday, 12 June 1987, after one of the longest and most expensive trials in Australian criminal history, the jury (which had to retire 31 times to consider its verdicts) found 30 people guilty and one (former Commonwealth Games boxer Phillip 'Knuckles' McElwaine) not guilty of murder, but guilty of affray.

Nine men were sentenced to life for murder and affray while the remaining defendants were found guilty of manslaughter and affray and sentenced to between 10 and 14 years jail. Twelve men were found guilty of affray but were immediately released having spent almost three years in jail awaiting trial.

The Milperra Bikie Massacre appalled Australia. Far from becoming an 'important part of Australian folklore' as one writer has described it, the Milperra Bikie Massacre was carried out by a lawless band of men who chose to deal with club conflict with baseball bats, machetes and guns. 'Jock' Ross and 'Snod' Spencer, who led their rival gangs into the massacre that Father's Day afternoon, served the longest of any of the bikies—but just five years and three months.

The other people found guilty of murder, manslaughter and affray at Milperra spent an average of four years and six months in jail.

REFERENCES:

- Stephenson, Ron (2003), *The Milperra Bikie Massacre*, New Holland, Sydney
- *Details of the Milperra Bikie Massacre* (1999), *www.thefiringline.com*

1984
Indira Gandhi Assassinated

FACT FILE

CRIME: Assassination
VICTIM: Indira Gandhi, aged 67
DATE: 31 October 1984
PLACE: New Delhi, India
PERPETRATORS: Beant Singh, Satwant Singh, Kehar Singh and Babir Singh
SENTENCE: Beant Singh was killed by soldiers. Satwant Singh and Kehar Singh were hanged on 9 January 1989. Babir Singh was acquitted.

The Gandhi–Nehru dynasty was as influential to Indian political history as the Kennedy family was to American political life. Indira Gandhi (1917–1984) was the daughter of Jawaharla Nehru, the first prime minister of India. After studying at Oxford University she married Feroze Khan in 1942 but her parents did not approve of the inter-religious marriage (Khan was a Muslim). 'Mahatma' Gandhi agreed to adopt Khan so that the marriage would not offend Hindus (Khan's mother's name was derived from the Persian form of Gandhi, spelt *Gandhi*, and he changed his name so that he could wed Nehru's daughter). While the marriage produced two sons, Sanjay and Rajiv, it was not a success and they later moved apart in the 1960s.

Indira Gandhi became president of the Indian Congress Party (1959–60) and following the death of Lal Shastri, became Prime Minister of India in 1966. During the 1970s Gandhi struggled to contain sectarian violence domestically and following her conviction for electoral malpractice in 1975, declared a state of emergency that was kept in place for two years. Defeated in 1977 she returned for a second term as Prime Minister in 1980. That year her eldest son and political heir, Sanjay Gandhi, was killed in a plane crash.

During the 1980s many of the country's 13 million Sikhs felt that Indian society discriminated against them both culturally and politically. Members of the Sikh community became increasingly militant, committing terrorist acts and calling for the secession of the northwest Punjab district. Disputes between Sikhs and Hindus were increasingly the source of political violence. In an effort to contain religious violence, Gandhi began to crack down severely on Sikh extremists. On 5 June 1984, Indian troops stormed the Golden Temple in Amritsar in order to end a four-day siege by Sikh militants. 'Operation Blue Star', as the military operation was known, was designed to flush out Khalistan separatists who were using the holiest temple in the Sikh religion as a base.

Sikh leaders Sant Jarnail Singh Bhindranwale and General Shabeg Singh had taken siege in the Golden Temple earlier in 1984 but by June, Prime Minister Indira Gandhi had had enough. On 3 June, a 36-hour curfew was imposed in the Punjab state and the Golden Temple was surrounded. This coincided with the anniversary of the martyrdom of Guru Arjan Dev, who built the Golden Temple, which meant that it was full of worshippers. From 4.30 to 7.30 pm, a senior army officer repeatedly ordered the militants and worshippers to come out of the temple. Finally, army tanks were deployed against the non-military target and many of the buildings surrounding the temple were destroyed. There were about 3000 people inside the temple when the assault on the temple began, including 950 pilgrims and 380 priests and other temple personnel. Tanks were used to attack the Sikh separatists but many worshippers were killed in the crossfire and the temple itself was severely damaged. Conservative estimates state that as many as a thousand people were killed during the battle, although the figure was more likely much higher because of the civilian casualties.

On 31 October 1984, Indira Gandhi was gunned down by her Sikh bodyguards to avenge the army's assault on the Golden Temple during Operation Blue Star the previous June. That morning, the Indian prime minister was walking through the garden of her New Delhi home at No.1 Safdarjung Road when her guards opened fire with their automatic weapons. Gandhi was on her way to her office to meet with actor Peter Ustinov, who was making a documentary about her. Guard Beant Singh was killed by the Indo Tibetan Border Police soon after the assassination while Satwant Singh was captured along with two alleged accomplices, Kehar Singh and Babir Singh.

Indira Gandhi's death was not confirmed by All India Radio until 6 pm that night by which time her son, Rajiv Gandhi, had been sworn in as Indian prime minister.

When general elections were held later that year, Rajiv Gandhi's Congress Party won a record 401 seats in the Lok Sabha.

REFERENCES:

- BBC Online (31 October 1984) *On This Day, www.bbc.co.uk*
- Gupta, Kanchan (2004) *Light a Candle, www.rediff.com*
- Khare, Harish (2004) *Trauma Revisited, www.freeindiamedia.com*

1985
The Sinking of the *Rainbow Warrior*

FACT FILE

CRIME: Espionage/murder
VICTIM: Fernando Pereira, aged 35
DATE: 10 July 1985
PLACE: Auckland, New Zealand
PERPETRATOR: French agents Major Alain Mafart and Captain Dominique Prieur
SENTENCE: 10 years for manslaughter

The Greenpeace organisation was founded in 1971 in Vancouver, Canada by environmental activists who wanted to stop the US nuclear tests on Amchitka Island, off the coast of Alaska. Passionately pro-environmental and opposed to any nuclear testing, Greenpeace quickly earned its international reputation as pro-active but non-violent interventionists. The organisation focused its activities upon the world's environmental trouble spots and had quickly caught the ire of the French government when it interrupted its nuclear test program in Polynesia in 1972. In 1978, Greenpeace acquired a deep sea fishing boat called the *Grampian Fame* and refitted and renamed it the *Rainbow Warrior*.

In 1985, the French government resumed atmospheric nuclear testing on Moruroa Atoll in the South Pacific Ocean. In July 1985 the international crew of the *Rainbow Warrior* docked the 40-metre schooner at Marsden Wharf in Auckland's Waitemata Harbour and readied themselves to lead a flotilla of protest vessels inside Moruroa's 12-mile (17km) exclusion zone. On the night of 10 July, the 13 crew members of the Warrior celebrated the birthday of American anti-nuclear campaigner Steve Sawyer while the boat was docked in New Zealand. After sharing a birthday cake on board, most of the crew went ashore at 11 pm to continue Sawyer's birthday celebrations. Of those left behind, skipper Peter Wilcox and two others went to their cabins while Portuguese photographer Fernando Pereira remained in the mess with several others and shared some beers.

Just before midnight the *Rainbow Warrior* was shaken by a huge blast. The ship's generator went dead, and below deck the darkness was split by the rush of water. Wilcox immediately thought that the *Rainbow Warrior* must have been hit by another vessel, such as a harbour tugboat. Davey Edwards, the chief engineer, found a massive hole in the engine room and the lower deck stairs were quickly covered by water. Guided by the glow of emergency lighting, those in the mess rushed below to see if anyone was still in their cabins. Those asleep in their cabins quickly made their way out and were told to abandon ship.

It was then that Fernando Pereira made the fatal mistake of returning to his cabin to rescue his valuable photographic equipment. While he was below, a second blast rocked the boat. It was only when the crew assembled on the wharf that they realised that one of their colleagues was missing. When the New Zealand police sent divers down to retrieve Pereira's body they confirmed that the disaster was a deliberate act of sabotage; the *Rainbow Warrior* had been sunk by two magnetic limpet mines attached to the ship's hull because both holes had the metal turned inwards. The ship was beyond salvaging and the young photographer's death was now a murder investigation.

Greenpeace activists did not immediately suspect the French government (would any country be so stupid as to attack a peace vessel moored in a foreign country?). But the criminal investigation undertaken in New Zealand—the largest the country had witnessed—proved otherwise. Helped by a series of public tip-offs, it was discovered that two agents working for the French Direction Generale de la Securite Exterieure (DGSE or secret police) had launched a covert operation on foreign soil but had left an obvious trail that eventually led to their capture.

On the night of the bombing, two men were seen carrying a light grey inflatable dinghy from a white van to a slipway of the harbour at about 7 pm (the licence plate of the van was noted by a local taxi driver). When French-bought oxygen tanks were found abandoned on the floor of the harbour near where the *Warrior* was sunk, a search of customs records found that a French vessel, the *Ouvéa*, was also in the vicinity. On the morning of the bombing a foreign couple who said that they were Swiss had returned a rented white van to the airport and asked for a refund. As the van's licence plate had already been given to police, the couple was detained for questioning.

The 'Swiss' pair was identified as high-ranking DGSE officers Major Alain Mafart and Captain Dominique Prieur. It was later established that crewmen from the *Ouvéa* had provided the pair of French agents with explosives, scuba equipments and a dinghy (Petty Officer Jean-Michel Bartelo was the diver who placed the explosives on the *Warrior*'s hull). The *Ouvéa* was intercepted at Norfolk Island (Australia) but there was then insufficient evidence to detain the crew. The French vessel was later scuttled in the Pacific Ocean so that it could not be examined. Greenpeace immediately closed its offices in France (they were not reopened until

1989) as the international backlash against French nuclear testing mounted.

Six weeks after the bombing, Mafart and Prieur went on trial in Auckland but avoided cross-examination and the possibility of implicating others in the espionage act by pleading guilty to the lesser charge of manslaughter (Greenpeace later stated that a French volunteer had also infiltrated its organisation so as to determine the *Rainbow Warrior*'s movements).

When the French press turned on its own government France finally ordered a second inquiry in September 1985 and the Prime Minister admitted that agents had been ordered to 'neutralise' the *Rainbow Warrior.* With the United Nations acting as an intermediary, France later formally apologised to the New Zealand government and paid NZ$13 million compensation.

Several years later France agreed to pay Greenpeace US$8 million, which was used to purchase and fit out *Rainbow Warrior II.*

HISTORICAL AND SOCIAL SIGNIFICANCE:

- The name 'Rainbow Warrior' came from a Native American legend about the 'Warriors of the Rainbow'—members of all nations who would one day band together and save the Earth.
- The 'fallout' from the bombing of the *Rainbow Warrior* saw France increasingly isolated by the international community. Although France resumed atmospheric nuclear testing in the Pacific in 1995 after a three-year moratorium, the program ended the next year.
- This act of violence by an international power on Kiwi soil led to the New Zealand government declaring the country 'nuclear free' in 1987.
- In 1987 the *Rainbow Warrior* was later patched up, towed to Matauri Bay in the Cavalli Islands and scuttled in order to become an artificial reef.
- Greenpeace, which is now based in Amsterdam, now has 2.8 million members globally and offices in 41 countries.

REFERENCES:

- Greenpeace Australia, *Pacific* (2005) *Rainbow Warrior www.greenpeace.org.au*
- *NZ Disasters: The Rainbow Warrior, www.library.christchurch.org.nz*

1986

The Death of Olof Palme

FACT FILE

CRIME: Murder
VICTIM: Sven Olof Palme, Prime Minister of Sweden, aged 59
DATE: 28 February 1986
PLACE: Sveavägen (the street name), Stockholm (Sweden)
PERPETRATOR: Unknown

The murder of Swedish prime minister Olof Palme in February 1986, shot on a Stockholm street while walking with his wife Lisbet after watching a film, has haunted Swedes for over 20 years. That the person responsible for Palme's murder has not been brought to justice remains a grave concern for everyone in the international community of nations who value peace.

Sven Olof Palme was born in Åstermalm, Stockholm on 30 January 1927. Despite his privileged background, Palme was influenced by socialist ideals and became a member of the Social Democratic student association while studying law at Stockholm University. Palme's 'world view' of social issues may have been formed by his time in the Swedish Army during the latter part of World War II, the BA in Political Science he obtained from Kenyon College Ohio in 1948 or the three months he spent hitch-hiking in America after his graduation, but his political career was launched with his election as President of the Swedish National Union of Students in 1952. The following year he was recruited by Prime Minister Tage Erlander, a social democrat, to work as his personal secretary, and was elected to the Swedish Parliament ('The Riksdag') in his own right in 1958. Palme held several ministries, including Communication (1965) and Education (1967) during his six years in Erlander's cabinet. When the Swedish prime minister stood down in 1969, Palme was unanimously elected his successor.

Energetic, imaginative and politically courageous, Olof Palme served as Swedish prime minister from 1969 to 1976 and again from 1982 until his death in February 1986. His twelve and a half years as prime minister, and the stance he took on a number of domestic and international issues, made him one of the dominant figures in Swedish history during the twentieth century. At home, he reduced the number of parliamentary chambers from two to one in 1969 and removed the last of the

Swedish monarchy's constitutional powers in 1975, but his left-wing views gave his political enemies ammunition that he was 'pro-Soviet' and soft on national security.

Internationally, Palme criticised America during the Vietnam War, campaigned against the proliferation of nuclear weapons during the Cold War, recognised the Palestinian Liberation Organisation, visited Fidel Castro in Cuba, and was a leading advocate of economic sanctions against the white South African regime. More than that, Palme's government politically and financially supported the African National Congress (ANC), and gave several anti-apartheid figures such as Oliver Tambo a voice to attack the South African regime whilst in exile from their homeland. Palme was a respected figure internationally; during 1980 to 1982, he mediated for an end to the Iran–Iraq War, on five occasions on behalf of the United Nations.

On the night of Friday, 28 February 1986—a week after he addressed an anti-apartheid rally and declared, 'apartheid cannot be reformed, it has to be eliminated'—the prime minister was shot twice in the stomach as he walked along Sveavägen Street after watching a film with his wife. The unknown assailant, who was wearing a long overcoat in the wintry conditions, also shot Lisbet Palme with a Smith and Wesson revolver, but she survived her injuries. A taxi driver used his two-way radio to raise the alarm while two young women offered medical assistance to the victims. Olof Palme was pronounced dead on arrival. The attack was first viewed as a senseless murder but the likelihood that the leader of Sweden should be the victim of a random attack on the usually safe Stockholm Streets raised immediate concerns of a political assassination.

While Sweden and many other people in the corners of the globe mourned the murdered leader, investigating police made little headway in unmasking the unknown assassin and made several major blunders investigating the senseless crime.

In 1987 Christer Pettersson, a petty criminal, alcoholic and drug user, was arrested in relation to Palme's murder after being identified from police photos by Lisbet Palme. Pettersson was tried and convicted but was released after a successful appeal to the High Court because prosecutors could not link him to the murder weapon. Christer Pettersson died of a brain haemorrhage and organ failure on 29 September 2004, aged 57.

More than twenty years after Olof Palme's death, the Swedish people—and the world—are still waiting for justice.

REFERENCES:

- BBC Online (2003), *Obituary: Anna Lindh, www.bbc.co.uk*
- Burns, Kari Sable (1994), *Unsolved Case of Olof Palme, www.karisable.com/palme.htm*

1988

The Lockerbie Bombing

FACT FILE

CRIME: Mass murder
VICTIMS: 243 passengers, 16 flight crew and 11 citizens on the ground
DATE: 21 December 1988
PLACE: Lockerbie, Dumfries (Scotland, UK)
PERPETRATOR: Abdelbaset Ali Mohmed Al Megrahi
SENTENCE: 27 years' imprisonment (currently under review by the Scottish Criminal Cases Review Commission)

The small town of Lockerbie, 75 miles from Glasgow and 20 miles from the English border, was one of those picture postcard places that dot the south-western region of Scotland. But in December 1988 Lockerbie was the scene of indescribable horror when Pan Am Flight 103, with 259 people en route to New York City, exploded at 31,000 feet and then killed another 11 people living in the town. The investigation into the disaster, which revealed that a terrorist bomb had been planted on board, would continue for another two decades.

Pan American Airways Flight 103 left London's Heathrow International Airport at 18:25 hours—25 minutes overdue—en route to New York's Kennedy Airport. After heading northwest, it reached the Scottish border shortly before 19:00 when Captain James McQuarrie was granted permission to begin the Atlantic crossing. At 19:02, while flying at 804 kilometres per hour and at a height of 9400 metres, Flight 103 disappeared off the radar screen at Shanwick Oceanic Control at Prestwick, Scotland, only to return moments later as multiple squares in a fanning pattern. The worst fears of radar control were quickly realised when the crew of another plane reported a large fireball on the ground.

A minute after the initial explosion, the wing section of the plane containing 91 tonnes of fuel fell on Sherwood Crescent, Lockerbie. Two families, several houses and 60 metres of the wing were vaporised on impact. Four members of one family, the Somervilles, perished in the fire. Twenty-one houses had to be demolished—the only house left standing on the block belonged to Father Patrick Keegans, the town's Roman Catholic priest. So intense was the heat from the fire that locals thought that the nearby Chapel Cross nuclear power plant had gone into meltdown.

Wreckage of Flight 103 was strewn over a 130-kilometre area with many bodies, including the cabin crew, still buckled into their seats (two passengers survived the fall but died soon after they were found). The investigators quickly surmised that the plane had been ripped apart by an explosion and had disintegrated in the air. It was determined that three seconds after the explosion, the nose cone broke off with the cabin crew intact (it crashed into a vacant field near the village of Tundergarth) before any emergency procedures could be activated.

Twenty-one nations were represented among the victims. Thirty-five students from Syracuse University and two from State University at New York who were flying home from an overseas study in London perished in the disaster. Five members of the Dixit family were flying from New Delhi to Detroit, but had missed their earlier flight because of illness and were seated on Flight 103. At least four members (possibly five) of the US intelligence community were on board the plane. Matthew Cannon, the CIA's deputy station chief in Beirut, Lebanon was on board, as was Major Chuck McKee, on secondment to the Defence Intelligence Agency (DIA). Two CIA officers, possibly bodyguards for the other two, were also on board.

Accident investigation authorities later found that plane parts had traces of plastic explosives on them. When the aircraft was 'reconstructed' from 10,000 pieces of debris it was clear that the explosion had gauged a 50-centimetre hole under the 'P' in the letters 'Pan Am' on the left side of the fuselage. A 'high energy event', caused by a 12–15 lb plastic explosive planted in luggage in the forward cargo hold, was enough to bring the aircraft down. The power of the explosion was 'enhanced' by the difference in air pressure inside the plane and the atmospheric conditions outside the plane. Fragments from a Samsonite suitcase—with clothing 'made in Malta' inside it—and a circuit board from a Toshiba radio cassette player were found to have contained Semtex explosive.

There were two obvious motives for the deliberate bombing of Flight 103—retaliation for military strikes by US warplanes of Tripoli and Benghazi, Libya, in April 1986, and the July 1988 downing of Iran Air Flight 655 by an American warship which had incorrectly identified it as a military target (290 passengers from six nations were killed including 66 children).

Authorities discovered that an unaccompanied bag had been loaded on an Air Malta flight to Frankfurt and then on to Heathrow. The clothes in the suitcase used for the bomb were traced to a Maltese merchant who sold them to Abdelbaset Ali Mohmed Al Megrahi—a Lybian intelligence officer and the head of security for Libyan Arab Airlines (LAA). When the circuit board was identified as similar to one found in the possession of a Lybian intelligence agent, the Libyan regime under Colonel Muammar Gadaffi became the number one suspect.

After a three-year investigation by Scottish authorities and the FBI, murder indictments were issued on 13 November 1991 against Abdelbaset Ali Mohmed Al Megrahi and Al Amin Khalifa Fhimah, the LAA station manager in Malta.

United Nations sanctions against Libya forced Libyan leader Colonel Gadaffi into protracted negotiations for the next decade before the accused men were handed over to Scottish authorities on the neutral venue of the Netherlands. The trial was conducted by three Scottish judges with no jury present. On 31 January 2001, Megrahi was sentenced to 27 years prison but Fhimah was acquitted. Megrahi is serving his sentence in Barlinnie Prison in Glasgow and despite the failure of two appeals, continues to profess his innocence.

On 15 August 2003 Libya accepted responsibility for the bombing and paid each family $8 million dollars (an extra $2 million would have been provided if the US had removed Libya from its list of countries supporting international terrorism but it failed to do this by the nominated time). Because Libya did not officially issue a statement of remorse for the loss of life many saw the payment of compensation as the price Libya had to pay to rejoin the international community. One month later, the United Nations removed sanctions against Libya.

HISTORICAL AND SOCIAL SIGNIFICANCE:

- It is now clear that the terrorists who planted the bomb had timed the explosion to occur over the Atlantic Ocean and thereby to avoid detection. However, the plane left Heathrow 25 minutes late and exploded just before it headed out to sea.
- The Motown group The Four Tops and the Sex Pistols' former frontman Johnny Rotten were booked on Flight 103 but arrived too late to board the plane.
- Until the 11 September 2001 bombings, the Lockerbie disaster was the worst act of terrorism ever committed against United States citizens. Americans who died on board the flight numbered 189.
- The Lockerbie bombing was the biggest police investigation in UK history headed by one of the smallest police forces in Scotland—the Dumfries and Galloway Constabulary.
- Each year Syracuse University holds a Lockerbie Remembrance Week starting on 21 December. The University also awards two year-long Lockerbie Academy scholarships to international students wishing to study in New York.

REFERENCES:

- Department for Transport (2005), Air Accidents Investigation Branch: Aircraft Accident Report No 2/90 EW/C1094 *www.dft.gov.uk*

1990

Andrei Chikatilo: The Russian Serial Killer

FACT FILE

CRIME: Serial murder
VICTIMS: 52 victims
DATE: 1978–1990
PLACE: Rostov, southern Russia
PERPETRATOR: Andrei Chikatilo (1936–1994)
SENTENCE: Executed by firing squad, February 1994

The Soviet Union refused to concede that it had a case of serial murder on its hands in southern Russia in the late 1970s and early 1980s. Serial killers belonged in the capitalist West, it argued, and the Communist Party did not tolerate such extreme individualism. Because of this tunnel vision the 'Forest Strip Killer', as the murderer was known, killed over 50 people during the next 12 years after the wrong man was executed for one of the earlier crimes. By the time the man responsible was captured and executed in 1994, the Soviet Union did not exist anymore.

Andrei Romanovich Chikatilo was born on 16 October 1936 in the village of Yablochoyne in the Ukraine. Chikatilo's mother once told him that before he was born an older sibling, Stefan, disappeared and was believed to have been kidnapped and eaten by starving Ukrainians at the height of Russia's famine. Whether this was true or not—it is not clear whether Chikatilo even had a brother—the psychological damage this caused the boy cannot be underestimated. Chikatilo was scared of other boys, shy around girls and experienced violent fantasies. He later told investigators after his capture, 'I know I have to be destroyed. I understand. I was a mistake of nature.'

Chikatilo's father was captured by the Germans during World War II and spent three years in a concentration camp. After his father returned home, young Andrei was forced to publicly renounce him as a Nazi collaborator. Teased and bullied because he wore glasses, Andrei was painfully shy at school and a bed wetter at home. When he grew to puberty, Chikatilo found it difficult to form meaningful relationships with women and was impotent. After failing the entrance exam into Moscow University, he worked as a telephone engineer near Rostov in southern Russia. His sister introduced him to a local girl named Fayina and he later fathered two children by her through a crude form of insemination. After completing a correspondence course in 1971, Chikatilo obtained degrees in Engineering, Russian Literature and Politics and became a teacher.

After a period of domesticity, Chikatilo's violent sexual urges overtook him and he abused students under his care. Forced to resign from the school because of the allegations, he easily obtained another teaching position because the principal was too scared to report him to authorities least it reflect poorly on the state-controlled school system. In 1978 Chikatilo moved to the mining town of Shakhty, not far from Rostov, and started work in another school. On 22 December he claimed his first victim, nine-year-old Lena Zakotnova. Luring her into a shack near the Grushevka River on the pretence of giving her American chewing gum, Chikatilo tried to rape her but could not physically complete the act. He then stabbed the girl and threw her into the river where she drowned.

Incredibly, Chikatilo should have been captured and executed after this first murder. A schoolgirl gave police a good description of the 40-year-old, bespectacled man but Chikatilo's wife provided him with an alibi (why, remains a mystery). A 25-year-old man with a conviction for rape, Aleksandr Kravchenko, 'confessed' to the murder after a period of interrogation and was executed in 1984.

With no free press in the Soviet Union, there was no public outcry about this miscarriage of justice and Chikatilo was able to continue killing with impunity. In 1981, Chikatilo was sacked from his job because of further sexual misconduct and found work as a supply clerk in a factory. Six months later he killed his second victim, 17-year-old Larisa Tkachenko, when she agreed to swap sexual favours for food. Chikatilo strangled her and filled her mouth with dirt to silence her screams.

By September 1983, Chikatilo had murdered 14 victims—including two young men—and the Moscow Militia finally sent Major Mikhail Festisov to investigate the growing list of murdered children, teens and young people whose bodies had been found in the strip of forest near Rostov. Festisov, an experienced detective, was scathing in his evaluation of the investigation being conducted by local police.

The crimes were committed by the same person, he told his superiors. A review of local sex offenders, cross-referenced with those questioned about the known murders, threw up Chikatilo's name. However, when he was investigated more closely he was eliminated as a suspect because his blood sample (AB) did not match the semen sample left on his victims' bodies (A). But Chikatilo had a secret—he was a non-secretor, which meant he had a different blood type to his semen sample.

In 1984 Chikatilo was detained after acting suspiciously among young girls on a train. Suspected of stealing a battery from the factory where he worked, Chikatilo was jailed for three months, but again the blood type anomaly cleared him of further suspicion in the 'Rostov' murders. Released from prison, he murdered again between 1985 and 1987, increasing the body count significantly. In 1990, Chikatilo murdered nine people, mostly boys.

Director of the Central Department of Violent Crime, Issa Kostoyev, had taken over the case and decided to review the files. Although this did not save his final victim, 22-year-old Svetlana Korostik (Chikatilo cut pieces from her body and ate them), it finally tightened the net that caught him. After Kostoyev's case review Andre Chikatilo was once again identified as a prime suspect.

On 20 November 1990, Chikatilo left work to obtain treatment for an injured finger (which had been bitten by one of his victims) and was followed by under-cover police. Police observed him carrying a briefcase down a road and approach a young boy.

The child's mother called the boy to come to her but three undercover police arrested him anyway. A search of his briefcase revealed a jar of lubricant, a length of rope and a long-bladed knife. A further search of Chikatilo's home found 23 knives, a hammer and a pair of shoes that matched a footprint left at the crime scene of one of his victims. Questioned by police, the 'Rostov Ripper' confessed to all of his crimes.

Andrei Chikatilo was kept in a cage during his trial in order to protect him from the relatives of his 52 victims. Found guilty of murder, Chikatilo—the serial killer the Soviet Union refused to believe even existed—was executed on 15 February 1994 by a single bullet to the back of the head.

HISTORICAL AND SOCIAL SIGNIFICANCE:

• Chikatilo suffered from water on the brain when he was born and his head was misshapen. Scientists believe this affected his bladder–seminal control and led to his impotency problems.
• In 1999, *Newsweek* published a story that 29 'multiple murderers' and rapists had been caught in Rostov since Chikatilo had been executed. If true, this would make Rostov the 'serial killer capital of the world'.

REFERENCES:

- Durden Smith, Jo (2005), *100 Most Infamous Criminals,* Arcturus, London
- BBC Online, *Case Closed: Andrei Chikatilo* (2005), *www.bbc.co.uk*
- Ramsland, Katherine (2005), *Andrei Chikatilo, www.crimelibrary.com*

1991

Aileen Wuornos: Female Serial Killer

FACT FILE

CRIMES: Serial murder, robbery and car theft

VICTIMS: Walter Antonio, aged 62; Troy Burress, aged 50; Charles Carskadden, aged 40; Dick Humphreys, aged 56; Richard Mallory, aged 51; Peter Siems, aged 65; David Spears, aged 43

DATES: 1989–90

PLACE: Florida (USA)

PERPETRATOR: Aileen Carol Wuornos (1956–2002)

SENTENCE: Executed by lethal injection on 9 October 2002 at Florida State Prison

Aileen Wuornos was an oddity—a murder study in gender role reversal, although she claimed that she only murdered men because they raped her while she worked the Florida highways as a prostitute—and was erroneously called America's first female serial killer. Two weeks after she was charged with the murders of seven men, lawyers acting on her behalf sold her story to Hollywood. Although she never lived to see it, her life was turned into an Academy Award-winning movie that made Aileen Wuornos something she had always wanted to be ... *somebody*.

Aileen Carol Wuornos was born in Rochester, Michigan, on 29 February 1956 (an unusual date that only occurs every four years). Her father, Leo Dale Pittmann, was a child molester and sociopath who left her mother before Aileen was born. Pittmann, who drifted in and out of their lives, was strangled in prison in 1969—the year before Aileen's mother died. Aileen and her brother, Keith, were raised by their grandparents, Laurie and Britta Wuornos, who subjected the children to further torment. Aileen told authorities that her grandmother was an abusive alcoholic and that her grandfather sexually abused her. Pregnant at 14, she gave her baby up for adoption and ran away for a year before being placed in a reform school.

After her release, Wuornos turned to prostitution. Her brother died of cancer in 1975, and at the age of 19 she was all alone in the world. Wuornos was arrested on several occasions during the 1970s and 1980s for drunkenness, shoplifting and prostitution, and was convicted of armed robbery in 1982. Wuornos was a transient—a barmaid, cleaner and prostitute—who slept on the beach, on the roadside and on the front porch of a biker bar called the Last Resort. Wuornos was a drunk known for her bad temper and her hatred of men, but the biker community tolerated her because she was an outcast and easy with her sexual favours. She lived this lifestyle right up until the time that she was arrested in 1991.

Wuornos was openly bisexual and formed a relationship with 22-year-old Tyria Moore in 1983. She believed that this new relationship would put an end to her feelings of being rejected by men, and so Wuornos spoiled, protected and dominated her new partner. Ironically, this domestic situation led to the start of Wuornos's career as a serial killer.

Wuornos needed money to provide luxuries for her girlfriend, and her hatred of men, coupled with her love of Tyria, drove her to murder her clients. Between 1989 and 1990, Wuornos murdered seven men using the same modus operandi—after offering sex for money, she would have her clients drive to a secluded spot, pull a handgun on them, and then rob and kill them. The body of her first victim, Richard Mallory, was found in a wooded area in November 1989 almost two weeks after his death. Six months later, the naked body of David Spears was found with six bullet wounds to his torso on Highway 19 in Citrus County. Five days later, on 6 June, the body of part-time rodeo worker Charles Carskadden was found in Pasco County. At this stage, however, there was nothing to link the murders.

On 4 July 1990, police found an abandoned car in Orange Springs belonging to 65-year-old Peter Siems. The previous month Siems had left Jupiter, Florida, for New Jersey but never arrived. Witnesses provided police with descriptions of two women seen fleeing Siems' car after they had been involved in a minor accident, and Aileen Wuornos and Tyria Moore were eventually identified as the women via some of their known aliases. A palm print found on the car door handle was later matched to Wuornos. But before she could be located and arrested, Wuornos broke up with Tyria and murdered three more men in consecutive months.

The body of Troy Burress, a sausage salesman from Ocala, was located in a wooded area off State Road 19 in Marion County in August 1990. The body of Dick Humphreys, a retired air force major and former police chief, was found, fully clothed, in Marion County in September, shot six times in the head and torso. Finally, the body of Walter Antonio was found in November. He too had been shot, and his car was located in Brevard County on 24 November.

In January 1991, Tyria Moore was located in Pennsylvania and cracked under questioning. Some of the jewellery she was wearing belonged to her former girlfriend's victims, and she claimed that Aileen Wuornos had dragged her into a life of crime. Tyria took authorities to where Aileen Wuornos stored some other jewellery, and police linked it to the missing men. On 9 January, Wuornos was arrested on the porch of The Last Resort bar after an undercover detective dressed as a biker engaged her in conversation and drank with her for most of the day. When she was arrested leaving the bar, Wuornos thought it was for an outstanding warrant for firearms offences. She was wrong.

Questioned about the murdered men, Wuornos confessed to killing Richard Mallory but said that it was in self-defence. Later she admitted to all seven crimes (police also believed that she was responsible for at least another three murders) but was tried for only one murder. While awaiting trial, Wuornos was adopted by born-again Christians, but it did not help her demeanour—she was argumentative during her trial and verbally abused the jury. Found guilty and sentenced to death in January 1992, she spent ten years on death row before being executed on 9 October 2002.

Aileen Wuornos chose lethal injection over the electric chair for her exit door to a world that had rejected her and, in a final act of defiance, declined a last meal. She showed no remorse for her actions, adding that she would kill again because she had 'hated humans for a long time'. Her final words, though, gave an indication that she may have had her eyes not only on heaven but also on that great Hollywood prize: 'I'd like to say I'm sailing with [wrestler/actor] The Rock, and I'll be back like Independence Day—with Jesus, June 6—like the movie; big mothership and all. I'll be back.'

HISTORICAL AND SOCIAL SIGNIFICANCE:

- Aileen Wuornos is the second woman to have been executed in Florida since the death penalty was reinstated in some states of the United States in 1976.
- An unrecognisable Charlize Theron starred in *Monster*, the 2003 movie based on Wuornos's life. Theron received the Oscar for Best Actress on 29 February 2004—on what would have been Wuornos's 48th birthday.

REFERENCES:

- *Murder Casebook* (1990), Marshall Cavendish, London
- *Aileen Carol Wuornos, www.clarkprosecuter.org*
- *Aileen Carol Wuornos, www.tripod.com*

1991

Jeffrey Dahmer: The 'Milwaukee Cannibal'

FACT FILE

CRIME: Mass murder

VICTIMS: Joseph Bradeholt, aged 25; James Doxtator, aged 14; Richard Guerrero, aged 23; Stephen Hicks, aged 19; Tony Hughes, aged 31; Oliver Lacy, aged 23; Errol Lindsey, aged 19; Ernest Miller, aged 22; Anthony Sears, aged 26; Konerak Sinthasomphone, aged 14; Eddie Smith, aged 27; Raymond Smith (alias Ricky Beeks), aged 33; Curtis Straughter, aged 19; David Thomas, aged 23; Steven Tuomi, aged 24; Matt Turner, aged 20; Jeremiah Weinberger, aged 23

DATES: June 1978 to July 1991

PLACE: Milwaukee, Wisconsin USA)

PERPETRATOR: Jeffrey Dahmer (1960–1994)

SENTENCE: Imprisonment for 936 years. In November 1994, Dahmer was beaten to death by a fellow prisoner

---

On Monday 22 July 1991, two Milwaukee patrolmen came across something they didn't see every day. An hysterical, partially naked black man was running down the street with a handcuff hanging off one wrist. The man, Tracy Edwards, flagged down the two policemen and told them that he had escaped from a nearby apartment belonging to 31-year-old Jeffrey Dahmer. Edwards had been lured there on the pretext of a party, but once he was inside Dahmer made homosexual advances and threatened him with a knife. Edwards escaped from the apartment when Dahmer allowed him to go to the bathroom. He then went back with the police and confronted Dahmer in the doorway of his apartment. What the police discovered inside the modest Milwaukee apartment repulsed them, the nation and the world.

Jeffrey Dahmer was born in Milwaukee, the son of middle-class Christian fundamentalist parents, in 1960. At the age of eight, Dahmer moved with his family to Bath, Ohio. He was a shy child with low self-esteem, and it was later alleged that he had been molested by a neighbour as a youth. Whatever the circumstances, Dahmer grew into an expressionless, nondescript young man—homosexual, alcoholic and a budding necrophiliac—who committed his first murder at the age of 18. In June 1978, Dahmer picked up teenager Stephen Mark Hicks, who was hitchhiking home after attending a rock concert. Taken to Dahmer's home and plied with alcohol, Hicks was struck over the head with a dumbbell when he attempted to leave. Dahmer then dismembered the body, wrapped the parts in black plastic and buried them under the house. When the stench became too great, he dug up the remains, stripped the victim's bones of flesh, smashed the bones with a sledgehammer and scattered what was left on his garden.

During the next decade, Jeffrey Dahmer moved back to Milwaukee to live with his grandmother. He frequented gay bars and was arrested in 1986 for exposing himself to young boys, but nine years passed before he killed again. In September 1987, Dahmer picked up Steven Tuomi at a gay bar and took him to a local hotel for sex. During the night he strangled Tuomi, and then bought a suitcase to remove the body to his home, where he dismembered it. The body parts were put into plastic bags and left out with the garbage. No forensic evidence of the victim was ever found, and Dahmer was never charged with this murder.

The following month Dahmer murdered male prostitute James Doxtator in the basement of his grandmother's house. Dahmer later told police that he dismembered the body, used acid to remove the flesh from the bones, and then destroyed what was left in the same manner as he had destroyed the remains of his first victim nine years earlier. After the death of next victim Richard Guerrero the following year, however, Dahmer's grandmother complained about the stench coming from her garage. Dahmer's father even investigated the smell, and his son told him that he was dissolving the bodies of animals in vats of acid, as he had done as a child. By September 1988 Dahmer's grandmother had had enough of his eccentricities and ordered him out of her house.

Dahmer moved into an apartment and sexually assaulted a 13-year-old boy named Keison Sinthasomphone, whom he lured there. The boy escaped because Dahmer wasn't able to drug him with alcohol, and Dahmer was later charged with enticing a child for immoral purposes. There was nothing to link Dahmer with the disappearances of the other men, and he was sentenced to one year in a 'house of correction' (which allowed him to work at his day job) and five years' probation. Dahmer did not kill again until May 1990.

The frequency and severity of Jeffrey Dahmer's crimes escalated during 1990 and 1991. He murdered four people in 1990 and doubled this the following year. Dahmer would invariably meet his victims, mostly African–Americans, in gay bars and invite them back to his apartment on the pretext of watching a movie or taking photographs, before spiking their drinks and strangling them. Anthony Sears, Raymond Smith (alias Ricky Beeks) and Errol Lindsey were killed in this manner. Dahmer bleached dancer Ernest Miller's skeleton and kept his biceps in his freezer.

The killer filmed the dismemberment of the bodies of victims David Thomas and Curtis Straughter, and took photographs of their severed heads. Dahmer propositioned deaf–mute Tony Hughes in writing—offering him US$50 to pose for photographs—and then killed him, keeping his dismembered body in his bedroom for another 24 hours before disposing of it.

Dahmer had the ability to talk himself out of almost any situation. When neighbours complained about the stench coming from Dahmer's apartment, he said that it was merely a defrosted fridge that needed fixing. In May 1991, 14-year-old Konerak Sinthasomphone, the brother of one of Dahmer's earlier sex victims, was lured to his apartment, drugged and abused. When Dahmer left the apartment to go to a gay bar, the drugged youth escaped.

Sinthasomphone appealed for help from two teenage girls, who tried to protect the boy from Dahmer, who had returned to his apartment block. When police intervened, Dahmer was able to convince them that it was nothing more than a lovers' quarrel and they allowed the boy (who appeared to be intoxicated) to go with him into his apartment. As soon as they were gone, Dahmer murdered the boy.

Four more victims were killed after this mistake before police knocked on Dahmer's door. The killer lured victims from Chicago (Matt Turner and Jeremiah Weinberger) but was becoming increasingly sloppy. As police finally investigated the Tracy Edwards incident in July 1991, they were overcome by the smell of death coming from Dahmer's apartment and found five dried, lacquered skulls, a barrel containing three male torsos, an electric saw stained with human blood and a drum of acid. In the freezer they found a human head and a container of human hands and genitals. Strips of human flesh, which Dahmer liked to eat with his favourite brand of mustard, were neatly wrapped inside the fridge.

In January 1992, Dahmer pleaded guilty on the grounds of insanity but was found to be sane and sentenced to a record 936 years in prison. Dahmer was offered special protection at Columbia Correctional Institute in Portage, Wisconsin, but refused because he wanted to remain part of the general prison population.

Two years later, in November 1994, Dahmer and another prisoner were bashed to death by a black prisoner named Christopher Scarver. Dahmer's murderer was allegedly upset that many of the 'Milwaukee Cannibal's' victims were black.

REFERENCES:

- BBC Online (2005), *Case Closed: Jeffrey Dahmer, www.bbc.co.uk*
- *Jeffrey Dahmer, www.rotten.com*

1992
The Backpacker Murders

FACT FILE

CRIME: Serial murder
VICTIMS: Caroline Clarke, aged 22; Deborah Everist, aged 19; James Gibson, aged 19; Anja Habschied, aged 20; Gabor Neugebauer, aged 21; Simone Schmidl, aged 20; Joanne Walters, aged 22
DATES: 26 December 1989 to September 1992
PLACE: Belanglo State Forest, New South Wales (Australia)
PERPETRATOR: Ivan Robert Marko Milat (b. 1944)
SENTENCE: Life imprisonment

Australia had long been seen as a safe destination for domestic and overseas travellers, but the crimes of Ivan Robert Marko Milat changed that perception forever. On Saturday 21 September 1992, members of a bush-orienteering club stumbled across a body covered with leaves and twigs near a large sandstone boulder in the Belanglo State Forest, south of Sydney. Five months earlier, the disappearance of two British backpackers travelling throughout Australia, Joanne Walters from Wales and Caroline Clarke from England, had been highly publicised. When another body was located some 30 metres (33 yards) from the boulder—hidden under a huge tree trunk and covered in branches—the two girls' fates were finally revealed.

It was more than a year before another body was found, just a few kilometres from where the remains of Joanne Walters and Caroline Clarke were recovered. A fossicker searching for firewood found a woman's body near the base of a tree, but when police arrived at the scene they quickly located another. The bodies were later identified as those of Australians James Gibson and Deborah Everist, who had disappeared on 30 December 1989 while hitchhiking together between Sydney and the city of Albury, on the New South Wales–Victoria border. Unlike Walters and Clarke, the Australian pair had been stabbed and bludgeoned to death, not shot. Despite this, the fact that the bodies of two young couples had been found so close to each other indicated that police had uncovered the burial ground of a serial killer.

In the five weeks after the discovery of the bodies of Gibson and Everist, 300 police, including trainees from the nearby Goulburn Police Academy, turned the Belanglo State Forest into a bustling tent community, their primary mission being the search for more bodies. On 1 November 1993, more human remains were located in another part of the forest. Superficial evidence at the scene identified the body as belonging to a young German backpacker, Simone Schmidl, who had last been seen on 20 January 1991 hitchhiking from Sydney to Melbourne. A post-mortem examination revealed that Schmidl had been stabbed to death.

Just days later, two more bodies were given up by the forest. The bodies, found buried about 60 metres (65 yards) apart, were of a man and a woman who had been killed by a combination of gunshot and knife wounds. The skeletal remains of the woman, buried in a shallow grave on the lee side of a fallen tree but covered with bush litter like the others, were missing the skull. The head had been hacked off by a large blade, probably a sword, but because it was never recovered police were of the opinion that the murderer must have taken it as a trophy, because an animal could not have carried it away. The victims, German nationals Gabor Neugebauer and Anja Habschied, had last been seen hitchhiking on Boxing Day, 26 December 1991.

Seven victims—each vulnerable in that they were a long way from home and travelling in an unfamiliar environment—snatched from the Hume Highway in south-western Sydney and murdered in the anonymity of the Australian bush. The Belanglo State Forest had clearly become the burial ground of a serial killer—but the excessive number of bullets fired into the victims, and the extreme number of head-shots coupled with the multiple stab wounds, marked these murders as among the most spine-chilling crimes in Australia's history.

Among the thousands of leads offered to police, a few proved to be crucial. One of these came from a man working at the Boral industrial depot in Parramatta, who told police that he was driving past the Belanglo State Forest in the company of a workmate, 'Paul Miller', when Miller remarked that 'there are more bodies out there' and 'they haven't found the Germans yet'. Another informant, by the name of Basil Milat, volunteered that he had seen a man driving the missing English girls in Queensland. (This latter appeared to be a red herring designed to lure police away from the Milat family). An anonymous caller suggested that police investigate the entire Milat family because 'they're a pretty weird bunch … they've got guns and they go shooting'.

But the vital breakthrough came from Englishman Paul Onions, who had contacted police in 1992 after the discovery of the first two bodies but, because of an administrative bungle, was not interviewed by police until 1994. The 24-year-old Englishman said that on 25 January 1991 while hitchhiking to Mildura he had accepted a lift from a well-built man with a handlebar moustache who tried to abduct him. When the man, known as 'Bill', stopped his silver four-wheel-drive and produced a gun and ropes, the scared Englishman made a break and flagged down a passing car. As police were already investigating the Milats, a picture of Ivan Milat was included among photographs of potential suspects shown to Onions. Onions identified Milat as his attacker after police were able to obtain a 1989 passport photograph of the suspect with his trademark moustache.

During the 1970s and 1980s, Ivan Milat worked for the New South Wales Roads and Traffic Authority (RTA) on a road maintenance crew, but he was also employed by Boral under his brother Bill's name. It was later discovered that Milat's other brother, Richard, also worked at Boral, under the name 'Paul Miller'. Worksheets obtained by police showed that Ivan Milat was not at work on any of the dates that the seven backpackers went missing, as well as on 25 January 1991—the date of the failed abduction of Paul Onions. Milat was taken into custody from his home in south-western Sydney on Sunday, 22 May 1994. Detectives found parts of a Ruger rifle hidden in wall cavities, including the breech bolt assembly, a complete trigger assembly and a Ramline aftermarket magazine. Cartridges of various calibres tied to the Belanglo State Forest crime scene were also found inside the house. Camping equipment belonging to Simone Schmidl was found in Milat's garage. Later, a photograph of Milat's girlfriend, Chalinder Hughes, wearing a Benetton top similar to the one owned by Caroline Clarke was recovered.

Milat's defence relied almost entirely on casting doubt as to whether the police had got the right 'Milat' and on his assertion that someone other than the police had planted the evidence in his Eagle Vale home. However, the presence in his house of so much property belonging to the victims—although circumstantial—carried a lot of weight with the jury. Ivan Milat was jailed for the term of his natural life on seven counts of murder and one of attempted murder. Police now started the huge task of re-examining the files of missing women dating back to the 1970s.

HISTORICAL AND SOCIAL SIGNIFICANCE:

- The Australian Outback continues to provide a stage for bizarre crimes. In July 2001, while driving in the Northern Territory, British tourist Peter Falconio was shot and his girlfriend, Joanne Lees, abducted. Lees escaped, but Falconio's body was never found. In December 2005, Bradley John Murdoch was found guilty of the crime.

REFERENCES:

- Shears, Richard (1996), *Highway to Nowhere*, HarperCollins, Sydney
- Dutton, Gerard (September 1999), 'Belanglo Forest Forensic Firearms Evidence', *Australian Police Journal*
- Kennedy, Les (3 December 2003) 'Milat link to nurses missing since 1980', *Sydney Morning Herald*, Fairfax Press

1993

James Bulger: The Death of Innocence

FACT FILE

CRIME: Abduction and murder
VICTIM: James Bulger, aged 2
DATE: 12 February 1993
PLACE: Liverpool (England)
PERPETRATORS: Robert Thompson and Jon Venables, both aged 10
SENTENCE: Imprisonment for 15 years. Both boys were released in 2001 after serving 8 years and 4 months

On 12 February 1993, a two-year-old boy was lured away from his mother in a busy shopping mall in Liverpool, England, savagely beaten and callously murdered on a railway track. What made this crime all the more appalling was the fact that the mall's security cameras captured images of a pair of 10-year-old boys, Jon Venables and Robert Thompson, holding the infant James Bulger by the hand and walking him away to his death.

On the day that he died, toddler James Bulger was at the Strand shopping centre in the Liverpool suburb of Bootle with his mother, Denise. Standing beside her as she was served in a local butcher's shop, James inexplicably left her side at about 3.40 pm that afternoon. Jon Venables and Robert Thompson were playing truant from school and had spent almost 6 hours trying to lure a victim from one of the many shops at the mall. Once they had succeeded in gaining James Bulger's confidence, they left the shopping centre within minutes—while his mother frantically searched for him.

The now distressed James Bulger was taken to an isolated railway track some 4 kilometres (just over 2 miles) away from the shopping mall and exposed to a series of violent attacks. He was pelted with rocks and bricks, and blue Hombrol modelling paint was splashed on him. The toddler's screams were silenced by prolonged kicking and stomping by the older boys, who finally used a metal bar to kill him.

As a final act of callousness, the older boys covered James Bulger's face and body with bricks and rocks and left his body on the railway track, where the post-mortem found it was severed in half by a train. The body of the young boy was not found for another two days—on Sunday 14 February, St Valentine's Day—by which time detectives had isolated video camera images of the abduction.

The world was shocked to learn that the two killers, first thought to be teenagers, were just ten years old. Almost as shocking, 38 people came forward and stated that they had seen Thompson and Venables with the two-year-old victim. One woman saw them swing Bulger high into the air holding him by the arms; another was close enough to notice a large wound on the young boy's head; a truck driver saw one of the boys give James a 'persuading' kick under the armpit; yet another expressed his concern about the little boy but was told by the young murderers that the boy was indeed lost and they were taking him to the police station. And yet no-one intervened—seeing two children with the little boy did not raise any alarms.

The trial of the two 10-year-old killers took place at Preston Crown Court on 7 November 1993. Thompson and Venables, referred to as 'Child A' and 'Child B' in court reports, pleaded not guilty to the murder of James Bulger and the attempted abduction of another child from the shopping mall. Both boys fidgeted as they sat through five hours of testimony each day of their 17-day trial. Towards the end of the trial, in which rival defence barristers tried to blame the other boy for the actual murder of the toddler, Venables sobbed uncontrollably and later expressed his remorse. Thompson remained impassive, and according to doctors did not come to terms with the gravity of his crime until some years later.

Why did this crime happen? Psychologists pointed to various elements of the boys' backgrounds: the violent videos the boys watched; the fact that one of the boys had an absent father and an alcoholic mother; the fact that the other boy was a bully, had learning difficulties and had been expelled from school for trying to strangle another child.

The trial judge, Mr Justice Morland, sentenced the two murderers to eight years' jail, which was extended to ten years by Lord Taylor, the Lord Chief Justice at the time, and then to 15 years by the home secretary, Michael Howard. In October 2000, Lord Woolfe was asked to recommend a new 'tariff' (minimum sentence) after the European court of human rights ruled that judges—and not politicians—should make sentencing decisions. Having recently turned 18, and facing a move to 'corrosive' adult prisons, Venables and Thompson were released in 2001 after having served 8 years and 4 months, despite a public outcry.

REFERENCES:

- Harrison, David (1993), *Agony of Following Jamie's Final Footsteps, www.guardian.co.uk*
- Pilkington, Edward (1993), *Blood on Boy's Shoe Was from Victim, www.guardian.co.uk*

1994
Fred and Rosemary West: The House of Horrors

FACT FILE

CRIME: Mass murder
VICTIMS: Alison Chambers, aged 17; Carol Cooper, aged 15; Catherine 'Rena' Costello, aged 32; Linda Gough, aged 21; Shirley Hubbard, aged 15; Ann McFall, aged 18; Juanita Mott, aged 19; Lucy Partington, aged 21; Therese Siegenthaler, aged 21; Charmaine West, aged 8; Heather West, aged 16
DATES: 1967-87
PLACE: Gloucester (England)
PERPETRATORS: Fred West (1939-1998) and Rosemary West (b. 1954)
SENTENCE: Fred West committed suicide on 1 January 1998 before he could be tried for his crimes. Rosemary West was sentenced to life imprisonment

Of all the 'partnership' killings that punctuate the crime annals of the twentieth century, the deeds of suburban English couple Fred and Rosemary West are unsurpassed for sheer depravity. After her husband had raped, tortured and murdered his victims—some of whom were Fred's own children—frumpy, bespectacled Rosemary West would make him a cup of tea. Complicit in her husband's crimes and having already been conscripted into prostitution to satisfy West's sexual lust, Rosemary West may have been the submissive member of the partnership but ironically she proved to be the mentally stronger of the two.

Fred West met his second wife, Rosemary ('Rose') Letts, at a bus stop in 1969. Although she was only 15 at the time, 'Dozy Rosy', as she was known at school, had already lived with an older man and was sexually experienced. Despite the fact that he had two young daughters (Charmaine and Anne Marie) by his first wife, West's rustic, toothy charm appealed to the naive teenager. Rose moved in with West, but they did not marry until 1972, after she had given birth to a daughter, Heather, and was expecting a second child, whom they would name Mae June.

Incredibly, West's first wife, Rena Costello, and her two daughters also lived with them. (Anne Marie was West's child, but he knew that Charmaine wasn't his biological daughter. When people referred to her 'Asian' features, he would say that she was adopted.)

What Rosemary West didn't know was that her husband had already claimed his first victim. Ann McFall, a Scottish nanny and West's lover, was eight months pregnant with his child when he murdered her in 1967. (Her dismembered body was found in the 1990s in a field near West's home town, a farming community known as Much Marcle.) In 1970, Fred West murdered his first wife, Rena. (Her body was later found in a field near Much Marcle). It was not until 1972 that eight-year-old Charmaine West, Rena's elder child, was murdered. Her body was found beneath the Wests' first home at 25 Midland Road, Gloucester, after his capture in 1994.

Even in their early years together, Fred urged Rose to have sex with other men. He took a suggestive photograph of her and put it in the papers to attract clients. West then drilled a hole in the wall so that he could watch Rose having sex with strangers. The nondescript suburban family home at 25 Cromwell Street became part hostel, part brothel. But the Gloucester home was also a place of savage rape, incest and brutal murder. When Fred West could not get instant sexual gratification from his son and daughters, he conscripted his wife to help him kidnap young women off the street, sexually abuse them, murder them and bury their bodies under the house. Rosemary West played a key role in offering hitchhikers and young runaways a bed or a job as the West children's nanny. The reality was indescribably worse.

Linda Gough, a 21-year-old seamstress from Gloucester, was the first of the Cromwell Street victims to be murdered and buried beneath the Wests' modest three-storey home, in 1973. Lucy Partington, also 21 and a university student from Gotherington, near Cheltenham, was killed the same year. In 1974, 15-year-old Worcester schoolgirl Carol Cooper became the couple's next victim. Juanita Mott, aged 19, from Newent, Gloucester, and Shirley Hubbard, another teenage schoolgirl from Worcester, were both killed in 1975. Therese Siegenthaler, a 21-year-old Swiss hitchhiker, and 17-year-old Alison Chambers, originally from Swansea, were both murdered in 1977. Shirley Robinson, a teenage lodger and West's lover, was heavily pregnant when she was murdered in 1978.

Rose West would often assist in the rapes, holding the victims down while her husband had his pleasure, but it is unclear whether she was complicit in the actual act of murder. (Fred's brother John committed suicide before he could be implicated in any of the crimes.) But for Fred West it was all about control—sexual, physical and psychological control—which was something the Wests' daughters, Anne Marie, Mae June and Heather, experienced first-hand. West took pleasure in stealing his daughters' virginity, but when 16-year-old Heather West finally stood up to him, he murdered her in the family laundry. After dismembering her body with an ice-saw, he buried her remains in the garden and told his wife that Heather had decided to 'strike out on her own'. Heather's murder would ultimately be Fred West's undoing.

When Gloucester police investigated the rape of 13-year-old Louise West, the family's other children—Tara (born in 1977), Louise (1978), Barry (1980), Rosemary Junior (1982) and Lucyanna (1983)—informed them that Rena, Charmaine and Heather had gone missing. (Fred West was not the father of Tara, Rosemary or Lucyanna). When police arrived to dig up their garden, Fred confessed to his wife that Heather's body was indeed buried there and Rose turned on him. West was arrested on 25 February 1994, and the home that the English press dubbed the 'House of Horrors' finally gave up its grisly secrets. Fred admitted to Heather's murder and pointed out where two other bodies were buried, but did not freely reveal that six other girls were also buried under the house's cellar and bathroom. The police had to find that out for themselves.

Although Fred West was charged with 12 counts of murder, he withheld information about at least another 20 missing women while he awaited trial. (West told detectives that he would reveal the burial sites of his victims at the rate of one per year.) Caroline Raine, one of the few victims to escape Gloucester's 'House of Horrors', told a packed court of the Wests' sexual sadism.

On New Year's Day 1995, West hanged himself at Birmingham's Winson Green Prison with strips of sheeting from his bed while the guards were changing shifts, leaving his wife to face justice on her own. Rosemary West was sentenced to ten life terms. She resides in the high-security Durham Prison and will never be released.

HISTORICAL AND SOCIAL SIGNIFICANCE:

- Anne Marie West, the daughter of Fred West and his first wife, changed her name after her father's capture and took an overdose of sleeping pills during her stepmother's trial. She had failed in a previous suicide attempt, when she jumped into the River Severn. The Wests' son, Stephen, also tried to commit suicide after a relationship failed.
- Gloucester Council demolished the Wests' 'House of Horrors' at 25 Cromwell Street in October 1996.

REFERENCES:

- BBC Online (2005), *Case Closed: Fred and Rose West, www.bbc.co.uk*
- *Fred and Rosemary West, www.crimelibrary.com*

1995

The Oklahoma City Bombing

FACT FILE

CRIMES: Murder, conspiracy
VICTIMS: 168 people, including 19 children
DATE: 19 April 1995
PLACE: Alfred P. Murrah Federal Building, Oklahoma City, Oklahoma (USA)
PERPETRATORS:
Timothy McVeigh (1968–2001) and Terry Nichols (b. 1955)
SENTENCE: Timothy McVeigh was sentenced to death and executed by lethal injection on 11 June 2001. Terry Nichols was sentenced to life imprisonment for conspiracy and involuntary manslaughter, but was found not guilty of the use of a weapon of mass destruction

---

On 19 April 1995, a huge bomb destroyed the front of the Alfred P. Murrah Federal Building in Oklahoma City. A tall, thin man had been seen to park a truck and then hastily walk away before it detonated—the explosion timed for maximum impact as people arrived for work and the office crèche filled with children—ripping the north wall of the building away. One hundred and sixty-eight people, including 19 children, were killed, with hundreds injured in the blast. The blast was first viewed as an act of international terrorism, but America was forced to look inwards.

The Oklahoma City bombing had its genesis two years before. On 28 February 1993, agents belonging to the US Bureau of Alcohol, Tobacco and Firearms (ATF) attempted to serve a search and arrest warrant on the premises of a religious community called Mount Carmel, outside the city of Waco, Texas.

The rambling group of farmhouses was occupied by a sect calling themselves Branch Davidians, which was led by a charismatic preacher named David Koresh (alias Vernon Howell). In the light of sex abuse allegations against its leader and firearms and tax violations by its members, the sect was attempting to break away from the constraints of constitutional regulations, which brought it into conflict with the US federal government.

The arrival of heavily armed federal agents at the Mount Carmel compound resulted in a fierce gun battle, in which four ATF agents and six Branch Davidians were killed. The resulting stand-off, in which the Branch Davidians refused to surrender to federal agents, lasted for 51 days. The FBI Hostage Rescue Team assumed control of the situation, but its aggressive assault on the compound on 19 April 1993 led to a fire that consumed the 76 occupants, including many women and children. One of those deeply disturbed by what happened in Waco, Texas, was former Gulf War veteran Timothy McVeigh.

Timothy McVeigh was born in upstate New York in 1968, and grew up in rural communities in Buffalo and Niagara, near the Canadian border. The product of a broken marriage and a loner by nature, McVeigh was already showing paranoid tendencies before he joined the army as a gunner in 1988. He and a friend bought a 10-acre (4.5-hectare) property and used it for target practice and to stockpile firearms and food. McVeigh told a workmate at the local Burger King that he was getting ready for the end of 'civilised society' and had adopted a 'survivalist' philosophy in which the individual's rights to use guns superseded any federal government regulations.

During his time serving in the Gulf War, McVeigh's hatred for the US government only increased. Back in the States he applied for the Special Forces section of the US army but failed the physical endurance test. Taking an early discharge from the army, McVeigh returned to his job as a security guard but became increasingly isolated from society as he travelled around the country. The Waco incident inflamed McVeigh's disgust at US federal powers, and he visited the burnt-out ruins of the religious community in his travels. About the same time, he began making bombs.

In September 1994, McVeigh began gathering the necessary ingredients needed to make a huge car-bomb. After buying 2 tons (just over 2 tonnes) of ammonium nitrate fertiliser from a co-op in McPherson, Kansas, McVeigh disguised himself as a biker and spent US$2775 buying nitromethane car-racing fuel at a Texas car track. The following year, he purchased a getaway car (a 1977 Mercury Marquis) in Junction City, Kansas, and drove it to Oklahoma City on 16 April 1995.

After conscripting an army buddy named Terry Nichols to drive him back to Kansas, McVeigh used the name 'Robert D. King' to take ownership of a 20-foot (six-metre) Ryder truck, which he filled with chemicals, and drove to Oklahoma City.

At 9.02 am, on 19 April 1995—Patriots' Day in the USA, and the second anniversary of the fiery end to the Waco siege—the home-made bomb destroyed the Alfred P. Murrah Federal Building on 200 NW 5th Street and killed 168 people. Witnesses originally described two men fleeing the scene, and there was some confusion about whether there was a second bomb ready to explode on the other side of the building. After leaving a scene of utter desolation, Timothy McVeigh was picked up for speeding 120 kilometres (75 miles) away by an alert highway patrolman, who also saw a gun in the 1977 Mercury's glove box.

Arrested for speeding and firearm offences, McVeigh was about to be bailed when authorities noticed his uncanny resemblance to one of the two men they were looking for in regard to the Oklahoma City bombing. Two days after the blast, Terry Nichols gave himself up to authorities after the FBI announced that it was looking for McVeigh's 'accomplice'. (The police sketch of the 'second' man turned out to be of an innocent bystander.)

Incredibly, the licence plate of the truck used as a car-bomb was recovered intact from the crime scene and authorities were able to trace it to Kansas and build their case against McVeigh. After a controversial trial, Timothy McVeigh was found guilty on 11 counts of murder and conspiracy and was formally sentenced to death on 14 August 1996. The following year, Terry Nichols was found guilty of conspiracy and voluntary manslaughter, but he declined to cooperate with authorities and was sentenced to life imprisonment.

In July 1999, McVeigh was moved to the US Penitentiary in Terre Haute, Indiana, and in accordance with his wishes, he was granted permission to stop all appeals. (The US government spent US$82.5 million prosecuting the case.) The execution was originally set for 16 May 2001, but it was delayed after it was revealed that the FBI had not made all its files about McVeigh available before his trial. McVeigh was executed on 11 June 2001.

Tim McVeigh did not utter any last words before the lethal injection was administered, leaving the thousands of relatives of his victims without any explanation as to why he took the lives of 168 innocent men, women and children.

HISTORICAL AND SOCIAL SIGNIFICANCE:

- On 23 April, President Bill Clinton declared a national day of mourning and a memorial service was conducted for the victims.
- Michael Fortier, who knew of the plot but did not inform authorities, was sentenced to 12 years' imprisonment despite being a key witness against McVeigh and Nichols. James Nichols, the younger brother of Terry Nichols, was indicted on charges of being an accessory to the bombing but was released. James Nichols later gained some notoriety for his rambling, pro-gun views in Michael Moore's documentary *Bowling for Columbine.*

REFERENCES:

- Creig, Charlotte (2005), *Criminal Masterminds*, Arcturus, London
- *Waco: Massacre at Mount Carmel, www.constitution.org*

1995

The OJ Simpson Trial

FACT FILE

CRIME: Murder
VICTIMS: Nicole Brown-Simpson, aged 35, and Ronald Goldman, aged 25
DATE: 12 June 1994
PLACE: Los Angeles, California (USA)
PERPETRATOR: Unknown

When police were called to Nicole Brown-Simpson's Bundy Drive condominium shortly before midnight on 12 June 1994, they found her bloodied barefoot body slumped on the pathway at the bottom of her front steps. Her throat had been cut while her children slept upstairs. Lying nearby was the body of 25-year-old Ronald Goldman, a waiter and occasional male model. Colleagues later said that Goldman had struck up a 'friendship' with Nicole Brown-Simpson, the former wife of former gridiron star and media personality OJ Simpson, but investigating detectives later viewed his death as a case of being in the wrong place at the wrong time. Goldman was returning a pair of sunglasses left by Brown-Simpson's mother at his workplace, the Mezzaluna restaurant, when he met his death. He, too, had been stabbed to death. Over a decade after the pair's death, the question remains ... who killed them?

Orenthal James Simpson was one of the greatest running backs in American football before he took up a high-profile media career. Born in San Francisco in 1947, Simpson was the first player selected in the 1969 professional football draft, having won the prestigious Heisman Trophy while at the University of Southern California. Simpson, known as 'OJ' or 'The Juice' to his thousands of fans, played for the Buffalo Bills throughout the 1970s and then finished his career with the San Francisco 49ers in 1979. Simpson was voted into the NFL Pro Football Hall of Fame, and his good looks and charming personality opened the door to an acting career (he appeared in films such as *The Towering Inferno*, *Roots*, and *The Naked Gun*) and made him a popular sports commentator after his retirement.

Simpson was married as a teenager and fathered three children by his first wife, Marguerite. In 1979 his 2-year-old daughter Aaren drowned in the family pool, and the marriage later ended in divorce. Simpson met teenager Nicole Brown while she was a waitress in the late 1970s, but did not marry her until February 1985. Nicole bore Simpson two children—daughter Sydney, born that year, and a boy, Justin, three years later—before this marriage also floundered. Nicole Simpson later complained that her famous husband was promiscuous with other women and abused her physically and emotionally. The pair tried to reconcile in 1991, but Simpson made a violent attack on her on New Year's Day, which she reported to local police, and the marriage ended in divorce the following year.

Nicole Simpson reverted to her maiden name and moved into a condominium in Brentwood, Los Angeles—not far from her former family home—with her two children. In accordance with her prenuptial agreement, she received a cash settlement of US$433,000, and as part of her divorce settlement, US$10,000 per month child support. Although Simpson had started a new relationship with model Paula Barbieri, he was hopeful that he would reunite with Nicole and bring his children home. That was before the night of 12 June 1994.

OJ Simpson was notified of his wife's murder the following day while on a business trip to Chicago. On his return to Los Angeles he was questioned by police (the LAPD) about his movements the previous day and his relationship with his ex-wife, then was allowed to go. Police were later criticised for being in awe of Simpson's celebrity. After attending Nicole Brown-Simpson's funeral with his children on 16 June, Simpson was told to surrender to police the following day at 11.00 am when he would be further questioned and arrested for the murder of his ex-wife. Simpson then did something quite strange for an innocent man—he panicked and ran.

On the morning of 17 June, Simpson wrote a suicide note maintaining his innocence and tried to escape in his Ford Bronco van, which was driven by his friend A.C. Cowlings. Simpson was pursued by a long line of law enforcement vehicles, while the whole episode was shown live on television to an estimated audience of 95 million. Inside the van were a change of clothing, a large amount of cash, a disguise kit and Simpson's passport—hardly the items belonging to someone contemplating suicide—but this was not revealed until after his trial. After a long, slow chase, in which crowds of people lined the freeway and cheered him on, Simpson returned to his Brentwood mansion and was arrested. On 22 July 1994 he pleaded 'absolutely 100 per cent not guilty' to the murder of Nicole Brown-Simpson and Ronald Goldman.

The trial of OJ Simpson opened on 24 January 1995 and was covered by a huge national (including most of the country's 'entertainment' media) and international news contingent. Simpson published his own story (*I Want to Tell You*) the same week, and it remained to be seen if he could get a fair trial given the extensive coverage the case had already attracted. Simpson was represented by a 'dream team' of lawyers headed by celebrity lawyer Robert Schapiro, the high-profile Johnnie

Cochrane and the experienced F. Lee Bailey. The defence team secured an early victory when they labelled detective Mark Fuhrman a 'racist' and discredited his evidence that a black glove belonging to Simpson was found at the crime scene. When Simpson later tried the glove on during the trial, it didn't fit. The implication was clear—the LAPD had planted the glove to frame Simpson. Johnnie Cochrane later famously summed up the entire case when he told the jury, 'If it doesn't fit, you must acquit.'

But a lot of the evidence did not show Simpson in the best light. Simpson's house guest, actor Kato Kaelin, testified that he saw Simpson wearing dark clothes at 9.30 pm; Simpson tried to call his girlfriend at 10 pm from his cell phone in his Ford Bronco; Simpson did not answer his intercom when limo driver Allan Park called at his home at 10.30 pm to take him to the airport; Park saw a man wearing dark clothing walk across the driveway at 10.55 pm shortly before Simpson answered the door.

Simpson later said that he was in the backyard hitting golf balls at the time of the murders, which were committed between 10.15 pm and 10.40 pm. But hair, fibres and other evidence placed Simpson at the crime scene; a footprint in the blood matched Simpson's size 12 Bruno Magli shoes; the left-hand glove found at the crime scene matched an Aris Light brand right-hand glove found at Simpson's house; and lastly, Simpson had a fresh cut on his hand the day after the murders and his blood was found at the crime scene, in the Ford Bronco and in his home.

After a nationally televised trial in which the conduct of everyone—Judge Lance Ito, the LAPD, Simpson's defence team (who did not let him take the stand), the prosecution team and the media—was criticised, the predominantly black, female jury found OJ Simpson not guilty on two counts of murder on 3 October 1995.

Despite a civil suit the following year that found Simpson 'liable' for the deaths of Nicole Brown-Simpson and Ronald Goldman and which ordered him to pay US$8.5 million compensation to the two families, OJ Simpson cannot be retried for the still unsolved murders regardless of any new evidence that may one day be revealed.

HISTORICAL AND SOCIAL SIGNIFICANCE:

- In 2007, Simpson co-authored a book on the still unsolved crime. The title was *If I Did It*.

REFERENCES:

- *OJ Simpson: Ten Years Later, www.eonline.com*
- *Orenthal J. Simpson, www.law.umkc.edu*

1995

Yitzhak Rabin Assassinated

FACT FILE

CRIME: Assassination
VICTIM: Yitzhak Rabin (1922–1995)
DATE: 4 November 1995
PLACE: Kings of Israel Square, Tel Aviv (Israel)
PERPETRATOR: Yigal Amir (b. 1970)
SENTENCE: Life imprisonment. Hagai Amir was sentenced to 12 years (increased to 16 years on appeal), and Dror Adani to 7 years, for their roles in Rabin's assassination.

On 4 November 1995, Israeli prime minister Yitzhak Rabin was assassinated by 25-year-old law student Yigal Amir as the Nobel Peace prize winner left a rally at Tel Aviv's Kings of Israel Square. The rally was designed to promote the Oslo Accord—the peace agreement between Yassir Arafat's PLO and Israel's Rabin government—but Rabin was gunned down at almost point-blank range with two fatal shots to the body. The assassin's goal was made clear as soon as he was questioned after his capture. Yigal Amir killed Rabin to stop the peace process.

The state of Israel was founded in turmoil in 1947 and, surrounded by its traditional enemies, has existed in that atmosphere for the past six decades. It has fought wars against its Arab neighbours, in 1967 and 1973, and has lived in a perpetual state of tension alongside displaced Palestinians who dispute Israel's very existence. The target of international terrorism during the 1970s and 1980s, Israel faced a new enemy in the 1990s from within its own boundaries—Orthodox Jews opposed to the country's plans to make peace with neighbouring Jordan, Syria and even the Palestinian Liberation Organisation (PLO).

Yitzhak Rabin was born in Jerusalem in 1922 in what was then the British-controlled section of Palestine. After graduating from Kadoori Agricultural High School in 1941, he wanted to become an irrigation engineer, but at the height of World War II he joined the Haganah (the forerunner of the modern Israeli Defence Forces). By 1947, with Israel declaring its independence, Rabin was the country's chief operations officer, and directed operations in the Arab–Israeli War in 1948. By 1962, he had risen to the position of chief of staff in the Israeli Defence Forces (IDF). Rabin served as Israeli ambassador to the United States after his retirement from the IDF, and was elected to the Knesset (the Israeli legislature) in 1973. On 2 June 1974, he succeeded Golda Meir as Labor prime minister and was the country's first Israeli-born leader. Although forced to resign in 1977 following the revelation of a banking scandal involving his wife, Rabin returned to power in 1992.

Rabin played a leading role in the signing of the Oslo Accord, which amongst other things recognised the PLO and created the Palestinian Authority to oversee partial control of the Gaza Strip and West Bank. It also brought internal and international condemnation from hard-line Jews who found it abhorrent that Israel would be negotiating with its sworn enemies. One of those Israelis who thought that Rabin was helping to set up a Palestinian state and wanted to 'give our country to the Arabs' was Yigal Amir.

A resident of the central Israeli town of Herzeliya, Yigal Amir was a law student at Bar Ilan University and an activist in several right-wing groups, including 'Eyel'. His older brother, Hagai, a student on the West Bank, supplied the 9-millimetre bullets for the murder weapon—even modifying them by boring holes in them and inserting iron pellets to make them more accurate—but after Rabin's assassination, he denied knowing what the bullets were for. However, Yigal Amir had twice told his brother that he had aborted plans to kill Rabin and had convinced himself that, according to the *Halacha* (Jewish law, handed down to Moses from Mt Sinai, but determined through an exacting process of metaphysical science), 'when you kill in war, it is an act that is allowed'.

Prime Minister Rabin had been warned of an assassination attempt at the peace rally on the night of Saturday 4 November, but promoting the Oslo Accord was far too important an issue for him to cancel his appearance. Rabin was shot in the arm and back as, surrounded by well-wishers, he walked to his car clutching the lyrics of a song he had quoted in his speech that night. The assassin could clearly be seen on amateur video waiting near Rabin's car and then lurching forward and getting off two shots. Rabin suffered massive blood loss and a punctured lung, and died in hospital with his deputy, Shimon Peres, by his side. Yigal Amir was captured at the scene and made no attempt to escape. Like a lot of fanatics, Amir hid behind his religion ('It was God,' he answered to questions asking if anyone had ordered him to assassinate the prime minister), but he was found to have been neither insane nor emotionally disturbed when he carried out the act.

At Yigal Amir's arraignment on 7 November, magistrate Dan Arbel put the crime into the gravest context when he stated:

Before me is a suspect in one of the worst crimes ever committed in Israel, possibly the worst committed at all times in this country. The suspect confesses to the murder of

Yitzhak Rabin and does not deny that he planned it in advance and did it with a clear mind.

Amir was held for 15 more days while police drew charges and investigated his involvement in illegal right wing organisations. At his trial the following February, Amir pleaded guilty to murder and was sentenced to life imprisonment the following September. Hagai Amir also played a role in the assassination: repeatedly requesting an M-16 rifle from the army that Yigal Amir intended to use to shoot Rabin from long distance; reconnoitering the area around Rabin's home with his brother in an earlier assassination attempt; and finally, supplying the bullets for the gun that killed the Israeli prime minister. Hagai Amir and an associate, Dror Adani, were also jailed for conspiracy to assassinate Rabin.

Like Egypt's Anwar Sadat—assassinated 14 years before—Rabin was portrayed as a 'martyr of peace' for the Middle East peace process. Rabin's assassination was condemned in neighbouring Arab countries, and his funeral was attended by US President Bill Clinton, Jordan's King Hussein and Egypt's President Hosni Mubarak, who made his first trip to Jerusalem to honour the fallen leader. On Sunday and throughout the night, an estimated one million people (in a country of 5 million) filed past Rabin's body as it lay in state at the Knesset. The following day Rabin's coffin was taken through the Jerusalem streets in the back of a military vehicle covered in black to Mount Herzl cemetery, which is reserved for Israel's prime ministers. All of Israel observed a two-minute silence once the coffin reached its destination.

As the King of Jordan observed, Yitzhak Rabin, once a soldier, died a soldier for peace.

HISTORICAL AND SOCIAL SIGNIFICANCE:

- Four days after Rabin's murder, the assassin's family published a letter of apology to Rabin's family and the Israeli people. In it, Amir's parents, Shlomo and Geula Amir, said: '... deeply ashamed, mourning and with bowed head, we ask for forgiveness and absolution.' The family stressed that they rejected all acts of violence.
- Kings of Israel Square in Tel Aviv, where Rabin was assassinated, has since been renamed Yitzhak Rabin Square.

REFERENCES:

- *Rabin Assassination (1995), www.cnn.com*
- *Amir Trial (1996), www.usatoday.com*

1995
The Tokyo Subway Gassing

FACT FILE

CRIME: Poisoning
VICTIMS: Twelve people killed, thousands injured
DATE: 20 March 1995
PLACE: Tokyo subway
PERPETRATORS: Shoko Asahara (b. 1955) and members of the Aum Shinrikyo sect
SENTENCE: Shoko Asahara was sentenced to death by hanging for the Tokyo subway attacks and 12 other charges. As of 2006, 11 other sect members have been sentenced to death and are also awaiting execution

---

The world has lived with the threat of biological weapons for decades now, but the nerve gas attack on the Tokyo subway in March 1995 was totally without precedent in the civilised world. The attack brought Tokyo's rail system to a halt; 12 people were killed and thousands affected by poisonous sarin gas. But far from being an attack by international terrorists, Japanese authorities had to look no further than a powerful local religious sect that had grown under the guidance of a long-haired, blind mystic named Shoko Asahara.

Two days after the Tokyo gas attack, 2500 police and military personnel simultaneously raided the Kamukuishiki complex of the Aum Shinrikyo sect and 24 of the cult's properties across Japan. Large stockpiles of gas-making chemicals and related equipment were found, and many of the cult's members were arrested. The sect, which started as a yoga school, had grown enormously during the early 1990s because of a fear of the coming apocalypse at the start of the new millennium. The cult was directed by Shoko Asahara—a messianic misfit who shored up his support amongst his gullible followers with threats that the government's efforts to disband Aum Shinrikyo would coincide with the end of the world.

Shoko Asahara was born Chizuo Matsumoto in Yatsuhiro, Japan, in 1955. Suffering from infantile glaucoma, he attended a school for the sight-impaired and graduated in 1977. After failing to gain a place at university, Matsumoto married and dabbled in Chinese medicine and New Age philosophy. After a pilgrimage to the Himalayas in 1987, he changed his name to Shoko Asahara and founded the Aum Shinrikyo sect. 'Aum' is a sacred Hindu symbol and 'shinrikyo' means 'supreme truth'. The cult blended Hindu, Tibetan, Taoist and Buddhist scriptures with the

Bible's Book of Revelations and even the predictions of sixteenth-century futurist Nostradamus.

Asahara claimed to be a reincarnation of the Hindu god Shiva and promised to lead his followers to salvation after the impending Armageddon. But Asahara was no prophet. *Time* magazine wrote of the cult leader in 1995:

> *Bushy-bearded and usually pictured wearing satiny pajamas, Asahara, 40, admires Hitler, boasts that he can levitate and offers to bestow superhuman powers on his disciples. Yet a look at his life reveals a rather pathetic figure at war with the world because he could not find an easy place in it.*

But Asahara, with his promise of reincarnation, had no shortage of recruits wanting to join him in his battle against the evils of society.

Aum Shinrikyo tried to gain a political foothold in Japanese politics, but its candidates failed miserably in the 1990 elections and so the sect decided to overthrow the government by other means. By the 1990s, Aum had over 10,000 members in Japan and many more internationally. The sect amassed assets of more than US$1 billion worldwide, and authorities later learned that Asahara's followers bought and manufactured chemical weapons, investigated the development of Tesla (magnetic field) weaponry and even enquired into the purchase of a uranium mine in Australia in an effort to acquire nuclear weapons.

As his fortune grew, Asahara grew more reclusive and became obsessed with threats from the United States, which he portrayed as 'a creature of Freemasons and Jews bent on destroying Japan'. Asahara predicted the end of the world some time between 1997 and 2000, and began citing the specific peril of poison-gas attacks on the Japanese population. In 1989, anti-Aum lawyer Tstumi Sakamoto was murdered along with his wife and infant son. Other members of the sect who tried to leave the cult also mysteriously disappeared. Then, in 1994, a sarin gas attack killed seven people in Matsumoto, in central Japan. But these were just preludes to a major attack on Japanese society.

On the morning of 20 March 1995, members of the Aum Shinrikyo cult used the tips of umbrellas to puncture plastic bags filled with liquid sarin, which they left behind on five subway trains. As a poisonous, invisible cloud spread through train carriages and subway stations, thousands of people became ill and 12 commuters and rail staff died. The attack was an obvious attempt to create mayhem on a public utility and so to discredit the Japanese government, but it emerged during Asahara's trial that the major reason for the attack was to distract a police investigation into the sect's operations. The attack had the completely opposite effect. Days after the Tokyo subway gassing Asahara was arrested while 'meditating' in an isolated building owned by the sect at the foot of Mount Fuji.

Shoko Asahara faced 27 counts of murder in 13 separate indictments relating to gas attacks and the murder of the sect's opponents. The Japanese media called it the 'trial of the century', and Asahara—his hair, once long and frizzy, cut short and his Rasputin-like beard neatly trimmed—certainly played the part. During the trial, Asahara's court-appointed defence team stated that their client's underlings committed the attacks without his knowledge, but a number of sect members testified that the attacks had been carried out on his specific orders. The court heard that Shoko Asahara ordered the 1989 murder of lawyer Tstumi Sakamoto and his family, a sarin gas attack in Matsumoto in June 1994 and the March 1995 sarin attack on the Tokyo subway. Asahara also ordered the murder of three cult followers; sprayed VX gas on three people, killing one of them; masterminded the February 1995 abduction of an Aum sect member in a bid to find the whereabouts of a relative who had escaped from the cult and then fatally injected him with an excessive amount of anaesthesia; ordered the construction of a sarin plant between 1993 and 1994; and ordered a sarin attack on another anti-cult lawyer in 1994 in an unsuccessful bid to kill him.

On 27 February 2004, Shoko Asahara was found guilty on 13 charges and was sentenced to death by hanging. Eleven other sect members have been sentenced to death for the Tokyo subway gassing and the murder of other anti-Aum figures. Asahara, now in his 50s, has spent the past decade in a Tokyo jail cell waiting for his death sentence to be carried out after all avenues of the appeal process are exhausted.

HISTORICAL AND SOCIAL SIGNIFICANCE:

- The Aum Shinrikyo cult, whose membership currently numbers about 1100, changed its name in 2000 to Aleph, which is the first letter of the Hebrew alphabet. Japan's Public Security Investigation Agency has about 50 agents monitoring the sect's activities.
- The cult still operates 7 main facilities throughout Japan and some 20 smaller branches where followers meditate, conduct yoga classes and computer seminars, and run student clubs on university campuses.

REFERENCES:

- *Shoko Asahara (2004), www.news.bbc.co.uk*
- *Supreme Truth, www.masonicinfo.com*

1996
The JonBenét Ramsey Case

FACT FILE

CRIME: Murder
VICTIM: JonBenét Ramsey, aged 6
DATE: 25-26 December 1996
PLACE: Boulder, Colorado (USA)
PERPETRATOR: Unknown

JonBenét Ramsey was a pretty child. So much so that her mother frequently entered her in child beauty contests. Boulder businessman John Ramsay and his second wife, Patsy (a former Miss West Virginia, in 1977), also funded scholarships for contest winners. Named 'National Tiny Miss Beauty' and 'Little Miss Colorado', six-year-old JonBenét would be dressed glamorously to perform on stage and made up to look much older than she was. Whether or not Patsy Ramsey's preoccupation with promoting her daughter's beauty attracted the attention of a paedophile or the family became the target of a failed extortion attempt, the murder of the little girl on Christmas night 1996 shocked the country and brought immediate suspicion upon her parents.

On the morning after Christmas Day, Patsy Ramsey discovered a three-page ransom note downstairs in the family home. Among other things, the note stated that JonBenét had been kidnapped by 'foreign interests' and a US$118, 000 ransom—an unusually specific amount—had to be paid for her safe return. The letter, written on a legal pad belonging to the household, said that the Ramseys would be contacted that night and were not to involve the local police. A search of her bedroom discovered that she was indeed missing, and against the wishes of the 'kidnappers', Patsy dialled 911. Upon their arrival at the 15-room family mansion, local police failed to secure the crime scene and allowed John Ramsey to search his home unaccompanied. While searching the basement, John Ramsey found his daughter's lifeless body hidden in a corner. Ramsey immediately carried his daughter's battered body upstairs to the police, thus destroying crucial evidence.

Despite evidence of a break-in via the mansion's basement, the Ramseys were asked to give hair, blood and handwriting samples for the purpose of elimination. The Ramseys flew to their former home in Atlanta to bury their daughter, while the police sealed off the Boulder home and investigated the only murder committed in the city that year. On the final day of 1996, JonBenét Ramsey was buried beside the grave of her half-sister (from John's first marriage), Marietta, who had been killed in a car accident four years before. The Ramseys also hired an attorney to represent their interests.

On New Year's Day 1997, John and Patsy Ramsey granted their first public interview. Patsy declared that 'there is a killer on the loose' and that they would hire their own investigation team and offer a reward for information leading to the killer's arrest. The following day five Boulder detectives arrived in Atlanta to search the Ramsey home. JonBenét's autopsy confirmed that she was strangled to death but also revealed haemorrhaging in her brain, scrapes and bruises on her head and one of her legs and 'chronic inflammation' of her vagina. A national tabloid published autopsy photographs of the little girl, but little was made of tiny burn marks on the child's neck. Had JonBenét been immobilised with a stun-gun before being taken to the basement and strangled?

While the Boulder police slowly built a case, rumours that potentially incriminated the Ramseys in their daughter's death were published in the press: JonBenét had a bed-wetting problem; she was molested and then murdered by a family member; the ransom note was a 'red herring' because the amount demanded exactly matched John Ramsey's contract bonus that year; Patsy's 911 call was suspicious; and her handwriting possibly indicated that she was the ransom note writer. Documents related to searches of the Ramsey homes were released to the media, and approaching the first anniversary of the child's murder John and Patsy remained under an 'umbrella of suspicion'. Despite the loss of vital evidence, police were keen to charge the parents with murder, but in October 1998, the Boulder district attorney announced that there was insufficient evidence for charges to be laid against any known persons.

In 2000, John and Patsy Ramsey started to fight back against the innuendo and tabloid reporting of the stalled murder investigation. The Ramseys released a book, *The Death of Innocence*, in which they named their own suspect—a local man who dressed up as Santa to endear himself to children—and launched multimillion-dollar lawsuits against the *Star* magazine, the *New York Post* and Time Warner for portraying the couple's eldest son, Burke, as a suspect. (Boulder police had ruled out any of John Ramsey's children, including two adult children from a previous marriage, as playing any part in the murder.) Still the Boulder police believed the Ramseys to be at the top of the suspect list.

Finally, six years after the murder, Boulder district attorney Mary Keenan took over the investigation and publicly stated that police had completed an exhaustive investigation of the Ramseys and that her office would now 'pursue new and previously unchecked leads'. In March 2003, US district judge Julie Carnes of Atlanta conceded that 'the weight of the evidence is more consistent with a theory that an intruder murdered JonBenét than it is with a theory that Mrs Ramsey did it'. District attorney Mary Keenan agreed. By this time, Patsy Ramsey was fighting a personal battle against cancer and John Ramsey had not worked for four years.

Much had been made of the fact that footprints had not been found outside the basement window, but there was hardly enough snow to register a footprint on the night the little girl died. Despite this, a boot print *was* discovered outside the Ramseys' home and there were signs that someone had entered and left the house via a basement window. Most significantly, however, male DNA recovered from the child's underpants did not match any member of the family. A report that an intruder had hidden inside another Boulder home while the owners were out, and then abused a child after the family returned home and went to sleep, was not originally linked to the JonBenét Ramsey case. Did the killer hide inside the house while the Ramseys were out, stun the little girl in her bedroom and then strangle her with a crude ligature in the basement?

Despite the fact that the Boulder district attorney hired a retired detective named Tom Bennett to work on the case alongside homicide investigator Lou Smit, no-one has been charged with the murder of JonBenét Ramsey. However, one suspect, a known paedophile living near the Ramsey home in December 1996, later committed 'suicide' in suspicious circumstances. Although the case ruined the Ramseys physically, emotionally and financially, a decade after their little girl's death the cloak of suspicion has at last been lifted from their shoulders.

HISTORICAL AND SOCIAL SIGNIFICANCE:

- In December 1999, 29-year-old Regana Rapp pleaded guilty to 'racketeering'—supplying confidential police information about the case to the media—and was sentenced to two years' probation and 50 hours of community service. In the same month, tabloid editor Craig Lewis was arrested after being indicted on extortion and bribery charges. He allegedly offered the Ramseys a copy of the ransom note (confiscated by police as evidence) for US$30,000.
- Two months after Patsy Ramsey died of ovarian cancer, in June 2006, 41-year-old schoolteacher John Mark Karr pleaded guilty to JonBenét's death after he was arrested in Bangkok on child sex charges. Karr was flown back to the United States amid a media storm but was later ruled out as a suspect through DNA testing.

REFERENCES:

- *The JonBenét Ramsey Case, www.cnn.com*
- CBS News (2002), *www.cbsnews.com*

1996

Marc Dutroux and the 'Beasts of Belgium'

FACT FILE

CRIMES: Abduction, rape, torture and murder
VICTIMS: Sabine Dardenne, aged 12*; Laetitia Delhez, aged 14*; Eefje Lambrechts, aged 19; Julie Lejeune, aged 8; An Marchal, aged 17; Melissa Russo, aged 8; Bernard Weinstein, aged 36**
*Dardenne and Delhez were rescued by police on 15 August 1996
** Weinstein was an accomplice of the gang but was killed by Marc Dutroux in 1995
DATES: August 1995 to August 1996
PLACE: Marcinelle (Belgium)
PERPETRATORS: Marc Dutroux (b. 1956); Michelle Martin (b. 1960); Michel Lelièvre (b.1974); Michel Nihoul (b.1944); Bernard Weinstein
SENTENCE: Marc Dutroux was sentenced to life imprisonment, Michelle Martin to 30 years' imprisonment and Michel Lelièvre to 25 years' imprisonment. Michel Nihoul was acquitted on kidnapping and conspiracy charges but was sentenced to five years' imprisonment on related drug charges

In 1986, a 35-year-old former male prostitute and small-time criminal named Marc Dutroux was charged with a series of sexual assaults on five girls in the Wallonion province of Belgium. Dutroux committed the crimes with Michelle Martin, who would become his second wife and the mother of three of his five children. Sentenced to thirteen and a half years' jail, Dutroux was able to convince prison psychiatrists that he was rehabilitated, and was released back into society in 1991 after serving just three years. The subsequent investigation into the abduction, rape and torture of six girls—four of whom were starved to death by Dutroux and his accomplices—ignited widespread anger in Belgian society about the inadequacies of the country's criminal justice system.

An unemployed electrician, Marc Dutroux earned his living by stealing cars, drug dealing and prostitution, but he also convinced a prison psychiatrist that he was mentally disabled and upon his release from prison was granted a government pension. Dutroux eventually owned seven houses, mostly vacant shacks, where he would go to torture the girls he kidnapped. In his main house, in Marcinelle, he constructed a concealed dungeon in the basement—2.15 metres (7 feet) long, 1.64 metres (5 feet) high and less than a metre (3 feet) wide behind a concrete door which he disguised as a bookcase. By the summer of 1995, fuelled by hundreds of pornographic videotapes, Dutroux, his wife and their two accomplices, Bernard Weinstein and Michel Lelièvre, had everything prepared for the victims they would abduct to satisfy their own sexual depravity.

Eight-year-old friends Julie Lejeune and Melissa Russo were kidnapped together on 24 June 1995 and hidden in Dutroux's dungeon. There, Dutroux sexually abused them and filmed them for pornographic videos. On 22 August, 17-year-old An Marchal and 19-year-old Eefje Lambrechts were kidnapped while on a camping trip. Because the dungeon was in use, Dutroux chained the girls to a bed in one of his houses, which meant that his wife was fully aware of what was happening. Some weeks later, in circumstances never fully revealed, Dutroux killed the two girls and buried their bodies under a shack next to a house he owned in Jumet. The house was occupied by Bernard Weinstein. Another accomplice, Michel Lelièvre, was later implicated in several of the abductions but did not take part in the sexual abuse or torture of the victims. Instead, he was 'paid' with drugs supplied by businessman Michel Nihoul.

In December 1995, Dutroux was jailed for his involvement in a stolen luxury car racket. While he was in prison from 6 December to 20 March 1996, Julie Lejeune and Melissa Russo remained hidden in Dutroux's dungeon and starved to death. Incredibly, police searched Dutroux's home on 13 and 19 December while the girls were still alive, but found nothing. In May 1996, Dutroux and Lelièvre snatched 12-year-old Sabine Dardenne on her way home from school and hid her in the dungeon. On 9 August, she was joined by 14-year-old Laetitia Delhez, who had been taken while walking home one night from the public swimming pool. However, Dutroux and his accomplice were taking more and more risks. A witness memorised part of the number plate belonging to Dutroux's car when Laetitia was taken and he, his wife and Lelièvre were arrested just four days later. A search of Dutroux's home showed no sign of the secret dungeon or the missing girls, but after two days' interrogation, Dutroux and Lelièvre confessed everything. Sabine Dardenne and Laetitia Delhez were found alive on 15 August 1996.

On 17 August, Dutroux led police to the remains of Julie Lejeune, Melissa Russo and his former accomplice Bernard Weinstein, which were buried in the backyard of another of his houses in Sars-la-Buissière. No doubt in an attempt to minimise his own culpability, Dutroux told police that it was Weinstein who had abducted the girls and let them starve to death. Dutroux claimed that he murdered Bernard Weinstein only because Weinstein let the girls starve to death. However, Weinstein's testicles had been crushed, his body was laced with barbiturates and he had been buried alive. Police later determined that Weinstein had been tortured to make him reveal the whereabouts of some missing money and then murdered by Dutroux lest he talk to the police about his injuries. Faced with these facts, Dutroux revealed the resting place of the remains of An Marchal and Eefje Lambrechts.

The crimes committed by Dutroux and his accomplices shook the faith of the Belgian people. Religious ministers asked from the pulpit, 'Where was God?' when the children starved to death in Dutroux's dungeon. There was stinging criticism of the country's judicial system and the investigation into Dutroux's activities. As early as 1993, local police had been told by an informer that Dutroux was constructing a cell, but no action was taken. (Dutroux's mother had even written to authorities objecting to her son's release from prison.) In October 1996, 300,000 people took part in a massive protest march (known as the 'White March') demanding the reform of Belgium's law enforcement agencies and the review of the early release of sex offenders. While a parliamentary commission found that Dutroux had not been protected by a network of high-ranking paedophiles or Satanists, the police's handling of the case again came into question when Dutroux escaped from custody in April 1998. Dutroux was captured the following day and the minister of justice, the minister for the interior and the police chief in charge of the investigation resigned.

Dutroux's trial began in March 2004—almost eight years after his capture. Tried for the deaths of An Marchal, Eefje Lambrechts and Bernard Weinstein, he denied committing these crimes despite having already confessed to Weinstein's murder. When Sabine Dardenne, now a mature 19-year-old, took the stand, she related how Dutroux had told her that she was being held on behalf of an international group but that he was 'protecting her' while they negotiated with her family. It was clear that he was the ringleader of the group. Facing her abductor on the witness stand, the teenage girl showed more courage than Dutroux had displayed in his entire lifetime. On 22 June 2004, Marc Dutroux was sentenced to life imprisonment without parole.

HISTORICAL AND SOCIAL SIGNIFICANCE:

- Marc Dutroux and Michelle Martin divorced in 2003 while both were in prison awaiting trial.

REFERENCES:

- Bell, Rachael (2005), *See No Evil, Hear No Evil, www.crimelibrary.com*
- 'Marc Dutroux Trial' (2004), *The Scotsman, www.news.scotsman.com*
- Slattery, Finbarr (2004), *Crime and Punishment, www.kingdompaper.com*

1996
The Dunblane Massacre

FACT FILE

CRIME: Mass murder
VICTIMS*: Victoria Elizabeth Clydesdale; Emma Elizabeth Crozier; Melissa Helen Currie; Charlotte Louise Dunn; Kevin Allan Hasell; Ross William Irvine; David Charles Kerr; Mhairi Isabel MacBeath; Brett McKinnon; Abigail Joanne McLennan; Emily Morton; Sophie Jane Lockwood North; John Petrie; Joanna Caroline Ross; Hannah Louise Scott; Megan Turner; Gwen Mayor, schoolteacher, aged 45
*All victims were 5 or 6 years old
DATE: 13 March 1996
PLACE: Dunblane (Scotland)
PERPETRATOR: Thomas Hamilton (1952–1996)

Nine years after a troubled 27-year-old man named Michael Robert Ryan armed himself with an AK-47 rifle and a Beretta pistol and killed 16 people in the sleepy English town of Hungerford, another group of innocent people became the victims of a madman with a legally owned gun. On 13 March 1996, 43-year-old shopkeeper and former scout troop leader Thomas Hamilton walked into a school in the Scottish city of Dunblane and started shooting. His 16 victims could scarcely have been more vulnerable—a group of 5- and 6-year-old kindergarteners and a female teacher. The killer then turned his gun on himself. How could this have happened again?

Thomas Hamilton was born on 10 May 1952 in Glasgow, Scotland. His young parents separated before Hamilton was born and the infant was legally adopted by his grandparents at the age of two. Hamilton grew up believing that his grandparents were his parents and that his mother was his older sister—he never knew his father. As a teenager, he developed an interest in rifles and boys clubs, which were to become obsessions later in his life. In 1973, he was dismissed as an assistant scout leader when his judgment was questioned after a scout trip. Hamilton had led a group of boys on a winter camping trip, and was met by a barrage of criticism from concerned parents when the boys returned suffering various stages of hypothermia. The 21-year-old was incensed that his leadership qualities were questioned. He wrote several letters to Scotland's Scout Association in defence of his actions, but their decision on his actions was final.

In 1974, Hamilton was told by his grandparents that his sister was his mother. Whether this had a profound effect on him is unknown, but Hamilton grew increasingly authoritarian and demanding. During the 1970s, he obtained his firearms certificate, increased his gun collections and constantly practised his shooting skills. When his 'do-it-yourself' shop, 'Woodcraft', closed he decided to start up a series of boys' 'activity' clubs in Stirling and Dunblane. Targeting boys between the ages of 7 and 11, Hamilton rented gymnasiums in local schools or halls and community sporting grounds for a program of gymnastics, sports skills and fitness. However, in the 1990s Hamilton's behaviour was erratic, rigid and bordered on the sadistic. Boys complained that he would discipline them, make them do things that caused them to feel uncomfortable, and then reward them to keep them quiet. Parents painted Hamilton as something of a pervert—taking photographs of half-naked boys, rubbing suntan lotion into their bodies and revelling in making them obey his every command—but when they complained to local police, authorities could not do anything about it. There was no overt evidence of misconduct.

After the Dunblane massacre, however, there was evidence that Hamilton had taken guns on his camping trips with young boys and encouraged them to 'shoot at any animal they saw'. Local detective sergeant Paul Hughes recommended that Hamilton's gun licence be revoked because of his 'unsavoury character' and 'unstable personality', but for a variety of reasons this was not followed through. (Had it been, it would have become evident that much of Hamilton's arsenal was obtained with invalid licences.) Parents took matters into their own hands and pelted him with eggs in the doorway of his home—the whole scene captured on video by a local news crew and shown on television. Hamilton was publicly humiliated, and many parents, schools and community groups would have nothing more to do with him. This only heightened Hamilton's paranoia. In response he wrote threatening letters to parents, local schools, rival scout leaders and even Queen Elizabeth saying that he was being victimised.

On 13 March 1996, Hamilton finally snapped. He would get back at everyone for spreading derogatory rumours about him.

The failed scout leader armed himself with two 9-millimetre Browning automatic pistols, two .357 calibre Smith and Wesson revolvers and more than 700 cartridges, and travelled to Dunblane Primary School. The rampage lasted for only three or four minutes, but Hamilton was able to fire 105 rounds with one of his pistols as children scurried for their lives. Fifteen children and a teacher, 45-year-old Mrs Gwen Mayor, were killed inside the school gymnasium and another 15 students were seriously injured. (One of the children later died in hospital.) After the rampage, Hamilton put one of his revolvers in his mouth and took his own life.

As a result of the Dunblane Massacre—an act of madness unprecedented in British history—sweeping changes were made to United Kingdom gun laws following the publication of the Cullen Report in October 1996.The law was changed to allow police, at any time, to revoke or alter a gun licence if they felt that the owner did not have 'good reason' to own his guns or ammunition.The laws had an enormous impact on the country's 120,000 rifle and pistol owners—hand-gun ownership was banned, and police would keep a closer check on rifle clubs and gun owners.The report was also critical of the police's failure to reassess Hamilton's gun ownership in the light of complaints about his behaviour.The decision to protect the identity of the victims by withholding 'sensitive information' in the Cullen Report for 100 years only heightened concerns of a police cover-up and propagated rumours that Thomas Hamilton was a known paedophile or that he was protected by friends in the police force—and feeding the unfounded fear that he did not act alone.

The decision to release further files—but not all of them—later that year w as some comfort to the grieving parents of the Dunblane schoolchildren and t he family and friends of Gwen Mayor. There was no such comfort for Thomas Hamilton.

HISTORICAL AND SOCIAL SIGNIFICANCE:

- The people of Dunblane have formed a long-distance connection with the people of Port Arthur, Tasmania, which was the scene of the worst massacre in Australian history six weeks after the Scottish tragedy.
- The Gwen Mayor Trust was established to advance education by providing financial support for projects connected with the arts, culture, music or sport.
- In 1992, a hybrid apricot rose was named in honour of Gwen Mayor.
- In September 2004, the Dunblane Centre was opened in memory of the victims. Seventeen etchings of birds, flowers and animals in the glass frontage of the centre represent those who died that day. Fourteen etched snowdrops represent the children who were seriously injured.

REFERENCES:

- *The Cullen Inquiry (1996), www.scotland.gov.uk.*
- *Dunblane Massacre, www.crimelibrary.com*

1996
The Unabomber

FACT FILE

CRIMES: Transportation of an explosive with intent to kill or injure and mailing an explosive device in an attempt to kill or injure.
VICTIMS: Hugh Scrutton, aged 38; Thomas Mosser, aged 50; Gilbert Murray, aged 47
29 people were wounded
DATES: 1978–1995
PLACES: Chicago (Illinois), Washington (DC), Salt Lake City (Utah), Nashville (Tennessee), Berkeley (California), Sacramento (California), San Francisco (California), New Haven (Connecticut) and North Caldwell (New Jersey), USA
PERPETRATOR: Theodore Kaczynski (b. 1942)
SENTENCE: Life imprisonment

For almost eighteen years, from 1978 until his capture in 1996, the 'Unabomber' waged a one-man war against what he saw as the 'evils' of technological progress. After the most expensive FBI manhunt in modern times had failed to identify the person responsible for a series of bombs that originally targeted university and airline personnel, the FBI referred to the perpetrator by the acronym UNABOM, which the media later latched on to. In 1995, after two men were killed in separate incidents, the 'Unabomber' succeeded in having his 35,000-word 'manifesto' published as a trade-off for stopping the attacks. However, this proved to be his undoing. David Kaczynski recognised the writing style of the author of the rambling attack on technology as his elder brother, Ted, a former university lecturer now living in seclusion in a shack in Montana. On 3 April 1996, Ted Kaczynski was arrested and the 'Unabomber's' reign of terror came to an end.

Theodore ('Ted) Kaczynski was born in Chicago, Illinois, in 1942. A brilliant student, he was severely allergic to medication as a child, and because he was hospitalised for long periods, was withdrawn and lacked the social skills of other teenagers. Some experts have suggested that Kaczynski suffered from a form of Asperger's syndrome, a mental condition that affects emotional and social development. Whatever the case, by the time he attended Harvard in 1958 (at the young age of 16, having skipped two years of grade school) he was painfully shy and socially inept. At Harvard, Kaczynski took part in a series of psychological experiments under the direction of Dr Henry A. Murray. After Kaczynski's capture in 1996, psychiatrists attributed some of his emotional instability and fear of technological control to Murray's controversial stress tests.

After his graduation from Harvard in 1962, Kaczynski earned a master's degree and a Ph.D. in mathematics from the University of Michigan, and by 1967 he was rated one of the university's brightest mathematical minds. A National Science Foundation fellow, Kaczynski taught undergraduates and published articles but was too aloof and reserved to relate to his students. Despite gaining employment as assistant professor of mathematics at the University of California in Berkeley in 1967, Kaczynski resigned after just two years of teaching. For the next decade, Kaczynski withdrew from society and was financially supported by his family. In the 1970s he lived alone in a 3-metre by 3.5-metre (10-foot by 12-foot) plywood shack on a block of land that he and his brother, David, purchased in Lincoln, Montana, in 1971.

Whatever prompted Ted Kaczynski to send letter bombs to universities, airlines and later computer companies, his first attempts were crude and ambiguous. On 25 May 1978, a package was found in a parking lot of the University of Illinois, Chicago. It was mailed to its return address, Northwestern University, where it exploded and injured a campus policeman, Terry Marker. A year later, Northwestern received another mail-bomb, which injured graduate student John Harris. During the next six years 'The Unabomber' targeted universities and airlines, and then 38-year-old Hugh Scrutton was killed by a bomb found near his computer store. It was the fourth bombing in 1985 alone, and the most lethal. Inside, on some of the bomb parts, was the inscription 'FC'—first thought to stand for 'F★★★ Computers' but later found to mean 'Freedom Club'.

The Unabomber did not strike between 1987 and 1993—a period in which Kaczynski attempted to rejoin society and even tried to look for a female companion—but he returned with deadly force in 1994. On 10 December 1994, advertising executive Thomas Mosser was targeted after an article incorrectly identified him as a 'spin doctor' hired to promote the oil companies after the Exxon Valdez disaster. Kaczynski justified this killing by stating that advertising companies manipulate people's attitudes—but he saved his deadliest bomb for last. On 24 April 1995, California Forestry Association president Gilbert Murray was killed when he opened a large package addressed to his former boss. Soon after this murder, Kaczynski mailed letters to the press and some of his victims demanding that his manifesto be published verbatim by a major newspaper. After he sent a further letter threatening to kill more innocent people, the article was published in the *New York Times* and the *Washington Post* on 19 September 1995.

The 35,000-word 'Unabomber Manifesto' was entitled 'Industrial Society and Its Future' and was published as a special lift-out. Kaczynski railed against population growth, man's dissociation with nature, the pace of technological change, social conformity, consumerism, corporate domination and computers, amongst other things. The Unabomber argued that there needed to be a 'social crash' so that people could escape the demands of technological progress and return to a simpler, happier lifestyle. On reading the piece, David Kaczynski informed authorities, who arrested his brother in Lincoln, Montana. David Kaczynski received an assurance from authorities that he would not be identified as the informer and that they would not seek the death penalty for his brother. Neither assurance was honoured.

In January 1998, Bureau of Prisons doctor Sally C. Johnson compiled a confidential report on Ted Kaczynski's state of mind after he attempted to hang himself with a pair of his underpants. Among other things, Johnson found that Kaczynski had failed to maintain adequate relationships with women, had once considered undergoing a sex change and dreamed of killing psychiatrists. Although diagnosed as a paranoid schizophrenic, Kaczynski was judged fit to stand trial and avoided the death penalty by pleading guilty to his crimes on 22 January 1998. Kaczynski tried to withdraw his guilty plea and use his mental condition as a defence, but by March 2002 all avenues of appeal had been rejected.

Theodore Kaczynski is serving a life sentence with no prospect of parole in the Federal ADX Supermax prison in Florence, Colorado. One of the Unabomber's fellow inmates was Oklahoma City bomber Timothy McVeigh, whom he befriended before McVeigh's execution in 2001. For a brief time, Kaczynski finally had a friend.

HISTORICAL AND SOCIAL SIGNIFICANCE:

- After Kaczynski's arrest, similarities were noted between his life path and that of the protagonist of Joseph Conrad's novel *The Secret Agent*. Conrad's protagonist was a professor named Verloc who resigned his position to become an anarchist. Kaczynski sometimes used the pseudonyms Conrad and Konrad when he travelled around the country planting his bombs.
- After subtracting legal expenses from the reward money he collected, David Kaczynski donated what remained to the families of his brother's victims.
- The University of Michigan's Special Collection Library has collected copies of over 400 letters Ted Kaczynski has written from prison to various academics and media outlets since he was captured in April 1996. Kaczynski continues his correspondence in prison.

REFERENCES:

- Creig, Charlotte (2005), *Criminal Masterminds*, Arcturus, London
- *The Unabomber: Ted Kaczynski (2005), www.rotten.com*
- *Ted Kaczynski: The Unabomber (2005), www.crimelibrary.com*

1996
The Port Arthur Massacre

FACT FILE

CRIME: Mass murder
VICTIMS: 35 dead, 28 wounded
DATE: 28 April 1996
PLACE: Port Arthur Tourist Attraction, Tasmania (Australia)
PERPETRATOR: Martin Bryant (b. 1969)
SENTENCE: 35 life sentences plus 777 years, to be served in Tasmania's Risdon Maximum Security Prison.

Port Arthur was established in 1830 as the main penal settlement on the island of Van Diemen's Land, which was later renamed Tasmania. Very few convicts tried to escape from Port Arthur, situated as it was in the south-western corner of the island, 95 kilometres (60 miles) from the main town of Hobart ... there was nowhere to escape to. In more recent times, the former prison has become one of the island's major tourist attractions, and millions of visitors have strolled through its grounds. When gunman Martin Bryant went on a murderous rampage at Port Arthur in 1996, the scale of his crime was unprecedented in Australia's peacetime history. At the end of the day, 35 people lay dead and another 28 wounded—an atrocity that reverberated not only around Australia but also around the world.

Sunday 28 April 1996 was a sunny, autumn day that attracted more than 500 visitors to Port Arthur. The Broad Arrow Cafe, situated at the northern end of the complex, adjacent to the main car park, was filled with visitors enjoying their lunch. Few of the tourists noticed the tall, blond-haired young man walk into the cafe carrying a large sports bag and a video camera. Cafe patrons later remarked that the young man commented on the lack of Japanese tourists at the cafe that day. After quickly finishing his meal, he stood at the back of the cafe in the north-western corner and placed his belongings on a spare dining table. He then took out an AR15 semi-automatic rifle from his sports bag and began to fire.

In the space of 15 seconds—the time period was verified by video footage taken outside the cafe by tourists—17 shots were fired, 12 people died and 10 others were injured. Twenty people ultimately lost their lives in the Broad Arrow Cafe—including several people serving behind the counter and a group hiding from the first onslaught in the adjoining gift store—but this number could have been much greater were it not for the selfless acts of bravery by many of the people trapped inside. Leaving the cafe, the gunman killed four more people in the lower car park before driving off in his yellow Volvo towards the tollbooth at the entrance to the complex. A number of people dialled the Australian emergency number 000, thinking he was getting away, but suddenly he stopped and continued his killing spree.

A group of people who had heard the gunshots thought that they were out of harm's way as they approached the tollbooth. But the gunman overtook them in his car, and ordered a mother shielding her children to get down on her knees. As she pleaded for the lives of her children, Nanette Mikac and her daughter Madeline were killed by a single gunshot, while 6-year-old Alannah Mikac attempted to hide behind a nearby tree. The gunman callously stalked and killed the helpless child. He then approached the occupants of a gold BMW waiting at the tollbooth and demanded their car. He shot and killed four of the occupants before driving off onto the main highway.

The gunman then confronted lawyer Glenn Pears and his girlfriend, Zoe Hall, in a nearby service station. Pears was made to get into the boot of the gold BMW before Hall was killed. The gunman then drove with his hostage towards a guesthouse in Seascape, north of Port Arthur. Police later learned that the gunman had already killed the owners of the guesthouse, David and Sally Martin, on his way to Port Arthur earlier that day. The gunman swung the gold-coloured BMW off the Arthur Highway and stopped at the entrance to the Seascape guesthouse, shooting at passing cars and injuring several people. He then drove inside and took Glenn Pears into the house and handcuffed him to the stairs. After taking the AR15 and FN rifles out of the gold BMW, he doused the car with a can of petrol and set the car alight.

Police surrounded the guesthouse and spoke to the gunman over the next six hours until the cordless telephone went dead. Some time during the next several hours, Glenn Pears, his final victim, was shot in cold blood. Police expected a long siege, but at about 8 am on Monday 29 April, smoke was seen billowing from the Seascape guesthouse. Shortly after, a man rushed out of the house, his clothes on fire, and stripped off his shirt. It was the gunman. At 8.25 am he fell to the ground and, offering little resistance, was arrested. His name was Martin Bryant.

Martin Bryant was born in 1969 and was described as an 'intellectually stunted child' with poor social skills. The pressures of coping with Bryant's developmental problems indirectly led to his father, Maurice, committing suicide in 1993. In 1987, Bryant met an elderly, eccentric New Town woman named Helen Mary Harvey, and started doing odd jobs around her house. Bryant became her 'companion', and when she died in 1992—the victim of a car crash that occurred when Bryant was driving—the 23-three-year-old was the beneficiary of her estate, valued at AUD$1.3 million.

The Australian government had already placed restrictions on which guns could be imported into the country, but the fragmentary way in which the states checked licences, granted permits and monitored the use of prohibited weapons had somehow made it possible for someone like Martin Bryant—who never owned a gun licence—to purchase five semi-automatic weapons. After the Port Arthur Massacre, the states cooperated in setting up an Australia-wide system to record gun sales and a national buy-back scheme was established to compensate those gun owners required to surrender their weapons. On 30 September 1996, Martin Bryant pleaded not guilty to 35 counts of murder and 37 counts of attempted murder, aggravated assault, wounding, causing grievous bodily harm and unlawfully setting fire to property. The day before his trial, which was set down for 8 November, he changed his plea to guilty. When the 72 charges were being read out, at the fiftieth charge—the 27th count of murder—Bryant laughed out loud. Bryant was sentenced to imprisonment for the term of his natural life on the 35 counts of murder and to 21 years on each of the remaining 37 charges—effectively, 777 years.

Martin Bryant continues to show no remorse for the killings because he has no insight into the impact of his actions. Prison authorities have maintained 24-hour observation of Bryant so that he does not commit suicide.

REFERENCES:

- Scott, Margaret, *A Story of Strength and Courage* (1997), Random House, Sydney
- *Where were you when ... the News that Stopped a Nation* (2003), New Custom Publishing, Victoria

1997

Gianni Versace: Fashion Victim

FACT FILE

CRIME: Serial murder
VICTIMS: David Madson, aged 33; Lee Miglin, aged 72; William Reese, aged 45; Jeffrey Trail, aged 28; Gianni Versace, aged 50
DATES: 27 April to 15 July 1997
PLACE: Miami, Florida (USA)
PERPETRATOR: Andrew Phillip Cunanan (1969-1997)

The murder of fashion icon Gianni Versace on 15 July 1997 sent shockwaves through the celebrity world. Had Versace, who was openly homosexual, been murdered by an ex-lover or was he another victim of a modern-day phenomenon—a celebrity murder designed to bring fame to the killer?

Gianni Versace was born in 1946 into a southern Italian family which owned a tailoring store in the town of Reggio di Calabria. By the mid-1970s he had created his own collection, established his own brand name and opened his own boutique. In 1985, his Instante collection became an international success, and the name Versace became as identifiable as those of Ralph Lauren and Giorgio Armani.

Particularly known for his innovative leather designs, Versace became a favourite designer amongst the world's rich and famous, including Sly Stallone, Madonna, Elton John and Diana, the Princess of Wales. In America, he became known for the soft-pastel colours of the 'T-shirt and jacket' look he designed for the hit television show *Miami Vice* in the late 1980s.

In 1992, Gianni Versace moved to Miami Beach, Florida, and bought an old apartment building called the Amsterdam Palace at 1116 Ocean Drive for US$2.9 million. Demolishing the adjacent Revere Hotel, he built a major addition to his new home, which he named Casa Casuarina. Versace wrote to his sister, Donatella, who was living in Florence: 'Here in Miami, I've finally found what I was looking for ... the center of my circle. I want to stay here and live out my time ... forever.'

On the other side of the country, Andrew Phillip Cunanan, the son of Filipino parents, was living a lifestyle that was about to crash in on him. A homosexual, drug addict and part-time prostitute, Cunanan liked to pay cash for everything. And when the cash ran out in 1997, Cunanan snapped. On 27 April, he murdered gay friend Jeffrey Trail in Minneapolis, Minnesota, and two days later, former lover David Madson. When Trail's body was found in Madson's loft apartment, Cunanan became a prime suspect. On 4 May, Cunanan drove to Chicago and murdered another associate, prominent real estate developer Lee Miglin, and stole his car. Now the focus of an intensive manhunt, Cunanan killed New Jersey cemetery worker William Reese on 9 May merely to swap cars. The murderer drove to Miami Beach and hid for two months before choosing his fifth victim.

On the morning of 7 July 1997, Gianni Versace got up early and, as he had done regularly since living on Ocean Drive, went to a nearby News Cafe to buy several Italian magazines. Versace's partner, 38-year-old Antonio D'Amico, was having breakfast with Versace's house manager and his tennis partner in the main dining room, in the eastern part of the house, when he heard two gunshots. Immediately, D'Amico looked out of a window and noticed that one of the iron gates leading into the mansion was partially open. Instinctively, he stood up—and saw Gianni Versace lying on the steps near the ground. D'Amico screamed and ran outside with the house manager and his friend. There they found Versace lying on his left side and bleeding from a head wound.

D'Amico told police that he saw a woman standing 7 or 8 yards (6 or 7 metres) southeast of the front gate and that she was motioning towards the north. D'Amico also saw a man walking briskly away from the house—the man was dark-skinned, with short, dark hair, and was wearing a cap and carrying what looked like a brown paper bag in his hand. D'Amico's tennis partner immediately gave chase but lost the possible suspect in the morning crowd.

D'Amico had been Versace's partner for 14 years and told police that Versace had used male escorts in the past. The question also had to be asked: had Versace been killed by a jilted lover? Versace's former lover lived in Italy (as did D'Amico's former female partner), and D'Amico told police that Versace had not used escorts for some years and never in Miami. It took some time for police to link this murder with four unsolved shootings that had occurred across the country.

Eight days after Gianni Versace's murder, Miami Beach police found Andrew Cunanan deceased, lying in a queen-size bed in the main bedroom of a Miami houseboat. Wearing only a pair of grey cotton shorts, Cunanan was propped up by three pillows and had a gun in his hand. He had shot himself in the mouth. The body was in a complete state of rigor mortis and he had obviously been dead for some time. Interestingly, a wound was found on Cunanan's stomach, which explained the medical supplies (cotton swabs, alcohol and sterile pads) found downstairs on a table. The killer may have suffered a wound while committing one of the murders and was in some discomfort before he died.

Miami Beach police established that the weapon used to kill Versace, a Smith and Wesson .40 calibre Taurus semi-automatic pistol, was the same one used in the murders of Madson and Reese. Although none of the eyewitnesses positively identified Cunanan as the shooter in the Versace case, Miami Beach police established that 'trace, paper and eyewitness evidence' put Cunanan in their jurisdiction at the time of the murder. Most important, the weapon Cunanan used on himself was the .40 calibre Smith and Wesson.

One of Cunanan's lovers told the FBI that Cunanan liked to cross-dress, and authorities were criticised for labelling the suspect 'a transvestite'. However, the autopsy revealed high levels of the male hormone testosterone in Cunanan's body. Did the killer take steroids to change his appearance and spark a homicidal rage?

On 30 December 1997, Miami Beach police officially closed their investigation into the murder of designer Gianni Versace. While the investigation successfully tracked down killer Andrew Cunanan, authorities did not establish any motive or 'direct connection' to explain why Cunanan targeted Gianni Versace in his cross-country rampage. Several theories were explored: that this was a contract killing; that the homicide was the result of an abortive robbery; or that Cunanan shot Versace as revenge or to gain notoriety. Nothing could be proved.

Drawing an ironic analogy with the fact that the murderer took his life on a houseboat, Miami Beach police chief Richard Baretto summed up: 'The real answer to that went down with the ship, so to speak, when Andrew Cunanan committed suicide.'

HISTORICAL AND SOCIAL SIGNIFICANCE:

- A week after attending Versace's funeral, Princess Diana was killed in a car crash in Paris. Elton John, who also attended Versace's funeral, sang at Princess Diana's funeral.
- The Versace Design Company was inherited by Gianni's sister, Donatella, and has continued to grow. Gianni's former lover, Antonio D'Amico, later formed his own design company.

REFERENCES:

- Brown, Joseph (1998), *Gianni Versace: Walking in Miami's Golden Light, www.southbeach-usa.com*
- *The Death of Gianni Versace, www.washingtonpost.com*
- *Versace: Case Closed, www.thesmokinggun.com*

1998

Harold Shipman: 'Doctor Death'

FACT FILE

CRIME: Serial murder
VICTIMS: 236 patients
DATE: 1975 to 1998
PLACE: Todmorden and Hyde (England)
PERPETRATOR: Dr Harold Shipman, GP (1946–2004)
SENTENCE: Life imprisonment. Shipman hanged himself in prison on 13 January 2004

In 1977, after having been fined for an alleged pethidine addiction but given a second chance, general practitioner Dr Harold Shipman was offered a position at the Donneybrook Medical Centre in Hyde, Manchester, in the north of England. Despite his conviction, and now 'cured' of his addiction, Shipman quickly earned his colleagues' respect—and his patients' trust. Over the next 20 years, Shipman killed over 200 patients without detection —many of them old and infirm, others healthy and alert. It subsequently emerged that his deadly murder career had started even earlier, bringing the confirmed figure to 236. Shipman killed his elderly victims with a lethal dose of morphine and then exaggerated their medical condition in his formal records to cover his tracks. He might well still be killing today had he not made one glaring mistake. Shipman got greedy ...

Harold Frederick Shipman was born in Nottingham, in the north of England, in 1946. The middle child of Harold and Vera Shipman, young Harold was known to everyone as 'Fred' Shipman to distinguish him from his father. When Shipman was a teenager, his over-protective mother developed lung cancer. She died in 1963, but as she lay dying Harold Shipman witnessed the relief she gained from the regular injections of morphine the local GP administered. Perhaps this inspired him to enter medical school two years later—perhaps this is also why he became an 'angel of mercy' and murdered more than 200 of his patients.

Shipman was an average student, but he graduated from Leeds University medical school and gained a hospital internship. Settling down to married life with wife Primrose, he gained his first GP position in the small town of Todmorden, in Yorkshire. Shipman was respected in his role, but in 1975 a suspicious receptionist noticed that the junior GP had been purchasing large quantities of pethidine—a painkiller that acts like morphine. When the practice's senior doctor investigated, he found that many of the patients for whom Shipman was ordering the drug did not have pethidine prescribed for them.

When confronted by the evidence, Shipman confessed that he was addicted to the drug. Those who worked with him recalled his frequent blackouts, which he had blamed on epilepsy at the time. The 29-year-old pleaded for a second chance, and although he was fined £600 for prescription fraud he was allowed to continue working as a GP. It was later thought that Shipman admitted to the pethidine addiction to cover the fact that he was murdering his patients. A later inquiry into the patients who died under his care at Todmorden found that 70-year-old Eva Lyons, who died on 17 March 1975, was probably his first victim. There was also a strong suspicion of unlawful killing—though insufficient evidence to constitute proof—in regard to another 11 Todmorden patients.

During his 20 years at the Donneybrook Medical Centre in Hyde, Shipman went on to kill 235 patients.

On 24 June 1998, Mrs Kathleen Grundy, a former mayoress of Hyde, died suddenly. Although 81 years old, Mrs Grundy was healthy and alert, and her death came as something of a shock to those who knew her. She was found on the sofa at her home by friends from the Age Concern Club, who called in to visit her when she failed to turn up for a function. According to her daughter, solicitor Angela Woodruffe, the last person to see her mother was her GP, Harold Shipman, who took some routine blood samples. When Mrs Woodruffe questioned the doctor about her mother's health, he told her there was no need for an autopsy because her mother had been under his care.

It was not until after Mrs Grundy's funeral that her daughter learned that her mother had made a new will and that the sole beneficiary of her £386 000 estate was none other than Harold Shipman. Angela Woodruffe had a copy of what she believed to be her mother's final will, which had been filed with her law firm in 1996. She could not believe that her mother would have made a new will without telling her—a practising solicitor—let alone fail to leave any part of her estate to her only daughter. When Mrs Woodruffe checked the signatures on the two wills, she had a strong suspicion that Shipman had forged her mother's signature on the new will. Police were also highly sceptical that the typed message in Mrs Grundy's will was in the elderly woman's own words:

All my estate, money and house, to my doctor. My family are not in need and I want to reward him for all the care he has given me and the people of Hyde. He is sensible

enough to handle any problem this may give him.
My doctor is Dr. H. F. Shipman. 22 Market Street Hyde.

The implication was frightening—Shipman, a respected doctor, had murdered Kathleen Grundy to inherit her estate. But even this thought gave little indication of the magnitude of his crimes.

As news of the investigation into Dr Shipman spread through Manchester, others came forward to tell detectives of their concerns over the deaths of their relatives. Many had heard rumours about his patients—the doctor's surgery across the road from Shipman's practice felt that he was signing too many death certificates, while one undertaker had even confronted Shipman about the number of bodies that had come to him for cremation and burial. Detectives decided to review the cases of 15 patients—six of whom had been buried, with another nine cremated. Kathleen Grundy's body was exhumed, and it was discovered that she had died from morphine poisoning. Shipman's career as a doctor—as a deluded 'angel of mercy', a megalomaniac and finally a fraudster—was over.

Police found that the forged will had been typed with Shipman's own typewriter. His office computer still contained the genuine medical records of those who had died by his own hand, and telephone records failed to support his claims that he had called for—and then cancelled—ambulances on the days that his patients had died. Unique in that he derived no sexual release from the killings, gained no sadistic pleasure from watching his victims die and did not try to benefit financially until the case in which he was caught, Shipman expressed no guilt or contrition for his crimes. (Psychologists believed that Shipman was mesmerised by watching the final breaths of his dying patients.) However, the good doctor undoubtedly took his wife's future financial situation into account when he hanged himself in prison on 13 January 2004. In dying before his 58th birthday, Shipman ensured that his insurance and pension would be paid out to her. Shipman took his real motives for the killings to his grave.

REFERENCES:

- Sitford, Mikaela (2000), *Addicted to Murder: The True Story of Dr Harold Shipman,* Virgin, London
- BBC Online (2005), *Case Closed: Harold Shipman, www.bbc.co.uk*
- *The Shipman Inquiry, www.the-shipman-inquiry.org.uk*

1998
The Omagh Bombing

FACT FILE

CRIME: Mass murder

VICTIMS: 29 killed, 220 injured

VICTIMS: James Barker, aged 12; Fernando Blasco Baselga, aged 12; Geraldine Breslin, aged 43; Deborah Anne Cartwright, aged 20; Gareth Conway, aged 18; Breda Devine, aged 20 months; Oran Doherty, aged 8; Aidan Gallagher, aged 21; Esther Gibson, aged 36; Mary Grimes, aged 65; Olive Hawkes, aged 60; Julia Hughes, aged 21; Brenda Logue, aged 17; Anne McCombe, aged 45; Brian McCrory, aged 54; Samantha McFarland, aged 17; Sean McGrath, aged 61; Sean McLaughlin, aged 12; Jolene Marlow, aged 17; Avril Monaghan, aged 30; Maura Monaghan, aged 18 months; Alan Radford, aged 17; Rocio Abad Ramos, aged 23; Elizabeth ('Libby') Rush, aged 57; Veda Short, aged 46; Philomena Skelton, aged 39; Frederick White, aged 60; Bryan White, aged 26; Lorraine Wilson, aged 15

DATE: 15 August 1998

PLACE: Omagh (Northern Ireland)

PERPETRATORS: Unknown elements of the National Liberation Army (INLA)

In April 1998, the British and Irish governments signed the Good Friday Agreement (also known as the Belfast Agreement), which called for political reform, paramilitary decommissioning and demilitarisation by British forces. Most important, it established the principle that Northern Ireland's constitutional future should be determined by a majority vote of its citizens. The people of Northern Ireland and the Republic of Ireland endorsed the agreement in two referenda held in May 1998. One of the agreement's provisions was the release of paramilitary prisoners held by organisations observing the ceasefire. On 15 August 1988, a splinter group of the IRA—the Irish National Liberation Army (INLA), which called itself the 'Real IRA' answered the call to disarm by planting a 500-kilogram (1100-pound) bomb in the heart of Omagh, in Country Tyrone, Northern Ireland. Twenty-nine people were killed, with another 220 injured—the largest single atrocity in Northern Ireland's troubled history.

In 1997, Tony Blair led the Labour Party to a stunning victory in the British parliamentary election after 18 years in opposition. Blair's government immediately implemented a program of constitutional change—reducing the number of hereditary peers in the House of Lords to just 92 and offering referendums on home rule to Scotland and Wales before taking on the most divisive and violent domestic issue to face Britain in the whole of the twentieth century—'the Irish question'. The outcome was the historic Good Friday Agreement.

Saturday afternoon was a busy time for shoppers in the market town of Omagh. The car bomb was planted close to the junction of Market Street and Dublin Road, in the middle of town. A warning given to a Belfast newsagency 40 minutes before the bomb was detonated stated that the target was the Omagh courthouse—400 metres (440 yards) away from where the car was actually left—and members of the Royal Ulster Constabulary (RUC), who belatedly evacuated the area, moved the crowd away from courthouse closer to the bombsite. Two other warnings, one to the Ulster Television newsroom in Belfast, only confused matters, but when the bomb detonated at 3.10 pm, it had maximum impact. Twenty-one people died instantly, and another eight died later from their injuries. Omagh was left looking like a war zone, with many of the town's shops destroyed or damaged.

A group of Spanish students, who were studying English and staying in Buncarana, County Donegal, had been taken on a coach trip to Omagh for an afternoon's shopping. One of them, 12-year-old Fernando Baselga, was killed, along with group leader Rocio Ramos.

Three Buncarana students—12-year-olds Sean McLaughlin and James Barker and eight-year-old Oran Doherty—also lost their lives, as did five other children. Three generations of the same family—30-year-old Avril Monaghan, her 18-month-old daughter, Maura, and her own mother, Mary Grimes, perished in the bombing. (Mrs Monaghan was also expecting twins.)

Three co-workers from Watterson's clothing shop—Geraldine Breslin, Anne McCombe and Veda Short—were killed, as was Aidan Gallagher, who was inside the shop when the car exploded. Father and son Fred and Bryan White died together, as did best friends Samantha McFarland and Lorraine Wilson. Most of the victims were from Omagh, but the explosion did not discriminate between Catholic and Protestant, Nationalist and Unionist.

The Omagh bombing was condemned nationally and internationally. British prime minister Tony Blair stated that the tragedy would not break the Good Friday Agreement between the two countries, as the terrorists had hoped. The INLA claimed responsibility for the bombing but then issued a second statement saying that 'all military operations had been suspended'. On 1 September, Gerry Adams, the president of the IRA's political wing, Sinn Fein, declared that the 30-year war waged by Republican forces against British rule in Northern Ireland had ended.

On 22 September 1998, police on both sides of the Irish border arrested 12 men in connection with the Omagh bombing. All were released without charge, but the following March builder and publican Colm Murphy was charged with 'conspiracy to cause an explosion to endanger life or cause injury'. The RUC was strongly criticised for its handling of the bomb threats and its investigation into those responsible for the bombing.

By April 1999, the men who had assembled the bomb and driven it to Omagh had been identified, but there was insufficient evidence to charge them. A BBC documentary later named the men, by which time the victims' families were investigating filing a civil suit against those thought to be responsible for the atrocity.

The report of an investigation into the original police inquiry, released in December 2001, claimed that the RUC ignored warnings, failed to question key suspects and did not disclose crucial intelligence at the subsequent inquest.

Relatives of those killed in Omagh demanded an explanation from Northern Ireland's chief constable, Sir Ronnie Flanagan. Although the police ombudsman resisted calls for a further inquiry into police conduct before and after the bombing, Flanagan was forced to resign in February 2002 in response to public criticism of his handling of the case.

Seven years would pass before another man was brought to justice for the murder of 29 innocent people at Omagh. On 26 May 2005, Sean Hoey, an electrician from County Amagh, was charged with murder, along with explosives and terrorism offences related to the Omagh bombing. The conviction of Colm Murphy was quashed on appeal in 2005.

While Sean Hoey was found not guilty of all 56 charges against him in 2007, a decade after the crime, in 2008, Chief Inspector Sir Ronald Flanagan publicly apologised to the families of the victims for the lack of convictions in relation to the Omagh bombing.

REFERENCES:

- Melaugh, Martin (1998), *The Omagh Bomb—Main Events, www.cain.ulst.ac.uk*
- *Omagh Timeline, www.guardian.co.uk*

1999

Columbine High School Massacre

FACT FILE

CRIME: Mass murder

VICTIMS: Cassie Bernall, aged 17; Steven Curnow, aged 14; Cory DePooter, aged 17; Kelly Fleming, aged 16; Matthew Kechter, aged 16; Daniel Mauser, aged 15; Daniel Rohrbough, aged 15; Rachel Scott, aged 17; Isaiah Shoels, aged 18; John Tomlin, aged 16; Lauren Townsend, aged 18; Kyle Velasquez, aged 16; William ('Dave') Sanders, aged 47; 27 others were wounded

DATE: 20 April 1999

PLACE: Columbine High School, Jefferson County, near Denver, Colorado (USA)

PERPETRATORS:
Eric Harris (1981–1999) and Dylan Klebold (1982–1999)

On 20 April 1999, two students walked into Columbine High School in Jefferson County, Colorado, and went on a highly planned shooting rampage. Within 90 minutes, 12 fellow students and a teacher were dead, 27 people were wounded, and the teenagers who were responsible, 18-year-old Eric Harris and 17-year-old Dylan Klebold, had committed suicide. It was the deadliest school shooting in the controversial history of school shootings in the United States, and the events at Columbine High School were to have far-reaching ramifications for US gun laws and school culture, and American society as a whole.

There were worrying signs of a potential tragedy before the April 1999 attack, but these were either ignored or not pieced together by authorities until after the murder rampage. As early as 1996, Eric Harris used a website he created to promote solutions to the computer game Doom and to post his diatribes against society.

Harris also gave details of the list of weapons he had accumulated and instructions for making pipe-bombs, but it was not until he wrote a death threat to a classmate on his website that the police were alerted. (A search warrant relating to Harris's home was drafted but never actioned.) In January 1998, both Harris and Klebold were caught stealing computer equipment from a van and were required to undergo psychiatric counselling when the sentencing judge noted that both lacked 'moral judgement'. It was later revealed that the two boys had referred in their private journals and in video messages to planning a massacre that 'rivalled' the Oklahoma City bombing in retaliation for 'getting into trouble' with authorities.

In early 1999, Harris and Klebold illegally ordered a semi-automatic handgun, a carbine rifle and two sawn-off shotguns. Using *The Anarchist Cookbook* from the Internet, they also built 99 explosive devices, which they planned to plant around their school. (Two of their friends were later jailed for supplying the young killers with weapons.)

Harris and Klebold arrived at Columbine High School in separate cars at about 11 am on 20 April and parked in car parks at either side of the school. A fire bomb set up in a nearby field acted as a momentary diversion for the fire brigade, but when bombs placed in the empty school cafeteria failed to detonate, the two boys armed themselves from their cars.

Wearing long trench coats, they carried duffle bags filled with weapons. One of the first people Eric Harris encountered in the school car park was the friend who had been the focus of his death threats. They had since patched up their differences, and Harris told the boy to go home. A witness heard Eric Harris scream to Dylan Klebold, 'Go! Go!' at 11.19 am.

Seventeen-year-old Rachel Scott was killed while eating lunch on a grassy hill outside the school with friend Richard Castaldo, who was seriously wounded. Three friends were fired upon as they descended a glass staircase inside the school, and another group was shot at as they walked away from their classes.

Klebold shot two of the wounded on the staircase, killing Daniel Rohrbough with a single shot to the back of the head. The two killers joined each other at the entrance to the cafeteria, shot at students having lunch and threw pipe-bombs out into the car park. Coach Dave Sanders was shot as he evacuated the cafeteria and ran to the library to warn others. (Two students administered first aid, but he died at 3 pm before the school could be fully evacuated.) Although injured, teacher Patti Nelson dialled 911 from the library, and a deputy police officer, the first policeman to arrive at the scene, fired on the shooters to keep them from preying on the injured in the cafeteria.

Captured on closed circuit television, students scurried for their lives as the two killers, having shed their trench coats, continued to fire. Four minutes after Neilson dialled 911, Harris and Klebold entered the library. Harris was heard to yell at students hiding behind shelves 'Get up!' and 'All jocks [sports athletes] stand up'. When no-one did, the pair started to fire indiscriminately. Kyle Velasquez, Steven Curnow and Cassie Bernall were killed in the library—the recoil of the shotgun as he shot Cassie broke Harris's nose. Next to be killed were Isaiah Shoels (whom Klebold first taunted about his race) and Matthew Kechter (a 'jock'). Klebold's question 'Do you believe in God?' was directed not, as first thought, to Cassie Bernall but (according to official reports) at survivor Val Schnurr. Lauren Townsend and John Tomlin lost their lives in the library, where most of those wounded had been seriously injured. As they reloaded their weapons in the library, the killers let another friend, John Savage, leave without harm. Daniel Mauser and Cory DePooter were the last to die before the killers walked out of the library at about 11.42 am. Thirty-four uninjured and ten injured students fled the library after the pair left.

Walking back into the cafeteria, Harris and Klebold attempted to detonate one of their propane bombs, and when this failed they threw a Molotov cocktail, which later caused a small fire. Walking back into the library after finding no-one in the adjoining rooms, the two boys killed themselves some time before 12.20 pm, shooting themselves in the head. Police outside the school envisaged a long siege, but when injured student Patrick Ireland crawled out of the library through a broken window at 2.30 pm, the shooting was over. Officials found the bodies of Dylan Klebold and Eric Harris inside the library at 3.30 pm.

Originally, the death toll was posted at 15 (including the killers), and police feared that those responsible may have had help from others. In the aftermath of the tragedy, everyone and everything was blamed for the killing rampage—from the teenage killers' parents to Goth rocker Marilyn Manson—but few, with the exception of the victims' families, cared to look at America's lax gun laws and culture of violence. Whatever the cause, there was much soul-searching in the years after 'Columbine'.

HISTORICAL AND SOCIAL SIGNIFICANCE:

- It is thought that the killers originally planned the massacre for 19 April because, among other things, that was the 110th anniversary of Adolf Hitler's birthday and also the anniversary of the Oklahoma City bombing. A delay in the production of the propane bombs may have caused the date to be put back by 24 hours.
- In 2001, film-maker Michael Moore released his Academy Award-winning documentary *Bowling for Columbine.* The title is derived from Moore's observation that the Columbine massacre had just as much to do with the fact that the killers liked bowling, as that they liked heavy metal music or violent films. In his view, America's violent culture and lax gun laws were to blame.

REFERENCES:

- *Columbine High School Massacre, www.wikipedia.org*
- *Columbine Victims, www.geocities.com*
- State of Colorado, Office of the Governor, *Columbine Review, www.state.co.us*

2001
9/11

FACT FILE

CRIME: Mass murder

VICTIMS:

2975 civilians

343 members of the Fire Department of New York (FDNY)

37 members of the Port Authority Police Department (PAPD)

23 members of the New York Police Department (NYPD)

DATE: 11 September 2001

PLACES: World Trade Center, New York; The Pentagon, Washington, DC; Shankville, Pennsylvania (USA)

PERPETRATORS: Mohamed Atta (pilot of AA F11); Wail al Shehri; Waleed al Shehri; Satam al Suqami; Abdulaziz al Omari; Marwan al Shehhi (pilot of UA F175); Fayez Banihammad; Ahmed al Ghamdi; Hamza al Ghamdi; Mohand al Shehri; Hani Hajour (pilot of AA F77); Nawaf al Hazmi; Khalid al Mihdhar; Majed Moqed; Salem al Hazmi; Ziad Jarrah (pilot of UA F93); Saeed al Ghamdi; Ahmad al Haznawi; Ahmed al Nami

---

At 6 am on Tuesday, 11 September 2001, Saudi nationals Mohamed Atta and Abdulaziz al Omari boarded a flight from Portland to Boston's Logan International Airport. As Atta stood in line preparing to board, he was identified by a computerised pre-screening system as someone who should be subject to special security measures. The only consequence was that his luggage was held off the plane until he boarded. As history has shown, this security measure did not hinder the plans of Atta and his fellow terrorists, nor save the world from the most shocking terrorist attack in modern times.

Atta and Omari arrived at Boston at 6.45 am and were joined by three other Saudi nationals: Satam al Suqami and brothers Wail al Shehri and Waleed al Shehri. Al Shehri also activated extra security concerns. Before the five men boarded American Airlines Flight 11 to Los Angeles, Atta took a phone call from Marwan al Shehhi, who was in another part of the terminal. Shehhi was joined at the terminal by another four terrorists, and the five men boarded United Airlines Flight 175, which was also bound for Los Angeles. The Boston flights left for Los Angeles at 7.59 am and 8.14 am respectively. About 15 minutes after take-off, Flight 11 was hijacked by Atta and his cohorts. Phone calls made by two flight attendants revealed that the

Shehri brothers, sitting in row 2 in first class, stabbed two flight attendants as they prepared for cabin service. While it is not known how the highjackers gained access to the cockpit, they somehow lured the captain or co-pilot from the locked cockpit and Atta then assumed control of the plane. The highjackers told the passengers that they now had control of the plane and said for everyone to 'just stay quiet' as they allegedly returned to the airport. Their true destination was New York City.

It was a similar story on United Airlines Flight 175. The last communication from the plane, at approximately 8.42 am, was a confirmation of a 'suspicious transmission' coming from Flight 11. The terrorists attacked at about this time; phone calls from passengers and flight attendants told of them using paper cutters, Mace and the threat of a bomb to gain access to the cockpit and kill both pilots. At 8.51 am the plane started to divert from its course back to New York.

Meanwhile, at Dulles Airport in Washington, DC, and in Newark, New Jersey, two more planes were about to be hijacked. American Airlines Flight 77, also bound for Los Angeles, took off from Dulles at 8.20 am. By 8.54 am the aircraft began to deviate from its flight path, and on-board phone calls confirmed that the hijackers used 'box cutters' to gain access to the cockpit and mace to move all the passengers to the back of the plane. UA93, bound for San Francisco, was the last plane to be hijacked, at 8.42 am.

At 8.46.40 am (EST), American Airlines Flight 11 crashed into the North Tower of the World Trade Center in New York City. Before a warning could go out to evacuate the South Tower, United Airlines Flight 175 struck the second of the twin towers, at 9.03.11 am. Survivors in the South Tower later stated that they were told via an internal intercom system that although there was 'a problem' in the North Tower, they did not have to evacuate. Rooftop evacuations were not part of the World Trade Center's safety plan, and the doors to the roof were in fact locked. The only way out was via three internal stair complexes down to the street. For those trapped above the damage, there was no escape.

At 9.34.46 am, Ronald Reagan Washington National Airport advised the Secret Service that an unknown aeroplane was heading towards Washington DC. It was 123 kilometres (77 miles) away and there was no time to intercept it. The 'unknown aeroplane' was American Airlines Flight 77. Changing course at the last moment, it crashed into the Pentagon three minutes later, at 9.37.46 am, travelling at approximately 530 miles (850 kilometres) per hour.

The terrorists had planned to hijack four planes within a time span of 25 minutes. When United Airlines Flight 93 departed from Newark for San Francisco—some 27 minutes late—the flight crew were unaware of the other hijackings. By 9 am, with the North Tower on fire, United Airlines had ordered the nationwide grounding of all its planes and broadcast an alert for all air-bound craft to increase cockpit security. At 9.24 am, the pilot of Flight 93 was asking for confirmation of the security instruction when air traffic control officers heard a struggle develop in the cockpit.

There were only 37 passengers on Flight 93, including four hijackers. (A man intended to be the fifth member of the team, Mohamed al Kahtani, had been refused entry into the United States the previous month.) Because this was the last aeroplane to be hijacked (and it had departed late), at least ten passengers and two crew members were able to communicate vital information to relatives and airport staff on the ground while the plane was still in the air. When it became known that the plane was going to be crashed into a building, the passengers stormed the cockpit to regain control of the plane or crash it into vacant ground. The terrorist pilot, Ziad Jarrah, tried to knock the passengers off their feet by rolling the plane to the left and right, but at 10.03.11 am the flight crashed into a field outside Shanksville, Pennsylvania.

Although hit second, the South Tower collapsed at 9.59 am under the heat and destruction caused by thousands of gallons of exploding aeroplane fuel. The many firefighters and police who had ascended the tower to organise its evacuation were killed instantly. In the next 29 minutes, before the North Tower collapsed at 10.28 am, many people were able to escape, but the collapse claimed the lives of all the people trapped above floor 94, including the chief of the New York Fire Department and the Port Authority superintendent and many of their staff.

The 9/11 terrorist attacks caught the authorities responsible for US internal security unawares. The World Trade Center had already been a target in February 1993, when six people were killed in a basement car bombing and both towers had to be evacuated. (The World Trade Center is actually a complex of seven buildings, including the Twin Towers, which until 1974 were the world's tallest structures. The towers shared a common basement and were linked by an underground shopping mall.) Because the majority of the terrorists were Saudi nationals, Osama Bin Laden and the Al-Qaeda organisation quickly became the chief suspects.

In response, the US government under President George W. Bush launched its war on terrorism. The world would never be the same.

REFERENCES:

- 'A Nation Challenged', *New York Times*, (2001), Jonathan Cape, London
- *The 9/11 Commission Report* (2003), Norton, New York

2001

Gary Ridgeway: The 'Green River Killer'

FACT FILE

CRIME: Serial murder
VICTIMS: 48 women (44 bodies found and 4 women identified from photographs without their remains being found)
DATES: 1982–1998
PLACE: Seattle, Washington State (USA)
PERPETRATOR: Gary Leon Ridgeway (b. 1946)
SENTENCE: 48 consecutive life terms without the possibility of parole

When Gary Leon Ridgeway was arrested in the American autumn of 2001, it brought an end to a litany of unsolved serial murders committed in Seattle, Washington, that stretched back almost 20 years. Faced with irrefutable DNA linking him to three of the earliest known victims, the 54-year-old truck driver admitted to murdering 48 women (although the real number may be as high as 60), who were mostly inexperienced prostitutes or runaway teens. Ridgeway picked up his victims from the street in his car and murdered them in his home. He later claimed that prostitutes and runaways were easy to kill because he 'knew they would not be reported missing right away, and might never be reported missing'.

In July 1982, the body of 16-year-old Wendy Coffield was found near Green River in Kent, Washington. However, Green River was of no significance to the killer. Police later identified five victims in the Green River 'cluster'—the first of eight 'burial grounds' the killer was thought to have used until his final victim was found in 1998. A wooded area off State Lake Road, areas north and south of Seattle–Tecoma International Airport, a site near Mountain View Cemetery, a stretch of Highway 410, two areas along Highway 18 and two along Interstate 90 also gave up their grisly cargo over the next 16 years—despite the fact that most of the victims were killed in the 12 months after the initial body was found. Ridgeway later admitted that he buried his victims in clusters to keep track of all the women he killed.

Investigating detectives thought the killer may have stopped in 1983, but all that had happened was that the bodies of the victims were no longer being found. The killer also changed his modus operandi—even moving one of his victim's bodies to the nearby state of Oregon—in order to avoid detection.

Such was the scope of the crimes, however, that mistakes were made in the original investigation. The original FBI profile stated that the killer was most likely a taxi driver who was familiar with the Green River district of Kent. (Another six profiles were to follow.) The killer hated women and his actions arose from a compulsion to control them. (Ridgeway believed the women he killed had power over him even after their death.) The targeting of prostitutes and young women suggested that the killer had problems with his sexual performance unless he was in a dominant position. (Ridgeway killed his victims by using a choke hold before they knew what his intentions were.) Lastly, given the position and movement of the bodies after death, the killer was a necrophiliac. (Ridgeway later admitted to going back several days later to where several of his victims were hidden and sleeping with them to maintain control over them.) After he was captured, Ridgeway told detectives that he became 'upset and frustrated' when the remains of his victims were found—they were his property, he owned them.

When 18-year-old Marie Malvar disappeared on the Pacific Highway South in April 1983, her father and pimp/boyfriend took police to Ridgeway's home and demanded that they arrest him. Ridgeway had previous convictions for soliciting prostitutes and was interviewed by detectives, but they had insufficient evidence to arrest him. Malvar's remains were not found until 2003, when Gary Ridgeway led police to her body near Auburn.

The Washington state attorney general's office was even offered assistance from serial killer Ted Bundy, who was on Florida's death row at the time. Detectives suspected that Bundy was jealous of the Green River Killer, who had remained undetected for much longer than he, but the infamous serial killer had hiked in the area and had some interesting insights into the murderer's psychology. Bundy was also able to uncannily 'read between the lines' in the police investigation, and suggested that detectives stake out the crime scene, but that was not practical. The attorney general's office originally took Bundy seriously but abruptly terminated contact with him when they felt that he 'getting off' on being involved in the murder investigation.

After several years out of circulation, Gary Ridgeway began killing again in 1990. Marta Reeves, aged 37, and Patricia Robe, 38, were older than his previous victims, but by then it was a different era and detectives had improved DNA technology and finally zeroed in on him. Police originally charged him with seven murders, but he later admitted to 48 murders.

Despite the fact that he did not like to look at his victims' faces when he killed them, he was able identify four women not previously linked to him from photographs (and dismiss another, whom he did not remember) and took detectives to where he had hidden several of the bodies. Gary Ridgeway was the rarest of criminals; a serial murderer whose primary motive was sexual assault (for most serial killers the primary motive is murder).

The plain-looking painter of only average intelligence admitted to detectives that during puberty he wanted to stab and have sex with his mother. (His mother had shamed him as a teenager for his regular bedwetting.) The 'Green River Killer' had had several failed relationships with women and had been twice divorced. He was in a de facto relationship when he was charged.

On 6 November 2003, to avoid the death penalty, Gary Ridgeway confessed to more murders than any other serial killer in US history. Authorities agreed to waive the death penalty in order to bring resolution to the families of the many other victims who had been waiting for justice. For six months, Judge Richard A. Jones delayed sentencing Ridgeway to 48 consecutive life terms without the possibility of parole to allow detectives to question him about the list of murders.

Ridgeway was cunning in the way he planned his procurements, abductions and killings, and was clever enough to avoid detection for almost 20 years. He could also be insightful when the occasion demanded. He lacked 'caring', he told detectives. Forced to listen to a series of victims' impact statements from the families of the women he had killed, Gary Ridgeway did something as startling for a serial killer as was the enormity of his crimes.

Fighting back tears, Ridgeway said that he was sorry.

REFERENCES:

- *Murder Casebook* (1990), Marshall Cavendish, London
- BBC Online (2005), *Case Closed: The Green River Killer, www.bbc.co.uk*
- *Law Center: Green River Killer Avoids Death Penalty in Plea Deal, www.cnn.com*

2002

The Washington Sniper

FACT FILE

CRIME: Serial murder

VICTIMS: Kenneth H. Bridges, aged 53; James ('Sonny') Buchanan, aged 39; Pascal Charlot, aged 72; Linda Franklin, aged 47; Conrad Johnson, aged 37; Paul LaRuffa, aged 55*; Lori Ann Lewis-Rivera, aged 25; James D. Martin, aged 55; Dean H. Meyers, aged 53; Claudine Parker, aged 52*; Sarah Ramos, aged 34; Premkumar Walekar, aged 54

Several others were seriously wounded

* Paul LaRuffa was killed in Clinton in Prince George's County, Maryland on 5 September and Claudine Parker was killed in Montgomery, Alabama, on 21 September 2002 before the Washington Sniper attacks started.

DATES: 3–24 October 2002

PLACES: Washington DC, Maryland; Ashland, Virginia; and Montgomery, Alabama, USA

PERPETRATORS: John Allen Muhammad (b. 1961) and John Lee Malvo (b. 1985)

SENTENCE: In March 2004 John Allen Muhammad was sentenced to death for the murder of Dean Meyers in Virginia. In May 2006, a Maryland jury found Muhammad guilty of six counts of murder and sentenced him to six consecutive life terms while he awaits his execution for the crimes committed in Virginia. John Lee Malvo was sentenced to life imprisonment

---

In 2002, the United States of America was engulfed by 'post-Oklahoma City, post-Columbine, post-9/11' paranoia. Having dealt with what were seen as three major attacks on their very way of life—launched from within their own boundaries—Americans could not have envisaged that the next attack would come from a random sniper who coldly killed 12 innocent people as they went about their daily lives. When the desperate Montgomery County (Maryland) police and a host of FBI agents finally closed the net on the 'Washington Sniper' after three weeks of terror, the perpetrators turned out to be another embittered Gulf War veteran and his teenage 'stepson'.

Raised in Louisiana, John Allen Williams joined the National Guard straight out of high school in 1978. Despite receiving a dishonourable discharge from the Guard for disciplinary reasons, he joined the US army in 1985—around the time he converted to the Nation of Islam—and served in the Gulf War as a combat engineer. After his discharge from the army, Williams volunteered as a security guard for the

Nation of Islam's 'Million Man March' on Washington in 1995, but did not change his name to John Allen Muhammad until October 2001. After his capture, much was made of Muhammad's religion (Muslim) and ethnicity (African–American), but the main reasons for the Washington DC murders were Muhammad's deep-felt bitterness at how his life had turned out and his desire to exact revenge on his second wife.

In 2002, John Allen Muhammad was a broken man. Having ended one marriage, he became involved in an acrimonious custody battle for his son before opening an auto repair business in Tacoma, Washington State, with his second wife.

When the business failed, his second wife filed for divorce and Muhammad absconded with their children to the Caribbean Island of Antigua (his mother's homeland) for a year. Muhammad at first refused to return the children to their mother, and after returning to the States in 2001 his behaviour became increasingly irrational. After his ex-wife obtained a restraining order and moved with their children to Clinton, Maryland, near Washington DC, Muhammad lived an itinerant life until he formed a relationship with the Jamaican mother of illegal teenage immigrant John Lee Malvo (born Lee Boyd Malvo). By the following summer, Muhammad and the 17-year-old Malvo were travelling the country together, living from hand to mouth.

The killing rampage in Washington DC started with the death of 55-year-old program analyst James Martin in the parking lot of a Shoppers Food Warehouse on the evening of 2 October 2002. The following day, 39-year-old landscaper James ('Sonny') Buchanan was shot dead at 7.41 am while mowing the grass at the Fitzgerald Auto Mall in Rockville, Maryland.

Half an hour later, part-time taxi driver Premkumar Walekar was killed as he filled up his car at a Mobil station in Aspen Hill. Half an hour after that, 34-year-old babysitter Sarah Ramos was shot dead while reading a book on a bus stop bench outside the Leisure World Shopping Center in Aspen Hill. A little before 10 am, Lori Ann Lewis-Rivera was killed at a Shell service station in Kensington, Maryland.

By now the local Montgomery County police were fully mobilised and media reports warned the public to look out for a sniper, but these measures could not prevent a fifth death that day. Retired carpenter Pasqual Charlot was shot as he walked along Georgia Avenue at 9.15 p.m. He died less than an hour later.

On 4 October, Caroline Sewell was wounded in the parking lot of a Virginian shopping mall, after which the sniper laid low for three days. On 7 October, 13-year-old Iran Brown was wounded as he walked into his school in Bowie, Maryland. The 'Washington Sniper' used the circular Capital Beltway (the killer was also called the 'Beltway Sniper') to move from target to target but police were not helped by several eyewitness accounts of 'a crazy white guy' armed with an AK-7 and driving a boxy white van. In fact, the perpetrators were two black men driving a former police car—an old blue Chevy sedan that had been specially modified into a 'killing machine'.

Muhammad had modified the boot of the car, allowing him to lie down and peer through a viewing port from the back seat of the car while John Lee Malvo drove. The murder weapon was a Bushmaster XM-15 semi-automatic .223 calibre rifle used from a range of 40 to 90 metres (50 to 100 yards). The rifle had been stolen from a gun supply store in Tacoma, Washington, but the proprietor had failed to notify authorities of its theft, as required by federal law.

The 'Washington Sniper' now received hourly national news coverage, and he revelled in toying with the investigating police. Tarot cards, including a death card with the words 'Dear Policeman. I am God' written on it, were left at crime scenes.

A three-page letter threatening the lives of children and demanding US$10 million was found after one victim was shot. Muhammad even called 911 at one stage from a public phone booth in Virginia, but when he was put on hold, he hung up. Four more people died before police connected bullets recovered from the crime scenes with those used in the unsolved murders of Maryland pizzeria owner Paul LaRuffa and liquor clerk Claudine Parker in Montgomery, Alabama, the previous month. The suspects in the latter crime were two black men driving a blue Chevy sedan.

Finally, on 24 October, Muhammad and Malvo were found asleep in their car on Interstate 70 near Hagerston, Maryland, after a tip-off from local citizens. They were arrested without incident. Investigating police later discovered that the car's licence plate had twice been logged at roadblocks, but the car had not been searched because it was not a white van and it was being driven by a black man.

John Allen Muhammad and John Lee Malvo were first tried for the two murders committed in the state of Virginia, with prosecutors keen to pursue the death penalty for Malvo despite the fact that he was only 17 years old at the time he took part in the murders. Though he claimed to be innocent, John Allen Muhammad was found guilty of capital murder for the shooting of Dean H. Meyers, the first of the Virginia victims, and was sentenced to death in March 2004. John Lee Malvo was sentenced to life imprisonment with no prospect of parole.

REFERENCES:

- Fido, Martin (2004), *The Chronicle of Crime*, Funtastic, Melbourne
- Neighbour, Margaret (2004), 'Washington Sniper Sentenced to Death', *The Scotsman, www.scotsman.com*
- Walsh, David (2002), *The Washington Sniper, www.wsws.org/articles/2002/oct2002/snip-o28.shtml*

2002

The Soham Murders

FACT FILE

CRIME: Murder
VICTIMS: Holly Wells and Jessica Chapman, both aged 10
DATE: 4 August 2002
PLACE: Soham, Cambridgeshire (England)
PERPETRATOR: Ian Huntley (b. 1974)
SENTENCE: Ian Huntley was sentenced to a minimum of 40 years' imprisonment on two counts of murder. Maxine Carr (b. 1977) was found guilty of conspiracy to pervert the course of justice and was sentenced to three-and-a-half years in prison

---

On 4 August 2002, two inseparable 10-year-old friends, Holly Wells and Jessica Chapman, disappeared from the tiny English village of Soham in Cambridgeshire. The girls were wearing brand-new, identical Manchester United soccer shirts with the name and number of their idol David Beckham on the back when they left a family get-together to go for a walk. The girls had been on the Internet for part of the afternoon, and when they did not return home before dark, grave fears were held for their safety. Twenty-eight-year-old groundsman Ian Huntley, the live-in boyfriend of an assistant who worked at the girls' school, looked shocked and worried as he recounted to television news crews how he had seen the pair walk past the rented home he shared with Maxine Carr. He even helped in the official search for the missing children. But Ian Huntley and Maxine Carr harboured a dark secret.

Ian Huntley had worked at various unskilled jobs during the 1990s after dropping out of school as a 16-year-old. He had also allegedly committed a series of sexual offences since 1995, including burglary, underage sex, indecent assault of a 12-year-old and three cases of rape. In the most recent case, in July 1999, Huntley supplied a DNA sample, but the victim dropped the charges after his mousy girlfriend, Maxine Carr, provided him with an alibi. The pair met at a nightclub in Grimsby, Huntley's home town, and decided to move in together. Carr worked as a factory processor but dreamed of being a teaching assistant in a primary school. Huntley's father worked as a school caretaker in the village of Lillyport, and he had enjoyed helping his father maintain the grounds. In 2001, when the rape charge fell through, Huntley applied for a caretaker's job at Soham Village College using his mother's maiden name (Nixon), and was successful.

The tragedy of Huntley's appointment—irony is too mild a word—is that when his background was 'vetted', the fact that he had taken an assumed name was enough to conceal his troubled past. In the words of one of the parents of the Soham victims, Ian Huntley was a 'time bomb waiting to explode'. Huntley and Carr rented the caretaker's cottage at 5 College Close, and Carr secured a job as a teaching assistant at St Andrew's Primary School. Holly Wells and Jessica Chapman befriended Maxine Carr at their primary school, and made her 'friendship cards' and wrote letters to her.

Whether the girls decided to visit their new friend at College Close or they just happened to be passing the house, Maxine Carr was not at home that summer evening when the girls called in at about 6 pm. Minutes before, Ian Huntley had angrily slammed the telephone down after Carr had informed him that she would be staying in Grimsby overnight.

What happened next is not known for sure, but detectives believe Huntley lured the girls inside the cottage and then murdered them. Incredibly, when Carr returned home the following day, she again provided Huntley with a false alibi that she had been home with him all evening.

As authorities searched for the missing girls, Huntley felt so secure about not being caught that he even helped with the search and appeared on television with his distraught girlfriend, expressing his concern for the missing girls. His confidence would be his undoing.

In one of the most intensive searches in English criminal history, investigators failed to do a check on the most obvious suspect—the last person to see the girls. Cambridgeshire Constabulary and Humberside Police were severely criticised for not sharing information during the investigation—information that could have revealed 'Ian Nixon's' true identity.

It was a member of the public who alerted them to Huntley's past. Twelve days after the girls disappeared, items of their clothing were found in the college grounds. Huntley and Carr were arrested for questioning, and the following day the bodies of the two girls were found 32 kilometres (20 miles) away, hidden in a ditch. Huntley was charged with two counts of murder and was kept in a mental institution after he went into an apparent 'comatose' state to avoid interrogation.

Carr was charged with the lesser charge of perverting the course of justice. It seems that she provided her boyfriend with a false alibi because she was convinced of his innocence and was afraid that police would find out about his past.

Huntley and Carr were the 'Brady and Hindley' (the 'Moors Murderers') of a new generation—no more reviled a pair of monsters existed in Britain at the start of the new millennium. Huntley, a coward to the end, refused to adequately explain what happened to the little girls once they were inside his home.

Instead, he told the unlikely story of helping Wells with a nosebleed and accidentally knocking her into a bath, where she drowned. Jessica Chapman, he maintained, was accidentally suffocated when she started screaming. He had then burnt both the bodies because he knew that no-one would believe him, but one can scarcely imagine what really happened to the two 10-year-olds in their final moments.

Carr, for her part, turned on her former partner on the witness stand and accused him of lying to her and abusing her. Compared to the victims, she got off lightly.

On 17 December 2003, Ian Huntley was sentenced to life in prison on two counts of murder, with a minimum term of 40 years. Huntley showed no remorse for his actions and tried to avoid responsibility for the killing of the two innocent girls with a series of lies.

The judge could have set a 'whole life' term but decided that this was not appropriate in Huntley's case. Huntley is today held in strict protection in Wakefield Prison and will be eligible for release in 2042. Maxine Carr was sentenced to three-and-a-half-years' jail but was subsequently released in May 2004 and today lives in a place unknown under a new identity.

HISTORICAL AND SOCIAL SIGNIFICANCE:

- An inquiry chaired by Sir Michael Bichard was set up in 2003 to review 'child protection procedures in Humberside Police and Cambridgeshire Constabulary in light of the recent trial and conviction of Ian Huntley for the murder of Jessica Chapman and Holly Wells'. The inquiry severely criticised the effectiveness of the relevant intelligence-based record-keeping, the vetting practices in those forces since 1995 and the lack of information-sharing between agencies. The chief constable of Humberside Police, David Westwood, was temporarily suspended, and Tom Lloyd, his counterpart at the Cambridgeshire Constabulary, was criticised for being too slow at the time to cut short his holiday and for displaying a general 'lack of grip' on the biggest investigation in the force's history.

REFERENCES:

- Fido, Martin (2004), *The Chronicle of Crime*, Funtastic, Melbourne
- BBC Online (2003), *Previous Allegations Against Huntley, www.news.bbc.co.uk.*
- BBC Online (2005), *Soham Killer Gets 40 Years, www.news.bbc.co.uk.*

2004
The Beslan School Siege

FACT FILE

CRIME: Abduction, murder
VICTIMS:
1128 held hostage
344 killed, including 186 children
More than 700 people were injured.
DATES: 1–3 September 2004
PLACE: Beslan, Chechnya (Russia)
PERPETRATORS: The 32 hostage-takers, of whom 5 were women, included:
'Abdullah' (alias Vladimir Khodov); Nur-Pashi Kulayev; 'Magas' (alias Magomed Yevloyev); Khaula Nazirov; 'Polkovnik' (alias Ruslan Tagirovich Khochubarov), the terrorist leader
SENTENCE: Nur-Pashi Kulayev was the only terrorist captured alive. He was placed on trial in 2005 and was sentenced to life imprisonment the following year

---

On 3 August 2004, Russia's Interior Ministry received intelligence about possible terrorist attacks close to the Chechen border. On 21 and 31 August, it warned local police to increase security around local schools in the south of the country. For a variety of reasons, security measures were not fully in place when Russian children returned for their autumn semester on 1 September—known as Russia's 'Day of Knowledge'. At School No.1 in Beslan, shortly after the student parade to mark the beginning of the school year, a group of 32 terrorists, on the orders of Chechen warlord Shamil Basayev, took more than 1000 teachers, parents and students hostage in the school gymnasium.

With the dissolution of the Soviet Union in 1991, Russia refused to recognise Chechnya as an independent republic and a bitter civil war broke out between Russian military and security forces and Chechen rebels.

With Chechnya being one of the world's richest oil-producing regions, Russia realised the historical, economic and strategic imperatives of maintaining control over the region. In 1990, ethnic Russians comprised about one-quarter of Chechnya's population of 1.3 million, but widespread crime and the 'ethnic cleansing' carried out by the Dudayev government during the 1990s caused most non-Chechens (and many of the Chechens Sunni Muslim population) to flee the country.

In the new millennium, Chechen separatists launched a series of terrorist attacks designed to weaken Russia's will to retain control of the region.

The 32 hostage-takers at the Beslan school were led by 'Polkovnik', alias Ruslan Tagirovich Khochubarov, although this identity is disputed. One of the five women who took part was 45-year-old Khaula Nazirov, a member of the Chechen Black Widows, whose husband had been tortured to death by Russian troops five years earlier. She was joined by her 18-year-old son and 16-year-old daughter. Seventeen-year-old Adam Kushtov was another member of the terrorist group, and several mercenaries, including a Slav, a Korean and an unidentified black soldier, gave the group hardened combat experience. Two of the team did not take part in the siege; Musa Tsechoyev owned the GAZ-66 that drove the hostage-takers to the school, and Mairbek Shainekkhanov was arrested shortly before the school attack.

As the terrorists wired the gymnasium with explosives, negotiations floundered because of confusion over the phone number the militants were using, and contact was not established until the end of the first day. Federal Security Service chief Valery Andreyev made a grave error when he deliberately underestimated the number of hostages. (The figure released to the media was just 354.) This infuriated the terrorists and caused emergency personnel to underplan for the rescue. As the hostages became more and more dehydrated inside the cramped gymnasium, Russian officials refused to negotiate with the terrorists and turned the situation into a powder keg.

On the third day of the crisis, one of the explosives in the gymnasium detonated and snipers killed two female terrorists who were carrying explosives to the gymnasium. The terrorists returned fire, and Valery Andreyev personally gave the order to overrun the school with Russian troops. Many of the hostages escaped—some with the help of loved ones who ran into the gymnasium, which was now ablaze, and rescued them despite being under intense gunfire—but 344 people died. Most perished when the gymnasium roof caught fire and collapsed, but others were executed or shot in the back by terrorists as they fled the blaze. Others were caught in the crossfire and killed by 'friendly fire'. Nur-Pashi Kulayev was the only terrorist captured alive, and narrowly avoided being lynched by members of the public after he was discovered hiding underneath a truck not far from the school.

REFERENCES:

- BBC Online (2005), Beslan Siege Suspect Trial Begins, *www.news.bbc.co.uk*
- Watson, Mark (2004), The Chechen Problem, *www.markswatson.com*

2007

The Disappearance of Maddie McCann

FACT FILE

CRIME: Abduction
VICTIM: Madeleine 'Maddie' McCann (b. 2003)
DATE: 3 May 2007
PLACE: Praia da Luz in Algarve, Portugal
PERPETRATOR: Unknown

On the evening of Thursday, 3 May 2007, three-year-old Madeleine McCann was taken from her bedroom while holidaying with her family at the Praia da Luz Resort in Algarve, Portugal. Her parents, English doctors Gerry and Kate McCann, had left her sleeping in a bedroom along with their two-year-old twins, Sean and Amelie, while they dined with friends at a resort bar 120 metres away from their ground floor apartment. The adults took turns checking on the children every 30 minutes starting at about 9:00 pm but when Kate McCann went to the apartment shortly after 10:00pm, 'Maddie' was missing from her bed and the window was open. The plight of the McCanns and a controversial investigation by Portuguese criminal investigation police (Policia Judiciária or PJ) made worldwide headlines.

A nanny employed by the Mark Warner Ocean Club which had organised the family's trip to Portugal was the first to hear Kate McCann's cries in the hallway outside the apartment. 'They've taken her, they've taken her!' she screamed. 'Madeleine's gone!' The McCanns did not take advantage of the nanny service nor had they locked the front door of their apartment, which was in the centre of the resort and was surrounded by apartments let to strangers who were not part of the Ocean Club. Although local police were called within ten minutes of the discovery of Maddie's disappearance by one of the McCanns' friends, official records logged the call at 23:50 hours and the police did not arrive until midnight. The Policia Judiciaria were criticised for downplaying the disappearance as a child who 'wandered off' while staff and guests searched the resort. But finally the Policia notified airports and secured the Portugal–Spain border and a full investigation into a possible abduction began.

Witnesses at the resort confirmed that the McCanns were a happy family who had been seen playing with their daughter and her siblings at the resort pool earlier that day. Maddie was a 'beautiful' girl – fair, with auburn hair and a distinctive colour imperfection in the iris of her right eye – qualities which would have appealed to the blossoming black market 'adoption' trade in Europe. But given the worldwide attention the disappearance the little girl had garnered, grave fears were held for her safety from the outset. Despite this, sightings from as far as Morocco, Belgium, Malta, the Balkans and even Argentina gave false hope to the parents that Maddie would be returned to them.

Police appeared to make a breakthrough when English journalist Lori Campbell drew their attention to a local man with dual Portuguese and British passports who had joined in the search and had acted as an interpreter for visiting news teams. Robert Murat had recently lost custody of his own three-year-old daughter and was 'deeply concerned' with the McCann case. Named as a suspect, the house he shared with his mother was sealed off and thoroughly examined along with two cars and several computers. A Russian associate named Sergey Malinka, 22, had recently helped Murat set up a website and the two had been in constant phone conversation since Maddie's disappearance but the PJ could not find any evidence to charge either of the men with a crime.

Heartbreakingly, the McCanns remained in Portugal for four months and marked Maddie's fourth birthday (May 12) as they awaited news of their missing daughter while supporters ran a high-profile publicity campaign in Great Britain to keep the missing girl's photo in the media. Although the family received widespread support from people in all walks of life (including financial support from Sir Richard Branson and spiritual support from Pope Benedict XVI) they felt that 'too little, too late' had been done in Portugal. After shouldering their 'anguish and despair' for months, the McCanns also had to weather public criticism of their decision to leave their children behind unsupervised on the night their daughter went missing. It seemed almost tragically inevitable then, given the failure to find any trace of the little girl, that local police and the sections of the media would turn on the grieving parents.

In September 2007, the McCanns were reinvestigated as suspects in their daughter's disappearance but fully co-operated with authorities – as they had done from day one – in the hope that Maddie was still alive somewhere in Portugal. Rumour (drugs, abuse) now took precedence over investigating real leads and the testimony of the McCanns' friends who were at dinner with them that night (the 'Tapas Seven') was even brought into question. The discovery of an 'inconclusive' mystery DNA sample in the bedroom where Madeleine disappeared and the description of a dishevelled unknown man seen near the apartments by one of the McCanns' friends finally took the spotlight off the family and back on the efforts of the Portuguese police. But nine months after her abduction, there was still no trace of Maddie McCann.

REFERENCES:

- BBC News, 'Holiday girl abducted, police say.' *www.news.bbc.co.uk*
- Edwards, R. 'Gerry and Kate McCann deny they are suspects' (7 September 2007), *Daily Telegraph*
- Interpol Alert, 'Madeleine Beth McCann' (8 September 2007)

Index